DATE DUE			
Nov 11 '76			
May 16 '77			
Dec 15 7 8			
Aug 15 79			

Who Will Marry Whom?

Bernard I. Murstein needs no introduction to serious students of mate selection. "Probably America's principal theoretician" in the field, to quote the noted sociologist William Kephart, he has written and lectured widely on the subjects of marriage and attraction, including his own theory of marital choice. Dr. Murstein, who is professor of psychology at Connecticut College, is also currently associate editor of the *Journal of Marriage and the Family* and editorial consultant to leading professional periodicals. His published works include, in addition to numerous articles, several books, most recently *Love, Sex, and Marriage through the Ages* (Springer, 1974). Other volumes are: *Theory and Research in Projective Techniques* (1963), *The Handbook of Projective Techniques* (editor; 1965), and *Theories of Attraction and Love* (editor; Springer, 1971).

Who Will Marry Whom?

Theories and Research in Marital Choice

BERNARD I. MURSTEIN

Springer Publishing Company

New York

In Memory of
Rebecca Cassel
a much admired friend

301.4143

M 96w

98 651

oct 1976

Springer Publishing Company, Inc.
200 Park Avenue South
New York, N.Y. 10003

76 77 78 79 80 / 10 9 8 7 6 5 4 3 2 1

Library of Congress Cataloging in Publication Data
Murstein, Bernard I
  Who will marry whom?

  Bibliography: p.
  Includes index.
  1. Mate selection. 2. Social perception. 3. Interpersonal attrac-tion. I. Title. [DNLM: 1. Love. 2. Marriage. 3. Social perception. 4. Social desirability. HQ728 M984w]
  HQ728.M88   301.41'43   75-46588
  ISBN 0-8261-2030-X

Printed in the United States of America

Preface

This book is the product of a decade of research and writing on a topic that concerns many and has been researched by few—the choice of a marital partner. As the materialistic needs of societies are slowly met and as the restrictions on marital choice are lessened, the problem of choosing a marital partner becomes increasingly a major decision in one's life. The data and conclusions in this book will, it is hoped, further stimulate interest and research in this area.

The book is intended for students and researchers in the fields of marriage and the family, interpersonal attraction, and person perception. It may serve as one of a number of books in a course on marriage, and the tests listed in the appendix may be of use in further research in this area. I hope that the various hypotheses presented will be retested by further research efforts.

It is traditional at this point for the author to thank his spouse and children for their forbearance and patience during the agonizing months (years?) of travail; however, my family, by now, is so well trained and used to my writing needs that the gestation of this book, I trust, disturbed them only minimally. Besides, scholars all, Nellicent, Danielle, and Colette have been busy in their own scholarly pursuits, and mutual accommodation has been a way of life in our home for a good number of years.

Contents

Acknowledgments

I am deeply appreciative of the support of the National Institute of Mental Health, which sponsored much of the work reported here for a period of five years. The Connecticut College Research Fund was most helpful with continuous research support for "spot" problems as they developed. In terms of personnel, I was indeed fortunate to have had an extremely able and conscientious band of research assistants: Rosemary Burns, Richard Graf, Neil Young, Gary Beck, and Jane Arabian. My amanuenses were the quick-fingered Karen Daniels and Deborah Spiegel, whose speed on the keyboard was matched only by their grasp of the English language, of which they had much need in deciphering my scrawl.

In the closing stages of the project, I was fortunate to profit shamelessly from the kindness and competence of Regina D. Roth and Jerry Lamb, who designed and ran an endless series of computer programs that inevitably led to new insights and more programs.

The manuscript has been read and criticized by Seymour Fisher, James Hawkins, Ted L. Huston, Robert Ryder, and Regina Roth, whose comments were deeply appreciated.

I am indebted also to the colleagues of various institutions who gave me access to their students. My thanks to Michael Gordon, Gilbert Nass, Eleanore Luckey, and Leo Schneiderman. Last but not least, my thanks to the hundreds of couples who gave generously of their time in participating in the various studies.

CHAPTER 1

Introduction

Why did they choose to marry each other? For much of history this question was of small importance since most individuals did not exercise much free choice in marriage. Even in recent times, when the question had attained relevance, most individuals were at a loss for words to explain marital choice. They hid their ignorance under the simplistic explanation "love," which in actuality meant anything from a love of economic security to a love of sex.

Social scientists preferred not to deal with individual choices and instead demonstrated the strong influence of homogamy with respect to age, class, race, and religion. But they shied away from dealing with exceptions.

The average man simply translated the scholarly jargon into adage and remarked approvingly that "birds of a feather flock together." Yet he noted couples who were quite different in many aspects. Then he might remark that "opposites attract." By using one or the other explanation he thought it possible to account for most marriages, simply glossing over the inherent contradiction in the simultaneous use of these adages.

The first serious attempt to go beyond folkloric sayings by postulating and then testing a theory of interpersonal attraction and

1

marital choice was accomplished by Robert F. Winch,[1] a sociologist, who began his research in the 1950s. Winch's theory, which will be discussed in Chapter 4, is, notwithstanding his being a sociologist, a psychological one. How is it, one might ask, that by this late date psychologists had not put forth a theory complete with data?

The answer, I believe, stems initially from the early history of psychology, which was concerned with efforts to gain respectability for the fledgling science. The physical sciences, and especially physics, became the model for psychologists to emulate. The emphasis was on precise measurement, quantification, and the discovery of laws. The early psychologists became masters of the study of reflexes, pressing keys, flashing lights, and measuring reaction times; they were establishing themselves as true scientists—more meaningful content would come later.

Although these budding scientists fell passionately in love and married after much *sturm und drang,* they never conceived of studying these important experiences that affected their lives as well as those of the vast majority of the population. There were ample reasons to justify the omission of love, passion, and marital choice from their research objectives. These were enormously complex concepts for a fledgling science to study, considering the limited state of interpersonal theory and statistical methodology in the early twentieth century. How do you quantify love or operationally define interpersonal attraction? Moreover, until relatively recently, a veil of discretion hung over relationships between men and women that few academicians dared to tamper with—and for good reason. In 1931, zoologist Harmon de Graff and psychologist Max F. Meyer were dismissed and suspended respectively from the University of Missouri for circulating a questionnaire on sex. The president of the university referred to their work as "sewer sociology" (Murstein, 1974a).

Marital choice itself was not too "sexy" to be investigated, but it was amply protected by the mystique of love. Even as late as 1967, the mystique could deny that love could ever be investigated scientifically, especially by that symbol of technology, the computer. In the absence of research, professional writers continued to propagate the idea of the metaphysicality of love. Thus, Joyce Greller could describe the onset of love as follows: "Whether I meet Him [Mr. Right] at a hoedown, treasure hunt, under a camel, in the cabbage patch, behind the obelisk or on a traffic island . . . even if it gets no further than the other side of the street . . . that fast glance; fleeting white flash; the in-

---

[1]It was Winch's work that first stimulated my thinking in this area, and I gratefully acknowledge my debt to him.

stant but elusive eye exchange . . . whatever that tenuous human contact may have been to join us for an instant . . . a machine provides no substitute. And never will" (Greller 1967, p. 74).

With the ending of World War II, funding for psychological research increased greatly, but funding administrators were not inclined to support research on romance. Psychology was dichotomized into hard-headed "basic research," which seemed to signify investigation for the sake of "pure" scientific knowledge without any conceivable applied use, and "applied" research, which became the label for the efforts of humanistically oriented, "soft-headed" psychologists. Funding for the latter was severely limited. The low status of love and marital choice in research was matched by the low status of the investigators of these topics in academia. Within sociology, the study of the family occupied a lowly position in relation to other more vital questions such as juvenile delinquency, crime, poverty, urbanization, deviance, and race relations. In psychology, the study of love, marriage, and the family was not so much low status as nonstatus. Clinical psychology could study the problems caused by poor marriages, but marital choice itself was not worthy of academic study. Perusing journals purporting to publish articles on personality and social psychology and finding little dealing with the human condition, I formulated Murstein's Law (which I published many years later): "The amount of research devoted to a topic on human behavior is inversely related to its importance and interest [to mankind]" (Murstein 1971c, p. 75).

In recent years, however, psychologists as well as sociologists have increasingly turned their attention to the study of interpersonal attraction. Whether this shift might be attributed to new-found security that enabled them to reject the physicist model of the scientist is a moot point. Other factors that might be mentioned include increasingly sophisticated statistical measures adapted to the study of interpersonal relationships, the rise in the "humanistic" element in the social sciences, and (oh crass world!) the increased funding by the federal government of "soft-headed" topics like love or marital choice. Whatever the reason, this book is the product of the enlightened era of research.[2]

Much of the data to be described resulted from an NIMH grant between 1964 and 1969. Before considering the data and theoretical framework (Stimulus Value Role Theory) that in part guided it and in

[2]From the recent agitation provoked by an American senator questioning the use of funds for research on "love" the "enlightened era" may have terminated. Hopefully the setback will prove only temporary.

part preceded it, I believe it would be of interest to the reader to trace the historical antecedents of theories of marital choice (Chapter 2). Following this historical review is a review and critique of the most influential current theories of marital choice: psychoanalysis (Chapter 3), complementary needs (Chapter 4), value theories (Chapter 5), and process theories (Chapter 6). Some of the theories are no more than broad schemata, while others are replete with hypotheses and data. I have used "theory" in the broadest sense possible.

In Chapter 7, Stimulus-Value-Role (henceforth SVR) Theory is described and an attempt is made to compare the various theories. The succeeding chapters deal with a description of the subjects and the measuring instruments (Chapter 8) and the hypotheses and data that pertain to SVR theory (Chapters 9 through 14). Chapter 15 deals with the applicability of exchange and SVR theory to other dyads such as marital couples and same-sex friends. Finally, Chapter 16 is devoted to assessment of the results in terms of the fit between theory and data and consideration of possible modifications of the theory. Most of the noncommercial tests constructed specifically for the present research as well as background data for the three samples of subjects are reproduced in the appendix.

CHAPTER **2**

Historical Antecedents
of Theories of Marital Choice

PARENTAL DOMINANCE IN MARRIAGE

Several hundred years ago in France, the son of the president of Dijon's parliament asked his father whether it was true that he intended to marry him to a Mademoiselle X. "Son" replied his father, perhaps preoccupied with important matters, "mind your own business" (Epton, 1959). Such a remark may seem funny to a modern audience, but a typical French person several hundred years ago would have found nothing strange about the father's statement.

Marriage, until quite recently, was regarded as too important a family or clan matter to be entrusted to foolish, impetuous young adults. As Goode has noted, "Kinfolk or immediate family can disregard the question of who marries whom, only if a marriage is not seen as a link between kin lines, only if no property, power, lineage, honor, totemic relationships, and the like are believed to flow from the kin lines through the spouses to their offspring" (Goode, 1959, p. 42).

The structure of most societies, until recently, was based on one or more items in the preceding list—and some societies still are. It

Much of the material for this chapter is drawn from my earlier work *Love, Sex, and Marriage through the Ages* (Murstein, 1974a).

5

became incumbent on important families, therefore, to guard their daughters against romantic passion, which might lead to premarital sex and possibly even to marriage to an individual wholly unacceptable to the family. In medieval Europe, premarital sex involving a woman of standing was condemned as contrary to the moral dicta established by the Church. It also depreciated the woman's economic value in the marriage market. In addition, it was hazardous to those who wished to remain unmarried, because the Catholic Church recognized secret marriages (without benefit of the clergy) as valid until the Council of Trent in 1563. Before this ruling, it often proved impossible to determine whether a couple had exchanged marriage vows before jumping into bed, or whether the memory of such a vow by one member of the couple was a fictitious postsexual concoction. Moreoever, an impetuous youth, eager to seduce a damsel, might secretly marry her by saying "I do" and later claim that he had never uttered such a vow.

The societal means of regulating marriage were manifold. The obvious method was to inculcate youth with the idea that it was wrong to marry without their parents' consent. Another way, as in France, was to have the government prohibit marriage without paternal consent before the age of thirty-five. Families also resorted to child betrothals, whereby infants were pledged to each other by their parents. Young women were sequestered under the care of chaperones; in Europe, Catholic girls were often sent to convents to assure their innocence and naiveté.

With the Church's ruling that marriage must be between mutually consenting adults, young adults gained a modicum of freedom in their choice of marital partner. However, the parents' control of the purse strings, in addition to tradition, served to maintain the idea of parental participation in the choice of a partner for their child. Moreover, as Martin Luther pointed out, the suppression of forced marriages was not the same as instituting free choice.

> To hinder or forbid marriage and to compel or urge marriage are two quite different things. Although parents have the right and power in the first instance—namely, to forbid marriage— it does not follow that they have the power to compel their children to marry. It is more tolerable to obstruct and block the love which two persons have for each other than to force together two persons who have neither liking nor love for each other. In the first case there is pain for a short time, while in the second it is to be feared that there will be an eternal hell and a lifetime of tragedy (Luther, 1955, p. 264)

Since he held the purse strings, the father could, by vetoing his offspring's choice, eventually induce his child to accept a spouse of the father's choosing. Luther himself goes on to say that a good Christian ought to accept his father's wishes even if they make him unhappy, because Scripture enjoins us to "resist not evil."

In the ensuing centuries, the independence of youth slowly increased, though parental veto power persisted to some extent into the nineteenth and twentieth centuries. A degree of independence, nonetheless, did not sanction the acceptance of passionate love as a valid reason for marriage. Indeed, in the seventeenth and eighteenth centuries marriage experts denounced passion as a basis for marriage, extolling "reason" in its stead.

RATIONAL MARRIAGE

A listing of the advocates of rational marriage reads like a who's who of the period. The list includes not only Spinoza (1952), but Milton, who noted, in connection with the creation of Eve for Adam in *Paradise Lost:*

> What higher in her societie thou findst
> Attractive, human, rational, love still;
> In loving thou dost well, in passion not,
> Wherein true Love consists not; love refines
> The thoughts, and heart enlarges, hath his seat
> In Reason. . . . (Milton, 1952, p. 245)

The supposition that love is at the beck and call of the rational will, and not of the glands, is made in *The Bachelor's Directory,* where the husband is told, "If she [the wife] loves you, you cannot without ingratitude forbear to love her" (*The Bachelor's Directory,* 1696, p. 237). Even women, frequently thought to be at the mercy of their emotions, sneered at romance. Mary Astell, although she champions the cause of women's rights, asks, "what does . . . Marrying for Love amount to? There's no great odds between . . . Marrying for the Love of Money, or for the Love of Beauty; the Man does not act according to Reason in either Case, but is govern'd by irregular appetites" (Astell, 1706, pp. 17-18).

Swift favored matches of prudence without passion (1964). In *Gulliver's Travels* he extols the Houyhnhnms, a race of horses who possess all the virtues for which men strive, and who marry for purely rational reasons (1952).

Samuel Johnson expressed himself quite concisely: "It is commonly a weak man who marries for love" (Boswell, 1952, p. 297). Kant stated that once a couple had the will to enter into a reciprocal relationship "in accordance with their sexual nature, they *must* necessarily marry each other . . . in accordance with the juridical laws of pure reason" (1952, p. 419).

What was *reason* in marital choice? The *raison d'être* for marriage was procreation. Children could best be reared in a congenial home, and reason dictated that congeniality was most likely to occur when both spouses were of the same socioeconomic rank. Nothing was said about compatibility of personalities, it being assumed that that might be arranged within the possibilities dictated by status. In any event, since emotional satisfaction was not the purpose of marriage, the partners had little to complain about as long as each carried out the institutionalized role—the husband that of the provider, the wife that of homemaker and bearer of children.

Even such liberals as Voltaire and Diderot did not refer to interpersonal needs or compatibility as components of marriage: "The *voluntary* union between man and woman contracted by *free* individuals, so as to have children" (Epton, 1959, p. 23). Defoe, who championed women's rights, nevertheless thought that a woman of menopausal age who dared to marry was a lecher, as was her husband (1727).

Rationalism deemed virginity not a sign of virtue, but a means of increased pleasure. Its value to Jeremy Bentham was that, "by restraining enjoyment for a time, it afterwards elevates it to that very pitch which leaves, on the whole, the largest addition to the stock of happiness" (Day, 1954, p. 307).

Montesquieu saw reason as the basis for the development of marital customs. In England, daughters sometimes married without their fathers' approval; but he found a rationale for this, because there marriage was the only vocation open to women. In France, the father's stronger role was rational since, if the daughter did not like the match he offered her, she was free to enter a convent and take up another vocation. What puzzled Montesquieu was the "irrational" behavior of Italian and Spanish daughters: "convents are there established and yet they may marry without the consent of their fathers" (1952, p. 189).

"Reason" took a somewhat more realistic path in the speculations of Locke and Paine. The former reasoned that if the purpose of marriage was *only* for the procreation and care of children, might not the contract of marriage be broken once this purpose had been achieved? (Locke, 1952). Paine had observed that some American Indian tribes he knew, unlike Christians, allowed unhappy marriages to be dissolved; their philosophy was that "we make it our business to oblige the heart we are afraid to lose" (1894, p. 53).

In sum, the concept of marriage as an emotional bond and a haven from worldly troubles had not yet evolved. "Radicals" concerned themselves with finding a rationale for dissolving marriage when it became oppressive, but they accepted the concept of marriage as essentially a rational, functional means of propagation.

WHERE WAS LOVE?

The adherence to parental dominance and rationalism as guiding concepts in marital choice did not clash with the belief that marriage and love were compatible if the concept of love could be bifurcated into two categories, passionate love and conjugal love, the latter being acceptable in marriage. Passionate love, for most individuals, did not properly belong in marriage, and was not a valid reason for marriage. The early Church fathers had warned that for a man even to *look* upon his wife with lust made him an adulterer.

In the twelfth century, the troubadours had excluded passionate love[1] from marriage for another reason. This reason becomes manifest in a letter from the Countess Marie of Champagne, who presided over a celebrated "love" court that concerned itself with affairs of the heart. The letter she wrote was in response to arbitration submitted to her regarding a dispute between a courtier and a noblewoman. Earlier he had pursued her endlessly, but she had rejected him saying that her heart belonged to another. He nevertheless persisted in courting her

---

[1] The troubadours concerned themselves with courtly love, which seems very close to passionate love as used here. Courtly love, according to the leading medieval writer on this topic, Andreas Capellanus, could be subdivided into two kinds of love: "pure" love and "mixed" love. "Pure" love referred to a union of hearts and minds but not of bodies. It was inexhaustible, because it continually increased tension without satisfying it. The lover might be permitted to kiss and embrace his beloved, even without her clothes, but the final "solace" was omitted. Although "pure" love was the ideal, "mixed" love was also acceptable. "Mixed" love was "pure" love with sex added. As with "pure" love, however, its course was the desire to please the beloved, and its effect was to ennoble the character of the lover. Nevertheless, there was an inherent contradiction between the "good" in "mixed" love and the fact that if the beloved were married she would become an adulteress. Apart from the inconsistency, a good case could be made for courtly love as complementary rather than antagonistic to marriage, because conjugal love was obligatory, whereas courtly love was based on freedom of choice.

until, to get rid of him, she said that she would consider taking him as her man if ever she should fall out of love. She soon married her true love and thought the matter settled. However, the obnoxious suitor now claimed her love on the grounds that by marrying she had automatically become unable to love her spouse. She resisted this interpretation, and the two agreed to the Countess's arbitration. The countess wrote:

> We declare and we hold as firmly established that love cannot exert its powers between two people who are married to each other. For lovers give each other everything freely, under no compulsion of necessity, but married people are in duty bound to give in to each other's desires and deny themselves to each other in nothing. Besides, how does it increase a husband's honor if after the manner of lovers he enjoys the embraces of his wife, since the worth of character of neither can be increased thereby, and they seem to have nothing more than they already had a right to? [Moreover,] no woman, even if she is married, can be crowned with the reward of the King of Love unless she is seen to be enlisted in the service of Love himself outside the bonds of wedlock. But another rule of Love teaches that no one can be in love with two men. Rightly, therefore, Love cannot acknowledge any rights of his between husband and wife. But there is still another argument that seems to stand in the way of this, which is that between them there can be no true jealousy, and without it true love may not exist. (Capellanus, 1959, pp. 106-7)

Since the arbitration was not legally binding, the woman presumably was not compelled to accept the Countess's verdict.

The conjugal love that was presumed to exist in marriage was a rational expression of the spousal role. The Puritan divine Wadsworth said of husbands' attitudes toward wives *"The Great God commands thee to love her . . .* How vile then are those who don't love their wives" (Morgan, 1944, p. 12). Not to love one's wife, therefore, no matter what his or her shortcomings, was to admit one's failure to be a good Christian.

Swedenborg noted the distinction between passionate and conjugal love "With those who are truly in love conjugial, conjunction of minds, and therewith friendship increases" (1954, p. 225). To the mystically inclined Swedenborg, conjugal love is experienced in a mental or internal sense, whereas those who love each other only physically experience a loss of conjugal love that "withdraws more and more from the interiors of the mind, and successively departs from them at length to the cuticles" (1954, p. 226).

It must be acknowledged that passionate love was not completely absent as a precursor to marriage from the sixteenth to the nineteenth century. Shakespeare, for example, allows such love to blossom into marriage in several of his plays, including *Romeo and Juliet.* Passion in these plays generally thrives on frustration and deprivation and becomes, seemingly, an act of rebellion against the repressive establishment. Shakespeare's plays, in which highborn gentlemen and highborn ladies fell in love and married despite parental opposition, represented a kind of wish-fulfillment rather than actual behavior in Elizabethan times.

Even by the nineteenth century, passionate love did not generally lead to marriage. The romantic's love affairs were generally extramarital or premarital. Passionate love still connoted an unhealthy, maladaptive state in contrast to reason. Stendhal in his book *On Love*, written in 1822, noted that passion led to distortion (1947). He described its effect by analogy to an experience he had had in a visit to Salzburg. He had observed the bare bough of a tree that after having fallen into a salt pit and lain there for several weeks, had acquired a covering of brilliant crystals. When it was taken out of the pit, the shabby branch appeared at first glance to be a priceless *object d'art*, but it was actually worthless. He compared this event to what takes place in love. The lover fantasizes and projects his ego-ideal on to the beloved, who is often no more worthy of these fantasies than was the bare bough; hence Stendhal called this process *crystallization*. When reality eventually intrudes, the person is seen for what he is, and love dies. Herbert Spencer, in a letter written at the tender age of 24 in 1845, also noted the connection between love and idealization, but he saw idealization not as an illusion but as a spur for the beloved to continue to act as to be worthy of this state (1926). Spencer was actually enunciating a newly evolving concept of love that had departed quite strongly from "rational" love.

VICTORIAN LOVE

The invigorating passion of the early-nineteenth-century romantics had caught the fancy of the middle class, but the romantic's attack on long-cherished institutions such as marriage was unacceptable to the latter. The bourgeois code emphasized personal responsibility for one's actions, respect for parents, and adherence to religion, if not enthusiastic acceptance. But the code ignored the growing desire of youth to gain a measure of the excitement and freedom of action that the personal life of the romantics seemed to personify. Sensitive to this dissatisfaction, an increasing number of novelists criticized marriages of convenience as morally wrong, and doomed its participants to perpetual unhappiness. The reading public identified with Jane Eyre in Charlotte Brontë's eponymous novel when she refused the suit of St. John Rivers, whom she liked but did not love.

The answer lay in a new alloy forged of the driving force of the romantic's sensual passion and tempered by the conservative family sentiment of the bourgeoisie. The florid phrases, energetic manner, styled unconventionality, and languid poses of the romantic were combined in a synthetic manner with bourgeois morality. Men saw their "beastial" needs elevated, not merely through their goal of propagation, but because they had as their object the "angel in the house," as the wife came to be euphemistically called after the astounding commercial success of the book-long poem of the same name by Coventry Patmore. Passion was purified when expressed within the confines of matrimony, and that only when and if its delightfully deified object shyly nodded assent. Lust was transformed into treacly sentimentality.

AMERICAN MARRIAGE

Marriage in America was not impervious to the influence of victorian love, but its effect was much muted in favor of the more relaxed interaction of companions. Girls in the United States had generally not been raised in partial segregation from boys or in convents, as had been the case in continental Europe. In pioneer times, now drawing to a close in the United States, women had been scarce, esteemed hard workers who could not be relegated to the pedestal of inertia reserved for the bourgeois wife.

Foreigners who visited America were amazed at the forthrightness and outspokeness of American women. They also noted the naturalness of male–female interaction and how much more women were esteemed by men than in Europe. Still, Americans seemed to lack passion. Stendhal doubted that crystallization could take place in the United States. His compatriot Moreau was astounded to find that a young couple could be together, without fear. "Sometimes on returning, the servants find them asleep and the candle gone out—so cold is love in this country" (Moreau, 1949, p. 99). Even the English, generally regarded by Continentals as an icy people, remarked that Americans lacked passion. J. S. Buckingham wrote that "love among the American people, appears to be required rather as an affair of judgment than of the heart" (1867, p. 479).

What the Europeans mistook for coldness arose from the fact that the sexes in America were raised together and interacted much more in childhood than did the Europeans, and so the fantasy built of seclusion and repression never developed. Instead, a camaraderie of sorts was developing between the sexes, which made for a degree of social ease and friendship but was too reality-oriented for passion.

THE RUDIMENTS OF THEORY

When in the nineteenth century the first marriage manuals were published in the United States, they focused on the qualities deemed essential to the quite stratified roles the marriage partners were destined to play. The chief criteria were religious, constitutional and physical, moral, and characterological (Gordon and Bernstein, 1969). An ideal husband, for example, was religious, sound of wind and limbs, and the recipient of no black marks for "idleness, intemperate use of intoxicating drinks, smoking, chewing, sniffing tobacco . . . taking . . . opium, licentiousness, . . . gambling, swearing and keeping late hours at night" (Fowler, 1855, p. 131). An ideal wife embodied the four virtues of piety, purity, submissiveness, and domesticity.

In the second half of the nineteenth century, the marriage writers went further and spoke of compatibility based on interpersonal factors. These may be subdivided into three categories: homogamy-complementarity combination, evolution, and phrenology.

Homogamy–Complementarity

One of the earliest proponents of a theory of the attraction of opposites was Hegel. As a result of his dialectics, Hegel stated that two opposing forces interact to form a new, more viable entity. "The force of generation, as of mind, is all the greater, the greater the apposition out of which it is reproduced. Familiarity, close acquaintance, the habit of common pursuits, should not precede marriage, they should come about for the first time within it" (Hegel, 1952, p. 134).

Most writers, however, made a distinction between background and temperament, physique, and personality. O. S. Fowler saw nature as buttressing the necessity of like marrying like: "Do lions naturally associate with sheep, or wolves with fowls, or elephants with tigers?" (1859, p. 280). Nevertheless, according to Fowler, when Nature saw one of her subjects depart drastically from the norm, she instilled in him the powerful attraction for an opposite type, as when the exceedingly tall, thin man was drawn to the short, plump woman. The same principle held for temperament and mental ability. A man with a magnificent memory but fuzzy conceptual powers ought to marry a woman with superb conceptual powers but a poor memory. The children, Fowler assures us, will have both conceptual strength and a marvelous memory.[2]

Fowler sums his approach with a strikingly modern amalgam of homogeneity and complementarity that would be later echoed by Kirkpatrick (1967), Goodman (1964), Murstein (1971a), and Karp, Jackson, and Lester (1970): "Wherein, and as far as you are what you ought to be, marry one *like* yourself; but wherein and as far as you have any marked *excesses* or defects, marry those *unlike* yourself in these objectionable particulars" (Fowler, 1859, p. 295).

Other writers such as the unidentified author of "The choice matrimonial" in the British magazine *Chamber's Journal* (1898), and Allen (1886), focused on a strictly complementary attraction theory. According to the latter "We fall in love with our moral, mental, and physical complement." Coan (1869), however, differentiated between environmentally induced characteristics and biological ones. He supported complementarity as regards "Natural organization," by which he meant temperament and physique, but he added that in terms of all that is induced (environmental influence) there must be similarity in purpose, thought, and how the couple will live; thus, "The secret of marriage is *opposition of temperament with identity of aim*" (Coan, 1869, p. 500).

Evolution and Genetics

The ramifications of Darwin's theory of evolution spilled over into theories of marital choice. Westermarck declared that monogamy was the most advanced evolutionary form of marriage, other forms, such as, for example, polygamy, being survivals of earlier stages of development (Westermarck, 1936). Sir George Campbell (1866) thought that scientific matchmaking was unnecessary, since evolution weeded out

---

[2] Fowler seems not to have considered that the child might have fuzzy conceptual powers augmented by a poor memory.

the mismatchings of the race. Charles Bellamy, brother of the more illustrious Edward Bellamy, wrote a utopian novel, *Experimental Marriage,* in which each individual within his lifetime evolves gradually toward a more perfect union, shedding less evolutionarily fit spouses along the way (Bellamy, 1889).

Other writers went a step further and speculated on the chemical and genetic makeup of individuals that influenced marital choice. A pre-Darwinian "chemist" was Johann Wolfgang von Goethe. In his novel, *Die Wahlverwandtschaften* (Elective Affinities), he likened interpersonal attraction to a chemical phenomenon in which four elements, originally joined in two pairs, are brought together (Goethe, 1963). The result is that each of the formerly paired elements seeks new combinations with a member of the other pair. In the novel, a wealthy man and his wife's niece feel a mutual attraction, as do his wife and his best friend. In accordance with Goethe's theory, when the husband and wife make love while under the influence of this "affinity" for nonmarital partners, the resulting child acquires the eyes of the husband's inamorata and the physiognomy of the wife's lover.

A book by Otto Weininger written a hundred years later and entitled *Sex and Character* was taken more seriously as a scientific treatise. He argued that no sex was of a pure gender. A man, for example, possessed predominantly masculine characteristics in his cells, but also some female characteristics. Each characteristic seeks its opposite in the opposite sex; hence a purely masculine type, hypothetically speaking, would be drawn to a purely feminine woman; however, the average man seeks a woman who possesses female characteristics to complement his masculine characteristics, and masculine characteristics to complement his feminine characteristics.

Weininger believed that he could account for much of woman's behavior on the basis of his genetic theory. Take the question of women's rights (circa 1900). No *pure* woman, in his view, desired independence and equality with men. A pure woman was predominantly sexual and cared little for masculine activities; however, those unfortunate women whose genetic makeup was heavily masculine naturally aspired to freedom of action, power, and intellectual accomplishment. Their agitation was unnatural and pathogenic, for most women are not constitutionally interested in such goals. The biological aspects of the theory proved stimulating to Patten (1908), but he considered it insensitive to the social influences that formed woman's role.

The lure of genetics proved difficult to discourage even in the twentieth century. Szondi advanced the theory that marital choice is directed "by the latent recessive genes, by the common ancestors that reappear, and formally reincarnate, in later generations after having been repressed for periods. The mates, though frequently quite dissimilar in their manifest traits, are attracted to each other by the stimuli of a unique 'identity' " (1937, p. 25).

Phrenology

Originally formulated by Franz Joseph Gall around 1800, phrenology was a theory based on the premise that the character and talent of a person are localized in specific portions of the brain. The size and development of the regions were held to be proportionate to the development of the particular faculty and to cause corresponding changes in the skull; hence, from an examination of the lumps and crevices of the scalp, an experienced phrenologist was thought to be able to make an accurate assessment of personality.

The areas related to marriage were said to reside in the posterior regions of the brain. As listed by Wells (1869), these included Amativeness, Conjugality, and Inhabitiveness. The first was responsible for sexual activity, the second for "the mating propensity or instinct for permanent union" (Wells, 1869, p. 11), and the last for the love of home. Physiognomy also played a role, so that, for example, a protruding jaw was a sure sign of sexual strength, whereas a dullard was diagnosed readily enough by the fact that his forehead was shorter vertically than was his nose. A person with a feebly sized cerebellum (believed to be the seat of Amativeness) ought never to marry, and phrenologists did not hesitate to advise clients to break their engagements if they found this important element wanting in their fiancé(e). Although phrenology has been wholly discredited today, its hold on the nineteenth-century public was so great that even Queen Victoria did not hesitate to have the royal children's heads examined by a phrenologist (Turner, 1954).

LOVE TRIUMPHS

By the end of the nineteenth century, love was unquestioned as the primary determinant of marriage. Lester Ward, one of the founders of sociology, threw the weight of sociology behind "love" in calling it an evolutionary product confined to the Aryan race (Ward, 1916). It was typical Caucasian policy at the turn of the century for Caucasian writers to point out that God, who was, after all, the supreme Caucasian, had assigned the capacity to love to his elected people, the Caucasians. One hundred years earlier, no less a man than Thomas Jefferson had rejected the idea that blacks were capable of love.

The triumph of love was not sealed, however, by a few textbook writers, but by the writers in the United States' most popular magazines. Alice Preston in the *Ladies Home Journal* of 1905 remarked that "no high-minded girl and no girl of truly refined feeling . . . ever . . . admits the advisability of marriage without love" (Preston, 1905, p. 26). Likewise, the *Woman's Home Companion* of 1911 advised: "Since we know that Love—that divine presence—may come, it is only rational and wise to be ready for his coming" (McCall, 1911, p. 24).

What had occurred to change the ideology of nineteenth-century marriage from "love after marriage" to "love preceding marriage"? I have found no explanations of this phenomenon in the literature, but based on an analysis of the development of American society from 1850 to 1900 and a perusal of the magazine literature relating to marriage during this period, the following causes seem plausible: legal enfranchisement of women, their increased earning power, improvements in education, and the egalitarian ideological climate.

During the nineteenth century, women gained the right to hold and sell real property, to maintain personal property, and to generally retain custody of children in case of marital breakup. In addition, the rapid industrialization of the country following the Civil War, the creation of many new service jobs, the perfection of the typewriter and the movement of women into secretarial positions, and the growth of the garment industry and of factories gave women a more important economic role in the family. The spread of mass compulsory education gave women a further opportunity to acquire useful knowledge in furthering their earning capacity. The increased status of women and the continued clamoring for justice by the women's rights movements helped create a climate for the emergence of a "new" much more independent woman. It should also be noted that American women, for reasons stated earlier, had already achieved a favorable social status as compared to many European women. By the beginning of the twentieth century, therefore, most men were willing to accept the social equality of women, although they balked at granting them economic equality in terms of job and pay.

Love as a reason for marriage is most apt to be found among relative equals. The ancient Athenian men rarely loved their wives. Women were sequestered and uneducated—hardly suitable love objects. There were, however, many celebrated homosexual loves, which is scarcely surprising considering that only men received education, interacted freely, and discoursed on interesting philosophical questions.

Love in the United States blossomed when the degree of free choice in marriage, which had been increasing steadily, was catalyzed by increasing status. But apart from woman's improved status, three further important conditions had to be satisfied before romance could blossom: youth had to have the opportunity to interact, sufficient leisure time to fall in love, and privacy. By the early twentieth century, these conditions were being met. Urbanization led to increased contact between the sexes and widened the field of eligibles. The spread of public high schools and the development of the land grant coeducational universities were to provide the time for love to bloom.

The perfection of the bicycle and the invention of the automobile permitted escape from the surveillance of parents and parent-surrogates, so that courtship could be pursued more naturally and in privacy. The invention of the telephone also aided in increasing communication and interaction.

The freedom of choice in marriage has continued to expand during the twentieth century. Women constitute an increasingly larger percentage of the work force, and they have moved into better paying jobs and ever closer to parity of status with men, though they are not yet equal in that regard. The burgeoning population of singles today, estimated at 49 million by Jacoby (1974), indicates that choice is more important than ever, and fewer are marrying because they have to. Parents of a young woman are no longer asked (even for the sake of formality) for the right to propose to their daughter. Rather, the couple announce to their parents that they intend to marry, or that they have married.

SUMMARY

There have been many changes in the conceptualization of the purpose and criteria for marriage. Marriage began as a contract, as much between families as between the nominal participants. The elders' primary concern was family interest rather than that of the welfare of the participants. The marriage's alleged rationale was propagation. When parental influence weakened, it was replaced by "reason" as the criterion of choice. Individuals of comparable backgrounds were presumed to rationally choose each other on the basis of being a good propagating stock and the hope of frictionless if not intimate interaction.

Love, including passion, is not a recent phenomenon. However, in medieval and later Europe its place was outside marriage. By the seventeenth century it was becoming accepted as a proper post-nuptial factor in marriage. Finally, toward the middle of the nineteenth century, it became accepted as a reason for marriage.

The rudimentary marital choice theories presented in the nineteenth century (homogamy-complementarity, evolution, and phrenology), despite their apparent diversity, had something in common; successful matching was alleged to result from the habits and traits of one or both of the partners. The use of tobacco and drinking was deemed inimical to marriage, as was a deficient bump in the cranium for conjugality. Regarding the complementarity aspect of mating, it focused on fixed attributes such as tallness or shortness. There is little concern in nineteenth-century marriage manuals about the quality and kind of verbal interaction between members of a couple, nor is there much mention of compatibility of needs. Questions regarding role aspirations and role compatibility were rarely raised.

The main reason for these omissions, in my opinion, was the great difference in power between the sexes. This disparity enabled men to secure most of the benefits of society—education, interesting jobs, legal benefits, political franchise—for themselves while relegating to women much drab work and few privileges. As a result of this power differential, men were much more attractive individuals than were women, and since they shared little with women except sex and family care, there was little stimulating interaction between the sexes. Most men, and some women too, also supported the roles assigned to each sex by the masculine-dominated society. Women who tried to escape their assigned domestic-subservient roles were presumed to invoke not only their husbands' ire, but that of evolution and God himself.

The second half of the nineteenth century witnessed considerable gains in ideology regarding women's place in society as well as considerable legal, political, educational, and economic gains. Although the power differential between men and women still existed, the gap was narrowed. As women gained power, they increasingly resisted pressures to marry for the sake of security and asserted their right of choice. At the same time, their increasing ability to partake of the fruits of society made them more interesting companions to men. By the twentieth century, their effectiveness in choosing their own marital partners was understood under the title of the love marriage.

The freedom of women in marriage, however, should not be overestimated. At the turn of the century most women did not work, and they had neither as much education as their spouses nor as good jobs. They still had not gained the vote. Yet progress from 1850 to 1900 was steady and considerable.

The twentieth century saw an acceleration in the number of theories of marital choice. Some of these are as rough hewn and non-empirical as the theories of the preceding century, while others contain hypotheses and research undertaken to test these hypotheses. In the next chapter we shall consider the non-empirically-based position of Freud on marital choice, a position that bridges the gap between nineteenth-century views and the more data-conscious theories of recent times.

CHAPTER 3

Theories of Marital Choice: Psychoanalysis

FREUDIAN THEORY

The key to understanding the Freudian position regarding marital choice is that Freud's guiding philosophy was hedonism: the goal of behavior was the pursuit of pleasurable excitement terminating in tension reduction and the avoidance of pain. Human interaction occurs not because there is a love of mankind or a desire for contact *qua* contact, but because relations with other humans are usually the only way in which painful tensions can be reduced to manageable levels. Man is a social animal from biological need rather than from social choice.

Further, man is generally at the mercy of instinctual drives that are irrational in nature. These biologically based drives release emotional or psychic energy; that energy relating to the sexual instinct is called *libido*. The libido is the raw material out of which complex emotional states such as love can develop. Moreover, Freud used the concept of a closed energy system; thus only a limited supply of libido is present in each individual; consequently, Freud saw the practice of *agape*, or universal love, as a foolish dilution and utilization of one's supply of love.

If I am to love him (with that kind of universal love) simply because he, too, is a denizen of the earth, like an insect or an earthworm or a grass-snake, then I fear that but a small modicum of love will fall to his lot, and it would be impossible for me to give him as much as by all the laws of reason I am entitled to retain for myself. What is the point of an injunction promulgated with such solemnity, if reason does not recommend it to us? (Freud, 1952b, p. 786)

However, the drives themselves are often wholly unconscious or visible to the conscious mind only in a distorted form. Man imagines that he functions by using his rational faculties; actually he mainly rationalizes.

The determinants of mutual choice are largely shaped by the success with which the individual navigates the shoals of the stages of psychosexual development. Each stage is named after the principal erogenous zone that gains sensitivity during the particular period in question. The result of passing through the various stages successfully is an adult whose principal source of sexual gratification is found in the genitals and whose nonneurotic character enables him to pair with a partner in marriage and to reproduce the species.

The first stage to be traversed starts at birth and involves the most erogenous organ of infants, the mouth. Psychologically speaking, in this period the infant develops either a sense of trust and confidence in his mother's ability to meet his needs and in the stability of his environment, or a sense of mistrust in his mother and in the environment.

In the anal stage, which begins generally toward the end of the second year of life, he comes to grips with the issues of hostility and of power. One focus of this stage is the question of the giving or the withholding of feces which, by being withheld, become a focus of hostile expression toward the parents or a vehicle for the expression of power.

The third, or phallic, stage draws its inspiration from Oedipus who, in Sophocles' tragedy, unwittingly kills his father and marries his mother. Development during this stage becomes a primary factor influencing marital choice, although its inception occurs between the ages of three and six. The principal erogenous zone involves the genitals, but not in the sense that adult sexual tensions are generated. Rather, the little boy develops a more demanding and possessive kind of love for the mother than heretofore. He may announce boldly that he will marry his mother when he grows up. However, there is a rival in the house—the father. Worse luck yet, the mother seems to prefer the father to him. She sleeps with the father, goes with him on trips, and in numerous ways shows evidence of preference for him over the son. Why? The young male child is unable to conceive of abstract concepts such as interpersonal needs, companionship, and the like. In all probability, he also has a distorted understanding of sexual relationships. He thinks concretely, and in a simple fashion he imagines that her preference for the father results from the fact that he is big and strong, whereas he, the son, is small and weak.

The son loves his father, according to Freud, but he also may hate him as a rival for his mother's affection. The boy thinks if he could weaken the father physically, perhaps the mother would take him as her husband. But if he can fantasy destroying the father's masculinity, cannot the father destroy his own masculinity? He has seen girls, who have no penes. He may assume they have been bad and had theirs cut off. If his hostile wishes were correctly diagnosed by the father, he might, in anger, cut off the boy's penis too; thus is born castration anxiety.

The normal boy is able to work his way through these difficulties. Because he loves his father, he begins increasingly to identify with him. He interjects many of the father's characteristics into his own personality, and he represses his interest in the mother into the unconscious. He may become more distant from her, he may fuse his love for both parents into a love of the family, or he may go outside the family for friendships (Kenkel, 1966).

This is the normal course. It is possible, however, for the father to be so severe and dominating that the son can neither express affection for his mother nor identify with his father. Or the mother may be so rejecting of the son that the boy turns to the father for warmth and affection, and may over-generalize and conclude that the opposite sex is too threatening to relate to. On the other hand, the mother, in her dissatisfaction with her husband, may encourage the boy's courtship of her, so that it becomes difficult for him to disentangle himself and eventually relate to other women. We shall see the consequences of these occurrences for marital choice later on.

The girl's situation is somewhat different from that of the boy. At around the age of five or so, like the boy, she becomes ambivalent about the parent of the same sex and sexually attracted to the opposite sex parent. But obviously she cannot have castration anxiety. According to Freudian orthodoxy, she regards the clitoris as a poor substitute for the penis and feels herself already castrated. She blames and rejects the mother for her lack of penis, and, manifesting penis envy, she turns to the father in the hope that he can supply her with a symbolic penis, a child.

Similarly to the boy, she gradually gives up the father and begins to identify with the mother. However, her lack of castration anxiety makes the psychological weaning process more gradual and incomplete than it is for the boy. Because her *envy* was not *anxiety,* there is much less compunction to renounce the father, give up the search for a penis, and identify strongly with the mother. Penis envy is not really sublimated, therefore, and it plays a major motivating role throughout feminine development.

The woman does not need to repress her desire for her father in a comparable fashion to that of the boy for his mother; consequently, her superego, which is, in part, a sublimated result of the necessity of repression of desire for the parent, is not as strong as that of the man. It remains more dependent on the external world for support, compared to the more independently functioning superego of the man. Women, thus, are more dependent on the love of others than are men. Women are also more narcissistic than men "because the sexual, reproductive, and personal demands made upon her are greater than those made upon men, and narcissism serves as a kind of defense in which integrity of the self does not dissolve in the face of agreeing to other people's demands" (Bardwick, 1971, pp. 14-15). The woman is now free to follow the passive, masochistic role she plays in the family—that of serving others.

Between the phallic and the genital stages of psychological development occurs the latency period, in which the individual's rate of psychological growth diminishes considerably. However, in the final genital stage of development at puberty, the rush of sexual energy reawakens the old Oedipal triangle. The inhibitions against incestuous love nevertheless remain in force for the normal personality, and the adolescent transfers the focus of this insistent sex drive onto another more socially acceptable object: the boyfriend or girlfriend.

To understand the influences behind the selection of a spouse for marriage, we must return to the infant's earliest days of life—the time when he existed in a state of primary bliss or narcissism, and all of his needs were met. Initially he is unable to distinguish between himself and the breast that feeds him—ego boundaries are very diffuse and vague. Soon enough, however, he learns that his needs are not always immediately met; that is, the feeding and diapering apparatus may not immediately sense his discomfort—his mother may be out of the room. His new ability to differentiate between himself and the other leaves him the choice of two love objects. The first is affection for those on whom the infant is dependent for feeding, care, and protection. Freud calls this kind of love *anaclitic* (literally "leaning up against"); the other is to take himself as love-object, which type of choice Freud calls *narcissistic.*

Object love of the anaclitic type, Freud tells us (1949a), is generally characteristic of the man, whereas the narcissistic type is characteristic of the woman. Freud acknowledges that these are general tendencies—there are numerous exceptions in which each sex adopts the other kind of love. No rationale is explicitly given as to why each sex generally follows a different model. It was noted earlier, however, that narcissism is more apt to characterize women than men in accordance with nature's compensation for the demands she makes on women. Perhaps, therefore, men are more drawn to the anaclitic type of woman because their mothers are more affectionate to them, generally preferring boys to girls.

Another troublesome item not explained by Freud is the seeming contradiction in love types represented by men and women, which ought to preclude their attraction to each other. For example, if the typical man follows the anaclitic model, he ought to be drawn toward a nurturant mother type (anaclitic). But the typical woman (narcissistic type) would be taking herself as a love object and, therefore, ought to exhibit little interest in a nurturant role vis-à-vis the man.

I think the confusion arises because Freud was so focused on unconscious drives that he failed to recognize that a resolution of the paradox depends on realizing that societal roles may be independent of or contradictory to unconscious drives. Thus, the late Victorian society of which he was a part would have prescribed that the man actively pursue the woman's hand in marriage. Once married, however, her *role* was to focus on her home, children, and husband. Her narcissism would not be allowed to interfere with her societal role but might focus itself in endless primping and concern about her toilette and dress.

However, narcissism does not have to be expressed directly through overconcern with the self. An older individual may love a younger person who seems to represent the qualities that the former possessed in his youth. A person may love another who represents what he would like to be, and a woman may love a child who was once part of herself. To summarize the paths leading to object-choice,

A person may love:
1. According to the narcissistic type:
    a. what he is himself (actually himself);
    b. what he once was;
    c. what he would like to be;
    d. someone who was once part of himself;

2. according to the anaclitic type:
    a. the woman who tends;
    b. the man who protects (Freud, 1949a, p. 47).

The Process of Loving

In growing up, the individual develops ideals of what he would like to be and what he wants in a spouse. These generally follow a path of social desirability. They represent what is commonly thought of by society as desirable traits for young people to have—kindness, courtesy, honesty, and sensitivity.

There are also characteristics that are attractive, but which the individual cannot accept in his self-concept. These are dissociated from the self, but when perceived in a love-object, they may draw the dissociator like a magnet. A man may be attracted to a very narcissistic woman because the narcissism which his conscious idealization forces him to renounce continues to pull him unconsciously. A woman may be drawn to a man for the boyish qualities she herself possessed before she had to abandon them for "girl's" behavior.

The individual is also drawn to the person who can aid him to become the person he must be, unconsciously speaking. A masochist, for example, would need a sadist as a marital partner. Within less extreme conditions, a nurturant person would need a receptive individual who could accept nurturance.

Quite often, however, the members of a premarital couple do not at first know each other well enough to be able to tell, consciously or unconsciously, whether the other will be able to satisfy his needs, or whether he will really fulfill his ideals. Consequently, in the absence of knowledge, the individual projects qualities of his ego-ideal onto the other. According to Freud, the sweetheart or fiancé(e) makes a superbly suitable object for projection. Lovers possess strong sexual desires for each other, but the aim (sexual intercourse) is deflected by societal mores or by the personal belief that to engage in sex before marriage is wrong. Indeed, the depth of love is often measured by the renouncing of sex in the face of opportunity—a fact undoubtedly more true in Freud's time (1856–1939) than it is today.

The libidinal impulse of the individual that is not expressed in intercourse is repressed and projected as idealization onto the beloved. The individual sexually overestimates the beloved; that is, he endows the beloved with characteristics above and beyond what objective assessment would warrant—an overestimation highly similar to Stendhal's "crystallization."

The effect of this flow of libido from the self to the beloved is to weaken the self regard. The individual's original superabundance of narcissism had, through socialization and identification, been considerably forfeited to idealization in the process of growing up. Now, through idealization of the beloved, the ego of the projector is virtually impoverished. The lover generally thinks of himself in very humble terms. He is worthless, the beloved is extolled. He is full of longing, he is deprived, he is empty! What is unconsciously needed is a return of libido from the beloved. The lover consciously experiences this as a desperate need to be loved in return, or at least to be accepted by the beloved. Only in this way can ego be re-enriched by the flow of some libido from the beloved to himself.

Since all love, according to Freud, is narcissistic at the core, the return of libido represents a happy fusion of ego libido (pertaining to the self) and object-libido (fixed on the beloved). This happy love corresponds to the primal condition of infancy when ego-libido and object-libido also were impossible to differentiate.

This is the overall picture, but the paths are accented differently for each sex. Since men generally follow the anaclitic path, they are more apt to experience a flow of libido from themslves to the woman, and they are more apt than are women to sexually overestimate the partner. They are also more likely to experience an impoverished ego and to idolize the woman. Men therefore are the pursuers who need to love the women.

Women, as we have seen, are depicted as being more narcissistic than men. Since they more often take the self as a love object, they are less likely to sexually overestimate the man. Their "love" is cooler, more detached. A textbook case of woman's narcissistic love is found in the book *The Magic Mountain*, by Thomas Mann, in which one character says of woman "You ask her if she loves him, and she answers, He loves me very much." Even for such a woman, according to Freud, there remains the possibility of object-love. In giving birth to a child, for example, a part of herself, nevertheless, becomes a suitable object on which to lavish love. This example also points out clearly that, at the base, anaclitic and narcissistic love are essentially narcissistic in origin.

Neurotic Choice

We have so far concerned ourselves with "normal" choice patterns. But what of neurotic choice? Neurotic choice comes about when the individual has failed to pass through all of the psycho-sexual stages successfully and has instead become fixated at one of the earlier levels: oral, anal, or phallic. He may also, as a result of trauma, regress to an earlier stage of development (Eidelberg, 1956). Several examples will illustrate these unhealthy patterns.

One case involves a man who has never resolved his Oedipal attachment to his mother. He may be attracted to a woman who reminds him of his mother, but attempting to make love to her brings a feeling of committing incest. The result may be impotence. On the other hand, he may split the image of the Oedipal mother into two persons: The one he marries is usually the recipient of the tender love he bore his mother, but making love to her proves impossible. The sexual drives are satisfied only by prostitutes, because, in his distorted perception, the Oedipal mother who gives herself to the father is basically doing the same thing as the prostitute (Freud, 1938).

On the feminine side there is the dutiful daughter who remains devoted and attached to her parents long after puberty. When she marries, if she does, she makes a renouncing, frigid wife (Bonaparte, 1953). The proverbial "marriage made in hell" occurs when this frigid female, married to her infantile fantasies of the father image, actually marries the guilt-ridden male who cannot deflower this mother-image (Simpson, 1960). According to most psychoanalysts, the core of these problems is unconscious to the participants, and only psychoanalysis can remove these distortions.

RESEARCH

Psychoanalysts have done next to no research on marital choice for a number of reasons: they are almost invariably self-employed, and the time required to investigate these phenomena would involve a sacrifice of income potential; moreover, most of them lack the necessary research skill to investigate Freud's theories. Thus, research on Freudian theories has been mainly carried out by psychologists and sociologists, who were rarely practicing analysts.

Much of the theory as it relates to marital choice is so vague and imprecise that it is untestable. How does one define an anaclitic type? How can one determine successful passage through the various psychosexual stages? How can one measure the extent of resolution of the Oedipal complex?

The lack of precision of the theory does not permit it to be disproved; thus, no matter what behavioral event occurs in clinical practice, it is almost invariably in accord with Freudian theory. A man with an unresolved Oedipal complex may be drawn to an older woman who physically resembles his mother. Yet he may react to his unresolved Oedipal complex in a completely opposite manner. He might resent the mother for submitting sexually to the father, and reason that she is essentially not much different from a whore. He may, therefore, marry a woman of marked social inferiority or of questionable moral standing. Conversely, however, he might idealize the mother, repressing her sexual aspects, and seek a frigid, virginal type for a wife.

These difficulties have not deterred a number of sociologists from trying to investigate the veridicality of psychoanalytic thinking as it applies to marital choice. The research efforts may be broken down into two areas: (a) the validity of the concept of an Oedipal complex, (b) the belief that romanticism is essentially aim-inhibited sex, which therefore should diminish sharply when sexual intercourse commences. (When most of the research was undertaken, 1937-60, sexual intercourse was "officially" presumed to commence at marriage.)

Research on the Oedipal Complex

Physical resemblance to parent.   Hamilton and MacGowan (1929) asked 100 men whether they had married someone who physically resembled their mother. Only 17 responded clearly affirmatively, but 16 of these (94%) were happy in their marriages. Of the 60 men who said that they married a woman definitely not resembling the mother physically, only 33 percent were happy. Data for 100 women asked this question were equivocal, because practically no women acknowledged marrying someone who resembled their fathers.

Commins (1932) reasoned that oldest sons would form their Oedipal image of a young mother, whereas succeeding sons would form an image based on an older mother. Accordingly, he predicted that oldest sons would marry younger women than would succeeding sons. Complaining that it was hard to truly determine a woman's age, he reasoned that it would be easier to determine a man's age. He extended the thesis, therefore, by postulating that the son marrying a young woman would himself be younger at the time of marriage than one marrying an older woman. Consulting the English *Who's Who?* he found statistical support for this hypothesis. Oldest sons tended to be 30.64 years old at marriage, whereas the mean age for all other sons was 32.44, a statistically significant difference.

Kirkpatrick (1937), using 768 cases from the *Compendium of American Genealogy*, was actually able to obtain women's ages. (Are American women less concerned about age?) He assumed that the

Oedipal complex would be manifested by a tendency of first sons, in accordance with a young mother image, to marry a younger woman than would succeeding sons. He reasoned, however, that different social classes tend to marry at different ages. Accordingly, he hoped to control for this belief by correlating the mother's age with discrepancy in age of the wife minus the husband. The younger the mother, the less discrepant the age difference in the married partners should be. Despite these tortuous, complicated maneuvers, a nonsignificant correlation of .04 was found. A second hypothesis, identical to that of Commins, was also not supported.

Strauss (1946a) asked 373 engaged or recently married men and women about the discrepancy between their physical ideal for a spouse and their actual partners. About 59 percent said that their mates were close to or identical with their physical ideal. Apart from the fact that this report is vague and not precise enough for statistical treatment, there was no specific interrogation reported as to the influence of the parent on the physical ideal.

In sum, the data on the physical resemblance of offspring and opposite-sex parent do not appear to offer much support for the psychoanalytic position. Hamilton and MacGowan's data suggest that men who acknowledge marrying a wife similar to the mother are happier in their marriages than those who do not, but they fail to tell us why the majority do not so marry. Further, the connection to the Oedipal theory is not clear. Had those marrying a woman physically similar to the mother resolved their Oedipal complex and thus achieved marital happiness, or did such a marriage reflect an unresolved Oedipal complex, which, paradoxically, still yielded marital happiness?

Commins' study was not substantiated by Kirkpatrick's findings. In addition, another explanation of Commins' data is possible, as he himself acknowledged. Many English followed primogeniture rules of inheritance, in which the oldest son inherited the estate rather than having it divided equally among the offspring. This being the case, the oldest son, being most secure financially, could afford to marry first. Concluding, the data on physical resemblance between spouse and opposite-sex parent neither support the Freudian position nor adequately test it.

Research on the interpersonal relationship between parent and child. A number of studies have tested the assumption that the attitude of parents and child toward dating and courtship would show unmistakable traces of the Oedipal situation. Oedipally speaking, the parent ought to be more hostile toward dating aspirations of the op-

Table 3.1

ATTITUDES OF FATHER TOWARD FIRST DATING

Attitude of Father as Reported by Students	Male		Female	
	N	%	N	%
Prohibited or disapproved		8.5		18.0
Indifferent		70.7		62.3
Encouraged		20.8		19.7
Replying	130		239	
Blank	11		19	
Total	141	100.0	258	100.0

Source: C. Kirkpatrick and T. Caplow, 1945, p. 115.

posite-sex child, which would be seen as a threat to their relationship. On the other hand, successful resolution of the Oedipal situation by the child ought to manifest itself by criticalness of the parents, with the ensuing benefits of independence and ability to form other relationships with the opposite sex.

Kirkpatrick and Caplow (1945) asked college students whether their parents prohibited or disapproved, encouraged, or were indifferent to their dating. They reported a possibility of an Oedipal situation in the fathers' greater disapproval of dating for daughters than for sons and the greater encouragement by mothers of dating for their daughters as opposed to a more modest encouragement of dating by sons, as shown in Tables 3.1 and 3.2.

Table 3.2

ATTITUDES OF MOTHER TOWARD FIRST DATING

Attitude of Mother as Reported by Students	Male		Female	
	N	%	N	%
Prohibited or disapproved		7.3		9.5
Indifferent		57.6		39.6
Encouraged		35.1		50.9
Replying	137		240	
Blank	4		18	
Total	141	100.0	258	100.0

Source: C. Kirkpatrick and T. Caplow, 1945, p. 115.

Inspection of these tables, nevertheless, reveals other possible explanations. Mothers encouraged dating by *both* offspring more than did fathers. It is possible to argue, therefore, that they were more concerned about the courtship of their children than were fathers, and that the greater interest in daughters' dating was due to identification with a same-sex younger model of themselves rather than to an interest in getting rid of a rival.

Winch in a series of analyses on a large pool of college subjects (1943, 1946, 1947, 1949a, 1949b, 1950, 1951) found only a faint indication that their courtship progress was associated with conflict with their opposite-sex parents. Typical of the weak associations was a $-.15$ correlation between courtship progress by the son and love toward the mother (1943). The son-father relationship and the daughter relationship with both parents were independent of romantic advancement by the offspring.

However, in another analysis of largely the same population (1950), results were somewhat different for specific questions. Winch found that sons stating that they loved their mothers more than their fathers, or that they were undecided as to which parent they loved best, were less apt to be advanced toward marriage in their courtship status than sons who loved their fathers more. Women, on the other hand, behaved in a manner contradictory to the Oedipal hypothesis. Those women who loved their fathers more than their mothers, or were undecided, were more apt to be making good courtship progress than those who preferred their mothers. Similar patterns of responses were found for the complementary question "Which parent loves you more?"

A study by Hobart (1958a) was largely consistent with Winch's findings. Men's courtship progress was associated with criticalness of their parents' marriages. Women, however, showed no relationship between criticalness and courtship progress.

Still another aspect of the Oedipal situation was tested by Winch (1949b). He reasoned that successful resolution of the Oedipal situation is achieved by identification with the same-sex parent. If, however, the parent is absent from the home, by reason of divorce or death, and the opposite-sex parent has not remarried, identification is impossible, and retarded courtship progress should result. He found support for this hypothesis for men but not for women. Unfortunately for his thesis, a replication of his study by Andrews and Christensen (1951) revealed no relationship between missing parents and courtship progress for either men or women.

To try to summarize these few but diverse studies is not easy. The clearest finding relates to the fact that criticalness of parents, and especially of the mother, is associated with courtship progress for men. For women, there is either no evidence of a relationship, or evidence going contrary to the Oedipal hypothesis. Women with good relationships with the father made better progress than did women without good relationships. In fairness to Freud, however, it should be noted that he did suggest that the resolution of the Oedipal situation was much more crucial for men than for women when he noted that "It does little harm to a woman if she remains in her feminine Oedipus attitude . . . She will in that case choose her husband for his paternal characteristics and will be ready to recognize his authority" (Freud, 1949b, p. 99).

Psychological resemblance to parent.   Psychological manifestations of an Oedipal situation have been tested in a number of ways. Hamilton and MacGowan (1929) found little difference in marital happiness between those marrying someone with the opposite parent's disposition and those not doing so.

Mangus (1936) had 700 college women rate their fathers, closest male relatives, male friends, and ideal-mate for interest, roles, and personality traits. Using the coefficient of contingency measure of association, the male companion was found to be most closely associated with the ideal-mate (C = .32), followed by the father (C = .24) and male relative (C = .20). Presumably, the low correlation for the father indicated that the father image did not determine the ideal-mate image.

Strauss (1946b) compared descriptions of parents and partners— either fiancé(e) or spouse—on a temperament personality check list. Although he computed no statistical tests, inspection of his table indicated that the resemblance of *both* parents to the partner was greater than that of the parents and randomly paired partners. In a separate analysis, he found that men's wives resembled their mothers more than women's husbands resembled their fathers.

Kent (1951) found considerable similarity in traits male college students applied to their mothers and to their ideal-wives. Since no control group was used, however, it could well have been that similarity existed between the stereotype of mothers (anyone's mother) and ideal-mate rather than pertaining to the subject's specific mother and his ideal-mate.

Prince and Baggaley (1963) using the Edwards Personal Preference Schedule, a personality test measuring 15 needs, correlated the perception of the self, mother, father, preferred parent, and nonpreferred parent. For both male and female college students, the highest correlations were found between self and preferred parent rather than self and opposite-sex parent, as the Oedipal theory would have called for. Moreover, in most cases, for *both* sexes, the most preferred parent was the mother.

CONCLUSIONS ON RESEARCH ON OEDIPAL SITUATION

A review of the literature does not indicate much support for the Oedipal situation, but as indicated earlier, no testing of a vaguely formulated theory can be more than suggestive. In addition, some of the researchers have made a difficult situation more difficult by ignoring the basic tenets of the Oedipal theory. For example, the influence of parental personality ought to be greatest in an unresolved Oedipal situation, but no researchers have tried to determine whether the Oedipal situation had been resolved. The Oedipal *image* of the parent by the child (possibly unconscious) is of utmost importance, but some researchers have unjustifiably accepted the perceived personality of the middle-aged parent by the adult college student as an adequate representation of the earlier Oedipal image. Admittedly, it would be next to impossible to test a past image, but in that case perhaps it would be better to conclude that the Oedipal situation is untestable than to introduce spurious tests of it. Whether the physique of a middle-aged parent has any relationship to the Oedipal image is highly questionable. Even had the researchers been able to determine whether or not a subject had resolved his Oedipal situation, it might be impossible to test the theory. As noted earlier, an unresolved Oedipal situation might lead one to marry a whore or a virgin. With a wide range like that, it is difficult to make predictions.

Because much of the research took place a good while ago, its quality is not very adequate for interpretation by current standards. In many cases, relationships are declared without tests of significance. In other cases, the absence of a control group makes it impossible to determine whether, for example, the relationship is a stereotype portrayal of the general mother-son similarity or of a specific mother-son relationship.

Two of the important findings were that parent-offspring personality similarity did exist, and that the son's criticalness of his parents and particularly of his mother was associated with his courtship progress, but that a father-daughter schism was either independent of or antithetical to her courtship progress. Let us see how these findings can be explained by attention to sociological factors rather than to psychoanalytic ones.

SOCIOLOGICAL EXPLANATION

The first item to note is that boys are, in general, preferred to girls (Winch, 1951). Note also the mothers are liked better by their off-spring of both sexes than are fathers (Prince and Baggaley, 1963); thus the two preferred members of the family and their relationship to each other (mother-son) would seem to be more important than that of the lesser lights of the family (father-daughter). A resolution or redefinition of this relationship would seem to be necessary, therefore, before the son would feel psychologically free to relate to other women.

The son's task is more difficult than the daughter's with regard to parental separation because although the daughter often has the option of pursuing a career or of marrying without working, society dictates that the man *must* work. The parents therefore encourage in-dependent behavior for their sons. Because traditionally women did not "seriously" consider a profession although they might work tem-porarily, it was considered normal to hold them "to a more exacting code of filial and kinship obligations" (Komarovsky, 1950, p. 511). This being the case, it is not crucial that the daughter break a depen-dency relationship with her father. She need only transfer her depen-dency from the father to her husband. If indeed she were expected to pursue a submissive role with her husband as with her father, asser-ting her independence would have poor implications for the success of the couple's marriage.

The fact that the fiancé(e) and opposite-sex parent resemble each other is not surprising. There may be a wide range of diversity in the personality characteristics of the couple, but the background charac-teristics including education, socioeconomic level and cultural milieu are generally quite similar. Greater than chance correlations, therefore, are to be expected between parent and spouse for interests and values. These variables would be of selective value only in the broad sense of defining a field of eligibles rather than accounting for the particular choice. The presence of such a correlation does not sup-port the Oedipal hypothesis, because it does not dictate that the spouse was chosen *because* of the similarity to the opposite-sex parent.

Strictly speaking, correlations do not imply causality. However, it may be possible to at least infer partial causality by the following paradigm: A group of newly married couples might be asked to describe the traits of their spouses and of the opposite-sex parent, the median discrepancy for the group being recorded. Then a control group of identical background might be created by randomly matching the two percepts; thus an individual's perception of his spouse would be matched with another same-sexed subject's perception of his opposite-sex parent. The median discrepancy might be obtained and compared with the median of the actual group's perceptions. By statistical procedures discussed elsewhere in this book, it could be readily determined whether the discrepancy of the actual subjects was significantly smaller than that of randomly-paired subjects. If so, it would suggest that either personality characteristics (Oedipal situation?) or a very special environment, not controlled by group matching, would account for these differences.

If, however, the discrepancies between actual and randomly paired perceptions were not significantly different, any tendency to find similarity between the spouse and opposite-sex parent could certainly be attributed to cultural factors and not to the Oedipal situation.

Although I have uncovered no such study relating to the Oedipal complex, a study of friends illustrates what I would expect to be the finding of such a study. Marsden (1966) found that friends on a college campus were significantly correlated for the General Values Inventory, which measures values important in friendship. However, when she randomly paired the members of her group, she still found a significant correlation that was little different from that between actual friends. The conclusion was that members of the campus community were selected for similar values, but these were not important in determining specific choices of friends. In sum, similarity of spouse and opposite-sex parent is accounted for more easily by the sociological explanation than by the Freudian one.

IDEALIZATION AND COURTSHIP PROGRESS

We have seen that for Freud the sexual overestimation and idealization of the beloved resulted from the deflected aim of the sex-drive. "Sexual tendencies which are uninhibited in their aims suffer an extraordinary reduction through the discharge of energy every time the sexual aim is attained. It is the fate of sensual love to become extinguished when it is satisfied" (Freud, 1952a, p. 683). In order for some semblance of love to survive, therefore, it must contain some element of deflected aim as in the tender love occurring for the parent when the child renounces his incestuous strivings. The survival of some tender components of love notwithstanding, it seems reasonable to conclude that, according to Freudian theory, idealization generally does not long survive a continuous sexual relationship.

Waller (1938), while accepting the core assumption of sexual inhibition as being responsible for idealization, expands on the process of the development of idealization. To him, this depends also on an ignorance of the beloved object, on whom the most extraordinary virtues are projected. At first acquaintance, the individual, although he knows little of the other, can perceive that little in a more or less objective light. However, as the love relationship develops, so does sex desire and the need to idealize the other. Each member of the couple, sensing this idealization of himself by the other, seeks to perpetuate it by exhibiting only those behaviors worthy of idealization. Since true lovers are always honest with each other, each decides to acknowledge that he is not as imposing a figure as his partner makes him out to be. Of course he hopes that the partner will vigorously push aside these protestations, deny that there has been the slightest shred of exaggeration, and proceed with the canonization of the individual.

When, with marriage, familiarity and sex expression occur, a sharp drop in idealization is to be expected; hence the hypothesis derived from Waller's theory is that idealization builds up during courtship and then drops sharply after marriage.

Research Findings

Burgess and Wallin (1953), in their empirically rich study of engagement and marriage of 1000 subjects, presented a wealth of evidence arguing against the Freud-Waller hypothesis. They reported that most married couples had been good friends before they fell in love, a finding not in accord with the thesis that idealization is based on ignorance. Almost half of their subjects engaged in premarital sex, and yet their engagement success scores (used as a measure of idealization) seem not to have changed much over the course of the courtship. According to Freud and Waller, however, sex should have led to de-idealization. Also contrary to the Freud-Waller thesis is the finding that the personality ratings of each other by the couple did not change much from before to after marriage, and the first year of marriage was judged by most couples to have been *considerably happier than the preceding year.* Lest it be thought that the de-idealization had not really had sufficient time to set in, the married couples were found to have rated the first *three* years of marriage as of about equal happiness. These findings all contradict the thesis that idealization ceases with marriage.

One item did appear to accord with the Freud-Waller hypothesis.

Men engaging in premarital sex with their partners tended to list a greater number of changes desired in their fiancées than did men not engaging in premarital sex with their partners. No significant difference was found for women. It could be argued nonetheless, as Burgess and Wallin point out, that engaging in premarital sex (at the time) was relatively unconventional behavior, and such individuals were more likely to avoid socially desirable, conformist behavior which called for an individual to insist that he desired no changes in his beloved. In other words, Burgess and Wallin claim that not the sexual behavior *but the kinds of people engaging in the sexual behavior* determined the differences in response.

In a series of studies, Hobart also failed to confirm the idealization hypothesis (1958a, 1958b, 1958c, 1958d, 1960). Using the Gross romanticism scale as a measure of idealization, he noted that romanticism increased for men in advanced courtship as compared with men in the preliminary stages. But romanticism did not seem to decline from going steady to the marriage state. Women did not show much in the way of significant relationships between romanticism and courtship.

Pollis (1969) tested the idealization hypothesis in a somewhat different manner. The primary respondent judged his (her) fiancé(e) for 17 traits, and the primary respondent's two best friends, who constituted the objective criterion, also judged the partner. Idealization was defined as the positive discrepancy between the respondent and each of his friend's ratings for the partner.

Pollis's results did not support the notion of increasing idealization with courtship intensity. In fact, exactly the reverse was found: casual daters were most idealistic, moderate daters were intermediate, and serious daters were least idealistic. Only the men's scores reached significance, though the women showed a trend in the same direction. Unfortunately, Pollis did not collect any information on sexual intercourse; hence it is difficult to determine whether de-idealization occurred because the subjects engaged in sexual intercourse or simply because they got to know each other better. If we assume that *moderate* daters were at the time of the study (1960s) more likely not to have yet engaged in sex than to have done so, a moderately reasonable assumption, then the evidence would be contrary to the Freud-Waller hypothesis.

Considering all of the evidence, it is possible to conclude that there appears to be no substantiation for the thesis that idealization is the result of aim-inhibited sex. Rather, the data support the view that for at least the early years of a sexual relationship and/or marriage, sex supports an idealization-romantic process. Probably idealization diminishes as a result of the slow adaptation to sex and with the realization that even the most "perfect" individual, when lived with over a period of time, turns out to have some less than ideal qualities—at least as far as his relationship with his partner is concerned.

CONCLUSIONS REGARDING PSYCHOANALYSIS AND MARITAL CHOICE

As Winch (1950) pointed out a generation ago, the high order abstractions of Freudian theory lack observable referents. "One cannot observe an Oedipus complex, he can only observe behavior which he may then try to interpret in terms of the concept of the Oedipus complex" (p. 481). We have seen that these attempts at interpretation are less consistent with the known facts and necessitate more inferences than simpler sociological explanations. It is not so much a question of the theory of an Oedipus complex being wholly wrong—there are data that seem to accord with some portion of it. The chief failure of the Oedipus complex as an explanation for marital choice is that it is far too simplistic. Psychoanalysis has seemingly been blind to the effect of society as a creator of needs and drives. The Freudian position seems to see society mainly as the frustrator of man's instinctual needs. Such thinking has not produced the kind of research that furthers insight into marital choice, no matter how many ad hoc analyses and inferences are made on how neurotic couples had chosen each other.

Perhaps the most egregious fault in the Freudian position is the categorization of *normal* women as essentially passive, masochistic, and narcissistic. Freud, in my opinion, was one of the most accurate observers of human behavior ever recorded. His observations of his women clients were, for the most part, probably quite valid. His error lay in assuming that the behavior that he observed stemmed from inevitable biological and developmental facts. He failed to fully appreciate that Viennese women were molded into their roles by a patriarchal Victorian society, which seized most of the spoils of life for *men* and then rationalized that the responsibility for women's inferior role lay with nature, not with men. It is ironical that the man who sensitized mankind to the fact that they rationalized their irrationality should himself not realize that his theory of women made him, in this regard, but another apologist for patriarchy.

CHAPTER 4

The Theory of
Complementary Needs

Many theories of marital choice existed prior to 1954, but they were often extremely simplistic ("birds of a feather flock together," "opposites attract"), conflicting, and inevitably free of contradiction from any data. The year 1954 saw the first formal publication of Robert F. Winch's theory that was as simple as its predecessors had been but, unlike these, was also accompanied by data testing the theory.

In this chapter, I shall first describe the theory and the research of Winch and his associates. After evaluating the research, I shall consider the research of others on complementarity and marital choice, following which I shall attempt an overall evaluation of the theory.

OUTLINES OF THE THEORY

Winch accepts the generally held sociological position that homogamy is a very potent factor in marital choice. Individuals tend to marry those of similar education, socioeconomic status, race, religion, age, and culture. But whereas some sociologists consider further selection a question of chance (e.g., Reiss, 1960), Winch sees the homogamous cultural variables as only a preliminary screening to determine a "field of eligibles"—the company one keeps, or who is eligible for consideration as a spouse. They do not determine individual choice. The actual selection of a spouse occurs on psychological grounds, and the basis of selection is from complementary needs.

The definition of need is taken from Murray. "A need is a construct . . . which stands for a force . . . which organizes perception, apperception, intellection, conation, and action in such a way as to transform in a certain direction an existing, unsatisfying situation" (Murray, 1938, pp. 123-24).

Two needs are complementary "when A's need X is gratifying to B's need Y and B's behavior in acting out B's need Y is gratifying to A's need X" (Winch, 1958, p. 93). It is not necessary that A's need X be a different one from B's need Y. If the same need is gratified in both A and B, but at very different levels of intensity, then it should follow that the couple should be negatively correlated for that need. If, for example, the man is very high on dominance, it should follow that the woman should be very low on dominance. Winch calls this case Type I complementarity.

If different needs are gratified in A and B, the interspousal correlation is hypothesized to be positive or negative depending on the particular pair of needs chosen. If a man is high on the need for nurturance, Winch postulates that he would be drawn to a woman who was high on the need for succoring. Similarly, if one member of the pair is high on hostility, the other ought to be high on abasement.

The situation involving two different needs is called Type II complementarity by Winch. Although theoretically the correlation between two different needs might be either positive or negative, depending on the particular pair chosen, in practice Winch has predicted only positive correlations between pairs of needs.

The theory seems quite uncomplicated. Yet before testing it Winch had to deal with a number of complex issues. For example, are the couple conscious of their needs? Winch concludes that some individuals are conscious of the needs that had drawn them to their spouse, and others are not. The degree of consciousness may vary from individual to individual. Where the pattern of complementarity is contrary to traditional male and female roles, the probability is increased that the couple will not acknowledge the complementary bond between them. An example of such a case would be where the woman is dominant and the man is not.

Another question was which needs should be chosen for study. After much deliberation, Winch selected 12 needs from Murray's list of needs and 3 general traits that would be quantifiable and unidimensional. Some rather important needs—sex, for one—were eliminated on the grounds of complexity. The list of needs chosen and their description is shown in Table 4.1.

Table 4.1

THE TWELVE NEEDS AND THREE GENERAL TRAITS

Needs	Abbreviation	Dichotomy	Definition
Abasement	n Aba	Overt-covert Within-without	To accept or invite blame, criticism or punishment. To blame or harm the self.
Achievement	n Ach	Overt-covert Only "without"	To work diligently to create something and/or to emulate others.
Approach	n App	Overt-covert Only "without"	To draw near and enjoy interaction with another person or persons.
Autonomy	n Aut	Overt-covert Within-without	To get rid of the constraint of other persons. To avoid or escape from domination. To be unattached and independent.
Deference	n Def	Overt-covert Within-without	To admire and praise a person.
Dominance	n Dom	Overt-covert Within-without	To influence and control the behavior of others.
Hostility	n Hos	Overt-covert Within-without	To fight, injure, or kill others.
Nurturance	n Nur	Overt-covert Within-without	To give sympathy and aid to a weak, helpless, ill, or dejected person or animal.
Recognition	n Rec	Overt-covert Within-without	To excite the admiration and approval of others.
Status Aspiration	n SA	None	To desire a socioeconomic status considerably higher than one has. (A special case of achievement.)
Status Striving	n SS	None	To work diligently to alter one's socioeconomic status. (A special case of achievement.)
Succorance	n Suc	Overt-covert Within-without	To be helped by a sympathetic person. To be nursed, loved, protected, indulged.

General Traits

Anxiety	Anx	Within-without	Fear, conscious or unconscious, of harm or misfortune arising from the hostility of others and/or social reaction to one's own behavior.
Emotionality	Emo	Within-without	The show of affect in behavior.
Vicariousness	Vic	Within-without	The gratification of a need derived from the perception that another person is deriving gratification.

Source: Winch, 1958, p. 90.

TESTING THE THEORY

Population

Because of the researcher's perennial ailment, limited funds, Winch decided to draw a small sample of 25 married couples in which one member of each couple was an undergraduate at Northwestern University. The exact means of selecting the couples is not given, but only eight couples had refused to participate by the time he had reached his quota of 25 couples. The study was conducted in 1950, and each couple was paid $7.50 for participating. Desiring a homogeneous sample, he excluded upper-class subjects, Jews, and blacks.

Testing Procedure

The main index for measuring needs was the Need Interview, a series of open-ended questions designed to tap the 12 needs and 3 traits to be measured. The interview took 2 to 3 hours and consisted of 45 questions. One such question, measuring need for aggression, asked the subject how he felt when someone stepped in line in front of him while he was waiting to be seated in a crowded restaurant.

Some of the needs were dichotomized and scored for *within* the marriage and also *without* (outside) it. In addition, some of the needs were scored separately for their *covert* presence and for *overt* presence, according to whether the subject seemed unaware or aware of the presence of the need within himself. The particular reason for scoring a given need for some or all of these combinations and not scoring another need in the same manner is not given. By this double dichotomization, Winch obtained 44 variables, which were each scored on a five-point scale. The interviews were scored by two raters working from the typed copy of the interview. They showed a corrected Spearman-Brown reliability coefficient of agreement of .75 (uncorrected .60), which was judged sufficiently high for the purpose of analyzing the data.

Other data collected included a case-history interview dealing with the subject's past development, and interaction with familial figures, beginning with childhood and continuing to the time of testing. In addition, eight cards from the Thematic Apperception Test

(TAT) were used. This test, developed by Henry Murray, consists in its entirety of 31 cards. The cards depict single individuals, groups, landscapes, and fantasy scenes. Some of the figures are easily identifiable, whereas others are ambiguous as to identity or behavior. The usual procedure is to select a number of cards and instruct the subject to make up a story about each of them. These stories may be scored for need, press, thema, and other personality assessment variables. The needs were scored "blind" by a rater who had not actually tested the subject.

To this point, needs had been scored for three independent data-collection methods (need interview, case-history, Thematic Apperception Method). Two further scoring approaches, derived from the three independent methods, were used. The fourth *"holistic"* method consisted of a separate analyst reviewing the data from each method and scoring needs on a holistic basis rather than on the basis of answers to specific questions. The fifth, *final conference* method consisted of all analysts discussing all of the data and arriving at a consensus set of ratings.

WINCH'S RESEARCH FINDINGS

Using the normalized ratings for the 44 variables from the need interview, it is possible, by correlating every variable with every other variable, to obtain 1936 interspousal correlations. Winch and his colleagues, however, were not prepared to make hypotheses for all of these variables. Instead, they selected 388 for which they hypothesized the signs of the correlations on the basis of the theory of complementary needs. They hypothesized that the 44 variables would be negatively intercorrelated for spouses (Type I complementarity, such as nurturance-nurturance). The remaining 344 correlations were selected so as to be positive correlations for different needs or traits (Type II complementarity, such as dominance-abasement).

Because of the nonindependence of his scores (i.e., there were many scores emanating from a single person), which violated the use of traditional statistics, he used an innovative yet conservative statistical approach to test the hypotheses. The method is described and illustrated in Winch, Ktsanes, and Ktsanes (1954). The results as indicated in Table 4.2 showed statistical support for the complementary need hypothesis, though the degree of support is far from overwhelming.

Table 4.2

NUMBERS OF CORRELATIONS
IN PREDICTED DIRECTION AT .01 LEVEL

	Observed	Expected by Chance
Significant in predicted direction	12	3.88
Not significant in predicted direction	376	384.12

$p < .01.$

Inspection of this table indicates that on the basis of chance alone, one would expect 3.88 correlations to be significant at the .01 level of significance in the direction of the hypothesis. Actually 12 correlations were found in that direction. By a chi-square statistic, the probability of such an event occurring by chance is less than 1 in 100 ($p < .01$); hence we conclude that the hypothesis is backed feebly in terms of magnitude (only 12 of 388 correlations were significant), but our confidence that this is not a chance finding is considerable ($p < .01$).

In another analysis of the ratings on the subjects (Winch, 1955a), attention focused solely on the Type I correlations. In this case, each subject's 44 ratings were correlated with those of his spouse, and a mean correlation was obtained. This was done separately for the data in the need interview and in the final conference. A control group consisted of the mean of the scores of all of the subjects randomly paired so that a given man would be most probably correlated with someone else's wife. It was predicted, in accordance with the complementary theory, that the interspousal correlations of the actual couples would be significantly lower than those of the randomly paired couples. This prediction was supported for the need-interview. The mean correlation for actual husbands' and wives' ratings stemming from the need interview was .10; that of the randomly paired husbands and wives was .23. The difference in the size of the means was significant ($p < .05$). The result for the final conference method was .11 for actual couples; that of its control group was .18. Although the difference was in the direction of the hypothesis, it was not significant, and the complementary hypothesis was not accepted for the conference method. Considering both methods, the results are marginally supportive of the complementary needs theory, but rather weak.

In yet another analysis of the same data (Winch, 1955b), Winch tested the efficacy of the five methods he had used to evaluate the data. Three of these proved significant (need interview, holistic, final conference), and two showed no significance (case history, TAT). Electing to focus on the Type II correlations, and correcting for the non-independence of scores, Winch arrived at the results shown in Table 4.3.

Table 4.3

DISTRIBUTIONS OF 344 HYPOTHESIZED CORRELATIONS
FOR THREE TYPES OF ANALYSIS
(Type II Complementarity)

		Source of Rating		
Number of Correlations	Chance	Need Interview	Holistic Analysis	Final Conference
Significant in hypothesized direction, $p < .05$	17.2	26	47	35
Other	326.8	318	297	309
Total	344	344	344	344
Probability of such an occurrence		.05	.001	.001

The table, not surprisingly, repeats the statistical significance found earlier for the same correlations plus the additional 44 Type I correlations. Again, however, since the majority of correlations were nonsignificant, the effect of complementarity appears to be relatively weak.

The same pattern of weak but significant associations is reported in a totally different kind of analysis, but with the same data. Ktsanes (1955) used factor analysis, a method for breaking down a complex set of variables into a smaller number of more general dimensions. His factor analysis of the 25 couples using the 44 variables yielded four major dimensions. The labels he gave to the dimensions and the correlations between husband and wife on each of them were Yielding Dependency −.22, Hostile Dominance −.43, Mature Nurturance −.29, Neurotic Self-Depreciation −.10. The second and third correlations were significant at the .02 level and beyond. Thus, if a husband was high on Hostile Dominance, his wife was likely to be low on it.

In an inordinately complex further analysis of the old data

(Winch, Ktsanes, and Ktsanes, 1955), the authors concluded that the major dimension of complementarity was assertive-receptive. In a final tour de force, Winch (1958) was given batches of the typed data containing the ratings on the subjects, with six to seven couples included in each batch. With all identifying data removed except the sex of the person, he was able to correctly match 13 of the 25 couples. Having been given further information about the subjects' emotional-psychological life beyond that implied in the ratings, he matched 20 of the 25 couples correctly, far exceeding chance probabilities.

EVALUATION OF WINCH'S RESEARCH[1]

Winch's research has been uncritically accepted by many, unjustifiably attacked by some, and meaningfully evaluated by still others. Perhaps most important, his work served as the impetus for a large number of studies which sought to test his theory.

The attack on Winch that seems the least justified has been that by two fellow sociologists (Bowman, 1955; Kernodle, 1959), who accused him of dabbling in areas where, in their eyes, no self-respecting sociologist ought to tread—psychology and psychoanalysis. They question whether any sociologist is competent to probe into the depths of the psyche to get at covert needs. Moreover, they seem to resent what they perceive as a slighting of sociological variables, in that these variables serve only as a "field of eligibles," whereas the important determining factors (needs) are psychologically oriented and are said to be independent of the sociological influences. Kernodle sees the sociological variables as more influential and the psychological needs as essentially derivatives of the social structure. Regrettably, Bowman and Kernodle do not comment on the quality of Winch's work, which, after all, gets to the heart of the matter.

At first glance, it would appear that Winch has generally found statistical support for both Type I and Type II complementary needs. There are, nevertheless, certain factors that may have influenced his findings but have not been discussed. I shall briefly list and discuss these.

---

[1] Many but not all of the comments made on Winch's research and theory have been discussed in disparate commentaries. The interested reader may wish to consult the following: Rosow 1957, Tharp 1963, 1964, Levinger, 1964.

1. *Pick the needs that look the most promising.* Winch's theory implies that all needs are complementary, yet he chose 12 needs and 3 traits to test the theory. (For the sake of simplicity, we shall henceforth refer to this list of needs and traits as "needs." He does not tell us why he chose them. Conceivably, he might have chosen those needs (perhaps unconsciously) that would fit complementary roles in our society—for example, a dominant husband and a deferential wife—while ignoring those needs that might contradict complementarity. He tells us that he omitted sex from the list of needs because it did not appear to be unidimensional. Yet it seems unlikely that an individual with a high need for sex would be drawn to one with a low need for it.

The factor of bias in the selection of needs goes beyond the choice of 15 for study out of a far greater number; from these 15 needs he derived 44 variables. Considering all possible pairings, we arrive at a total of 1,936 possible pairing of needs. Only 388 were actually selected (44 Type I, 344 Type II). The selection of the 44 Type I needs is entirely consistent with the theory of negative interspousal correlation, but why did he choose the particular 344 out of the remaining 1,892 possible pairings? It seems logical to assume that he chose them because they seemed most likely to be complementary, whereas he rejected 1,548 pairings because they were more risky in this regard. Considering the operation of this selective bias and the minimal nature of support for the theory, confidence in the theory is somewhat weakened.

2. *When is homogamy complementary?* In his test of Type I complementarity, with the need interview data, Winch found an average correlation of .10 between husband and wife and an average correlation of .23 for the randomly paired couples. The significant difference between the correlations is taken as support for his theory. Strictly speaking, however, the only conclusion that would seem warranted is that the actual couples were less *homogamous* than the control couples. But being less homogamous is not the same as being complementary. Complementarity ought to involve a negative interspousal correlation—as Winch posits in the theory—not a smaller positive correlation.

3. *Loading the dice against the TAT.* Winch and More (1956a, 1956b) reported that the TAT failed to be of value in the study. When the procedure for using the TAT is examined, however, it is evident that its use was inappropriate. The TAT is a general test of personality; it is not designed to obtain measures of the specific needs

Winch wished to study. In addition, Winch used a small sample of 8 cards. This is far too small a number to serve of itself as an index of the strength of 15 needs. Worse yet, no rationale for the selection of the cards is given. It appears that the somewhat naive hope of the research team was that the cards chosen would be ambiguous enough to allow the projection of all 15 needs.

There has been a great deal of research on the TAT, which I have summarized elsewhere (Murstein, 1963). The crux of my research and that of others is that knowledge of what needs the stimulus properties of the cards suggest is of essence if one is to hope to study these needs. I have advocated custom construction of thematic cards as an aid in measuring the strength of particular needs and in improving subject and interjudge reliability in scoring the stories. With careful attention to scaling the cards for their various stimulus properties, it is possible to achieve interjudge reliabilities of the order of .85 to .95. However, to choose 8 cards without regard to their stimulus representation of the needs to be studied is an invitation to disaster.

If we look at the reliability of .20 reported for the TAT by Winch, we can see why the TAT proved invalid. With so low a reliability value, it is next to impossible to expect a test to be valid. Given this meager reliability, therefore, Winch should have constructed cards more sensitive to the needs he wished to study and worked on a scoring system that would yield higher reliabilities. Failing in that, he should have given up the attempt to utilize the thematic method.

4. *How many methods were significant?*   Winch's statements make it appear as if three of his five methods of analyzing the data yielded significant results (need interview, holistic need interview, final conference), with the case history and TAT proving fruitless. However, the holistic and final conference methods are based primarily on the findings of the need interview. Consequently, it would be fairer to say that one of the three methods of collecting data (need interview) was favorable to complementarity (Tharp, 1963), a figure not as imposing as that presented by Winch.

5. *How atypical was his sample?* It should be emphasized that all of Winch's and his colleagues' analyses were done on the same 25 couples, much of it on the same data (need interview). If his sample proved to be atypical of even a college sample, itself atypical with respect to the general population, then the generalizability of his findings might be questioned.

The first thing suggesting atypicality is the fact that one of each pair of married subjects was an *undergraduate*. In 1950 it was less atypical for a college student to be married while yet an undergraduate than it is today, but it was unusual nevertheless. There is considerable data that indicate that early marriage is associated with feelings of inadequacy and ego deficiency, not to mention pregnancy.

Also, Winch mentions that 13 of his couples could be classified as wife dominant, 9 as husband dominant, and 3 as mixed. Other research indicates that the majority of marriages, particularly successful ones, have egalitarian power distributions with asymmetry, where it occurs, usually favoring the husband, in accordance with role expectations (Blood and Wolfe, 1960, Lu, 1952). Further, the husbands in Winch's study generally felt inadequate about fulfilling a masculine role of dominance; in short, the suspicion grows that this was an atypical sample even for college volunteers.

6. *Were the raters biased?* Winch has been attacked by several researchers for using needs that were undoubtedly related as if they were independent. For example, it seems likely that individuals who are dominant are not very likely to be deferent. Consequently, in rating, it is likely that implicit theories of personality take over (Katz, Glucksberg, and Krauss, 1960), so that a person called dominant also has a greater than chance probability of being rated low on deference, and succorance. In addition, since the raters were all aware of the theory they were testing, the number of subjects was small, and the data collected on each subject quite large, it is difficult to see how rater bias could not influence the ratings that they assigned.

Winch has pointed out that the ratings were done without knowledge of who the spouse was. Removing names and not telling a rater who is married to whom is, nevertheless, often not enough to remove the bias. Each individual reveals things about himself—his philosophies, common friends, age, environment—which tend to narrow the number of his plausible partners within the group. This factor also might well account for Winch's ability to match partners in the sorting study. Despite the successful matching, we cannot tell whether it is the variable we are interested in (need ratings) or extraneous information which allowed Winch to match the pairs accurately.

It would take elaborate precautions to eliminate rater bias, and Winch gives no report that such elaborate precautions were taken. Thus, while it is far from certain to what extent rater bias operated, it is at least a possible contaminating factor.

In sum, Winch's data support his theory minimally, but questions have been raised concerning bias in the selection of needs and methodology. These difficulties weaken still further confidence in data that were somewhat marginal to start with. Before attempting an overall appraisal of the research on complementary needs, however, we should consider a substantial portion of the research on complementary needs by others, stimulated by Winch's efforts.

RESEARCH ON COMPLEMENTARY NEEDS BY OTHERS

Before embarking on a review of the research, we had best clarify as well as we can just what complementarity is. Winch's research makes it clear just what *he thinks* complementarity is. When we turn to some of the other researchers, however, we occasionally find definitions of complementarity that depart considerably from his interpretation.

Lipetz, Cohen, Dworin, and Rogers (1970) is a case in point. They note that similarity may be fulfilling under certain circumstances and dissimilarity under others; they therefore define need complementarity as *"what in one person satisfies the needs of the other"* (Lipetz et al., 1970, p. 202). Turning to their data, we find that they interpret a lack of discrepancy between Nurturance and Succorance as evidence of complementarity, just as Winch did in his Type II needs, but they also record a lack of discrepancy between husband and wife on Autonomy as complementarity, *which is exactly the opposite of what Winch would do for Type I needs.* Obviously they are using an implicit role model, but unfortunately they call it complementarity. Their work therefore cannot be used to test Winch's theory.

A similar problem exists in part of the work of Centers and Granville (1971) and Kerckhoff and Davis (1962). They use a model borrowed from Schutz (1958) called *reciprocal compatibility.* This is described by the formula Reciprocal Compatibility = $|e_M - w_F|$ + $|e_F - w_M|$ where e stands for the behavior that an individual wants to express vis-à-vis others, and w stands for the behavior he wishes others to express toward him. The subscripts M and F stand for male and female. Perfect reciprocal compatibility occurs when the absolute difference of the behavior the man wishes to express and the women wants from him equals zero and the behavior she wishes to express subtracted from that which he wants from her also equals zero. The authors of both studies equate reciprocal compatibility with complementarity.

A simple set of examples, however, will illustrate that this is not complementarity the way Winch operationally utilizes it. Suppose that the man is very dominant (10 on a ten point scale), the woman wants him to be that dominant, she is very passive (1 on a ten point scale), and he wants her to be that passive. Then, Reciprocal Compatibility = $|10 - 10| + |1 - 1| = 0$. We now have perfect compatibility and also perfect complementarity according to the above cited authors, and also Winch.

But suppose that the man is very high on Affiliation, she wants him to be high on Affiliation, she is high on affiliation, and he wants her to be high. Then $|10 - 10| + |10 - 10| = 0$ and again we have perfect compatibility and, according to the authors, perfect complementarity. But in this case we also have *perfect similarity*, which is exactly opposite to what Winch would predict for a Type I need. Thus, complementarity and similarity can be hopelessly confounded under the rubric of Reciprocal Compatibility. It is surprising, therefore, that Winch has accepted Kerckhoff and Davis's work uncritically as support for complementarity.

These are not the only cases of misused complementarity. Reiter (1970) has used significant sex differences on a personality scale (not couple differences) as an example of complementarity. Stuart (1962) thought he had found complementarity in the fact that of 70 male volunteers for a dating TV program, 1 man thought that he was sincere, but 14 wanted sincerity in their partner. No needs were measured here, and there were, in fact, no couples who were rated; consequently, neither of these studies necessarily relates to complementarity. Restricting ourselves then to definitions of complementarity that are identical to or approximate that proposed by Winch, what do the data show?

Research with the Edwards Personal Preference Schedule (PPS)

The Personal Preference Schedule consists of 225 paired statements that are alleged to tap 15 personality needs taken from Murray. These needs overlap with but are not identical to those used by Winch. The subject must choose one of a pair of statements, and his choice indicates a preference for one need as opposed to another. The items were supposed to be equated for social desirability, but there is some evidence that this was not completely achieved (e.g., Corah, Feldman, Cohen, Gruen, Meadow, and Ringwall, 1958). The PPS yields a separate score for each of the 15 needs. It is so constructed that it is impossible to get high scores on every need because there are only a fixed number of points available. If an individual, for example, received the highest possible score on Achievement, he could not achieve an equivalent score on Dominance.

Table 4.4 provides a summary of all the research that I have found bearing on marital choice and involving the PPS. The data refer to actual complementarity as defined by Winch rather than to perceived complementarity; hence they refer exclusively to the case in which the couple *each* filled out the test rather than one person filling it out for him- or herself and also for how he or she perceived the other. Parenthetically, research on the latter case has not supported complementarity (Murstein, 1967a, 1971a; Udry, 1963, 1967).

The populations include those dating, going steady, engaged, recently married, and married for some time. Both college and non-college populations are represented. These data very conclusively show no support for complementarity apart from a possible chance significance here and there. They, in fact, tend to support a homogamy need theory, although not in a very pronounced way.

Winch has questioned the meaningfulness of research with the PPS (1967, 1974) because he believes the test has no proven validity. I know of no simple answer to this question. The research literature, in general, has spewed forth a variety of findings on this test, many unfavorable, some favorable. It is certainly impossible to give a definite yes or no to this question.

Winch has also complained that his findings were not adequately replicated by the research of others, apart from the use of the PPS in lieu of the need interview. Setting aside the fact that an interview and a paper-and-pencil test operate on different levels, he has noted that the PPS has only 10 needs that are similar to the 15 he used. He noted further that instead of using relative newlyweds as he did (his median subject couple were married about a year and none more than two years), other researchers have varied from using dating partners to those married a decade or so.

At first glance his objections appear to have some merit, but upon closer examination they do not hold up very well. Schellenberg and Bee (1960) decided to tackle the question of whether the need scores on the need interview were quite different from those obtained via the PPS. They reasoned that if the size of the intercorrelation between needs on the need interview did not differ from those obtained with the PPS and a different sample (normative group of 1509 subjects used in standardizing the PPS), then Winch's objections would be invalid. Choosing seven variables from the PPS which clearly seemed to be the same as those used by Winch, the authors proceeded to rank the 21 possible pairs of variables for the size of their intercorrelation in Winch's data (Roos, 1956). They also ranked the same pairs of needs according to the size of the correlation listed in the PPS Manual

(Edwards, 1959). The rank-order correlation between the listing for Winch and the PPS ranged from .78 (PPS and Winch's overt-within need ratings) to .70 (PPS and Winch's overt-without ratings). Given a certain loss due to less than perfect reliability, different samples, different tests, and the extracting of 7 needs to be tested out of 15, these correlations are remarkably high. They suggest that whatever the degree of validity possessed by the PPS, it is shared also by Winch's data.

In addition, objection might be made to Winch's insistence that his study be duplicated exactly. The theory of complementary needs, as he presents it, is presumed to be a theory of *all needs*, not just selected needs. Why then object to the use of needs different from the ones chosen by him?

His objection to the use of long-married subjects has some substance, but that to the use of engaged subjects is without foundation. Certainly there is a weakness in the use of such subjects, since a minority of them will probably break their engagements and marry someone else. But objections can be raised also to Winch's use of subjects up to two years after they were married. How can one be sure that the needs they manifested at testing time were the same as those that had been operative in their selection of a spouse? In sum, the negative findings with the PPS are far from being artifacts. Let us consider the findings with instruments other than the PPS.

Research with Other Instruments

Research with instruments other than the PPS has run a wide gamut from scales made from Murray's description of needs to projective techniques, the Leary Interpersonal Check List, background questionnaires, value questionnaires, and depth interviews. Most of the research as shown in summaries appearing in Table 4.5 flatly contradicts the theory of complementary needs. A few studies show no support for complementarity or homogamy, and a few support homogamy.

One study (Holz, 1970) *seemingly* suggests that complementarity and homogamy are dependent on a mediating variable such as Family Ideology. From the findings, "traditionalists" are said to be complementary, whereas "egalitarians" are said to be homogamous. A factor analysis of the different needs yielded two important personality dimensions. The first dimension, "Instrumental," consisted of factor loadings of .50 or more for the following needs: dominance,

Table 4.4

SUMMARY DATA TESTING WINCH'S THEORY USING EDWARDS PERSONAL PREFERENCE SCHEDULE (PPS)
ALONE OR WITH ANOTHER TEST [1]

Test Used	Investigator	Subjects	Findings
PPS	Banta & Hetherington (1963)	29 engaged couples and friends	Type I: 8 of 15 needs significant *contrary* to complementarity. Average $r = .36$.
PPS	Becker (1964)	39 couples married $\leq$ 2 years, engaged or going steady	Type I: $r = .15$ for Dominance (not significant). Complementarity or similarity of couples is mediated by Authoritarianism score. High- and low-complementarity couples on Dominance had higher Authoritarian scores than moderately complementary couples.
PPS	Blazer (1963)	50 emotionally well-adjusted married couples obtained from city and college advertisements, married $\bar{x} = 10.1$ years	Type I: 4 or 15 correlations significant in direction *contrary* to complementarity. Type II: 5 of 32 correlations significant in *accordance* with complementarity and 5 in *contrary* direction.
PPS	Bowerman & Day (1956)	60 college couples formally engaged or going steady	Type I: 4 of 15 correlations significant in direction *contrary* to complementarity. Type II: 5 of 210 correlations significant in *accordance* with complementarity; 10 significant *contrary* to complementarity.
PPS, Leary's Interpersonal Check List used as measure of satisfaction	Heiss & Gordon (1964)	62 couples, dating, going steady, or engaged	Type I: 1 of 15 needs significant in *accordance* with complementarity.

[1] Significance is defined as p < .05.

PPS (shortened version)	Katz, Glucksberg, & Krauss (1960)	56 couples, married x̄ = 5 years	Type I: 3 of 11 needs significant *contrary* to complementarity. Type II: 1 of 10 needs significant *contrary* to complementarity.
PPS, Famous Sayings Test	Murstein (1961)[2]	68 married couples, including 20 newlyweds, married x̄ = 1.2 years, and 48 middle-aged, married x̄ = 11.4 years	Type I: Newlyweds; 3 of 19 needs significant *contrary* to complementarity. Average $r = .24$. Type I: Middle-aged; 9 of 19 needs significant *contrary* to complementarity. Average $r = .30$.
PPS modified	Murstein (1967)	99 couples, mainly college, engaged or going steady	Type I: 6 of 15 needs significant *contrary* to complementarity. Average $r = .13$.
PPS with extra derived scores	Saper (1965)	24 couples, married x̄ = 5.8 years	Type I: 1 of 16 needs significant *contrary* to complementarity. Type II: 1 of 6 needs significant *contrary* to complementarity.
PPS	Schellenberg & Bee (1960)	64 college married couples, median married < 2 years; 36 premarital couples, of whom 18 were engaged, 18 going steady	Type I: Correlation of couples across 15 needs transformed to "convergence scores" was significant in direction *contrary* to complementarity. *Separate* analysis for married couples established significance *contrary* to complementarity for married couples, trend in that direction for premarital couples. Further Type I: 0 of 2 needs was significant. Type II: 0 of 6 needs was significant.

2 The values reported here have been recomputed from the 1961 article because the analysis was done incorrectly. In the published study the actual couples were compared with randomly paired men and women. In actuality, for this type of data no control group should have been used. Randomly pairing individuals for a given need yields an expected correlation of zero; hence only the correlations of the actual groups should be used and compared against a table of significant values for coefficients of correlation. This correction has been made for the present table.

Table 4.5

SUMMARY DATA TESTING WINCH'S THEORY
USING TESTS OTHER THAN THE EDWARDS PERSONAL PREFERENCE SCHEDULE

Test Used	Investigator	Subjects	Findings
Murray need scale (1938); 11 needs studied with separate complementarity and similarity scores devised	Hobart & Lindholm (1963)	100 married couples; 50 from college, 50 of age < 40 from working-class church	Type I: For each of the 11 needs, randomly matched couples were more complementary than actual married couples; but significance was not reached in any case. Pooling the need scores, significance was not reached either, but a trend contrary to complementarity was evident. Regarding similarity scores, 1 of 11 need scores was significantly more *similar* for married couples than randomly paired subjects. The pooled needs score was significantly more *similar* for actual couples than for randomly matched subjects.
Murray needs battery of 12 needs, Levinson's Traditional Family Ideology Scale	Holz (1970)	49 couples, married $\bar{x}$ = 1.2 years; 25 couples classified as "traditional" on Levinson Family Scale, 24 couples classified as "egalitarian"	Type I: 5 of 12 needs significant via tests showing differences in mean need scores between men and women in "traditional" group. Interpreted as *supporting* complementarity. 0 of 12 needs significant for "egalitarian" group. Interpreted as *contrary* to complementarity.

			Type II: 12 of 36 needs showed a significant difference between means of men and women in "traditional" group; 26 of 36 needs showed a significant difference for the "egalitarian" group. Findings interpreted as showing significantly greater *complementarity* for "traditional" group than for "egalitarian" group. Factor Analysis yielded two primary dimensions: Instrumental and Expressive. "Traditional" couples were found to be similar for the Instrumental dimension and complementary for the Expressive dimension. The "egalitarian" couples were found to be complementary for the Instrumental dimension and similar for the Expressive dimension.
Murray needs for two bipolar scales; Dominance-Submission; Nurturance-Receptiveness. Many other questions about life asked. Interview method	Trost (1967)	267 men, 286 women from Sweden who had "published the banns" preparatory to marriage or were newlyweds	Correlation of couples yielded $r = -.05$ for Dominance-Submissiveness, and $-.07$ for Nurturance-Receptiveness. No support for complementarity or homogamy. A veritable armada of variables was compared to see whether couples dichotomized or trichotomized on these variables differed for their dominance or nurturance correlations. In general, they did not. Variables included, among many others: education, social class, number of previous engagements, attitude toward sexual fidelity, attitude toward divorce, religiosity, political preference, happiness during engagement, duration of knowing each other.

Table 4.5 (continued)

Test Used	Investigator	Subjects	Findings
Extensive interview of 2 to 3½ hours, Baughman-Rorschach Ink Blot Technique, Marriage Apperceptive Thematic Examination, Marriage Value Inventory, Sex Questionnaire, Background Questionnaire	Murstein (1972)	19 college couples going steady or engaged	The typed protocol of data from all subjects was used to rate subjects on 100 statements about personality. Of these, 87 were predicted to be homogamous for the couple. Some 27 were significant in the predicted direction, 1 was significant in direction contrary to prediction. Of the remaining 13 predicted to be complementary, 1 was found to be so. The results support *homogamy.*
Leary's Interpersonal Check List used to define group of dominant and group of submissive subjects	Palmer & Byrne (1970)	21 men, 21 women (college students) comprise dominant group; 50 men and women divided equally by sex comprise the submissive group	Subjects had to evaluate protocol of a "dominant" or "submissive" opposite-sex stranger and to state their liking of the stranger. The results indicated that attraction is primarily culture-determined. Attraction was greater toward the dominant stranger; men preferred the submissive stranger more than the dominant one, women preferred the dominant stranger more than the submissive one. A slight similarity effect was found, with submissive subjects compared to dominant subjects liking the submissive stranger more than the dominant one, and dominant subjects compared to submissive subjects preferring the dominant stranger to the submissive one. *No complementarity* was found.

Amalgam of questions from PPS (Edwards, 1959), FIRO-B (Schutz, 1958), social and personal characteristics, background, habits, tastes, and values	Strong, Wallace, & Wilson (1969)	College students matched by computer. Number varies with analysis. Total of men 93, women, 65	Subjects were matched according to three principles: (a) random; (b) similar background and values; (c) similar background, values, and complementarity of needs. Post-date evaluations showed random dates were liked less than matched dates. Men showed no difference in preference between "similar" and "complementary" dates. Of 18 women replying, all *preferred the "similar" date* to the complementary one.
Same as above study	Strong & Wilson (1969)	College students matched by computer. 72 men, 21 women	Subjects matched according to three principles: (a) background similarity (similar); (b) background similarity and value similarity (compatible); and (c) background similarity and complementarity (complementary). Men showed a significant *preference for compatible dates* over *complementary* ones, but only a trend toward preference over similar dates. Not enough women completed the procedure to analyze their preferences.

achievement, status, striving, and status aspiration. The second factor is called "Expressive" and consisted of the following highly loaded needs: autonomy, nurturance, succorance, deference.

As shown in Figure 4.1, the "traditional" couples are said to be complementary (Case C) for the "Expressive" dimension, whereas the "egalitarian" couples are complementary for the "Instrumental" dimension (Case D). On the other hand, the "traditionalists" are similar for the Instrumental dimension, whereas the "egalitarians" are similar for the expressive dimensions.

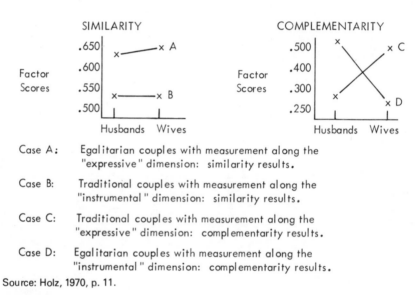

Case A: Egalitarian couples with measurement along the "expressive" dimension: similarity results.

Case B: Traditional couples with measurement along the "instrumental" dimension: similarity results.

Case C: Traditional couples with measurement along the "expressive" dimension: complementarity results.

Case D: Egalitarian couples with measurement along the "instrumental" dimension: complementarity results.

Source: Holz, 1970, p. 11.

Fig. 4.1. Similarity and complementarity in the marital dyad: Factor analytic results

There is, alas, a major problem with this stimulating finding. Holz takes mean differences in scores between the sexes within an ideological group as indicative of complementarity. However, the existence of sex differences is not necessarily equivalent to demonstrating complementarity between members of a couple. To illustrate this fact I have concocted a fictitious example, as shown in Table 4.6.

Table 4.6 shows that although significant sex differences exist for the "Expressive" dimension, there is no significant correlation of complementarity between husbands and wives. Men are shown to have generally lower scores than women, but the range of male scores is

Table 4.6

HUSBANDS' AND WIVES' SCORES
ON "EXPRESSIVE" DIMENSION
WHERE SEX DIFFERENCES DO NOT RESULT
IN COMPLEMENTARY CORRELATION
(Hypothetical Example)

Wives' Scores		Husbands' Scores	
Wife 1	6	Husband 1	5
Wife 2	10	Husband 2	5
Wife 3	9	Husband 3	6
Wife 4	7	Husband 4	6
Wife 5	8	Husband 5	5
$\bar{x}$ =	8.0	$\bar{x}$ =	5.4

Note: Interspousal correlation is .00, which is not significant. The *t* test for difference between means of the sexes is 3.47, which is significant ($p < .01$).

limited, and there is no significant negative correlation between a husband's and wife's score, as complementarity (Type I) would dictate. Holz's data ought to be reanalyzed with focus on interspousal correlations as a test of complementarity.

The research findings with tests other than the PPS often suggest the appropriateness of a role theory explanation for marital choice. Palmer and Byrne's experiment (1970) is strictly speaking not very strong evidence against Winch's theory, because their subjects were strangers who judged only responses of a stranger's protocol. However, their experiment, in which all of the variables were carefully controlled, serves as an excellent illustration of the importance of roles as opposed to needs—a conclusion buttressed more substantively by the majority of other cited studies.

Palmer and Byrne's subjects were selected from Leary's Interpersonal Check List as being either highly dominant or highly submissive. They read a test, purportedly filled out by an opposite-sex stranger, showing either very dominant or very submissive traits. The stranger's protocol was in actuality constructed by experimenters. The subjects then filled out a brief questionnaire that provided a measure of how much they liked the stranger.

The subjects, taken as a whole, preferred the dominant stranger. This finding is hardly surprising, because our culture teaches that dominant behavior is more socially desirable than submissive behavior. When separate analyses were done by sex, however, men were found to prefer the submissive stranger, whereas women preferred the dominant one. Again, this is not surprising, because women have been traditionally taught to be submissive and men dominant; consequently, men would generally prefer a woman to be submissive, and women would prefer a dominant male.

A slight pull toward similarity was also found, in that submissive subjects, although generally preferring dominant strangers, preferred them less strongly than did dominant subjects. The submissive subjects, although not liking submissive subjects very much, nonetheless liked them somewhat more than did dominant subjects. In short, the cultural and role influences seem most strong, but similarity seems to exert a slight pull, though hardly enough to offset the culturally determined trend. Complementarity played no part in their findings.

Considering the totality of research by Winch and others, it cannot be concluded that the failure to confirm his theory rested largely on testing by the PPS. Neither can the failure to confirm the theory be ascribed to the kind of population used, because no matter what population was used, the results were negative. The paper-and-pencil measures cannot be blamed, because several studies used interviews, but the results were never supportive of complementarity. In sum, there is no clear cut support of complementarity in any of the studies cited.

In the next section, we shall consider the conceptual problems of the theory itself apart from the failures experienced in testing it.

A CONCEPTUAL ANALYSIS OF THE THEORY
OF COMPLEMENTARITY

The various problems with the theory of complementarity may be condensed into eleven more or less independent points.

1. *No rationale for selecting needs or need-pairings.*   We have seen how selecting particular need-pairings may have predisposed toward significant findings in favor of the theory. Apart from the data,

however, a rationale is needed for determining whether the theory deals with all needs or only with some. If it deals only with some then the theory should be able to explain why some need-pairings are complementary and some are not. This the theory does not do.

The elimination of some needs on the grounds of "complexity" is also unsatisfactory. As noted in the earlier section, sex needs are as likely to be complementary as nymphomaniacs are likely to be drawn to eunuchs. Moreover, I can conceive of no reason why dominance and status striving are more simple or unidimensional than is sex. One spouse may dominate the other in order to protect, to bully, or to nurture a helpless individual. Status striving may represent an attempt to eliminate poverty, or to keep up with the Joneses.

2. *Are the needs independent of each other?* Winch asserts that the need ratings can vary independently of each other (Winch, 1954). Yet the various factor analyses and intercorrelations of needs noted earlier indicate that certain needs cluster together, whereas others do not. But there is no rationale to determine which needs are complementary to other needs and which are independent.

To Winch's credit, he is aware of this problem in his tests of significance, and he avoids statistical tests that assume independence of needs in favor of tests that do not. However, this does not clarify the conceptual ambiguity as to which needs are derivates of other needs.

3. *At what personality levels do needs operate?* Winch does make a distinction between overt and covert needs. Unfortunately, the functioning of needs seems much more complex than that. Rosow (1957) has noted apropos of Winch's "flat list of needs" that "'superficial' needs (including many cultural values) are not easily distinguished from 'deeper,' and presumably stronger motives ..." (p. 219). Spouses may not be complementary if a husband's need for nurturance is manifest and his wife's need for succorance is latent. Indeed, people with the same needs will often manifest different behavior. This leads us to Point 4.

4. *Is behavior altogether waiter and pimp to the tyranny of need?* It was the father of "need" psychology himself, Henry Murray, who is alleged to have denied that needs were directly translated into behavior. In fact, by the 1950s psychoanalysis had moved away from an "id" psychology, which suggested a direct one-to-one translation of needs into behavior, apart from the traditional psychoanalytic exceptions such as sublimation and reaction formation. "Id"

psychology was replaced by "ego" psychology, which stressed that needs and traits can only be understood as subservient to the ego. Personality is not a collection of needs, but an organized system for adjustment to the environment. Some systems are set up to translate needs directly into behavior; such individuals are termed impulsive. Others can only express some of their needs, and these only infrequently, and only in specific situations.

It is incumbent, therefore, in understanding an individual's behavior, to understand his self-acceptance of his needs and also the possible conflict in two simultaneously aroused needs. If a dominant woman sees a passive but eligible bachelor, shall her desire for status striving (marriage) win out, thereby directing her to play the traditional submissive female? Or, shall she respond to her dominance needs when confronted with an indecisive male, but thus risk wounding his male ego and threatening her status-striving? When is an appropriate time to express a need, and when should it be inhibited? Even if she dominates him, is she doing so because he is helpless, or because she has hostility needs? Trying to evaluate needs without reference to the goals of the individual seems a little like saying that the tail wags the dog.

5. *Is there such a thing as a general need?*   Winch, to be sure, refers to needs within marriage and those without, but this refers to the target of the need, not to its degree of generality (Rosow, 1957). Even within marriage, a man may exhibit a need to dominate a woman in bed (perhaps to her pleasure?), but he may meet stiff resistance if he tries to tell her how to prepare a soufflé. The thinking of current personality theorists seems increasingly to be moving toward the view that needs are in large part dependent on roles. A corporate president may feel obliged to play the role of a fierce tiger in the corporate jungle, but gladly settle for the role of a contented pet sheep at home. An individual may, in short, have different needs with respect to his spouse in their intimate interaction as opposed to when they function as a couple in company, which may differ yet again from how they interact as parents with regard to their children. It is their roles, not their general "within" needs, which make it easiest to understand their behavior. In fact, when an individual's needs are general rather than role specific, we are often dealing with a neurotic. The aggressive executive who reacts to his friends, wife, and children with the same aggressive suspiciousness as he does with his business rivals is exhibiting a generalized need but also a disturbed personality.

One frequent problem resulting from the difference between masculine and feminine roles is the fact that the husband may have more external opportunities to satisfy his needs (e.g., at work) than does his wife, who may be reduced to conversations with a two-year-old child for several hours a day. His needs for affiliation (approach) at home may be minimal, therefore, whereas hers by the time he comes home may be maximal—even though abstractly both might be defined as having equal affiliation needs.

6. *What of sensitivity to needs?* One factor which seems to have escaped not only Winch, but even his most ardent critics, is the fact that individuals differ dramatically in their sensitivity to the needs of others. Alberta may have a high need for succorance, but Albert may have all the sensitivity of an anesthesized armadillo for *her* need; this despite his expressing his own need to nurture his son and the "club" at the Little League games. It is not clear from Winch's work that need and sensitivity to need are equivalent, and the assumption that different individuals of equal need would all be equally sensitive to their partner's complementary need would seem unwarranted.

7. *Is woman's need for hostility the same as man's need for hostility?* Neither Murray nor Winch make any distinction in their need definitions between the sexes. Typically, they adopt a masculine viewpoint. Hostility, for example, is defind as "to fight, injure, or kill others" (Winch, 1958, p. 90). There are few women who would meet this definition of hostility, but who would say that a hostile woman is a *rara avis?*. Rather, women are often more subtle and cunning in their expression of hostility than are men, a style no doubt affected by their subservient status in society as well as by their less formidable physical weapons than those possessed by men.

8. *To need is not to get, unless you have assets.* Winch's theory makes it appear as if once entrance has been made into the field of eligibles, that is, once one has passed the criteria for race, religion, social class, occupational grouping, location of residence, income, age, level of education, intelligence, and interests and values, the remaining consideration is need complementarity. This suggests that a balanced consideration of the assets and liabilities that each member of the couple possesses is not important. Other research, however, has suggested that equity of net marital worth (assets minus liabilities) is of some importance (Murstein, 1970). For example, two individuals might have perfect Winchian complementarity, but one might be physically attractive, highly sexed, high in self-esteem, and moving to a new out-of-town job next Tuesday. The partner may be fat, relatively low in sex-interest, low in self-esteem, and without plans

to leave town in the forseeable future. Despite need complementarity, the interpersonal characteristics of the first individual are more highly valued by society and/or at least different from those of the second individual; consequently, in choosing a marriage partner, each might be apt to search out a person with assets more comparable to their own.

9. *What are the criteria of complementarity?* Type I needs are complementary when they differ in *intensity,* and Type II needs are complementary when they differ in *kind.* It follows, therefore, if needs differ neither in intensity nor kind (assuming such a beast exists), that no complementarity is present (Levinger, 1964). Yet as was noted in the earlier example of Kerckhoff and Davis, reciprocal compatibility may occur either through complementarity or similarity.

Consider the hypothetical case of two perfectly complementary (Type I) couples Carl and Cora and Sam and Sarah, as shown in Table 4.7. Carl and Cora differ greatly in their Type I needs, whereas Sam and Sarah differ from each other only slightly, but both couples show perfect complementarity. It is evident from inspection of Sam and Sarah's scores that they are quite a bit more similar in score to Irwin and Irma than they are to Carl and Cora. Yet Irwin and Irma are homogamous with respect to each other whereas Sam and Sarah are perfectly complementary. A fourth couple, Vincent and Vera, are also highly similar to each other, but show no significant correlation in terms of their needs.

This example illustrates that the concept of complementarity is

Table 4.7

INADEQUACY OF NEGATIVE INTERSPOUSAL CORRELATION
AS AN INDEX OF TYPE I COMPLEMENTARITY

	Carl	Cora	Sam	Sarah	Irwin	Irma	Vincent	Vera
Need 1	5	1	3	2	3	3	3	3
Need 2	5	1	2	3	2	2	3	2
Need 3	5	1	3	2	2	2	2	2
Need 4	1	5	2	3	3	3	2	3
	$r = -1.00$		$r = -1.00$		$r = +1.00$		$r = .00$	

Note: Sam and Sarah, Irwin and Irma, Vincent and Vera are all similar to each other.
          Yet Sam and Sarah are Complementary, Irwin and Irma are Homogamous, and
          Vincent and Vera show No Relationship in Terms of Interspousal Correlation.

most meaningful when extreme need scores are involved such as would most readily be found in neurotic couples. As one moves toward similarity in the need strength of the partners, Winch's use of a negative interspousal correlation as a measure of Type I complementarity becomes increasingly inappropriate and confounded with similarity.

10. *Effect of time on needs.* Rosow (1957) has pointed out that time may affect need patterns in many different ways. Internal growth and maturation may lead to change in need strength and need priority. As a result of the interaction of a couple, certain needs may lessen, whereas new needs may emerge. As new roles are adopted ("steady," "fiancé," "bride"), new self-images and new needs sprout. Last, environmental factors, unexpected promotions or demotions, trauma, and new relationships may alter the need structure. Thus, it seems erroneous to think of needs as fixed enduring quantities. It also puts in question whether Winch's measurement of needs in the post-wedding state would have yielded identical scores to those obtained prior to the wedding.

11. *Social status, the critical incident, the social network, and other non-need determinants of marital choice.* There is a plethora of factors that influence marital choice apart from homogamous "field of eligible" characteristics and need complementarity. Some of the more important are as follows:

a. *Timing.* Many people meet desirable marriage partners but do not marry because the timing is not right. Some may not feel psychologically ready for marriage and prefer to play the field; others may be heavily involved in training for professional careers and do not wish to add financial and interpersonal responsibilities to the demands of their training; still others simply have not gone with enough partners to have achieved a comparison standard against which to gauge the desirability of their partner.

b. *Critical incident.* Although many people drift into matrimony almost imperceptibly, others seem to require a critical incident before they are galvanized into action. These incidents may be external or internal. Common external incidents are career transitions such as graduation from a university, promotion to the branch office of a corporation a thousand miles away, or possibly a less salubrious incident such as pregnancy.

Internal pressures result from one partner pressing the other toward a commitment of marriage. The critical incident in this case usually serves as a catalyst to hasten the eventuality of marriage, or to cause the recalcitrant one to back out of the relationship altogether.

c. *Marriage as a status.*   Some individuals view marriage itself as an affirmation of their own desirability, as well as a desired status with innumerable social and economic benefits. An individual with this orientation is less apt to be as finicky about the degrees of compatibility he experiences with his partner than is an individual with less concern about marriage as a value in itself.

d. *The social network—"conveyor-belt" influence.* Society is interested in marriage and the family for a multitude of reasons. Married individuals are less antiestablishment, more stable, bigger consumers of products, and generally more economically productive than are single persons. Moreover, most individuals have been inculcated with the virtues of family life so that, after their own marriage, they strive to influence their friends and, later, their children to marry. The pressures may be direct in the case of parents vis-à-vis their children, or in the case of friends—take the more indirect form of inviting "marriageables" as dinner guests.

When two people begin to go together, they have stepped on a conveyor belt (Ryder, Kafka, and Olson, 1971) whose ultimate stop is often matrimony. The belt moves slowly at first, so that it is not too difficult to jump off if one wishes. However, as time progresses, the belt accelerates in speed so that jumping off just before the end (marriage) can be a most traumatic experience.

Movement starts with official notice of "pairing" by friends and parents. The couple eventually come to be treated as a "couple." They may be invited as a couple to social functions, bridge parties, and tennis. Eventually, if they continue together for some time, expectations mount that this is a "serious" relationship that will end in marriage. The parents seem to look more "expectantly" at the couple with each passing month. When the engagement is officially announced and a "shower" is held for the bride, it is almost too late to jump off. Even if a couple realizes at this time that their interpersonal compatibility is not as good as they first thought, it takes a brave individual to risk the questions, guilt, and embarrassment involved in explaining one's change of mind to the social network.

CONCLUSIONS REGARDING COMPLEMENTARY NEEDS

Evidence has been presented that Winch's research is but minimally supportive of his theory and it has been suggested that various biases may have affected these findings. Research by others on marriage has not supported Winch's theory. The theory itself as originally formulated is badly dated and far too simple to account for such complex behavior as marital choice. It shows more promise in determining friendship, a topic outside of our present concern (c.f. Rychlak, 1965, Bermann, 1966). Needs may supply an initiating push to behavior, but cortical evaluation of the situation and environmental factors determine in what form if any a need will be expressed. We have also discussed a whole list of nonneed factors that influence marital choice, including roles, equity of assets, and social networks, to name just a few.

It is not meant to imply that Winch has been oblivious to the limitations of a preoccupation with needs. In his book (Winch, 1958) he shows sensitivity to the fact that roles are important and needs change with time. His theory, however, makes no formal provision for any of these factors.

Modification by Winch

Winch's reaction to the avalanche of critical studies and commentaries has been to reject most but not all of the studies as inappropriate. However, he has acknowledged many of the points brought out by the critics, and revised his thinking considerably. This revision has been influenced by Bermann's (1966) study of roommate stability in student nurses. Bermann was able to determine normative behavior for the "good nurse" and investigated whether adherence by both roommates to the norm was more predictive of roommate stability than was complementary need fulfillment. He found that norm adherence predicted stability best, and that complementarity predicted it less well, but significantly. Combining both principles provided the best predictor of stability.

Winch now sees a combination of complementarity (a psychological theory to him) and role theory (a sociological theory to him) as the best basis for understanding marital choice. He notes that "Role directs our attention to behaviors and attitudes that are appropriate to a situation, irrespective of the actor, whereas personality directs our attention to behaviors and attitudes that are characteristic of the actor, irrespective of the situation" (Winch, 1974, p. 406). This leads him to formulate a new hypothesis:

A pair of spouses who are attracted to each other on the basis of complementary needs will be a less stable pair if the complementariness is counter to role specification than if it is consistent with role specification.

He does have doubts, however, on whether needs and traits will be of use in "further and more exhaustive analysis of marital and familial roles" (Winch, 1974, p. 408).

There is little question that Winch's reformulation is an improvement over the original theory. However, it is difficult to agree with the dichotomization and assignment of needs to the psychologists and roles to the sociologist. It seems more reasonable to think of the intraindividual (psychological) and societal (sociological) factors as interacting from birth to produce an integration of influences on interpersonal behavior.

Needs are certainly influenced by sociological factors: the kind of family, status, and environment one acquires from birth on. There are, no doubt, also biological factors that interact with learned behavior to produce "needs."

In the same vein, roles too are not solely defined by reference to societal norms. There is never an entity called a traditional housewife role. Each woman generally modifies the societal stereotype to adjust to her own perception of needs and environment and thereby creates a tailor-made role of a wife for herself. This role may or may not show much similarity to the societal stereotype of housewife, but it probably is a much better predictor of her behavior. Where conflict occurs with respect to the societal role, it is more likely to be a conflict between competing roles—her custom-made one and that assigned by society—rather than between her "raw" needs and the normative role that society has proposed for her. Whichever of these two proposals the reader prefers (or perhaps neither), it seems evident that the old theory of complementary needs is no longer of much impact in theoretical thinking regarding marital choice.

Its impending disappearance should not be interpreted as detracting from the contribution of Winch and the theory of complementarity to the area of marital choice. From the perspective of hindsight, it is not difficult to find flaws in Winch's theory. It should be noted, however, that when he first forwarded the theory, there was no earlier model to improve upon. He was the first to propose a theory of marital choice and at the same time embark on a research program to test the theory. His work strongly stimulated research and theoretical thinking on marital choice and interpersonal relationships. If complementary needs was only akin to a first-stage rocket blast, it nevertheless provided the main thrust toward more advanced levels of thinking about what brings two people together in marriage.

CHAPTER 5

Value Theories

The literature is replete with examples of the influence of homogamy on marital choice. Numerous studies indicate that an individual tends to marry another of the same race, religion, age, education, social status, intelligence, eye color, number of siblings, musical ability, and longevity, to name but a fraction of the list of homogamous variables. Some of these variables, such as, for example, longevity, are spurious. It would no doubt be very romantic indeed if two aged lovers could expire in each other's arms after each had exhibited the clairvoyance to choose a mate literally "for life." Such clairvoyance, however, has been only slightly in evidence in that their correlation for longevity has been reported to be in the neighborhood of .2 (Pearson, 1903). A correlation of that size is not very imposing, but it is statistically significant and leads to the question of just how prescient people can be with regard to their own and their spouse's life expectancy. It is true, of course, that certain nations are significantly longer lived than others; the Scandinavians, for example, are noted for their longevity. Pearson's data, however, is based on British subjects.

The error in Pearson's thinking arises from collecting data over a considerable period of time, including using tombstones as records (Beckman, 1962); consequently, the fact that life expectancy underwent considerable change during the nineteenth century made for a modest but spurious correlation. Husbands and wives in the early part of the nineteenth century, not having had the benefit of late Victorian advances in medicine, undoubtedly lived shorter lives than did those of Victorian times.

Eye color is associated with ethnic background. Since individuals show some tendency to marry according to ethnicity, the correlation for eye color is probably merely an indirect consequence of ethnic pairing.

The correlation in number of siblings of those marrying is also probably a derivative of a more influential variable—social status. Homogamy for social status is very selective, and number of children varies inversely with social status. A man of the upper middle class probably came from a relatively small family, as did his upper-middle-class wife. The poor have many children; therefore the fact that a poor woman's family had a lot of children, as did her poor husband's family, would assure an overall correlation if rich and poor are included in the data bank.

It has been observed for many years that the handicapped show a greater than chance propensity for marriage with each other. This has particularly been the case with deafness (Harris, 1912). Alexander Graham Bell was so struck by this phenomenon that he took the occasion to point out some negative consequences of this tendency in an article entitled "Upon the Formation of a Deaf Variety of the Human Race" (Bell, 1883). It is a moot question, however, whether value homogeneity lies at the basis of such marriages or rather opportunity for interaction, since the deaf generally share common schooling, family life, and association.

Despite the fact that some aspects of homogamy are spurious, the basic homogamous bent of variables such as age, education, race, and religion, among others, can scarcely be questioned. But when we have said that, we have only scratched the surface of understanding homogamy. Why does homogamy operate, and why doesn't it *always* operate?

Some researchers (Burgess and Locke, 1945) have listed the factors behind homogamy, but Kerckhoff (1964) has dichotomized them as follows:

> The first type views the patterns of mate selection as a function of *opportunities*. It explains similarities of mates on the basis of residential segregation and differences in activity patterns of various social categories which limit the range of contacts of any person to encounters with persons like himself. The second explanation is a *normative* one. It views the patterns of similarity as the result of preferences on the part of the chooser for persons like himself and/or the enforcement of such homogamous choices through social sanctions. (Kerckhoff, 1964, p. 289; italics mine)

When a group strongly adheres to a *norm* out of conviction, and there is simultaneously little *opportunity* for being tempted away from homogamy, we should expect strong adherence to homogamy. The inhabitants of Quebec in 1951 were 88 percent Catholic, religious, cohesive, and socially distant from the English Canadians (Locke, Sabagh, and Thomes, 1957), who were few in number. Not surprisingly, only 2 percent interfaith marriages were reported in the Canadian Vital Statistics of 1951.

The authors also report that New Mexico showed a 47 percent incidence of Catholics, which at first view suggests considerable opportunity for intermarriage. Yet the rate of intermarriage was only 13 percent. The explanation resides in the existence of a norm not only to marry within the religion, but also of a cultural norm for Mexican-Americans (largely Catholic) to marry other Mexican-Americans, and for Anglos (Protestants) to marry Anglos.

Where opportunity to marry within a religion was practically nonexistent—as was the case for Catholics in North Carolina, where the incidence of Catholics was 1 percent—the intermarriage rate burgeoned to 70 percent. Most Catholics, it would appear, would rather marry non-Catholics than not marry at all.

Kerckhoff (1964) sought to test the relative strength of the norm and opportunity components in a study with Duke College coeds. The proportions of homogamous choices in religion, urbanity, education, and class were traced from the first beau to the second beau and then to the fiancé. Urbanity declined in homogeneity, suggesting an opportunity factor, whereas education and class both increased, indicating that they functioned as norms. The trend for religion was unclear.

Kerckhoff's classification is of help in understanding the motivating factors in homogamy, but it does not go deeply enough into the meaning of "opportunity" that leads to marriage.

The pure sociological position is that "opportunity" merely allows normative values to function so as to screen out the less desirable candidates for marriage. This position is spelled out in Coombs's value theory of mate selection (1961). Borrowing from Williams (1954), Coombs defines value as:

> ... any aspect of a situation, event, or object that is *invested with a preferential interest* as being "good," "bad," "desirable," and the like ... Values are not the concrete goals of action but rather *criteria* by which goals are chosen. (They) . . . are *modes of organizing conduct*—meaningful, affectively invested pattern principles that guide human action. (Williams, 1954, pp. 374-75)

Values are held to be so meaningful that they are accepted

without question, and they are generally thought to be desirable for others as well as for oneself. Moreover, values are said to be internalized in the personality through socialization. When an individual's values are attacked, it is as if the individual himself were attacked; it follows, therefore, that individuals are drawn toward those persons who accept their basic values, thereby providing emotional security.

The question might arise why there should be so much selectivity in marriage, given that most value systems are not very complex in nature. Shouldn't all Jehovah's Witnesses be equally acceptable as marriage partners for each other? Coombs notes, however, that although many people share common values, no one has exactly the same experiences, and each person's value system could be said to be unique to some degree.

Coombs believes he can account for most existing theories on the basis of values. Homogamy of religion, for example, may be accounted for because "persons who share similar social backgrounds will be likely to be socialized under similar conditions, and will therefore develop similar value systems" (Coombs, 1961, p. 52).

Propinquity is said to be a factor because people living side by side interact and tend thereby to become similar in values. The apparently Oedipal situation, in which, for example, the son marries someone whose "characteristics" resemble that of his Oedipal mother, can also be explained by the fact that individuals marrying within their class would have parents who embraced comparable values and socialized their children with these values. Accordingly, the wife's values resemble the mother's, not for Freudian reasons, but for cultural ones.

The ideal mate theory, holding that an individual marries someone who resembles the image that he holds of an ideal spouse is also readily accommodated by a value theory. The image is said to be derived from one's values. "That is, an idealized mate is merely a visualized combination of all one's basic values projected into one ideal or 'perfect' person" (Coombs, 1961, p. 54).

The only theory that cannot be accounted for on the basis of values, in Coombs's opinion, is the "complementary needs" theory, namely, that opposites attract. Coombs points out, however, that this theory assumes free choice of marriage partner. In our society, he argues, external pressures are brought to bear in open or subtle ways, so that few marriages can meet the criteria for complementary needs to operate; hence Coombs dismisses the complementary need theory as inoperative.

Coombs's theory broadens our understanding of homogamous norms and opportunities somewhat, but it lends little to our understanding of the dynamics of how values lead to attraction. His model of a more-or-less passive individual who is the recipient of different kinds of socialization does not promote an understanding of an individual who reacts, modifies, and adjusts to competing values in his environment—an individual who is influenced by his genetic and physical makeup, luck, psychological needs, roles, and expediency. As Adams (1971) has noted: "Many youthful marriages may occur to escape an unhappy home, or because of a premarital pregnancy; in such cases the importance of background homogamy, value consensus, and empathy may be minimal" (p. 223). Among older individuals, the interest in acquiring marital status may predominate, so that if a "value consensus" mate is not on the horizon, someone else with more interest in immediate marriage will do. Further, Coombs's theory does not account for the exceptions to value homogamy — blacks marry whites, princes marry peasants, and confirmed xenophobes bring home war brides from across the seas.

It might be argued that these mavericks have learned competing values that simply rank higher on their hierachy of values than do homogamy of race, social status, and nationality. This argument seems weak, however, in that common observation suggests that tradition-breakers often defy tradition because to do so satisfies needs that are not reducible to inculcated social values. They adhere to values because the values make them feel good and comfortable within themselves. If the values do not serve well in this regard, they can be, and often are, dispensed with. A bit later on we shall consider some research indicating under what conditions value homogeneity can be overlooked. First, however, we ought to more explicitly state the reasons why value congruence is generally satisfying.

One of the strongest human needs is the feeling of competence—that one understands what life and people are all about. All of us want to master our environment as well as we can, whether our goal be accumulation of wealth, good will, or achievement of a state of Nirvana. We build up a cognitive map of what the world is like, and we try to pattern our behavior accordingly.

One person may conclude that the world is very competitive where it is every person for himself. He may accordingly construct a model of behavior calling for suspiciousness, distrust, and precautions against being exploited. Yet there are competing philosophies. Some espouse the "brotherhood of man," a competing value system. How can one be sure that one's own value system is correct and that of the others is false? One way of gaining assurance is by finding that another person, whom one regards as having some status, agrees with the individual's values. The individual's views thus receive social validation (Festinger, 1954, Berscheid and Walster, 1969, Byrne, 1971).

Another feature of values is that they are introjected into the self and define the self-image; hence the person who rejects our values is often perceived as rejecting us. Acceptance of our values, con-comitantly, implies that we are accepted. Provided that we have a reasonably positive self-image, we tend to be attracted to persons whom we perceive as validating it.

In a study on some 20 correlates of liking, the most potent correlation of liking another was the belief that one was, in turn, liked by that person (Murstein and Lamb, 1973). Perceiving that another has the same values as we may lead to the conclusion that the other would like us, as well as to the satisfaction of having our values confirmed.

In addition, persons who have similar values are likely to engage in similar activities and reward each other in several ways. Tennis players may reward each other's commitment to tennis as a meaningful form of exercise; they also serve as partners making a match possible. Moreover, since activities are valued differently by others, individuals participating in the same activity are likely to possess equal status in their milieu.

It seems plausible that individuals of equal status in society are likely to be drawn to each other because of their equal ability to reward each other. Later on, I shall present some empirical foundations for this assumption.

In sum, there are numerous reasons why a couple's value homogeneity should lead to mutual attraction. But under what con-ditions is value consensus important and when is it not important?

THE COMPLEXITIES OF VALUE CONSENSUS

One of the earliest researchers to question the importance of com-munality of values was Benson (1955). His research on engaged and married couples led him to conclude that engagement success and marital adjustment were not significantly related to the number of common interests indicated by the subjects. There was, however, a significant but minor correlation of about .2 between *belief* regarding the number of interests in common and engagement success.

When the areas of interest were broken into "familialistic," "undefined," and "individualistic," the familialistic area proved to be the one strongly related to engagement success. His work, therefore, suggests that value consensus need not be sweeping, but only related to the particular kind of relationship involved.

The finding that value consensus was not equally distributed across the various socioeconomic classes was reported by Dentler and Hutchinson (1961) and Kerckhoff (1972). The former compared the views of family members—mother, father, and one or two adolescent children—on a brief measure of values. The families were divided into three classes: professional-executive, lower-managerial-clerical-sales, and skilled and service workers. Value consensus decreased from the first to the last of these groups. However, consensus was not greater within a particular class for actual families than for randomly created ones. In other words, a husband might be paired with someone else's wife within his class and find as much consensus as with his own wife.

Kerckhoff (1972) worked with very recently married young couples and found very similar results. He did report, however, that consensus among actual couples was higher than among randomly paired couples for professional couples 60 percent of the time, for "middle" couples 56 percent of the time, and for working class couples 33 percent of the time. It appears that individual selection for value consensus as opposed to class selection becomes more and more important in the higher social classes, although at the same time class value consensus also improves from lower to upper classes.

Kerckhoff and Bean (1967), working with engaged college couples or those "going steady," demonstrated that role needs may influence the importance of value consensus for satisfaction with the partner. In one part of their analysis, they focused on men and women high in the need for "inclusion"—the need to be a part of groups and activities. Men in our society, according to Talcott Parsons (Zelditch, 1955), are said to have stronger *instrumental* concerns (getting things done, earning money) than women, who are said to have stronger *expressive* orientations (tending to social, emotional values). Kerckhoff and Bean, therefore, broke down their men's group into those with high and those with low instrumental values and their women's group into those with high and those with low expressive concerns.

The question they were asking was what kind of a correlation between partner satisfaction and value consensus would each of these subgroups manifest? The answer may be seen in Table 5.1. Inspection of this table reveals that men higher in instrumental concerns show a significant *negative* correlation between value consensus with their partner (measured by ranking ten values relating to marriage in order

Table 5.1

CORRELATIONS BETWEEN VALUE CONSENSUS AND
PARTNER SATISFACTION FOR HIGH INCLUSION SUBJECTS
SUBDIVIDED INTO HIGH AND LOW INSTRUMENTAL-
EXPRESSIVE SUBCATEGORIES

Category	N	r
High inclusion men		
High instrumental	21	−.48*
Low instrumental	22	−.18
High inclusion women		
High expressive	25	.05
Low expressive	21	.53**

* $p < .05.$
** $p < .01.$

Source: Kerckhoff and Bean, 1967, p. 184; modified slightly.

of importance) and satisfaction with her. Women low on expressive values show a significant positive correlation between consensus and satisfaction.

The authors explain their findings by stating that men who are extremely high on the role dictated for them by society (highly instrumental) expect their spouses to be different from them on their values—perhaps to have "feminine" values. Such men might find someone with identical values too masculine.

Women who are low on expressive values but yet are high on need for inclusion have a dilemma. They need to be included, but they don't value their "woman's" expressive role in society very highly. They tend therefore to find satisfaction in agreement in values with the man. The data in this study are treated in a very complex fashion, and there are interpretations possible other than those favored by the authors. The main point of the study for our concern, however, is that the need for value consensus is obviously not ubiquitous but depends on role adherence, psychological needs, and social class.

The relevance of needs to desire for similarity has been studied by a number of psychologists, but I shall choose only two representative studies for discussion. Walster and Walster (1963) reasoned that a primary factor making people want to associate with those similar to themselves was the fear that they might not be liked if they associated with dissimilar persons. Their experiment supported this belief. Subjects told that it was important to talk with people who liked them chose more often to interact with similar rather than with dissimilar people. Those who had been assured that everyone would like them were much more willing to associate with dissimilar people than were subjects in other conditions.

Goldstein and Rosenfeld (1969) measured their subjects on a scale of security. Those less secure preferred more similar subjects than did more secure subjects.

That there may be competing homogamous values was aptly demonstrated by Leslie and Richardson (1956) and Coombs (1962). The former authors found slight status homogamy among college students who married someone they had known at home before attending college, but no homogamy among those met and married while on campus. Likewise, Coombs found that status homogamy was much greater for college couples in which both partners lived at home during courtship as opposed to those in which neither lived at home.

Conclusions

Although there are many reasons for value homogamy to be important in interpersonal attraction and marital choice, it is far from being sweeping and all-determining. Its influence is most certain when there is a direct correspondence between the values and the nature of the relationship. Moreover, value consensus is more important and more personally selective in the upper than in the lower class. Last, personality factors also influence the desire for value consensus. There is something attractive and interesting in associating with an individual with different values from oneself that may be lacking in a relationship with one whose values mirror one's own. However, this interest is counteracted by the strain in encountering the unknown and the fear of not being accepted because of the difference in values. Since individuals differ in confidence, interest in new relationships, and fear of rejection, it follows logically that individuals will differ psychologically in their need for value consensus. Is there, nevertheless, some support for a value theory of marital choice?

RESEARCH ON VALUE THEORIES OF MARITAL CHOICE

Although Coombs has been the chief proponent of a value theory of marital choice, he has published only one study relating to the theory even tangentially (Coombs 1966). College students were computer-matched for five items: preferences for a "date" with campus popularity, "good looks," fraternity membership, stylish clothes, and dancing ability. Couples were divided into "similar," "medium," and "dissimilar" groups on the basis of their answers. Actually, a rather constricted range of scores was used. With the four-point scale of importance (0 to 3) employed for each item, the couples could have differed by as much as 15 points for the 5-item test. However, because of factors other than that related to the study, no couple differed by more than six points; hence the "similar" were identical, the "medium" differed by only a point or two, and the dissimilar (really only moderately dissimilar) differed by 3 to 6 points.

The couples went on a date. Shortly afterwards, they were asked how satisfied they were with the partner, and how easy it was to communicate with him or her. The satisfaction scores for men and for women were correlated with the degree of value consensus. Women showed a significant but low rank-order correlation of .17 ($p < .01$) between satisfaction and value consensus, but the association for men was not significant ($r = .07$). Regarding the correlation between communication ease and value consensus, both sexes were significant (men, $r = .13$ ($p < .01$); women, $r = .16$ ($p < .01$)), but were again low.

Despite the fact that the correlations are quite low, value consensus did seem to play a part in dating satisfaction and communication, and there is good reason to believe that its importance for marital choice is somewhat underestimated by this study. Dating, after all, is not marital choice, and subjects who were interested in having a good time may not have concerned themselves as much with the date's values as with physical attractiveness, poise, and entertainingness. Another factor retarding the magnitude of correlation was the restricted range of scores, as noted earlier. Last, using five superficial items as a measure of value consensus was unfortunate but understandable within the requirements of a brief questionnaire needed to entice the students to participate. The fact that significant findings occurred, therefore, testifies that value consensus plays at least some role in courtship.

The importance of value consensus is better highlighted in a study by Schellenberg (1960) who used 36 premarital and 64 married couples and a more extensive, standardized test of values, the Allport, Vernon, Lindzey *Study of Values*. This test measures the relative emphasis of a person with regard to six values: theoretical, economic, aesthetic, social, political, and religious.

An artificial group of 67 couples was created by matching men and women so as to achieve the same general background similarities and differences as for the actual couples. These were supplemented by twelve additional couples selected from a larger outside pool of subjects, so that the final artificial group of 79 couples closely matched the actual group of subjects.

A score of 100 represented chance value convergence in the Allport-Vernon-Lindzey test. The artificial couples achieved a mean score of 115.3, which was significantly better than chance. This score indicated that the college population as a whole showed a greater than chance similarity of values. The premarital and married groups mean scores were 132.0 and 134.5 respectively. Both of these scores were significantly higher than the artificial group, thus indicating that the individual factors making for value consensus added significantly to the proportion of value homogamy accounted for by the background factors alone. Hutton (1974) obtained correlations between 54 engaged or dating couples on the same test. Four of the six values were significantly correlated between members of couples (artistic .67, religious .48, economic .45, political .33); two were not (social .16, theoretical .14).

Studies by Rich (1973) and myself largely confirmed Schellenberg's and Hutton's findings. Rich's study involved the use of two measures of value consensus: the Farber Index of Marital Integration (1957) and also Morris's (1956) "Ways to Live." Two central groups were used; one, an engaged college group randomly paired, the other a number of randomly paired students who had never been engaged or married. The results generally showed that the actual couples were more homogamous than the two control groups on most preferred and least preferred values, with middle values (those of indifference) not differentiating between the groups.

Rich also was able to determine that his findings were not due to different group preferences for values by correlating the ranks assigned to the values by the engaged and nonengaged groups. The correlations ranged from .80 to .96, indicating that the difference between the groups in value homogamy was due to individual selectivity and not to group norms.

My own findings with three groups of students, though not as conclusive as Rich's findings (2 of the 3 groups supported value homogamy, one showed no difference), generally support value homogamy. Since they will be discussed in full detail in conjunction with my theory of marital choice, no further reference will be made to them at this time.

The studies we have reviewed so far do not provide a direct test of whether value homogeneity is *responsible* for interpersonal attraction, or whether, to some degree, it results *from the interaction* of the couple. Rich's work, as noted above, partially controls for this possibility, but it is conceivable that group stability for value preference might remain the same, while individuals changed position from that prior to interacting with the partner to that after interaction, with the changes occuring in all directions, giving the same net effect.

A study by Snyder (1964), controls for this possibility. She collected data from 561 high school sophomores who either had not dated each other or were only minimally acquainted. Forty of these students subsequently married someone from the original sophomore class. The old data on attitudes toward 14 areas of behavior (including church attendance, dancing, dating, divorce, smoking, staying out late), peers, family and community were then analyzed. Summarizing across all areas there appeared to be roughly a 50-50 split on similarity and dissimilarity; that is, the couples agreed on about half of the items across the various categories and were dissimilar on about half.

Focusing next on the similar items, Snyder wondered whether these were determined by individual preference or by class membership. She measured individual selectivity in the following way: If the couples exceeded the class homogamy on an item by 81 to 100 percent, she labeled the item "very selective homogamy." By succeeding twenty-percent jumps in descending order, other items were declared to be "rather selective," "chance selectivity," "rather nonselective," and "very nonselective." the results of the comparison across all areas is shown in Table 5.2.

This table indicates that 32 percent of the attitudes were

Table 5.2

MARITAL SELECTIVITY IN ATTITUDE SIMILARITY

	Percentage of Similar Attitudes				
Degree of Selectivity	Toward 14 Areas of Behavior	Toward Peers	Toward Family	Toward Community	Total
Very selective	5	4	6	3	5
Rather selective	27	28	16	40	27
Chance selectivity	44	35	33	40	38
Rather nonselective	15	29	39	15	25
Very nonselective	9	4	6	2	5

Source: Snyder, 1964, p. 335.

selective, 38 percent were of chance selectivity, and 30 per cent were nonselective.

The value of such an approach depends on the representativeness of the population studied and of the attitudes sampled. If, for example, members of the American Fascist Party were sampled on attitudes relating to fascism and authoritarianism, it is unlikely that any evidence of selective homogamy would be uncovered. In the present case, it is unknown to what degree the high school students who participated were representative of high school students in general, and to what degree the items used were representative of the attitudes of high school students. If we make the assumption that both were representative, then Snyder's findings suggest that the individuals had only moderately similar attitudes before they met, and that only a moderate amount of similarity was selective.

CONCLUSIONS

The research indicated that values may be most operative in bringing people together so that they can interact. From that point on values play a significant but lesser role. Even universities, where many of the studies originated, may have some variation in family values from member to member, though much of the variance has been narrowed in the selectivity of population that occurs in moving from high school to the university. The value homogamy found among campus couples seems to be fairly equally accounted for by campus (class) values and by individual variation. Studies outside the campus have indicated that value consensus increases as one ascends the occupational scale, probably because sex role differentiation declines as one ascends the occupational scale.

The research is not altogether consistent with respect to the importance of individual selectivity as opposed to class membership in determining value consensus. A variable that might clarify this question is "timing." Is there an optimal time in a relationship when value consensus is important, after which it diminishes in relevance? We shall consider this question in the next chapter on process theories.

Another question is how much does value consensus lead individuals to be attracted to each other, and how much does it result from the interaction of people who like each other? The data of Snyder suggest that both factors may be operating. However, the crispest evidence on this matter would come from a future longitudinal study.

A contribution badly needed at this stage of the research literature is a more profound, comprehensive scale of values. The tests used, such as three to ten "homemade items" or the ten-statement Farber index have been helpful in initial research. But they are too brief, and they are riddled with social desirability, which probably inflates the alleged contribution of class membership to value consensus by blurring the distinction between actual and control groups.

In sum, it is clear that value consensus of itself is insufficient to account for marital choice. We noted that, for example, when Catholics constitute a very minor portion of a geographical area, the majority of them abandon value homogamy in the area of religion. They would rather wed heterogamously than remain homogamously single.

Another weakness in value theory is that it cannot handle departures from homogamy. Blacks should always marry blacks, Protestants should marry Protestants, and the discreet charm of the bourgeois should be reserved for the bourgeoise. Yet blacks marry whites, Protestants marry Catholics or Jews, and princesses marry paupers. These exceptions are bypassed by value theory as errata.

Moreover, there are many variables other than values that influence marital choice, such as physical attractiveness, sexual compatibility, expediency, role satisfaction, parental pressure—ad infinitum. Value homogamy is probably important in many courtships but far from sufficient as an explanation of marital choice.

CHAPTER 6

Process and Filter Theories

Process Theories

A number of theorists have taken the position that marital choice cannot be understood by measuring the traits of each individual in the dyad, no matter how thorough and reliable the measurement. One of the principal spokesmen for this school of thinking has been Charles Bolton (1961), who makes the following statement:

> The outcome of the contacts of . . . two individuals is not mechanically predetermined either by the relation of their personality characteristics or the institutional patterns providing the context for the development of the relation—though these are both certainly to be taken into account—but that the outcome is an end-product of a sequence of interactions characterized by advances and retreats along the paths of available alternatives, by definitions of the situation which crystallize tentative commitments and bar withdrawals from certain positions, by the sometimes tolerance and sometimes resolution of ambiguity, by reassessments of self and other, and by the tension between open-endedness and closure that characterizes all human relations. . . . (pp. 235-36)

In short, there can be no single explanation of marital choice, according to Bolton. There are multiple causes, and the key to understand them is the study of the transactions between them—the processes by which the two individuals are drawn ever closer together.

REISS'S THEORY

Among the earliest of process theorists has been Ira Reiss (1960, 1971). Reiss's "wheel theory" contains four processes said to exist in a closely interrelated manner, as shown in Figure 6.1.

The initial process is called *rapport*. When two people meet (the theory could apply to any kind of relationship, not only to marital choice), they quickly come to an assessment of the rapport that exists between them. They sense the degree to which they feel comfortable with, interested in, and understood by the other. To Reiss the degree of rapport is generally largely predictable, given knowledge of the social and cultural background of the two individuals.

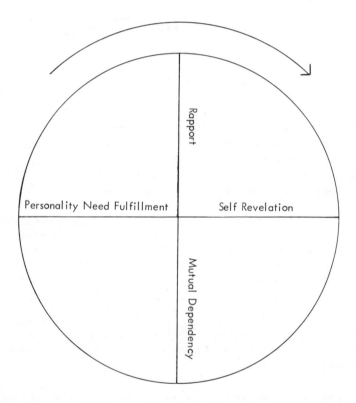

Fig. 6.1.   Graphic presentation of the wheel theory of the development of love
Source: Reiss, 1960, p. 143.

If a feeling of mutual rapport exists, it leads to a feeling of relaxation, which encourages the onset of the second process, that of *self-revelation*. The individuals in this stage proceed to reveal intimate facts and feelings about themselves. Here, too, according to Reiss, the social and cultural factors point out the reason for differences. Some groups are socialized to talk readily on first dates, whereas others are taught to be more reserved. In Reiss's view, males are taught to reveal sexual intimacies to females earlier than females are generally ready to accept them, resulting often in the "battle of the sexes."

Self-revelation in turn leads to *mutual dependency*, or inter-dependent habit systems. Each member of the couple becomes conditioned to the other as a source of reward for many activities and behaviors: sexual partner, companion, and audience for the expression of feelings as well as for the recounting of personal triumphs and failures. These habits also are culturally determined according to Reiss.

The fourth and final stage, also culturally determined, is *personality need fulfillment*, which includes the need to love, to confide in someone, and to stimulate one's ambition. The wheel may spiral several times, leading to increased rapport at each revolution, which leads to increased self-revelation, etc. It may also unwind[1] in that an argument may lead to less rapport, which may discourage self-revelation, which may, in turn, detract from developing a continuing mutual dependency, which may inhibit personality need fulfillment, which may further destroy rapport, and so on.

Reiss admits that much of the theory is tentative but claims that he has found some support for an aspect of the theory in a little survey that he conducted with 74 college students. These students received a sheet containing ten needs and were asked to list as many as they thought were important. Some needs showed little sex difference. For example, 60 percent of the boys listed needing someone to confide in, and 65 percent of the girls listed this need as important.

On the other hand, only 22 percent of the boys needed someone to look up to very much, whereas 70 percent of the girls scored this need as important. These findings are taken as supportive of the importance of cultural background in determining need fulfillment. Reiss further notes that Wheel Theory "seems to be capable of accounting for and interpreting much of the available field research on love relationships" (1960, p. 144).

---

[1]The analogy is a little forced here. To unwind ought to signify going in an opposite or counterclockwise direction. But "unwinding" follows the same path as "winding."

I must confess, however, that I cannot see how Reiss' data and the Wheel Theory can account for any research evidence on love relationships. Though the sequence he postulates seems reasonable, the theory as stated is very vague and imprecise, and it lacks empirical data. That cultural factors influence the four stages will not be contested by very many, but this is hardly confirmation of the theory.

Huston (1974) independently has seemingly come to a similar conclusion about the theory. He has remarked that Reiss

... fails to adduce supporting evidence for the developmental sequence he describes or to link the stage of the relationship either theoretically or empirically to the strength and character of the love bond. Moreover, Reiss fails to consider factors which qualify or modify the supposed developmental process. It would be interesting to know, for example, the conditions under which self-revelation does and does not lead to the development of interdependent habits (p. 19).

BOLTON'S THEORY

A more complex process theory is that of Bolton (1961). Indeed it is so structurally complex, with somewhat repetitious overlapping categorizations, that it would be exceedingly difficult to synopsize it. Despite these problems, the theory does draw attention to process patterns by which individuals become committed to a relationship.

The first pattern consists of *escalators,* which may be defined as situations with built-in momentum in which, once the individual takes the first step, he is swept along almost automatically to marriage. The *involvement* escalator results from interaction with the partner in so many varied and different ways (e.g. education, sex, recreational activities, daily schedule of coming and going, moral identity, and career plans), that the partner seems an intrinsic part of the individual's life almost without his volition. The *commitment* escalator can be interpersonal—going steady suggests love as the reason for the relationship, and love suggests engagement as the next step. Engagement adds public commitment to the interpersonal one and suggests early marriage. The *addiction* escalator might more properly be called "fear of isolation." The individual fears the withdrawal symptoms of exchanging "twoness" for isolation.

The *fantasy* escalator suggests that the individual compulsively adheres to the relationship as a symbol of a private fantasy or of the institutionally provided romantic one. The *idealization* escalator involves a worshipping of the other because an individual's self-esteem is united with the partner. Thus, the more one can adore the fiancé and get others to do so, the more the self-esteem. Finally, there is an *expediency* escalator (not formally listed by Bolton), which involves unexpected events, such as a pregnancy, which speed up movement toward marriage.

Another point made by Bolton is that the relationship may serve to resolve an identity crisis. The individual may escape from nothingness in the parental home and become a "person,"—a "man" or a "woman" as the case may be—by being loved by the other who testifies to this love by proposing or accepting marriage.

Precisely the same criticisms levied at Reiss can be extended to Bolton; the theory is, if anything, less precise than Reiss's, because not even a vague sequence is postulated. Yet the theory does suggest the futility of trying to translate relationships into intraindividual scores.

RAPOPORT AND RAPOPORT'S APPROACH

Rapoport (1965) and Rapoport and Rapoport (1964, 1965, 1968) have portrayed courtship as the coming-to-terms with a series of tasks inherent in the transition from singlehood to marriage. The nine critical transition tasks for early career and family are:

1. Establishing an identity as a couple.
2. Developing a mutually satisfactory sexual adjustment for the engagement period.
3. Developing a mutually satisfactory orientation to family planning.
4. Establishing a mutually satisfactory mode of communication.
5. Establishing satisfactory relations with others.
6. Developing a mutually satisfactory work pattern.
7. Developing a mutually satisfactory leisure pattern.
8. Developing a mutually satisfactory plan for the wedding and early marriage.
9. Establishing a mutually satisfactory decision-making pattern. (Rapoport and Rapoport, 1965, p. 390)

No elaboration is given with respect to sequence, nor are there data bearing on the solution of these tasks to courtship progress.

LEWIS'S PREMARITAL DYADIC FORMATION THEORY

A process theory in which an attempt at empirical verification has been made is that of Lewis (1972, 1973). Believing that a theory of marital choice was too difficult, Lewis limits himself to a theory of premarital dyadic formation. He posits six pair processes that "modal, middle-class, American couples progressively experience through their dating and courtship careers" (Lewis, 1972, p. 22). These processes and their subdivisions are as follows:

A. The achievement by pairs of perceiving similarities in each other's
    1. Socio-cultural background
    2. Values
    3. Interests
    4. Personality
B. The achievement of pair rapport, as evidenced in a pair's
    1. Ease of communication
    2. Positive evaluations of the other
    3. Satisfaction with pair relationships
    4. Validation of self by the other
C. The achievement of openness between partners through a mutual self-disclosure
D. The achievement of role-taking accuracy
E. The achievement of interpersonal role-fit, as evidenced by a pair's
    1. Observed similarity of personalities
    2. Role complementarity
    3. Need complementarity
F. The achievement of dyadic crystallization, as evidenced by a pair's
    1. Progressive involvement
    2. Functioning as a dyad
    3. Boundary establishment
    4. Commitment to each other
    5. Identity as a couple
(Lewis, 1972, p.23)

A principal notion underlying Lewis's theory is that the success for a given process depends upon the successful fulfillment of the one immediately preceding it. Thus, those couples who have successfully achieved the first (A) *(similarity perception)* process, may be expected later on to achieve greater *pair rapport* (process B) than those couples who have not successfully achieved process A (they are low on similarity perception). All six processes may operate to some measure during the course of a successful relationship, but there is an optimal period of functioning for each variable.

Testing the Theory

Questionnaire data were collected at what we shall call Time 1 from 173 dating couples, of whom at least one of each couple was a University of Minnesota student. Two years later (Time 2), attempts were made to reach the 346 students by telephone, and 314 were actually reached. Of the 173 couples, 58 had broken up; the mean number of months since breakup was 21. A 14-page questionnaire containing measures relating to the six processes described earlier was mailed to one partner; those who had broken up were told to reply to the questions in terms of the month prior to the separation. On the return of the first questionnaire, an identical one was mailed to the partner. Subjects were asked not to collaborate on the answers, but no safeguards were instituted to prevent possible collusion.

A total of 91 complete couples' data was utilized in the analysis (53 percent of the original sample), of which some 30 couples had dissolved their relationships. This group was presumably fairly well through the early stages called for by the theory, in that 24 percent were formally engaged at the time of the first contact, and 60 percent had some commitment toward marriage. Somewhat rashly, Lewis states that the attrition rate failed to influence the longitudinal analyses. "For instance, differences in social and interpersonal characteristics, produced by respondent attrition, were negligible" (Lewis, 1973, p. 20). No documentation is made of this fact, however, and as Rubin and Levinger point out (1974), since no data were collected from those bowing out prior to Time 2, it is impossible to check the validity of Lewis's claim.

The heart of the analysis involved testing the prediction that couples who had successfully moved through a task within Process A at Time 1 would also show high accomplishment for a task within Process B at Time 2. Couples who had not successfully resolved the given task at Process A, Time 1 should also be deficient in accomplishment for a task for Process B, Time 2.

I have used the language employed by Lewis to acquaint the reader with the path of his deductions. However, operationally speaking, what Lewis hypothesized was that, for example, if couples are trichotomized (both persons high, one person high, no persons high) for success for Process A, Time 1, the high group(s) should also be high for Process B, Time 2. Also, continuing couples, similarly, ought to score higher from Time 1 to Time 2 than dissolved couples.

Of a series of tests for differences in behavior from Time 1 to Time 2, 4 out of 24 predictions were significant at the .05 level or better.

Differences between the continuing and dissolved groups were much more pronounced. Of 28 tests, 23 were significant. A further analysis showed that the Time 1 scores of continuing couples were significantly better than those of dissolved couples on 8 of 10 tests computed.

The results lead Lewis to conclude that his data support the assumption "that a process which functions as a selection-rejection process at one stage of dyadic development may not be as salient at another stage" (p. 24). He notes also that "the longitudinal test substantially accounts for the dissolution and the continuance of dyads" (p. 16), and concludes on the optimistic note that

"The future value of this framework may lie in the larger amount of explained variance which the framework may eventually account for, over and above that which any of the current theories has generated to explain the development and continuance of premarital dyads" (p. 24).

Despite these roseate conclusions, a thorough analysis of the theory and data indicates many areas of ambiguity in the theory and a failure to crucially test the theory by the methods Lewis employed, so that his findings do not bear on the theory one way or another. Let us consider first the problems with the theory.

Criticisms of Premarital Dyadic Formation Theory and Research

Theory: Wolfe (1973) remarks that the theory is a checklist. "After completing all six tasks, not only is the couple ready to get married, but it would seem that they never need return to these tasks again—that they become a permanent characteristic of the relationship. (If this were so, people would never get divorced)" (p. 2). Wolfe also notes that the theory does not explain the mechanisms by which the stages are achieved and is thus a process theory only in the sense "that the couple 'proceeds' from one item on the checklist to another" (p. 2).

Another difficulty is that the order of the sequence of six steps is not explained. Rubin and Levinger (1974) ask "Why . . . should the achievement of pair rapport precede the development of role-taking accuracy, rather than vice versa? Or why should the perception of similarities come before rather than after the induction of mutual self-disclosure?" (p. 229).

Yet another problem is that no information is given as to when one of the processes ends and the other begins. The failure of the theory to deal with a rationale for the sequence might be sidestepped somewhat by empirical support for the theory, but the data fail to do this. Why?

Research: The difficulty with Lewis's research may be illustrated by reference to Table 6.1, which is a slightly modified version of Table 2 from Lewis (1973). The table indicates that couples who had scored better (higher) on Validation of Self (Process B) at Time 1 also scored better (lower) on Openness (Process C) at Time 2. Lewis takes this finding as supportive of his theory, but it can readily be demonstrated that the test of his theory is inappropriate, and that a simpler explanation will account for his findings perfectly well. We know that at the time of initial testing, many of the couples had been going together seriously for some time and were very close. Most of them would eventually become the "continuing" group. Let us suppose that other couples had been going together, but either intended no commitment toward marriage, or found their relationship to be in the doldrums—that, though still intact, it showed strains of various kinds and was going nowhere. These persons were destined to constitute the future "dissolved" group.

Table 6.1

MEAN SCORES FOR POST-TEST ACHIEVEMENT OF OPENNESS [1]
(STAGE C), GROUPED BY VALIDATION OF SELF BY OTHER (STAGE B-4)

	High in validation:		
	Both persons	*One person*	*Neither person*
Post-test openness of continuing couples	15.0	20.7	21.7
Post-test openness of dissolved couples	16.2	23.0	23.6

[1] High scores indicate low degrees of openness.

Source: Lewis, 1973, p. 21.

When the future continuing group was tested at Time 1, it scored higher on most of the tasks from Processes A through F than did the future dissolved group; sometimes a difference was significant, sometimes not, but a trend to do better on the tasks was generally noticeable. The subjects were retested at Time 2. Most of the subjects who had originally scored well at Time 1, were continuing their relationship (continuing group) and, *mirabile dictu,* they continued to score well at Time 2 for Processes A through F. Couples who had initially had a poor relationship generally would be expected to break up and become the dissolved group. Looking back at their relationship in the month preceding the breakup, it would be hardly surprising to assume that they perceived themselves as having done poorly in the various processes.

The simplest assumption, therefore, would be that the continuing group did better than the dissolved group on *all* of the processes. If this were true, then the Lewis theory would obviously be fulfilled but would have little significance. We would expect the continuing group to do better than the dissolved group not only on Process B at Time 1 and process C at Time 2, but also on the converse, Process C at Time 1 and Process B at Time 2. The latter prediction would not be in accordance with Lewis's theory, but would accord with the simpler explanation that continuing couples show consistency over two years' time. Had Lewis done such converse analyses, he might have strengthened the support for his theory. As it stands now, however, his analyses do not test the theory.

The same problem occurs with his report that continuing couples did better than dissolved couples on a number of tests at Time 1, when all couples were intact. By way of analogy, suppose we give a group of married couples a series of questionnaires about how well they relate. Two years later we find a number of them have divorced, while others have intact marriages. Going into the background of these subjects we find, not surprisingly, that at the original time of testing the subsequently divorced couples had been unhappy, quarreled often, and evinced little empathy for their partners; those with intact marriages, in comparison, had been happier, had fewer quarrels, and showed more sensitivity to their partners. This finding would hardly qualify as supportive of any theory—it would be simply common sense.

The fact that some of the subjects were tested long after the relationship had broken up—conceivably as much as two years afterwards—presents a thorny problem with regard to the validity of responses. Remember that the dissolved couples were asked to describe the relationship in the month prior to the breakup. In addition to the fact that some details might merely be forgotten over a period of time, the more serious problem remains of individuals trying to justify a broken relationship. It would scarcely be surprising for them to lessen self-responsibility, to denigrate the partner somewhat, or simply to distort the ongoing process between the two, in order to make these details consistent with the *fait accompli* of dissolution.

Last, the use of a three-by-two analysis of variance as reproduced in Table 6.1 was technically ill-advised. A significant difference was reported between the validation groups, but these group differences could have been significant and yet the theory would neither be supported nor completely rejected. Suppose the mean for "both persons high in validation" were 20, for "one person high" 60, and for "neither person high" 20. This distribution would probably result in a significant F test, but would hardly support the theory. The reason is that the F test does not take into account the *order* of the means, but such consideration is necessary for Lewis's theory. It is not clear from Lewis's article (1973) whether the monotonicity of the groups' means (that "both members of a couple high" had to have the highest mean, "one member high" had to be second highest, and "no member high" had to be lowest) was taken into account. If not, the F test was not testing the theory.

In conclusion, Lewis's data do not adequately test his theory. This in no way invalidates it. However, theories that prove to be untestable or untested generally lose favor rapidly. Perhaps Lewis or others may find the means for more precise evaluation of the theory in the years to come.

Filter Theory

THE KERCKHOFF AND DAVIS FILTER THEORY

Kerckhoff and Davis (1962) started out with an attempt to evaluate a hypothesis that progress in courtship is dependent on both homogamy of values (value consensus) and complementarity, after an initial screening for homogamous cultural variables. They collected a sample of 97 Duke University female college students, all of whom were engaged, "pinned," or "seriously attached." The woman received her test packet, filled it out, and her boyfriend was mailed the same questionnaire. The questionnaire data included Farber's "index of consensus," a task involving the ranking of ten standards of family success (Farber, 1957). By correlating the ranks of each member of the couple, a Spearman rank coefficient of correlation could be obtained for the couple. The more positive and higher the correlation, the greater the value consensus of the couple.

A second test germane to the present discussion was the Schutz FIRO-B test (1958). This test yielded a score called "reciprocal compatibility," which Kerckhoff and Davis believed accorded with Winch's definition of need-complementarity (Winch, 1958, p. 93). We noted earlier in Chapter 4 that Winch's *verbal description* of need-complementarity might lead one to presume it is equivalent to reciprocal compatibility. However, *operationally*, a perfect reciprocal compatibility score could be achieved by similarity as readily as by complementarity. Accordingly, in the discussion of the results that follows, I shall avoid the term "complementarity" and instead use "compatibility," with the understanding that we are dealing with a psychological role satisfaction score.

About seven months after the initial testing, the subjects were mailed a brief questionnaire that in essence asked them how well their courtship had fared. They were given three choices. Those checking "We are nearer to being a permanent couple" (56 couples) were regarded as good courtship couples. Those who answered that their relationship was the same as seven months earlier or that they were further apart (38 couples) were regarded as not making courtship progress. Only 3 of the 97 couples for whom the original usable data had been collected were lost in the interim. Each of the variables, "value consensus" and three compatibility scores, "inclusion," "control," and "affection," were dichotomized as close to the median as possible.

Tests of significance were made by comparing the proportion of couples within each variable who were "high" and made courtship progress with those who were "low" and made progress, as shown in Table 6.2.

For example, of those high in value consensus (see Total under Value Consensus in Table 6.2), about 73 percent made courtship progress, whereas of those low on value consensus, only about 46 percent did so. This difference was quite significant ($p < .01$). None of the three measures of compatibility was significant, although a trend was apparent in two of the three cases.

The most interesting finding occurred when couples were divided into those who had known each other for at least 18 months (long term) and those who had gone together less than 18 months (short term). As shown in Table 6.2, under these conditions value consensus was associated with courtship progress for short-term relationships but not for long-term ones. For short-term relationships high compatibility is not related to courtship progress in any of the three areas. However, for long-term relationships two of the three high compatibility scores are related to courtship progress.

It very much looks as if a filter effect were operating. For individuals in short-term relationships, value consensus seems to

Table 6.2

PROPORTIONS OF COUPLES INDICATING PROGRESS
(Total P = .596)

		Length of Association		
		Short-term	Long-term	Total
A.	Value consensus			
	High	.783 (23)	.680 (25)	.729 (48)
	Low	.350 (20)	.538 (26)	.457 (46)
	Significance of Difference	.01	—	.01
B.	Inclusion complementarity			
	High	.560 (25)	.750 (28)	.660 (53)
	Low	.611 (18)	.435 (23)	.512 (41)
	Significance of Difference	—	.02	.10
C.	Control complementarity			
	High	.588 (17)	.750 (20)	.676 (37)
	Low	.577 (26)	.516 (31)	.544 (57)
	Significance of Difference	—	.05	.10
D.	Affection complementarity			
	High	.588 (17)	.700 (20)	.649 (37)
	Low	.577 (26)	.548 (31)	.561 (57)
	Significance of Difference	—	—	—

Note: The number on which each proportion is based is presented in parentheses after the proportion.

Source: Kerckhoff and Davis, 1962, p. 300.

serve as a filter to screen out most couples whose members operate on a different set of values. By the time the courtship has persisted for some months, those couples who are going to split over differences in values generally will have done so. From then on (couples are now considered "long term"), dissimilarity of values is no longer predictive of breakup. At this point, differentiation on the basis of psychological compatibility takes over, and those that have it are more likely to make better progress than those who do not.

Reflecting on these results, the reader might ask why some couples with low value consensus survive into long-term relationships, since value consensus is especially associated with courtship progress in the early stages of courtship? The answer is implied in Table 6.3 which shows that low value consensus couples with high psychological

`Table 6.3

PROPORTIONS OF LOW CONSENSUS COUPLES SHOWING PROGRESS
BY LENGTH OF ASSOCIATION AND NEED COMPLEMENTARITY
(Total P = .467)

	Length of Association	
	Short term	Long term
Inclusion		
High	.357 (14)	.786 (14)
Low	.333 (6)	.250 (12)
Control		
High	.400 (5)	.833 (6)
Low	.333 (15)	.450 (20)
Affection		
High	.333 (9)	.750 (12)
Low	.364 (11)	.357 (14)

Note: The number on which each proportion is based is presented in parentheses after the proportion.

Source: Kerckhoff and Davis, 1962, p. 302.

compatibility are far more likely to survive in a long-term relationship than couples with low compatibility. By the time a couple who are low on value consensus are classified as long term, it presumably is clear to them that they disagree on values; hence there must be a compensating factor that substitutes for this potential source of friction.

To summarize, it would appear then that an initial screening of individuals takes place with respect to traditional homogamous cultural values, and this screening determines who meets with whom and starts dating whom. At this point value consensus further screens out couples, followed by a final filter late in the relationship with regard to compatibility. Yet along the way exceptions can occur if an unusual degree of satisfaction is found in an area other than the one typically associated with that stage. Thus, although value consensus is typically most important in early courtship, those couples manifesting a high degree of psychological compatibility somewhat precociously at the early stage might be able to survive as a couple even in the absence of high value consensus. Another possibility is that one or both members of the couple might possess some of the myriad other possible marital assets that would compensate for low value consensus. For example, the woman's beauty might cause the man to overlook her different values, and possibly, his potential occupational status might likewise influence her.

Kerckhoff and Davis do not speculate very extensively as to what accounts for their findings, but an exchange theory postulating that other marital assets besides consensus might suffice to continue a relationship would accord well with their data. This theme will be more fully developed in the next chapter on Stimulus-Value-Role Theory.

The Kerckhoff and Davis results were rightly hailed as an exciting advancement in the study of marital choice. Their article was cited frequently and reprinted in marriage readers. For four years, everyone was content to cite this article, but no one was inclined to see if it could be replicated until, finally, a trio of psychologists undertook this task (Levinger, Senn, and Jorgensen, 1970). They went through the same procedure at two different locales—the University of Massachusetts and the University of Colorado); they also added some measures of their own, which do not bear on our present concern.

Overall, Kerckhoff and Davis had found significantly better courtship progress for high value consensus couples than for low value consensus ones. In the Massachusetts and Colorado samples, however, no significant differences were found for either of these groups. The earlier study had reported no evidence of association between compatibility and courtship progress on any of the three areas of compatibility when length of relationship was ignored. None was found in the present study.

The heart of the matter lay with the differences between long- and short-term relationships. Kerckhoff and Davis found that for short-term relationships high value consensus was associated with courtship progress, with long-term relationships yielding a higher proportion of courtship progress for couples with high psychological compatibility. The present study did not support these findings.

In the Massachusetts sample, *long-term* (not short-term) relationships manifesting high value consensus showed more progress in courtship than did the low value consensus group—just the opposite to the findings with Kerckhoff and Davis's group. The Colorado sample showed even greater change. Here, as in Massachusetts, the long-term relationships showed significance instead of the short-term relationships, but the *low* value consensus group showed more progress than did the high value consensus group.

In the earlier study, in long-term relationships, high compatibility couples showed a significantly greater percentage of courtship progress in two of the three areas studied. In the present study, the

Colorado sample showed no significant findings for any of the three areas, whereas the Massachusetts sample showed significance in but one of the three areas.

To what can the failure of replication be attributed? The overall progress rates in courtship were fairly similar in both studies. However, the nature of the scores on the FIRO-B questionnaire had changed dramatically. Both men's and women's scores in both the Massachusetts and Colorado samples were higher on Inclusion and Affection and lower on Control. The authors conclude, therefore, that *time* and/or the *use of different samples* may have accounted for the failure of replication. They believe that at the present time the FIRO-B questionnaire and the Farber Index of Value Consensus are not adequate measures for the study of courtship progress. In their opinion, couple-centered rather than individual-centered measures may provide better answers for the future.

CONCLUSIONS

We have not yet finished with process and filter theories. The Stimulus-Value-Role theory to be discussed next is an exchange-process-filter theory. The details of the theory and the extent of data collection are sufficient to warrant a separate chapter. It may be helpful at this point, however, to pause and take stock of what research on process and filter theories has indicated so far.

The richness and depth of the process theories is impressive. At least at first glance, these theories seem to be closer to what actually transpires in courtship than do other theories. Courtship is certainly concerned with how couples get along, and the process of interrelationships and couple transactions are said to be at the heart of process theories.

It seems almost a rule of thumb in psychology and sociology that the simpler a theory, the easier to test it, but the more the exceptions and complications that spring up regarding it. On the other hand, complex theories such as the process ones tend to ramble, be conceptually unclear, and often difficult to reduce to operational terms. Process theorists decry the reliance on traits and needs as units of measurement—perhaps with good reason. But these are generally measurable. Transactions are not located in any one person and are not readily measured by paper-and-pencil tests. They are often highly inferential, and the more inferential theories are often the most difficult to validate.

With reference to the theories presented here, many unanswered questions present themselves. How do we know which processes precede others? Are all of the processes described within a theory really needed to account for courtship? What happens when one stage fails to develop successfully? Are all of the stages of equal importance? If not, which are crucial for the relationship and which not? Why are they crucial? How do we know when the time comes for a stage to end and another to begin? Why should one end and another begin? What are the mechanisms of such change?

No theory can be expected to have all the answers to these questions at this time, but when these questions are applied to the various process theories, the theories' vagueness is immediately perceived. Indeed, the processes in the Lewis theory are sufficiently vague to suggest that it might be just as easily labeled a sequence theory as a process one.

The Kerckhoff-Davis filter theory is logically easier to grasp. Its main difficulty appears to be a solid failure in a cross-validation study, perhaps contributed to by weak measures of value and compatibility. Yet these measures had been successful in the first study. The Kerckhoff-Davis theory is also vague on what draws individuals together prior to the time of value comparison and is not very rich in details about what happens later, apart from psychological compatibility. For example, where are physical attractiveness and sexual satisfaction in the theory? Surely these variables play a part in marital choice. It is insufficient to say that homogamous cultural variables bring people together; there are obviously more personal criteria that play a part.

Process and filter theories have an immediate logical appeal, because they are not monolithic or simple in concept. But the theories presented will need much more empirical support if they are to gain much acceptance.

CHAPTER 7

Stimulus-Value-Role (SVR) Theory of Dyadic Relationships

SVR theory is a general theory of the development of dyadic relationships in which it is presumed that the participants are free to develop
the relationship or not, as they wish. The theory, therefore, does not
apply to parent-child, lawyer-client, or doctor-patient relationships,
insofar as these relationships are determined by the roles the participants play as described by society. It seems applicable in some
respects to courtship, friendship, and also to the husband-wife relationship to the extent that the latter can be seen as an evolvement of
the Role, or tertiary, stage of courtship.

The theory is an exchange one, positing that, in a relatively free
choice situation, attraction and interaction depend on the exchange
value of the assets and liabilities each of the parties brings to the
situation. The kinds of variable that influence the course of development of the relationship can be classified under three categories: stimulus, value comparison, and role. The variables are
operative during the entire course of courtship, but they are
maximally influential at different stages of the courtship, and each of
the three stages reflects by its name the kind of variables most
influential during that period (for example, stimulus variables are
most influential in the stimulus stage).

Our chief concern will be the degree to which the theory can
explain marital choice. However, the prediction of attraction in a

107

dyadic relationship is not equivalent to predicting marital choice, for a number of reasons. First, the search for a marital partner is sometimes highly competitive. Individuals with many interpersonal assets generally have many potentially marriageable partners. It is possible, therefore, that any given relationship in which they are involved may be highly successful, and relationships other than those examined by the researchers may be even more successful. Focusing on a given relationship, therefore, might distort the conclusions about the probability of the relationship terminating in marriage.

Another important consideration is that marriage may not be the goal of the relationship. Traditionally, society has educated its youth to expect that close heterosexual dyadic relationships between unmarried youth terminate in marriage. Although there is no evidence that this philosophy has drastically changed, it is nevertheless evident that today more individuals are courting for longer and often cohabiting in a domicile without the benefit of matrimony. An increasing number (though still but a small fraction of the population) speak of having a close monogamous relationship without marriage. These factors, too, contribute to the imperfectness of dyadic closeness as a prognosticator of marriage.

Other factors influencing the incidence of marriage are timing, critical incidents, the social network, and the value of marriage as a status, all of which were discussed earlier in Chapter 4. These various factors contribute to the conclusion that dyadic compatibility and marital choice are not synonymous. Nevertheless they are sufficiently correlated so that an understanding of heterosexual dyad formation can lead to an understanding of marital choice.

The remaining portion of the chapter will consist of a discussion of the exchange aspects of SVR theory, followed by an elaboration of the kinds of variables that influence both dyad formation and the various stages of courtship. At the close of the chapter I shall try to make clear the similarities and differences between SVR theory and the theories of dyad formation already discussed in earlier chapters.

EXCHANGE IN COURTSHIP

The exchange model of interpersonal transactions involves the use of some elementary economic concepts for explaining social behavior (Thibaut and Kelley, 1959; Homans, 1961; Blau, 1964). Essentially, these approaches maintain that each person tries to make social interaction as profitable as possible, *profit* being defined as the *rewards* he gains from the interaction minus the *costs* he must pay. By *rewards* are meant the pleasures, benefits, and gratifications an individual gains from a relationship. *Costs* are factors that inhibit or deter the performance or more preferred behaviors. A young man living in the Bronx, for example, might like a young lady from Brooklyn whom he met while both were at a resort. Back in the city, however, he may doubt that the rewards he might gain from the relationship would be worth the costs in time and fatigue of two-hour subway rides to Brooklyn.

Closely allied to rewards and costs are assets and liabilities. *Assets* are the commodities (behaviors or qualities) the individual possesses that are capable of rewarding others and, in return, causing others to reciprocate by rewarding the individual. *Liabilities* are behaviors or qualities associated with an individual that are costly to others.

A man who is physically unattractive (liability), for example, might desire a woman who has the asset of beauty. Assuming, however, that his nonphysical qualities are no more rewarding than are hers, she gains less profit than he does from the relationship, and, thus, his suit is likely to be rejected. Rejection is a cost to him, because it may lower his self-esteem and increase his fear of failure in future encounters; hence, he may decide to avoid attempting to court women whom he perceives as much above him in attractiveness.

Contrariwise, he is likely to feel highly confident of success if he tries to date a woman even less attractive than himself, where he risks little chance of rejection (low cost). However, the reward value of such a conquest is quite low, so that the profitability of such a move is also low. As a consequence, an experienced individual is likely to express a maximum degree of effort and also obtain the greatest reward at the least cost when he directs his efforts at someone of approximately equal physical attractiveness, assuming all other variables are constant.

Although his interpersonal experiences, thus, push him towards someone of objectively equal physical attractiveness, his own perception of his physical attractiveness and that of his partner need not necessarily be equal. A person with high assets might be content if he got a partner whom he perceived as having as high assets as his own. He would be even happier, however, if he believed he were obtaining a partner with perceived assets higher than his own.

In this realm of subjectivity, it is not necessary for his partner to complement his perception by perceiving him as lower than herself in assets—this need not be a zero sum game with a winner and a loser.

Both partners may subjectively think they are getting a partner whose assets exceed their own. In fact, it seems reasonable that when two persons each perceive their partner as having more assets than themselves, they should be more satisfied than when they perceive the partner's assets as only equal to their own. There are data that support this conjecture. Kelly (1941) found that marital adjustment was correlated with the tendency to perceive the partner as superior to oneself.

It is, however, unnecessary for equity of physical attractiveness to be present in order for a viable relationship to occur. Given that a man and woman are sufficiently acquainted with each others' respective assets and liabilities, it becomes possible for the less attractive member to compensate for his "weakness" in a number of ways. Suppose, for example, that the man is unattractive and the woman is attractive. He might render services to his partner far above what she gives him, waiting on her hand and foot. Consistent with this thesis is a study by Dermer (1973) which reports that the greater a woman's attractiveness, the longer the vacations she expected to take when she married, and the fewer hours she expected to work to supplement her husband's income.

The attractive woman "pays" the man back through the status she confers on him by being seen with him, a cost (loss of status) she incurs in being seen with an unattractive man. Berscheid and Walster (1974), reviewing the literature, have indicated that individuals perceived to associate with physically attractive persons gain in the self-esteem in which they are held by others, whereas those persons consorting with unattractive partners lose status. The outsider looking only at the physical attractiveness of the couple may find them terribly unbalanced with regard to their exchange value and wonder what she possibly sees in him. The people who know the couple well may find that she exploits him miserably and wonder why he puts up with it. Yet the situation is balanced if all of the variables are taken into consideration.

We have made no mention so far of the status accruing to an individual solely on the basis of his sex, but men in our society have traditionally enjoyed a greater social, economic, and political status (Murstein, 1974a). These advantages may be eroding away, but they have not disappeared altogether. It follows, therefore, that men should be able to utilize this greater status to extract benefits prior to and during marriage. A physically unattractive man should find it somewhat easier to marry than a physically unattractive woman, and the 1969 statistics supported the hypothesis indirectly. In 1969, of men and women aged fifteen years and older, 31.4 men per 1,000 married as compared to 28.9 women (Vital Health Statistics, 1969).

As women's liberation spokeswomen have constantly stated, men are able to arrange marriage so that more of the benefits fall to them, and more of the costs fall to women. Research by Knupfer, Clark, and Room (1966) is consistent with this contention, in that married men were found to be more content and better adjusted than married women.

During courtship, as Waller has indicated through his "principle of least interest" (1938), the person least involved in the relationship can generally control it if the other is deeply involved. Traditionally, the power differential has been expressed by the man's sexual exploitation of the woman and by the woman's economic exploitation ("gold-digging") of the man. Since women acquire more status by marriage than do men, the lion's share of exploitation in dating is enjoyed by men.

The woman is not wholly without her weapons, however. Tradition calls for the man to be the pursuer during courtship. A woman who is perceived as generally "hard to get" becomes more valuable than one who can't say no to anybody, with the important proviso that the "hard to get" woman indicates that she is interested in the man in question (Walster, Walster, Piliavin, and Schmidt, 1973). The reward value of being associated with a sought-after person is greater than that of association with a partner who seeks after everyone.

There are still other reasons why equity of exchange value is not necessary for a relationship. One reason has to do with the availability of other alternatives. The concept of comparison level for alternatives (CL_{alt}) was introduced by Thibaut and Kelley (1959) to indicate that before imbalance of exchange can threaten a relationship, a viable alternative must exist for at least one member of the couple. A given boyfriend may be somewhat of a pompous bore, but if the alternative is not an interesting sexy "tiger" but *no boyfriend*, a woman may hesitate to terminate the boring relationship. Of course, those who perceive that they have many interpersonal assets may be willing to take more risks in this regard than those who perceive that they have fewer assets.

If an individual's experiences outside of the dyad are highly satis-factory and in some way related to the dyad, the rewards occurring extradyadically may suffice to balance out the unprofitability of the dyad per se. Thus, if a young orphaned woman finds a surrogate, kindly mother and father in the parents of her swain, she may overlook the less rewarding qualities of the swain himself. Likewise, a politician is unlikely to divorce his spouse in an election year, even though his wife may have become a virago. A married politician may not gain many votes due to the fact that he is married, but a divorced politician loses some votes solely on the basis of his divorce.

Rewards from within the Person

So far it may seem as if most interpersonal transactions are largely commercial and self-seeking. If a good bargain cannot be obtained directly from the partner or indirectly through him, the dyad may seem to be in danger of breaking up. But a moment's reflection suggests that much behavior is not exchange oriented—consider the heralded saints of antiquity and of modern times: Jesus, Saint Francis of Assisi, Albert Schweitzer, Pope John XXIII. These individuals seemingly not only worked without an equitable return, but often returned good for evil. Explanations of high CL_{alt} or indirect rewards from others do not readily explain their behavior.

It is evident that the rewards these individuals received were not external but internal; hence they cannot, by our definition, be considered exchange. These individuals carried a model of appropriate behavior within themselves, and their ability to emulate this model provided more gratification than did any extrinsic reward. For such individuals to repay evil with evil might have achieved exchange equity, but the failure to fulfill the ideal-self image would have resulted in the high cost of guilt.

Internal reward systems are not the exclusive property of saints. Through societal inculcation, many of our roles are defined by inequitable requirements. Mothers dote on their offspring, philanthropists open their purse strings to the needy, and men sometimes offer their seats to women in the subways to fulfill their ideal-self concepts rather than in the hope of recompense.

Personal commitment to the partner also may be subsumed under the rubric of internal rewards. If the individual believes that he is in some way responsible for his partner's welfare or that he has committed himself to marriage by dint of continuing the relationship over a long period, he may remain in it despite inequities of exchange. In general, however, commitment serves to make terms of exchange more flexible rather than to banish exchange from consideration. For example, an undergraduate man and woman may commit themselves to each other, forswearing other heterosexual interests. But as they plan to go to graduate school, they may find that the vicissitudes of fate and graduate departments consign them to graduate schools a thousand miles apart. The costs of infrequent contact and infrequent rewards may be augmented by the cost of foregone relationships with other attractive members of the opposite sex. If the costs of the old relationship exceed the rewards by a substantial margin, the commitment may not be enough to avoid the weakening and eventual termination of the relationship.

Some commitments are much more enduring—the commitments of marriage partners to each other, for example. The commitments in this case extend beyond that of concern for the partner. They involve concern over the welfare of the children, the disruption of status, uncomfortable explanations within the network of friends and associates, and possible conflict with religious commitments—Catholics are not permitted to divorce within the Church. There are additional considerations beyond these external factors. When an estranged couple had earlier obtained substantial rewards from the relationship, they may find it hard to believe that the costs each now feels will not eventually melt away. Marriages that have endured have undoubtedly had occasions when things seemed inequitable to at least one of the partners—costs exceeded the rewards within the marriage. Learning theory tells us that an intermittent reward system is extremely hard to extinguish. The individual is thus likely to assume that with patience the trouble will pass and things will get better again.

Also, with the passage of time, the feeling of personal commitment for the marriage partner becomes stronger. The individual increasingly internalizes the role of spouse, so that it becomes partially free of external reward considerations. The feeling of responsibility for the partner involves the cost of guilt if the partner is abandoned, and to this guilty consideration is added his own cost of starting a new life, with its attendant trouble and necessary adjustment. Thus, breakups should occur more frequently among premarital couples than among marital couples, and among marriages of short duration as opposed to those of long duration.

In sum, exchange is a very complex phenomenon. It may involve services for the other, but status or other assets may take the place of services. Moreover, the value of services, or even of relatively "fixed" assets such as beauty or occupation, change with time. The ravages of time may diminish one's beauty. Adaptation level may eat away at one's interpersonal assets and capacity to reward. An individual may relish the compliment of being declared a brilliant wit by his beloved, but the maximal delight in that statement occurs when first he hears it from her lips. When she says it again later on, it diminishes in value because the individual's adaptation level has shifted somewhat; thanks to the rewarding impact of the original compliment, the individual now thinks of himself as wittier than was the case before he received the initial compliment; consequently, with a higher self-perception of wittiness, a compliment of the same magnitude will be less rewarding than the same compliment was when delivered earlier.

Not only is the value of services (compliments are one example of services) a victim of adaptation level, but also our valuation of beauty. Once we perceive ourselves as meriting a beauteous companion, the reinforcement value of the companion diminishes.

If one person's assets are in services, and another's are in status, if everything is constantly changing in value, and much behavior is not exchange-oriented, can we presume that equity of exchange is a meaningful feature of dyadic attraction? I believe so, because exchange seems most important in the initial stages of interaction. At that point in time, there are no role requirements that dictate that we must marry the first person we date. Moreover, personal commitments are built up over a long period of time and should be of greater consideration, therefore, in the maintenance of relationships than in their formation. To spell out how and why equity of exchange affects interpersonal attraction we should consider the three stages of courtship.

THE STIMULUS, VALUE, AND ROLE STAGES OF COURTSHIP

To properly understand the development of the stages of courtship, a few words must be said about the locus in which the relationship unfolds. This context may be categorized into "open" and "closed" fields.

"Open" and "Closed" Fields

An "open" field encounter refers to a situation in which the man and woman do not as yet know each other or have only a nodding acquaintance. Examples of such "open field" situations are "mixers," a large school class at the beginning of the semester, and brief contacts in the office. The fact that the field is "open" indicates that either the man or the woman is free to start the relationship or abstain from initiating it, as they wish. The contrary concept is the "closed field" situation in which both the man and woman are forced to relate in some manner by reason of the roles assigned to them by the environmental setting in which they find themselves. Examples of "closed field" situations might be that of students in a small seminar in a college, members of a "Peace Corps" unit, and workers in a political campaign. This interaction generally enables the individual to become acquainted with the behavior of the "other," which is then evaluated according to the individual's own system of values. This system is a compendium of values acquired in the process of acculturalization to the traditional or current tastes of society, values acquired from one's peers and parents, values derived from experience, and values resulting from genetically based predispositions, which may be labeled "temperament."

Individuals, of course, may be attracted to members of the opposite sex without necessarily contemplating marriage. The fact that almost all persons in the United States eventually marry, however, suggests that many of the heterosexual social encounters of young adults contain at least the possibility of eventual marriage; consequently, the general heterosexual encounter has been treated as the first step toward possible marriage.

Stimulus Stage

When two members of the opposite sex meet in an open field, a "mixer" dance, for example, there generally has been a considerable amount of incidental screening that has eliminated many of the maritally noneligible persons. If the mixer is held on a college campus, for example, attendance may be restricted to college students. Such students not only reflect educational homogeneity, but they are apt to show greater than chance similarity on variables that are correlated with education: socioeconomic status, age, intelligence, and, to some extent, values. There remains, nevertheless, sufficient variance with respect to variables for an active selective process. Other characteristics such as physical attractiveness, temperament, and sex-drive have undergone very little selectivity, and thus interpersonal encounters between the sexes may result in widely varying responses, from joy to repulsion.

The motives in attending the mixer will vary from person to person. For some, attendance will avoid the isolation of being alone on a Friday night. For others it will be an opportunity to find a lover and sex partner. Still others hope for a possible spouse or at least a companion for the evening. Suppose we consider a fictitious example to help us understand an unfolding relationship. We'll call the man Bart, the woman Angie. They do not know each other. Both are sophomores who during their first year at college made no permanent heterosexual attachments—they're still looking.

Both look around the hall where Art Mustinelli and his Grinding Millstone Five are playing some music. Each would like to meet someone interesting, but how can they tell who would be interesting and who not? In an open field, information about personality, value consensus, sex drive, and attitudes towards women's liberation is not often available prior to interaction. Therefore they try to process whatever information they can get and make the best judgement with respect to the possible enjoyment interaction with a given person might bring.

The first cues they get are not dependent on personal interaction with the other, and I have subsumed these cues under the classification of *stimulus* variables. These include the other's physical attractiveness—is he (she) the right height, well-built, good-looking? What does Bart's voice sound like? A rich, well-modulated baritone or an accented, nasal tenor? Is he dressed in a relaxed, sexy manner, or is he "establishment" formal?

There is ample evidence that the initial impact in a dating situation depends largely on physical attractiveness (Berscheid and Walster, 1974). The importance of physical attractiveness resides not only in its being highly valued by society as a status-conferring asset and in the fact that it is the only evidence of potential viability of the relationship prior to interaction. One must consider also that all kinds of desirable personality and intellectual attributes are ascribed to the beautiful. They are viewed as "more sensitive, kind, interesting, strong, poised, modest, sociable, outgoing, and exciting, . . . more sexual, warm, and responsive than unattractive persons" (Berscheid and Walster, 1972, pp. 46, 74).

Initial impressions are not wholly dependent on the senses, however. An individual's stimulus value may include also information about his reputation or professional aspirations that precede him into the initial contact. That Ronald Rabbitfoot is a star running back for Podunk University may compensate for his less-than-classic-Greek profile.

In sum, initial judgements are formed on the basis of perceptions of the other and/or information about him. These may be obtained without any interpersonal contact whatsoever, or on the basis of brief introductions. It is questionable how much such initial impressions correlate with subsequent marital happiness. Nevertheless, the stimulus stage is of crucial importance in the "open field," for, if the other person does not possess sufficient stimulus impact to attract the individual, further contact is not sought. The "prospect" in question might make a potentially exemplary, compatible spouse, he might manifest value consensus and superb role compatibility with the perceiver. But the perceiver, foregoing opportunities for further contact, may never find this out. In consequence, persons with low stimulus attractiveness—especially those who are physically un-attractive—are at a considerable handicap in an open field.

The "closed" field is more promising because it allots more importance to other than stimulus attributes in a situation where interaction involves no serious commitments. It is for this reason, no doubt, that colleges have acquired the reputation of being excellent marital marts. Inidividuals in the pursuit of knowledge get a chance to get to know each other, to compare their values, and to discover which roles are most comfortable with respect to each other. The importance of stimulus characteristics does not vanish as a relationship develops. However, data more pertinent to dyadic interaction become more available, and the stimulus variables may diminish in importance from sole consideration as the basis for a relationship to a more modest role.

The Process of Approach in an Open Field

Because physical .attractiveness is so highly valued, it would seem logical that each individual would seek the most attractive partner when information about other characteristics is not available. Enjoy-ment of a date when interaction has been relatively brief would also probably be mainly contingent on the attractiveness of one's partner.

There is evidence that this is the case when either of two conditions exist: (a) The individuals have relatively little experience in dating and have not undergone the costs of rejection; and (b) An experimental paradigm is constructed in which the individual is more or less guaranteed a date (Berscheid and Walster, 1974; Huston, 1973a). However, it has been predicted that over 90 percent of the current population will eventually marry, and it is evident that they are not all physically attractive. We need to explain therefore how the ideal preference is converted to the actual choice.

Earlier, I suggested that the best combination of reward and probability of success often occurs for experienced daters when they approach someone of equal attractiveness to themselves in an open field. At this point, I shall spell out this process in some detail.

Despite somewhat varying language, the factors influencing

social behavior have been the object of attention for some decades (Edwards, 1954; Rotter, 1954; Atkinson, 1958). More recently, Huston (1973b) has directly applied these earlier writings to a model of initial interpersonal approach.

The writings of these researchers have emphasized that behavior is a function of the reward seen as resulting from the contemplated behavior and its probability of success. I have, following Huston (1973b), adapted the formula to account for approach behavior within the stimulus stage. As shown in Figure 7.1, the formula indicates that the potential of enacting a behavior is equal to its reward potential—the value of the perceived reward multiplied by the probability of success—minus the potential costs—the perceived cost of a negative response to the act multiplied by the probability of failure (1—probability of success).

Factors often influencing its magnitude are given in parentheses below each member of the equation in Figure 7.1. A few examples will indicate how these function. Consider first the case of Saul Schlepp who espies a beautiful girl, Paula Poitrine. The perceived reward potential is very high, let us say 10 on a scale of ten (see Figure 7.1). Saul has no girl friend (few Schlepps do), and the value of the satisfying agent (the girl) is quite high. However, when Saul considers his probability of success in establishing a relationship, he is not hopeful. He thinks that a beautiful woman is apt to be very choosy. Research by Huston (1973a) has confirmed that men think their chances of being accepted by attractive women are less than for unattractive ones.

His own appraisal of himself is low. He has low self-esteem, and research has indicated that when men have their self-esteem lowered by experimental manipulation they are less apt to attempt to date attractive women than are men whose self-esteem has been experimentally raised (Kiesler and Baral, 1970). Saul also knows that the situation is not conducive to succcess because there is plenty of competition, the hall being replete with Adonises. In sum, his perceived probability of being accepted by the beautiful woman is quite low, perhaps .10.

Focusing on the perceived costliness, let me assume that he has not become used to rejection. He fears that if he asks her to dance and she turns him down or disappears right after the dance, he will experience another blow to his self-esteem. There is no one else who attracts his eye at the moment, so that by asking the girl to dance he does not forego other social opportunities. Overall, we score the perceived costliness as 7. The probability of failure is equal to [1—probability of success (.10)], or .90. The equation multiplied out is:

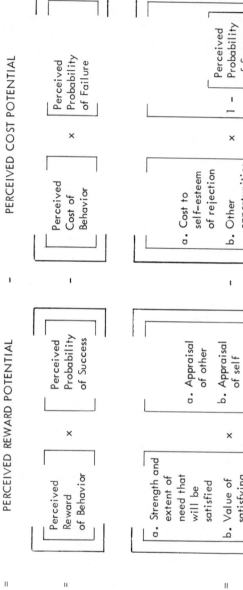

BEHAVIOR POTENTIAL = PERCEIVED REWARD POTENTIAL − PERCEIVED COST POTENTIAL

= Perceived Reward of Behavior × Perceived Probability of Success − Perceived Cost of Behavior × Perceived Probability of Failure

=
a. Strength and extent of need that will be satisfied
b. Value of satisfying agent (person)
c. Other rewards

×
a. Appraisal of other
b. Appraisal of self
c. Appraisal of situation

−
a. Cost to self−esteem of rejection
b. Other opportunities foregone
c. Other costs

× 1 − Perceived Probability of Success

Fig. 7.1. Behavior potential of Saul asking a girl to dance

Probability of Behavior = $[(10 \times .10) - (7 \times .90)] = 1 - 6.3$, or $- 5.3$. All plus scores, theoretically, result in the execution of the potential act; all minus solutions result in the inhibition of the act. The more positive the score, the more rapidly the act will occur and the greater the magnitude of the action. The converse is true for negative outcomes. In the present case, Saul never approaches Paula: instead, he focuses on Hortense Homebody.

Hortense is no raving beauty, and her perceived rewardingness is 5. Fortunately, the perceived probability of success is much higher than it was with Paula. Saul feels less threatened by girls who are slightly below average in looks. Considering all of the factors, Saul thinks the probability of establishing a relationship, if he so desires, is about .8. The perceived cost of a rejection is quite damaging but not as much as by a pretty girl (Sigall and Aronson, 1969). We score it 5. The probability of failure is $1 - .8$ or $.20$. The equation works out to $[(5 \times .8) - (5 \times .2)] = 4 - 1 = + 3$. The outcome is positive, and Saul approaches Hortense and asks her to dance. As he expected, she accepts.

The dance ends and Saul evaluates his outcome in order to decide whether he should attempt to spend some time with Hortense. During the course of the dance they have also talked briefly, and all the information gained must be processed (I believe she is wearing a girdle . . . nice bust . . . warm smile . . . skin complexion not so hot . . . she sweats a lot . . . she has a sexy voice . . . she dances well . . . I wonder if she's intelligent . . . I wonder what her reaction is to me. She seems to relax against me in the slow dance. I think maybe she is attracted to me).

This information is now used to evaluate the rewardingness and probability of success in asking her for a second dance, or to go for a walk. Again the components of the equations are computed, and the action is attempted if the anticipated outcome is positive. Individuals of course vary in their awareness of the components of the equation; some may be quite conscious of them, whereas others may be quite unconscious of the decision-making process, noting only that they either feel or don't feel like asking a girl to dance. To analyze the probability of acceptance of Saul by Hortense, we would have to construct a similar equation for her.

We can now appreciate more readily why individuals of equal physical attractiveness should be drawn to each other. Being of equal attractiveness, and assuming that perceived attractiveness of an *unknown person* is relatively invariant across persons due to cultural stereotypes of beauty (Udry, 1965), we see that an important component of the attraction equation (potential rewardingness) will be equal for both the man and the woman. Since at first they do not know each other, there should be little possibility of weakness in this area being influenced by personality considerations.

We should, nevertheless, consider that status values may influence approachability as well as self-confidence. A handsome male gasoline attendant may be more hesitant to approach a wealthy, educated coed than a somewhat less attractive male college student would be.

In short, we expect some tendency towards equity for a given characteristic—physical attractiveness, self-esteem, status, etc.—all things being equal, and in the next breath I must allow that often all things are not equal. A handsome man of low status, for example, might dampen his equity expectations regarding physical attractiveness. The likelihood of finding equity between two individuals for a given variable, therefore, depends on the importance of that variable to the courtship of the individuals concerned. If physical attractiveness is of paramount concern to both men and women, we should expect a greater-than-chance equity of physical attractiveness between members of a couple despite the fact that all other things are not equal. We shall have occasion to test this hypothesis later.

As a result of their experiences, individuals begin to build up an erotic ranking for themselves. They tend to gravitate toward their own level of equity. Old movie buffs will recall the Bing Crosby, Bob Hope pictures in which Crosby always got the girl, andHope got the laughs. In a group of males going out together, certain individuals generally end up with the better-looking girls and others with those of lesser attractiveness. Consistency in this regard suggests that experience has taught a certain economy of action, so that each individual focuses on the attainable rather than on the ideal.

Approval and acceptance by the other is the primary reward generally sought in first encounters. Even if one does not really care for the other, the fact that the other likes us stamps us as an attractive worthwhile person and is therefore rewarding. The value of the reward will vary with the rewarder's status and the esteem in which the individual holds the rewarder.

Expressions of approval and liking by *A* for *B* are rather risky in beginning relationships for a number of reasons. For one, they imply a commitment by *B* to reciprocate by behavior which is rewarding to *A*. But the small sample of behavior that *B* uses to judge the viability of his relationship to *A* may be too nebulous to warrant potentially costly commitments; hence the need for caution.

Another reason for hesitancy is that if an expression of affection by *A* seems to *B* to be greater than the circumstances warrant, *B* may suspect *A*'s motives. If a man, after only a brief interaction with a woman, tells her that she is the most wonderful creature he ever laid eyes on and that he adores her, the woman is apt to think either that he wants to seduce her or that his needs for acceptance are so great that he throws compliments around in an indiscriminating manner in the hope that someone, anyone, will accept him. In beginning interactions, therefore, individuals who are interested in another individual may communicate this without the use of words, as Knapp (1972) has indicated.

On a purely intuitive level, we know that there are some men and some women who can exude such messages as 'I'm available,' 'I'm knowledgeable,' or 'I want you' without saying a word. For the male, it may be such things as his clothes, sideburns, length of hair, an arrogant grace, a thrust of his hips, touch gestures, extra long eye contact, carefully looking at the women's figure, open gestures and movements to offset closed ones exhibited by the woman, gaining close proximity, a subtleness which will allow both parties to deny that either had committed themselves to a courtship ritual, making the woman feel secure, wanted, 'like a woman,' or showing excitement and desire in fleeting facial expressions. For the woman, it may be such things as sitting with her legs symbolically open, crossing her legs to expose a thigh, engaging in flirtatious glances, stroking her thighs, protruding breasts, using appealing perfume, showing the 'pouting mouth' in her facial expressions, opening her palm to the male, using a tone of voice which has 'an invitation behind the words,' or any of a multitude of other cues and rituals—some of which vary with status, subculture [and] region of the country (p. 17).

VALUE COMPARISON STAGE

If a couple approximates equality in their stimulus variables, that is, the weighted amalgam of each individual's perceived stimulus attributes (physical attractiveness, status, poise, voice, etc.) is approximately equal to that of the other, they may progress to the second (value comparison) stage of courtship. It is impossible to fix a specific time limit for passage from one stage to another, because the importance of each stage and kinds and rate of interaction between individuals will vary from couple to couple.

Figure 7.2, however, presents a theoretical average curve for the importance and duration of the three variables.

The curves in Figure 7.2, strictly speaking, apply separately to each member of the couple. It is possible for one member of the couple to be in the stimulus stage, whereas his partner is in the value com-

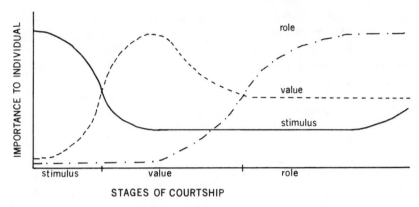

Fig. 7.2. *Stages of courtship in SVR theory*

parison stage. For example, he may be reacting primarily to her physical attractiveness, and she may have queried him on what he thought about women's liberation, equal careers, and childless marriage. He may not have found out much about her values, so that a disparity exists not only with regard to what each considers important in the relationship, but also with regard to the stage of courtship each is in. This disparity is not necessarily inimical to the relationship so long as each is highly rewarded by the relationship.

For many couples, however, the depth of the relationship advances in mutual fashion, and reciprocity in social penetration is typical. When she asks about his values, she may in turn supply her own views on the topic in question, or he may ask her about these views. Thus, most couples should show some correspondence of movement through the various stages.

The termination of the stimulus stage may be defined as occurring at the point in the relationship when the stimulus variables, as a group, become less important to the relationship than the value comparison variables. Passage from the stimulus to the value comparison stage might occur in a matter of hours, or it might take some weeks. It is also conceivable that such passage might not occur, but I shall deal with this eventuality when we have completed our description of the three stages of courtship.

The label "value comparison" has been used for want of a better name. I use the term "value" more as an inclusive rubric rather than in the narrow sense of the term. I infer under this term interests, attitudes, beliefs, and even needs when they are seen as emanating from beliefs. The primary focus of the value comparison stage, in short, is information gathering by verbal interaction with the other.

Verbal interaction will surely be an important feature of the role stage, which succeeds the value comparison stage. But in the role stage, the emphasis will be more on the dyadic relationship and will include commitment positions regarding depth of feeling for the other and desire for permanency, confirmation of the self image, and accuracy in predicting the feelings and perceptions of the other.

The value comparison stage occurs when the couple has not as yet developed sufficient intimacy to learn and confess the innermost precepts, fears, aspirations, and concerns that each has. Nevertheless, there is much public and private information that each learns about the other in this period. Information is gleaned about religious orientation, political beliefs, attitudes toward people, parents, friends, interests in sports, the arts, dancing, and the like.

The rate of progress through the value comparison stage depends on the rate of social penetration (Altman and Taylor, 1973). The couple exhibits increasingly larger areas of what they think and feel. They evaluate their comfortableness, the acceptance of what they reveal, and the effect of their disclosure on their partner's behavior. In a successful relationship, the partner evinces acceptance of the values of the individual and discloses his own values. Self-disclosure among individuals promotes reciprocal self-disclosure, and the relationship may proceed to increasingly deeper levels of personality (Cozby, 1973).

A sense of pace is important in the reciprocal disclosure process. To jump too far ahead of what the partner can accept may lead to high costs for the partner, which may outweigh the rewards he perceives himself as obtaining from a relationship to which he is not fully committed. A man telling a long-time female friend that watching horses mate "turns him on" (as it did Queen Victoria) may be met with a bemused but accepting smile. Pouring out this confession to a girl on a man's second date with her may lead to raised eyebrows and discomfort.

In the most successful relationships, consensus on the important values intrinsic to the relationship is generally reached. There are, of course, exceptions and mediating variables to consider, such as economic class, referred to earlier in Chapter 5. Nevertheless, there are numerous reasons why agreement on values is conducive to courtship progress, as was also noted in Chapter 5.

Although the stimulus and role variables are still operative during the "value comparison" stage, the importance of the stimulus variables has already waned somewhat. Those of disparate stimulus attractiveness have, likely as not, never developed a relationship. Many couples possessing disparate stimulus attributes have broken up. Couples of different stimulus attributes who continue their relationship presumably have unusual compensating value consensus or role compatibility.

During the value comparison stage in successful relationships, role compatibility has been increasing. But role compatibility involves not only intimate verbalizations, but getting to know how to behave vis-à-vis the partner as well as knowing what roles the partner can play in satisfying one's own needs: friend, teacher, lover, critic? These roles not only involve the greatest intimacies, they also necessitate a great deal of time to master; hence the rate of growth of role compatibility is slower than that of value comparison, which involves mainly verbal interaction. There does come a time, however, when role compatibility supersedes value comparison in importance, marking the onset of the role stage, as shown in Figure 7.2.

The importance of a stimulus attribute such as physical attractiveness may obtain renewed salience in the role stage, though is not likely to regain the importance it held in the stimulus stage. My reasoning is that, prior to the role stage, the individual may not have seriously contemplated marriage. Courtship in the stimulus and value stages is still burgeoning. Going with the partner at this point may be an expression of liking, but it is not necessarily a commitment toward an enduring relationship such as marriage.

When the individual finds himself in the role stage, however, he is more apt to realise that he is drifting in a current of commitment that, if unchecked, may lead to matrimony. Faced with this awareness, he is apt to reappraise the qualities of his possible spouse. Physical attractiveness may manifest a slight upward turn in importance at this time because the individual becomes aware that his children's attractiveness will reflect not only his features but his spouse's as well. Moreover, he may be sensitized again to the fact that others judge him in part by the qualities of his partner. The most salient aspect of his partner to others, particularly those who do not know her, is her physical appearance. This judgement will be more important for an intended spouse than for a girlfriend or boyfriend; consequently, the individual approaching a decision about marrying is apt to reconsider the physical attributes of his partner.

Value comparison does not lose all importance at this time, but value comparisons are more important in determining whether a relationship is possible than in deciding whether a long-standing relationship should eventuate into marriage. Role compatibility is, of course, of crucial importance in the role stage for reasons I shall now elaborate. Before leaving our theoretical series of curves, however, I wish to emphasize the highly speculative and arbitrary placement of the curves with respect to each other. Although I believe the SVR sequence is substantially sound, the precise height and salience of the various curves with respect to each other is highly speculatory and would doubtless be revised somewhat as new evidence on the courtship process becomes known.

ROLE STAGE

When a couple has survived the stimulus and value stages, they have established a reasonably good relationship. Some individuals may decide to marry at this point. However, for most persons these are necessary but insufficient grounds for marriage. It is also important for the couple to be able to *function* in compatible roles.

Role is defined by English and English as "the behavior that is characteristic and expected of the occupant of a defined position in [a] group" (1958, p. 468). Sociologists tend to focus on the "defined position" with the understanding that the role is defined by an individual's culture and that he adjusts himself into it much as one does in purchasing a ready-made suit. My use of the term "role," however, is much broader and individual-centered.

A wife's role as defined by her husband consists of *his* perception of the behavior that is expected of a wife. His perception may be in part molded by his culture, but part of it may stem from his own idiosyncracies, and this would not be found in his neighbor's definition of the role of wife. In like vein, the wife's definition of the wifely role would consist of *her* perception of what the role should embody.

The general role of spouse may be subdivided into specialized functions that the individual is expected to execute in different situations. Thus the husband's role may be subdivided into his role vis-à-vis his wife in private, in public, and in the family.

A primary feature of the role stage is the evaluation of the perceived functioning of oneself in a dyadic relationship in comparison with the roles one envisages for oneself, and the perceived role functioning of the partner with respect to the roles one has envisaged for him. Personal, intimate behaviors are revealed much more slowly than are values, which can be expressed in more abstract, less intimate fashion. Also, many roles may be included within an overall evaluation of role compatibility, and an evaluation, therefore, may be difficult to make, whereas values are generally simpler to understand.

We can measure role compatibility by comparing expectations and perceptions of the fulfillment of expectation over a wide range of behaviors. Some culturally esteemed behaviors may not require measurement of expectations because they are almost univerally perceived as rewarding: individuals with both high social status and high nurturance needs, for example, are generally sought after because such individuals are easy to relate to, rarely self-centered, and sensitive and giving toward others. Many neurotics, on the other hand, are high-cost persons who are difficult to relate to and thus, barring exceptional compensating assets, they are not much in demand, through interaction.

Role compatibility is probably the most complex of all the stages and is probably never completely traversed, since individuals seem to be constantly adding new roles or modifying existing ones.

EXPRESSIVE AND PERCEPTUAL STYLE AND EXPRESSIVE BEHAVIOR

In our discussion of the stages and components of courtship so far, we noted that each person aspires toward his ideal with respect to stimulus values, but that the demands of reality tend to force him back toward a person of comparable assets and liabilities. With respect to values, the argument was advanced that homogamy is highly desirable, because it signifies that the participants are moving toward identical goals. Also, when attitudes are similar, communication should be less stressful, since much would be understood and approved, and the fear of being misunderstood would be less likely. I should like now to focus on other behaviors that I have labeled "perceptual style" and "expressive behavior."

Perceptual Style

Both the content and style of an individual's perceptions may surely reveal his value system, as the "new look" research demonstrated a quarter of a century ago (Bruner and Postman, 1948). At that time there were numerous experiments in which coins were perceived as greater than objective size by the poor, and ambiguous signs were seen as swastikas by concentration camp victims. Perceptions, in short, can reveal the values of the perceivers.

Homogeneity of perceptions between two people should be beneficial for a premarital relationship on two counts. Even when the agreement in perception involves no common values, it at least supplies consensual validation; it is rewarding to know that one is in good contact with reality. If two campers can agree that the skies portend that a cold wind is coming, they can make appropriate responses even if one believes that it is healthful to be lightly clad, and the other believes it is healthful to be warmly bundled up. If the couple can interpret an experience within similar value systems, homogamy should be even more strongly rewarding. If two naive passengers discover that they have been overcharged by a Parisian taxi driver, and they confirm each other's belief that tourists are regarded as fair game by the natives, they may feel highly justified in exhibiting suspicious behavior when future business transactions take place in a Parisian boutique.

Expressive Behavior

Expressive behavior is more complex. By expressive behavior I refer to the *style* and *manner* of interacting with other people or objects rather than to the *content* of what they say; hence talkativeness, querulousness, and hyperactivity are three examples of expressive behavior. To the degree that expressive behavior reflects similar values, it should be homogamously selective. If two people have a cynical view of the world, they may enjoy each other's humor in spoofing even the noblest of endeavors.

On the other hand, if expressive behavior reflects a role the individual has adopted, similarity of expressive behavior is rewarding only to the extent that similarity of the roles is rewarding. For example, a politician who is articulate and likes to talk at the drop of a hat may be benefited by a wife who is equally articulate, independent, and talkative. He thereby gains another campaigner. A man who wishes to play the role of sage patriarch to his wife's "doll house Nora," however, may be made uncomfortable by a wife who boldly enunciates her own views and independence.

In making predictions about the similarity or complementarity of expressive behavior, therefore, we have to estimate whether the behavior is most apt to reflect a philosophical position (value), or a role. If it serves the latter, we will have to estimate whether the roles of the partners served by the particular expressive behavior are similar or complementary.

Not enough is known about perceptual and expressive styles to indicate in which stage they are most operative; consequently, I assume that they cut across the various stages and I shall not venture any predictions regarding their being especially influential during any one stage of courtship.

TYPES OF COURTSHIP AND CROSS-CULTURAL INFLUENCES

Figure 7.2 describes what I conjecture to be the typical path of courtship for most middle-class couples in the United States. Variations due to personality, economic, and cultural differences, however, would alter the graph somewhat. "Stimulus" types would hold stimulus variables to be most important over the course of the courtship. For such persons, marrying in the right class or profession would be paramount, and role interaction secondary. One thinks immediately of the exceedingly wealthy class in this regard. Here, values would be relatively unimportant in selection, because class selectivity would be great and individual variability much smaller in comparison to class selectivity. In other words, if almost everyone within a class holds similar views, individual selectivity with respect to values does not seem to be a major issue.

The same would probably be true for other societies in which social change is relatively slight and class structure is stable. A Greek peasant might be most influenced by stimulus variables because almost everyone in the village holds similar values. Role stratification also might be very rigid, a man's role and a woman's role being clearly defined and differentiated. In that case, the role stage along with the value stage might be of relatively small import.

In our own society, value consensus seems to be of greatest importance within professional and upper-middle-class couples and of least importance in the lower class (Kerckhoff, 1972, 1974). In the lower class, we may presume that the narrowed range of class variability with respect to values and the structuring of roles makes individual selectivity of lesser importance.

Since value comparison in many respects serves as an introduction to role comparisons and role compatibility, it is easier to think of a "value-role" type than of either a separate "value" or a "role" type. This type would include individuals whose greatest rewards come from close interpersonal interaction with people. It would be of interest to determine whether "stimulus" types invariably marry "stimulus" types or sometimes "intermarry" with "value-role" types.

DISTINGUISHING BETWEEN EQUITY AND SIMILARITY

Similarity and equity are often bandied about as if they were equivalent terms. It is necessary, however, to distinguish between them because equity plays an important role in SVR theory, whereas similarity is of lesser importance. Similarity within the context of our discussion refers to the number of common components or the degree of similar structure of two objects. If two individuals have similar values, it is meant that if we ranked the values of each in order of preference, a high rank order correlation would result.

Equity, as used here, refers to equal rewarding power; hence two equitable persons might be totally dissimilar. A couple comprising a beautiful but poor woman who marries an ugly but wealthy bachelor may represent an equitable balance of beauty and wealth.

The problem arises when members of a couple are equally represented on a variable so that they are both similar and equitable with respect to it. Generally, similarity functions as an independent variable. Individuals possessing similar values are drawn to each other because they receive consensual validation that their views are correct. In some cases, however, logic tells us that two people who share a socially undesirable characteristic may not necessarily be drawn to each other. They may in fact *settle* for each other because it is the best they can do. It is doubtful, for example, that two physically unattractive individuals are drawn to each other because they admire unattractiveness. Rather, they may have learned through experience that they are apt to be rejected by more attractive persons whom they attempt to court, if they do not possess outstanding compensating attributes for their unattractiveness. It is the presence of similars at the bottom of the totem pole that enables us to differentiate similarity as a socially desirable attracting agent from similarity as an equity-of-exchange factor.

Similarity can be nonrewarding even when the traits involved are socially desirable, because unless similarity leads to a rewarding experience it may be of little utility. In the area of personality, similarity may lead to competition and dissatisfaction. When both members of a couple possess strong needs to dominate each other, the couple may function less harmoniously than a tandem of a dominant and submissive member. The strongest interpersonal relationship therefore, does not necessarily occur between the most similar types but between those with equal rewarding power (equity), even where the variables contributing to these rewards are different for the partners.

Where Is Love?

Up to this point there has been no mention of love, but this does not mean that I perceive marriage as a loveless relationship. Indeed, in America everybody marries for "love"; consequently, the term love has come to represent a large number of diverse behaviors; we love apple pie, the Mets, sex, Uncle Otto, our spouses, children, colleagues, and our country. Apart from indicating a positive affinity for a diverse series of objects, these "loves" offer little insight into the nature of the relationships.

One could also speak of heterosexual love, parental love, conjugal love, and romantic love. These subdivisions only differentiate between the objects of love but do not illuminate the process.

In addition, our understanding of love is further clouded because the word "love" has assumed a high symbolic value, so that it operates as a reinforcement (reward) independent of any overt behavior. For example, Ephraim Exploitum, having just finished a tasty swordfish steak, tells his wife tenderly, "Earline, I love you." He then proceeds to the living room to watch the news on television, while his wife, who had returned from her job and prepared his meal, now turns her attention to the dishes. On the other hand, some persons may engage in what many individuals consider loving behavior, but for one reason or another do not label their action as "love."

Since "love" can be independent of behavior, and since, in any event, definitions of love vary enormously, I prefer to focus on the determinants of close dyadic attraction rather than on labeling preferences. Almost all of the subjects in my research "loved" their partners, but it would seem of greater interest to determine whether the focus of their attraction had to do with stimulus, value comparison, or role variables.

Relationship of SVR to Other Theories

SVR theory is in many respects a compendium of a number of past theories, hopefully with some helpful amendments that aid our understanding of the dyadic process. It is an extension and elaboration of Kerckhoff and Davis's filter theory. Their theory, however, makes no mention of the initial attraction process. I have added the stimulus stage, which precedes the value stage and accounts for initial attractions. Also, I have not emphasized the filter aspects because it is an incomplete filter at best. The importance of stimulus variables can be superseded by value comparison variables at a given time, but the former do not necessarily lose their influence on courtship.

The value theory of marital choice is represented in the value comparison stage, and, to some extent, also in the stimulus stage, insofar as these represent culturally induced values. However, the value theory of marital choice is based on homogamy rather than equity and cannot account for the fact that individuals may be drawn to each other despite certain value differences. This problem is handled in SVR theory by positing equity; a weakness in one area can be compensated by strength in another.

Lewis's process theory shares an emphasis on value consensus and role satisfaction with SVR theory. However, Lewis believes that perceived similarity in personality is an important initial process, whereas SVR theory holds that only similarity of values is generally conducive to courtship progress. Even here, its importance varies with the individual, class, and culture.

Winch's theory of need complementarity presupposes selection from a field of eligibles. However, the field of eligibles does not play an intrinsic role in Winch's theory, since it really serves as a preamble to his concern with complementary needs. In a very rough sense his field of eligibles is comparable to the S and V stages of SVR theory, though his lack of concern with how a relationship starts limits further comparison. His complementary needs theory is somewhat comparable to the R stage, but SVR theory rejects any monolithic attempts to account for attraction, since in some cases complementarity best serves the individuals' goals, and in other cases homogamy serves them.

Huston (1973b) has posited a theory of initiation of heterosexual pair relationships based on the earlier work of Lewin et al. (1964), Rotter (1954), and W. Edwards (1954, 1955). The present description of the tactics of initiating behavior is based on these same authors, my earlier field approach (Murstein, 1961a), and that of Huston.

Last, I have indicated earlier some differences between similarity (homogamy) and equity. However, the two are often tied together, as we noted earlier. Although similarity can be a basis for attraction (most notably in value consensus), it often is an epiphenomenon of the equity of exchange process and therefore does not play a central role. This is illustrated well in the following statements by J. N. Edwards (1969):

1. Within any collectibility of potential mates, a marriageable person will seek out that individual who is perceived as maximizing his rewards.
2. Individuals with equivalent resources are most likely to maximize each other's rewards.
3. Pairs with equivalent resources are most likely to possess homogamous characteristics.
4. Mate selection, therefore, will be homogamous with respect to a given set of characteristics (p. 525).

In sum, SVR theory is a relatively complex theory of dyadic relationship formation. From a transactional framework it is an exchange theory; viewed teleologically it is a sequential, partial filter theory. Whether SVR theory will prove useful remains to be seen. Few theories of marital choice and dyad formation can be said to be right or wrong. Rather, they are conceptual tasks for organizing existing data into a meaningful framework and for making predictions. As such, they generally have strong points and weak points, and they differ in usefulness.

The judgement of usefulness is a consensus judgement evidenced by critiques, references to the theory in research papers, and new research stimulated by it. Theories in the social sciences are rarely if ever proved or disproved by any single piece of research. There is generally a difference of opinion about the definity and validity of results. Even the best theories do not want for critics, and even the worst are rarely without an advocate or two.

Gradually, however, with the passage of time, poor theories or theories that have outlived their usefulness become less visible in the literature, and when reference is made to them, the proportion of critical to positive comments is high. In the end, no more is heard about them as new theories gain the ascendance.

In the following chapter I shall present information on the subjects and tests used in my research, followed in succeeding chapters by specific hypotheses and data bearing on the theory.

CHAPTER **8**

The Population and the Tests

I have presented the basic components of SVR theory as applied to premarital courtship. In the following chapters, a series of hypotheses based on the theory will be presented, along with data relating to these hypotheses. First, however, it will be necessary to describe the population studied, the tests used, and the general procedures followed.

From the beginning it was clear that the main thrust of the research would involve college students. The advantages of a college population are many. They are bright, articulate, and sophisticated. With such subjects it is possible to use extensive questionnaires that require intelligence, a good vocabulary, and good reading ability, not to mention high motivation. One can also use lengthy interviews that necessitate a willingness to talk about personal matters. Since the interviewers and administrators were themselves either a college professor or graduate students, it could be assumed that both interviewer and interviewee would be most comfortable talking with someone from the same cultural milieu. Moreover, college students are obviously an excellent source for obtaining premarital couples. It might be added that although college students represent perhaps a half or less of the 18- to 22-year-old population, they represent a majority of those who read research findings. Thus there would be some generalizability from the subjects to the reading public.

On the other hand, the generalizability of a college volunteer group to the national population of premarital couples is limited. Also, volunteers are more highly motivated and less defensive than the average college student, and they are both more anxious to please and more compliant than are nonvolunteers.

There are other problems apart from generalizability. A select sample will often exhibit a curtailed distribution of scores on various measures. For example, if one tries to differentiate "highs" from "lows" on a variable such as "neurosis" with such a sample, it is possible that rather than separating neurotics from normals, we may be faced with the more difficult task of separating high normals from only slightly neurotic subjects. The effect is to maximize the chances of a Type II error (accepting the null hypothesis of no significant difference between the groups when in fact there are real differences).

Moreover, very little is known about the interpersonal relationships of noncollegiate premarital couples, and it would be a worthwhile contribution to investigate their patterns of interaction. Consequently, an advertisement was placed in the local town newspaper offering $30 per couple to courting couples who had had no college education and who would participate in the interview and testing procedure. In addition, for approximately two weeks, announcements of engagements in the local newspaper were scrutinized for individuals whose description suggested the possible absence of a college education. Telephone calls were made to approximately fifteen couples. Also, posters describing the research and monetary offer were placed in several supermarkets throughout the town of New London.

The fruit of our efforts after two weeks was that we were contacted by two couples, of whom one successfully completed the testing procedures. The man in the other couple refused to take the ink blot test despite assurances that the data would be confidential. In view of the difficulties in recruiting subjects and the expense in time and finances for rather meager returns, the attempt to obtain a noncollege sample was reluctantly abandoned.

Concerning the mostly college population actually used, the money we paid probably helped somewhat in vitiating the volunteer bias. An earlier pilot study, in which we paid nothing for participation, had resulted in a large number of dropouts before the project was completed. When a questionnaire was mailed to these dropouts asking why they dropped out and what it would have taken for them to have completed the tests, we found some surprising answers. Many said that the questions were too personal, yet when we asked what might have influenced the subjects to participate, they checked off the item "If I had received $7." Aided by this information, we elected to pay handsome stipends as long as the funds held out, and as a result we incurred few dropouts among volunteers.

Most of the data were collected between 1964 and 1969, although some supplementary work was done from 1970 through 1972. The bulk of the subjects were studied in three waves, which will be referred to as Groups I, II, and III. The data for Group I was collected in 1964-1965, for Group II in 1965, and for Group III in 1967-1968. (A list of all the tests used with all three testing groups is found in Appendix A. All the tests used with Group II or portions of them with the exception of the inkblot test are found in Appendix C.

GROUP I

Subjects

The subjects were selected through announcements at several New England colleges and universities for couples who were going steady, engaged and/or seriously contemplating marriage with the partner. Of the 100 couples agreeing to participate, 99 successfully completed the entire test battery. One man refused to be photographed, although he and his partner had been read a synopsis of the entire procedure before testing. Accordingly, he and his partner were removed from the data processing. Each subject received $10 for participating, divided as follows: $3 for taking a battery of tests, and $7 when he answered his follow-up questionnaire six months later.

Tests

The battery of tests took 3 to 5 hours and was administered on one of 15 available dates. Both partners had to be present for the testing, which was administered by a research assistant or the author, who made sure that the partners did not communicate during the testing. (All of the tests used with Group I except for the MMPI and the Revised Personal Preference Schedule are found in Appendix B.)

The tests consisted of the following:

1. *Minnesota Multiphasic Personality Inventory (MMPI)*. This well-known personality inventory consists of 550 items that are to be answered *True, False,* or *Cannot Say.* The items cover a wide variety of topics including physical condition, morale, and social attitudes.

The original intention of the test constructors was to derive a number of empirical scales based on differentiating individuals with varying psychiatric diagnostic classifications from control groups. For a number of reasons not germane to our present concern, the psychiatric diagnostic meaning of the scales has been abandoned. A high score on the Paranoia scale, for example, does not ipso facto indicate that the individual is paranoid.

A great deal of research has been done with the scales so that it has been deemed convenient to retain the old psychiatric labels (although many prefer to use arabic numbers 1, 2, etc. to describe the scales) but to base the interpretative significance of the scores on the correlative data unearthed in thousands of studies. Much of the data has been compiled into various handbooks (Welsh and Dahlstrom, 1956, Dahlstrom and Welsh, 1960).

In addition to the 10 empirical scales, there are 4 rational scales that measure the validity of the test-taker's attitudes and approach to the test. These comprise the 14 basic scales, but the items have been keyed for hundreds of other scales. I shall describe the 14 scales scored in the standard MMPI plus 4 additional scales relating to mental health, which were added in the present study because I was particularly interested in their effect on marital choice.

The four rational scales are: ?, L, F, K.

?.   A high *Cannot Say* (?) score indicates evasiveness, defensiveness, and/or indecisiveness.

L.   The lie (L) scale contains items that are socially desirable, but that most people would admit are not always true of them. Most individuals, for example, would answer *True* to the statement: "I do not always tell the truth." To answer *False* does not necessarily indicate a dishonest response, but to answer in opposition to the keyed response over a large number of items suggests a tendency to seek to be always in a socially desirable light and, thus, to be less than frank.

F.   The F scale is made up of items observed to be rarely answered in the keyed direction (less than 10 percent) by normal persons. A high score on this scale suggests careless reading of the items, intentional desire to make oneself look unusual, or psychological illness.

K.   The K scale is a measure of a test-taking attitude, somewhat similar to the *L* and *F* scales, but more subtle. It is said to represent defensiveness against psychological weakness. A high score indicates great defensiveness against psychological weaknesses, whereas a low score indicates that the individual's defenses are down (*Military Clinical Psychology,* 1951). The K score is used to correct several of the empirical scales by adding or subtracting to the raw score to compensate for the degree of defensiveness. For example, to correct the Hysteria scale, one adds .5K or one-half of the K score to the original Hysteria score.

The 10 empirical diagnostic scales have been briefly described by Edwards (1970) as follows:

Scale 1 *(Hs)*. Hypochondriasis: individuals with undue concern about health and bodily symptoms.

Scale 2 *(D)*. Depression: individuals with depressed states and feelings of hopelessness.

Scale 3 *(Hy)*. Hysteria: individuals with multiple physical symptoms of various sorts and for which, in general, there was no known physical basis for the symptoms.

Scale 4 *(Pd)*. Psychopathic deviate: individuals in trouble because of delinquency, habitual lying, stealing, etc.

Scale 5 *(Mf)*. Masculinity-femininity: the items in this scale were selected to differentiate between males and females.

Scale 6 *(Pa)*. Paranoia: individuals described as having paranoid personalities and characterized as being suspicious and jealous of others.

Scale 7 *(Pt)*. Psychasthenia: individuals with obsessive thoughts, fears, feelings of guilt and anxiety.

Scale 8 *(Sc)*. Schizophrenia: individuals characterized as having marked distortions of reality, bizarre thoughts, and tending to be withdrawn.

Scale 9 *(Ma)*. Hypomania: individuals characterized as being overactive, excitable, and irritable.

Scale 10 *(Si)*. Social introversion: the items in this scale were selected to differentiate between individuals with high and low scores on another scale designed to measure introversion-extroversion (pp. 55-56).

The four additional scales derived from the answers to the items included the Neurotic Triad (the sum of the scaled scores for the scales of Hysteria, Depression, and Hypochondriasis). This scale, as the title suggests, is said to represent neurotic behavior (Hathaway and McKinley, 1967). Also included were the Repression and Anxiety scores (Welsh, 1956) and Ego-Strength (Barron, 1956).

The raw scores were converted to normalized T score equivalents as published in the MMPI norms (Hathaway and McKinley, 1967). A T score of 50 represents the mean, and the standard deviation is 10; hence a score of 60 would be exceeded by only 16 percent of the population in a normal distribution, and a score of 70 would be exceeded by less than 3 percent of the population. Because of the skewness of the raw scores, scores much below 40 are rare.

2. *Expediency Scale.* This test contained 22 items and was intended to provide a measure of the subject's desire to get married. Questions varied from the direct "Would you like to be married now?"

to the somewhat indirect "Would you like to get away from living at home?"

3. *Revised Edwards Personal Preference Schedule (PPS).* The standard PPS, as constructed by Edwards (1959), consists of paired sentences representing different needs and asks the subject to choose from each pair the sentence that best fits him. The matched items are roughly equated for social desirability, so that the individual is presumably forced to express his "personal" choice rather than being able to choose the more socially acceptable answer. Unfortunately, research by Corah, Feldman, Cohen, Gruen, Meadow, and Ringwall (1958) has shown that the "social desirability" factor has not been eliminated from the PPS. Horst and Wright (1959) have shown that the paired comparisons on the PPS are less reliable than the items considered individually. For the present study, therefore, the items were considered singly, and for each one a five-point scale, ranging from "very frequently" or "very important to me" to "almost never" or "almost no importance" was used. The Revised Edwards Scale thus consisted of 135 items tapping 15 needs of 9 items each. For a given subject, therefore, each need score might range 9 to 45.

In the opinion of the present author, "social desirability" is an intrinsic aspect of personality needs. To extract this component from a personality score is to eliminate an important source of variance, particularly since marital choice obviously depends a great deal on "social desirability." Therefore, unless it can be demonstrated that the spurious "set" cast by "social desirability" more than offsets the loss in knowledge when it is partialled out of the data, it seems wisest to avoid such a "corrective" procedure.

4. *Marriage Value Inventory.* The subjects ranked ten values according to their importance to them for marriage. Test-retest correlation after three weeks, in which the rank order of the ten variables for each subject was compared with his new set of ranks, yielded mean r's of .94 for a sample of six women and .91 for a sample of six men.

5. *Sex Questionnaire.* Sex drive may be measured in many different ways. Two different concepts of sex-drive were used in this study; a reported performance measure and a psychologically perceived state, both measured through the use of a sex questionnaire. After initial instructions regarding the definition of orgasm, the scientific value of studying sexual behavior, the presence of great variability in feelings and behavior within the normal range, and the assurance of confidentiality for the data, the questionnaire listed four questions: 1. When did you have your last orgasm? (twelve-category scale from "today" to "never") 2. What is your best estimate of your average rate of sexual orgasm per week? (eleven-category scale from

0 to 22 or more) 3. As you see yourself in relation to other members of your sex and your age, would you rate your sex drive as stronger than average, average, or not as strong as average? 4. Please rate the extent to which control of your sex drive is a problem. "Control" here means to exercise effort to get your mind off sex, to get to concentrating on something else, efforts to subdue, to cope with sexual desires in some manner (five-point scale from "control is little or no problem" to "control is a very difficult problem").

6. *Physical Attractiveness.* Three measures of physical attractiveness were obtained. Two questions asked of the subjects on a background questionnaire dealt with physical attractiveness. The first asked the subject how physically attractive he found his partner, and the second asked for his estimate of his own physical attractiveness. Each question was evaluated on a five-point scale ranging from "extremely good-looking," which received a score of five, to "considerably below average in looks," which received a score of one.

In addition, during the general testing procedure, each couple was called to another room and photographed twice by means of a Polaroid camera. One photo was taken with the couple in a natural pose looking directly at the camera, the second with the couple smiling. These pictures were evaluated by 8 judges (young professors and graduate students of whom 4 were men and 4 were women) on a 5-point scale. The judges were instructed that, in the general population, but not necessarily in the subject population, a score of 5 (extremely good-looking) would be obtained by about 8 percent of the population, a score of 4 (better looking than average) by about 17 percent, a score of 3 (average) by about 50 percent, a score of 2 (somewhat below average) by about 17 percent, and a score of 1 (considerably below average) by about 8 percent. Comparison of the average of the male and female judges' scores yielded a Pearson r of .80, suggesting that no pronounced sex differences were present; hence to determine interjudge reliability, the scores of all 8 judges were pooled and then separated into two random halves. The mean scores of each half were correlated by means of the Spearman-Brown formula, resulting in an r of .91, a reliability value sufficiently high for the purpose of the study.

7. *McGuire Index of Social Status.* A shortened version of this instrument (McGuire and White, 1955) was used with two weighted scales focusing on major source of family income and educational attainment of the father or parent lived with if not the father.

8. *Marriage Expectation Test.* This inventory contains items relating to expectations regarding roles desired to be played by the future spouse and the self in marriage along with desired personological, sociological, value, physical, and temperament characteristics

that the spouse should have. The items were in part obtained from earlier questionnaires, and in part were constructed for the present research.

The preliminary form of the test contained 262 items for men and 263 for women, many of which were identical. Each item was rated on a five-point scale from (5) "Yes, the possession of this behavior or characteristic by my future spouse is very important to me," to (1) "No, the *lack* of this behavior or characteristic is very important to me." The subjects also filled out the Marriage Expectation Test according to how they perceived their partner.

The data were factor analyzed using a computer that could accommodate no more than 158 items at a time; hence four factor analyses for each sex were undertaken to include all of the variables. The most representative 158 items were selected for the initial analysis. Items with no loadings greater than .30 on the first ten factors extracted were then eliminated, and new items added to bring the number of items up to 158 again. The final version consisted of 130 items for men and 135 items for women. Ten slightly altered versions of the test were prepared for use with Group III and will be described a bit later on. The male and female versions of the test are found in the appendix. Test-retest correlations after three weeks for a small sample of 9 randomly chosen women, each taking 3 of the Marriage Expectation Tests at a time, averaged from .71 to .91 for the women and from .62 to .79 for similarly chosen men.

9. *Background Questionnaire.* This inventory asked questions about the subject's age, length of courtship, definitiveness of plans for marriage, date of planned marriage (if planned), attitudes toward children, status of parents, confidence that the marriage would be happy, evaluation of parents' marriage, stresses and break-ups in the subject's present relationship, and confidence that a marriage would take place.

Six months after the subjects had been tested, they were mailed a follow-up questionnaire. The primary question asked was, "Is the relationship between you two different from what it was last fall or winter when you filled out the first questionnaire?" (This question had been used earlier by Kerckhoff and Davis (1962) in their study of courtship.) The subjects had four possible choices that were later scored from 1 to 4. These were: (1) "Yes, we are farther from being a permanent union." (2) "No, it is about the same but not necessarily very good." (3) "No, it is about the same, but it is very good," and (4) "Yes, we are married, or we are nearer to being a permanent couple." Other items related to size of home town, circumstances of first meeting, religion, height, weight, eye color, hair color, and whether there were differences about the date of future marriage. Of the 99 couples mailed the following questionnaires, 95 men and 95 women eventually returned their questionnaires.

GROUP II

Subjects

Group I had received structured, questionnaire-type inventories. Group II was selected to examine the utility of more indirect measures of assessment. The subjects came from the same source as the earlier college subjects. Originally it was hoped to get 30 couples, but the procedure and the analysis of the data for this phase proved so time-consuming that only 19 couples could be tested in the time set aside for the phase. Each subject was paid five dollars, two at the time of the testing and three dollars for returning the follow-up questionnaire.

Tests

A background questionnaire, sex questionnaire, and the Marriage Value Inventory used with Group I also were administered to Group II. Three "depth" measures not used earlier were added.

Interview. The interview consisted of approximately 200 questions in a semistandardized format, the interview taking as long as necessary to provide the necessary information. The questions dealt with childhood relationships with parents, present relationships with them, the origin of the relationship with the partner, its ups and downs, the couple's sexual relationship, and their hopes and aspirations for the future. The interview took anywhere from 2 to 3½ hours. (Many of the items for the interview came from an earlier one developed by Rhona and Robert Rapoport, to whom I wish to extend my thanks for allowing me to make use of their interview schedule.)

Marriage Apperceptive Thematic Examination. The thematic test consisted of 13 cards expressly created to portray interpersonal, heterosexual situations in accordance with findings of the kinds of cards most useful for projection (Murstein, 1965b). The instructions used with the TAT (Murray, 1943) were slightly modified so as to suggest that the test was a measure of personality rather than of intelligence.

The responses to the stories were scored for 16 personality variables that have been used in earlier research with thematic tests. A list of these variables appears in Table 13.2 on page 239.

The meaning of some of these variables is apparent by inspection. The meaning of the others is as follows: "emotional tone" refers to whether the mood of the story is positive, negative, or neutral; "projection" refers to the extent to which the subjects' stories manifested qualities that were projections of the subjects' world in that they went beyond the stimulus qualities of the cards; "remoteness of hostile expression" indicated the extent of avoidance of individual responsibility the subject manifested for his hostile expression—for example, seeing a murder taking place in a play rather than in actual life; "goodness of response" refers to the adequacy of the story as a whole in terms of the subject's ability to follow the experimenter's instructions in making up a story, and in terms of the logical properties and internal consistency of the story.

Some of the variables listed have been found to have moderate-to-high interjudge reliability and are described more fully in earlier research (Atkinson, 1958; Epstein, 1962; Eron, 1950). Others ("attitude toward men," "attitude toward women," "projection," and "qualifications in the story") were created especially for the present study.

Baughman Modification of the Rorschach. The standard Rorschach test consists of ten ink blots, some chromatic, some achromatic, which are shown sequentially to subjects who tell what the blots look like. The subsequent inquiry determines how much of the blot was used in the perception, what determined the perception (i.e., form, color, shading, movement), exactly what the subject saw, and how he saw it. Each of these variables has interpretative significance with regard to the test taker's personality.

The Baughman modification uses the standard Rorschach presentation but contains six other possible stimulus variations that are used in the inquiry (Baughman, 1958). Because of considerations of time, only the four most frequently applicable variations were used. One variation is achromatic but retains the shading nuances of the Rorschach. Another set is also achromatic but without shading. A third set has the figures in white and the background in black, which is the reverse of the usual figure-ground contrast. The fourth set contains grey where color appears in the original Rorschach, thus converting the color-achromatic contrast of the original Rorschach to a grey-black one.

The alleged advantages of the Baughman modification over the standard Rorschach is that it avoids making the determinants of perception excessively dependent on the verbalization of the subject. It has been noted earlier (Murstein, 1960) that many persons do not possess the verbal skills, motivation, or self-knowledge to be able to verbalize the determinants of their perceptions on the Rorschach that are converted into determinant scores used in the analysis of their personalities; hence, the subjects tend to pick up clues from the way the examiner nods his head, smiles, or grunts as to what kind of statements on their part seem to please him. The test, therefore, becomes more a test of subjects' reinforced verbal responses (Wickes, 1956; Gross, 1959; Simkins, 1960) than of their perceptions.

In the Baughman Modification, however, the subject who, for example, says he sees a clown, might be shown a comparable card from the grey-black series where the texture and contours are the same, but the color is absent. If he no longer sees a clown, it may be inferred that the color in the original Rorschach card was a contributing determinant of the perception. In using the stimulus variation as substitutes for most of the verbal inquiry, the subject is compelled to make perceptual discriminations rather than verbal explanations, a task that seems to be more consistent with the intended purpose of the Rorschach.

The 48 variables scored for the Rorschach make an extensive list (see Table 13.1, p. 238). I shall, therefore, avoid a description of each variable and, instead, limit myself to describing the kinds of variables included. A more complete description of the significant variables will appear in Chapter 13.

The Rorschach variables may be classified by four categories: location, determinants, content, and a residual catch-all category. The location variables measure how much of the blot was used in arriving at a perception. The determinants reflect to what extent the perception was determined by form, perceived movement in the blot (e.g., an animal flying), shading, and color. The content refers to whether the subject saw humans, animals, inanimate objects, blood, anatomy. The residual category contains measures of the process of taking the test, the average time the subject took to give his first response (reaction time) and to give all his responses (average response time). Body image was studied with regard to toughness (barrier, penetration). Also, various score ratios believed to have relevance in personality assessment were recorded. The M:FM ratio, for example, refers to the ratio of human movement responses to animal movement ones. Further details about the scores used may be found in the following works: Allen, 1966; Fisher and Cleveland, 1958; Holtzman, 1961; Murstein, 1956, 1968; Piotrowski, 1957.

Q Sort. The results of the various tests were used to judge the subjects on a 100 item Q Sort. The construction of the Q Sort was as follows: One hundred statements relating to personality, temperament, and values were selected from a variety of tests or constructed for the present test. The items were balanced so as to contain an even number of favorable and unfavorable statements. After evaluating all of the information gained from the tests and questionnaires, the assessors (Dr. Rosemary Burns and myself) sorted the items into nine columns on a forced choice basis such that a normal distribution was achieved. Thus the greatest number of items were placed in the middle column, 5, and a continually diminishing number were placed in the parallel columns 6 and 4, 7 and 3, 8 and 2, and 9 and 1. The range went from "most like the subject" (Column 9) to "least like the subject" (Column 1). (The 100 items of the Q Sort are listed in Appendix C.)

GROUP III

Three years after the start of the testing of Group I, a new sample of college students was recruited to determine whether some of the earlier findings could be replicated and to investigate in greater depth than heretofore the importance of person perception and role compatibility in marital choice and courtship progress.

Subjects

Volunteer couples were collected through announcements at Connecticut College for couples interested in participating in a study on interpersonal relationships and marital choice. It was stressed that any couple could participate who had had at least two dates. Each subject was paid $5.00 for participating ($2.00 initially and $3.00 when the follow-up was returned 6 months later). Subjects were assured that all data would be confidential and coded for anonymity.

The woman's packet of tests was given to those women (Connecticut College was a woman's college at the time) who said that they had discussed the study with their boyfriends, and that both members of the couple wished to participate in the study. Upon her return of the completed packet, a new one was mailed to the address of her boyfriend. Only a very small number of the boyfriends were located in the same town as their girlfriends.

Of 136 women filling out packets, 101 packets were received from their boyfriends. Since we wished to work only with completed couples, we now had a base of 101 couples. Of the 101 follow-up questionnaires sent out to each member of the couple six months later inquiring about courtship progress, 98 were received from both members of the couple, and these subjects constituted the group used in analyzing the data.

The tests for Group III were mainly intended to focus on person perception measures. Accordingly, since only a finite number of subject time could be utilized, those tests used earlier that did not specifically focus on premarital couples or which were time consuming (the MMPI and PPS) were eliminated.

Tests

The Marriage Value Inventory and McGuire Index of Social Status were given as in the earlier study along with background and sex questionnaires. The only major change in the sex questionnaire was the omission of the question asking for the date of the most recent orgasm and the substitution of a question asking for the source of orgasm. The rationale for this change is explained in the data section dealing with sexual drive.

Marriage Expectation Test. The Marriage Expectation Test refined by factor analysis to a 130-item form for men and a 135-item form for women, with 76 items in common for both sexes, was the central focus of the third study. Each subject took the test under 10 different perceptive "sets," each set being identical for each sex except for the slight rewording of the items for grammatical reasons.

The sets were:
1. Importance of item for self
2. Ideal self
3. Self
4. Ideal-spouse
5. Perception of Girlfriend (Boyfriend)
6. Importance of items about partner
7. Prediction of how girlfriend (boyfriend) sees ideal-spouse
8. Prediction of how girlfriend (boyfriend) sees ideal self
9. Prediction of how girlfriend (boyfriend) sees herself (himself)
10. Prediction of how girlfriend (boyfriend) sees you

(Because of some ambiguity in the comprehension of the two Importance sets, as determined by post-test interviews, these were not analyzed.)

BACKGROUND DATA ON SUBJECTS

Our three samples were largely drawn from the same sources, and, in the interests of space, much of the background data will be discussed in common, although not every question was duplicated for each sample. The mean age of the men was just over 21, the mean age of the women just under 20.

Most individuals came from towns or small cities, the modal population size being 25,000 to 100,000. The overwhelming percentage were church members, though the majority were irregular in attendance. About half of the subjects were Protestants, a quarter Catholic, 15-20 percent Jewish, and the rest unaffiliated. Relatively few black students were in eastern Connecticut universities at the time, and none volunteered to participate. The subjects reported good relationships with their parents, came largely from intact homes, and generally reported that their parents' marriages were quite happy.

Concerning their relationship with their partner, most had met through channels generally regarded as conducive to stable relationships (mutual friends or relatives, social affairs, school) rather than by chance or on blind dates. On the average, they had known each other just under two years at the time of testing. The modal response for the classification of the relationship was between dating exclusively and being "pinned" or informally committed to each other; a considerable number, however, were formally or informally engaged. Between 20 and 30 percent dated others, and very few classified their relationship to each other under the noncommittal category "date somewhat."

Only a distinct minority had ever broken off with the partner, although more than half had at one time or another contemplated breaking off the relationship. A high majority classified their partner as understanding them very well and believed that they understood their partner.

Groups I and II had been recruited with the requirement that the subjects be seriously contemplating marriage, whereas Group III subjects were only required to have had at least two dates. Not surprisingly, therefore, the first two groups contained only about 5 percent who were "uncertain about marriage" as opposed to other plans for marriage: "pretty sure to marry," "barring unforeseen circumstances," or "absolutely sure." Group III, however, contained about a third who were uncertain, or doubtful about future marriage with the partner.

Physical Attractiveness

Three measures of physical attractiveness were obtained for Groups I and III (see Tables 8.1 and 8.2). The subjects in both groups tended to perceive their partners as rather physically attractive. Their perception of themselves was somewhat more modest, but was nevertheless

Table 8.1

PHYSICAL ATTRACTIVENESS OF MEN (IN PERCENTAGES),
AS JUDGED BY PARTNER, SELF, AND FROM PHOTO

Attractiveness	Perceived by Partner	Self-Perception	Photo Attractiveness [1]
Extremely good-looking	17 (20)	4 (10)	3
Better than average	55 (50)	39 (36)	18
Average	26 (24)	53 (48)	61
Below average	2 (5)	3 (4)	17
Considerably below average	0 (0)	0 (0)	1

Note: Percentages not in parentheses are from Group I (N = 99); percentages in parentheses are from Group III (N = 98).
One subject's data from Group III was not reported.

[1] Since these values were the means of 8 judges, for both men and women, mean scores of 4.50 and over were arbitrarily assigned by me to the category "extremely good-looking," 3.50 to 4.49 to "better than average," 2.50 to 3.49 to "average," 1.51 to 2.49 to "below average," and 1.50 and below to "considerably below average."

rather high. When the judges of the photos rated them, however, there was a relative downgrading of attractiveness. These data suggest how important "good looks" are to couples in that almost no one is perceived by his partner or by himself as less than average in looks. Only uninvolved judges saw imperfection.

Table 8.2

PHYSICAL ATTRACTIVENESS OF WOMEN (IN PERCENTAGES)
AS JUDGED BY PARTNER, SELF, AND FROM PHOTO

Attractiveness	Perceived by Partner	Self- Perception	Photo Attractiveness
Extremely good looking	24 (29)	1 (6)	1
Above average	61 (58)	38 (55)	23
Average	11 (11)	61 (36)	57
Below average	2 (1)	0 (2)	17
Considerably below average	1 (0)	0 (0)	2

Note: Percentages not in parentheses are from Group I, percentages in parentheses
are from Group III.

Sex

The responses to the sex questionnaire are shown in Table 8.3.
Inspection of this table shows that the modal reported weekly orgasm
rate was approximately 3 for men and 1 for women. For both groups,
the values were comparable to those reported by Kinsey and his
associates (1948, 1953). The majority of individuals of both sexes,
nevertheless, tended to perceive their sex drive as average or above,
with a good number experiencing at least some difficulty in dealing
with these drives (control of sex drive). The vast majority of those
experiencing orgasm indicated that they did so either via intercourse
or via "petting."

Marriage Value Inventory

The ranked marriage values for Groups I and III were so similar that
no significant difference occurred between them in the mean value
attributed to any item; hence, in the interests of space, we shall list
only the values for Group III, which are broken down by sex and are
shown in Table 8.4. Investigation of this table shows few sex
differences in rank order of the items, and no mean value for an item
that is significantly different between the sexes. The hierarchy of
value importance suggests that our subjects were essentially interpersonally focused, with relatively little professed concern for

Table 8.3

MEN'S AND WOMEN'S REPLIES TO SEX QUESTIONS
(IN PERCENTAGES) (Groups I and III)

Question	Men	Women
Orgasms per week (average)		
0	7 (3)	30 (28)
1	16 (7)	24 (18)
2	16 (17)	16 (23)
3	20 (23)	16 (11)
4	14 (8)	6 (0)
5	9 (15)	1 (3)
6	4 (6)	1 (2)
7	8 (5)	2 (6)
8-14	3 (12)	2 (4)
15-21	2 (1)	1 (3)
22 or more	0 (1)	0 (0)
Self-perceived sex drive [1]		
Stronger than average	30 (43)	15 (29)
Average	66 (51)	77 (63)
Below average	4 (5)	8 (7)
Difficulty in control of sex drive		
Little or no problem	40 (40)	55 (66)
Something of a problem	40 (45)	37 (24)
Definite problem	11 (10)	4 (4)
Difficult problem	6 (3)	4 (5)
Very difficult problem	2 (0)	0 (0)
Chief source of orgasm [2]		
During sleep	(2)	(1)
Masturbation	(11)	(1)
Petting	(40)	(42)
Intercourse	(43)	(27)
No orgasm experienced	(0)	(27)
Response not given	(2)	(0)

[1] A five-point scale was actually used for Group III, but the two end categories have been collapsed for purposes of comparison.

[2] This question was used only with Group III.

economic security, status, and moral and religious unity. Since our subjects were rather well-to-do on the average, it is not surprising that economic security was not a primary concern. Yet it was placed higher in importance than "moral and religious unity," testifying to the weak influence of religion on marriage in the perceptions of our subjects.

Table 8.4

MEAN RANKING AND STANDARD DEVIATION OF IMPORTANCE OF
EACH ITEM OF MARRIAGE VALUE INVENTORY FOR MARRIAGE
BY MEN AND WOMEN OF GROUP III (N = 98)

	Men		Women	
Item	Mean	S.D.	Mean	S.D.
Companionship with spouse	1.59	1.34	1.16	.60
Healthy and happy children	3.23	1.53	3.19	1.58
Satisfactory sex life	3.58	2.07	3.35	1.59
A home where one feels one belongs	4.21	1.81	4.24	1.64
Economic security	5.93	1.82	5.97	1.95
Physical comforts of marriage	6.81	1.90	7.68	1.77
Moral and religious unity	6.82	2.65	6.29	2.30
Satisfaction of being a married person	6.92	3.12	7.09	2.07
A place in the community	7.36	1.94	7.21	1.81
Enjoying the admiration of others	8.56	1.94	8.81	1.62

The Minnesota Multiphasic Personality Inventory

The MMPI as noted above was administered only to Group I. The
profile sheet for the men's and women's mean scores for the basic 14
scales, converted to a normalized score-equivalent (T score), are shown
in Figures 8.1 and 8.2 respectively. These Figures indicate that our
subjects are well within the normal range (30 to 70). The men show
slight peaks for femininity and for mania, but this is quite expected in
college students and reflects the effect of cultural interests in the case
of the first variable, and the high energy and drive typical of college
students in the case of the second variable.

The women's scores were also wholly within the normal range.
Both groups made very few undecided responses, which probably
reflects their interest in the proceedings for which they had
volunteered.

A T score for the Neurotic Triad score does not exist, but since the
score is a composite of three standard MMPI scores and since these
scores were well within the normal range of our subjects, it may be
concluded that the Neurotic Triad scores are also within normal
limits. For the men, T scores for Anxiety, Repression, and Ego-
Strength were 50, 49, and 59, respectively, all within the normal range,
though the Ego-Strength score suggests somewhat better-than-

Profile and Case Summary

The Minnesota Multiphasic Personality Inventory

Starke R. Hathaway and J. Charnley McKinley

Scorer's Initials

Name

Address

Occupation _____ Date Tested

Education _____ Age

Marital Status _____ Referred by

NOTES

Male

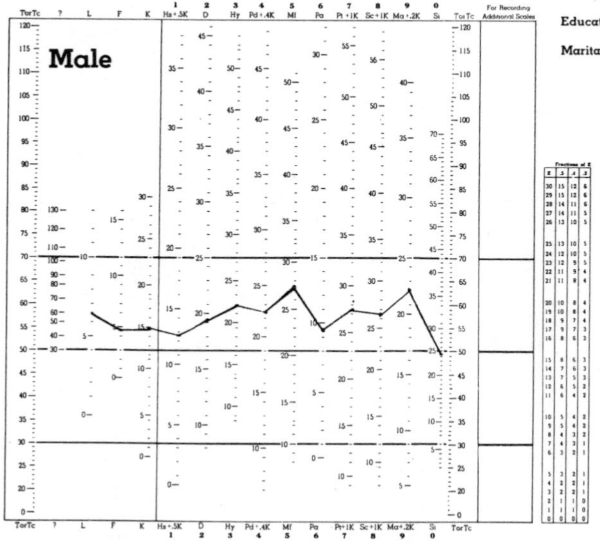

Raw Score

K to be added

Raw Score with K

Printed in U.S.A.

Signature _____ Date

65-1365

Fig. 8.1. Minnesota Multiphasic Personality Inventory mean T scores for male subjects from Group I.

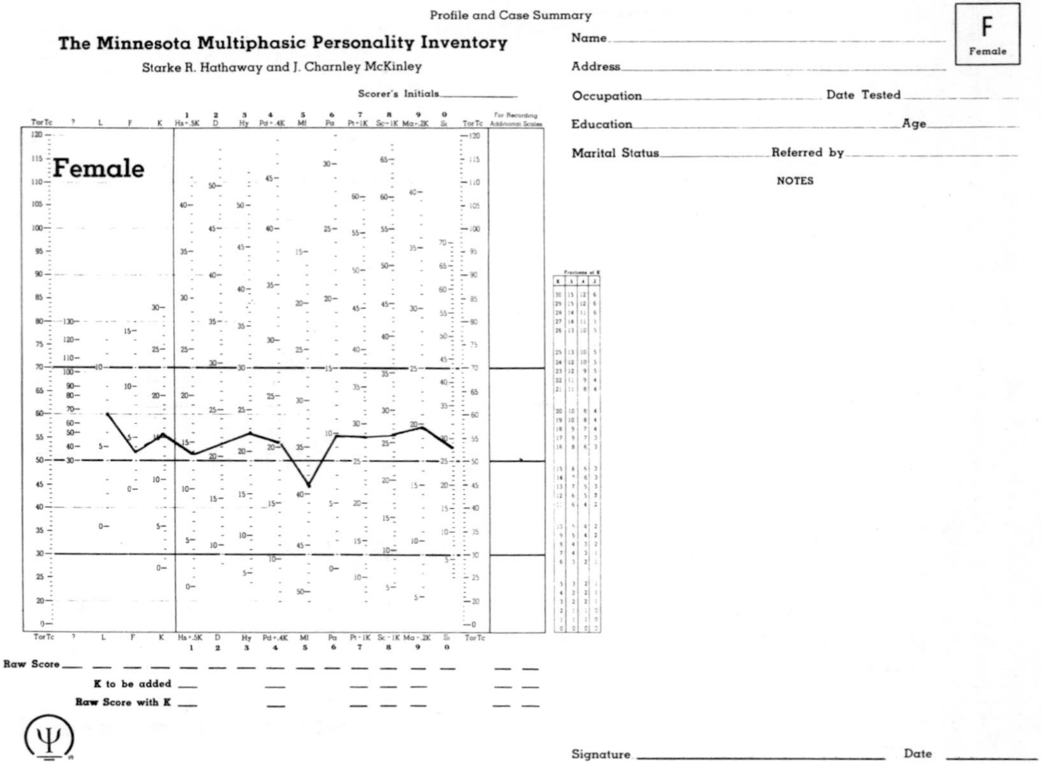

Fig. 8.2. Minnesota Multiphasic Personality Inventory mean T scores for female subjects from Group I.

average ego-strength; however, one cannot be sure because, although the T scores for Anxiety and Repression were obtained with a normal Minnesota population (Welsh, 1956), the nature of the sample used for Barron's Ego-Strength scale (Dahlstrom and Welsh, 1960) is not described.

For women, the T scores for Anxiety, Repression, and Ego-Strength were 47, 51, and 59, respectively, all within the normal range and quite similar to the men's scores. We may conclude, therefore, that Group I is a normal group insofar as personality functioning as tapped by the MMPI is concerned.

The 18 MMPI scores recorded for our subjects were correlated across the 99 couples in Group I, and the results are shown in Table 8.5. This table reveals findings rather typical of those often found in correlation of personality scores between couples—the correlations are mainly of zero order or slightly positive.

Table 8.5

MMPI CORRELATIONS BETWEEN PARTNERS IN GROUP I

Scale	r	Scale	r
Cannot say (?)	.14	Paranoia	.13
Lie	−.10	Psychosthenia	.17*
Validity	−.06	Schizophrenia	−.01
K	.08	Hypomania	−.02
Hypochondriasis	−.01	Social introversion	.19*
Depression	.21*	Neurotic triad	.10
Hysteria	.07	Anxiety	.16*
Psychopathic deviate	−.06	Repression	.04
Masculinity-femininity	−.27**	Ego-strength	.12

*p < .05
**p < .01

The typical low positive correlation may reflect the fact that most roles and expectations are slightly better served by personality similarity between the participants than by differences. Yet Table 8.5 still shows a negative correlation to be the highest of the 18 variables. The Mf correlation of −.27 indicates that men high in masculine interest were drawn to women high in feminine interest. This finding appears to be one of the few cases of complementarity found in our research. A similar finding was found also with Group II, to be reported later.

Revised Personal Preference Schedule (Group I)

The intercorrelation matrix between the eight perceptual sets of the Revised Personal Preference Schedule was computed to supply information for several hypotheses, but it may be of some interest in its own right. It is reproduced in Table 8.6.

This table indicates that our subjects were relatively high in self-acceptance, the mean self/ideal-self correlation being .66 for men and .58 for women. There were no pronounced sex differences, but the intraperceptions (comparison of two perception scores stemming from the same person) for men and women (bisected upper portion of the table and lower right end section) were far superior in magnitude to the interperceptions (comparison of two perception scores, each originating from a different member of the couple). Indeed, the lowest of the intraperceptual correlations (self$_W$, spouse$_W$), which was .38, was greater than the highest of the interperceptual correlations (self$_M$, spouse$_W$) which was only .35. Also noteworthy was the low order of similarity among identical percepts by the sexes. For similarity of self,

Table 8.6

AVERAGE CORRELATIONS FOR VARIOUS "SETS" FOR REVISED EDWARDS PERSONAL PREFERENCE SCHEDULE FOR GROUP I

	Self	Ideal-self	Ideal-spouse	Partner	Self	Ideal-self	Ideal-spouse
		Men				*Women*	
Men							
Ideal-self	.66						
Ideal-spouse	.57	.72					
Partner	.40	.47	.60				
Women							
Self	.13	.18	.17	.31			
Ideal-self	.14	.15	.14	.20	.58		
Ideal-spouse	.20	.21	.17	.15	.55	.67	
Partner	.35	.28	.21	.09	.38	.42	.63

$r = .16$ (p $<$ .05)
$r = .23$ (p   .01)

Note: Ellipse encircles correlations between identical percepts between members of couples.

ideal-self, ideal-spouse, and spouse the range of correlation was from .09 to .17 (dotted ellipse in table) of which only the ideal-spouse correlation, .17, was significant ($p < .05$). Similarity of personality needs on this test does not appear to be an important factor in marital choice.

Summary of Background Data

Our sample consisted almost exclusively of middle- and upper-middle-class white college students whose familial upbringing seems to have been relatively untroubled. They were from intermediate-sized towns, and though nominally religiously affiliated, they were not very active practitioners. Their orgasm rate appeared normative although problems of sexual control, not unexpectedly, troubled some. Their value system regarding marriage emphasized companionship and family interaction rather than material and prestigious pleasures. These answers are, of course, highly "socially desirable." On a personality test (MMPI), the adjustment of Group I seemed wholly within normal limits. On both the MMPI and the Edwards test, the couples showed only a very slight tendency toward similarity of responses. Similarity of personality did not therefore, of itself, seem to be associated with pairing in premarital couples.

CHAPTER 9

Hypothesis Testing
and Physical Attractiveness

The two basic components of SVR theory are equity of exchange and sequence. The data to be presented will deal mainly with the exchange component, for reasons I shall describe.

Ideally, to investigate sequence it would be necessary to have a large group of subjects who could be studied from a point just prior to the commencement of their heterosexual relationships until the point of their marriage. Assuming that there were some way of controlling for the effect of repeated testing, we could determine whether stimulus variables were truly most influential during the initial phase of a relationship, whether and/or at what point they were superseded in importance by value comparisons, and finally at what point role variables came into prominence.

One reason the ideal was not reached is because SVR theory was not fully developed at the onset of research. The initial purpose was to examine some possible determinants of marital choice rather than to test the theory in hypothesis form. The hypotheses to be described all preceded the data analysis, but some of them also preceded the formulation of the theory, although the majority were derived after the scaffold of the theory had been erected.

The subjects who volunteered to participate in the research knew each other on the average slightly less than two years. Such a lengthy relationship would clearly put most of them well within the role stage of relationship, making it impossible to test the sequential aspects of the theory except by indirect means.

Even had the theory been formulated long before beginning the research, it would have been extremely expensive in terms of time and funding to follow a sizeable group of adolescents from the onset of their dating to matrimony. Nevertheless, with the aid of hindsight it might be possible to study the S and V stages by gathering individuals of both sexes who did not know each other. They might be formed into a closely interacting group over a brief period of time in order to study the onset of relationships. By the time this thought had occurred, however, funds and time had been committed to the study of exchange and other aspects of marital choice. Thus extensive examination of the sequential stages of SVR theory remains a task for the future.

The study of equity of exchange poses some problems of its own, which I have discussed in a general sense earlier. As applied to the analysis of data, it is clear that complete equity can rarely be measured because of a variety of operational problems. Equity is to be expected for the sum of all assets and liabilities the individuals possess; consequently, weaknesses on a given trait or characteristic can be compensated elsewhere. Thus, equity for a given characteristic might be expected on a group basis only for very important items—such as, for example, physical attractiveness. Further, not all assets and liabilities are readily measurable. If an individual's assets are in status or physical attractiveness, they might be readily measurable by questionnaire and camera. However, if one member of the couple is handsome and wealthy, and the other, less endowed, performs various services for the "star" that are not measured by the questionnaire, the exchange may erroneously appear onesided to the unknowing outsider. The best way of measuring exchange, therefore, ought to be to avoid focusing on individual traits, and instead attempt to sum up all of the assets and liabilities a person possesses. However, the noting of all important variables and weighting them for importance would seem impossible without a complete knowledge of the individual's past and present. The most that could be realistically hoped for, therefore, is to attempt to measure a sufficient number of important variables so that a partial summation without weighting might give at least a rough measure of the reward potential of the individual.

Criteria for Equity

The two measures most frequently used involving equity were (a) the demonstration of a smaller disparity between members of a couple for a given variable or, a higher correlation than that manifested by randomly paired men and women, and (b) measuring whether individuals who subsequently reported good courtship progress (henceforth called CP) had six months earlier manifested smaller disparities (greater equity) for given variables than had individuals who reported poor CP. The use of CP as a measure of the progress in the relationship of our couples requires some elaboration.

CP as a Measure of Progress in the Relationship

Because most of our couples had known each other at least six months and often longer at the time of initial testing, it could be assumed that they were in the "role" stage of the relationship. To measure progress in this stage, as noted earlier, we asked the couple six months after the initial test to state whether or not their courtship had advanced or slackened. For statistical purposes, it would be most desirable to dichotomize the subjects into two equal groups of those who made good and poor CP. Such an aspiration, however, appeared to fly in the teeth of reality. Most of the couples in Group I, for example, were formally or informally engaged at the start of the study. It might be thought, therefore, that they would suffer from a kind of "ceiling effect" in that they could henceforth make but little progress. This conclusion, however, is clearly based on an "outside" perception, extrinsic to the couple. In actual fact, most of the couples in their own minds had advanced considerably during the six-month interval. Apparently, "emotional space" is boundless, and, at least before marriage, it is always possible to move closer to one's beloved no matter how close one is already.

Of the 99 couples in Group I, in 95 cases both members of the couple eventually returned their follow-up questionnaires. If we combine the CP scores of both members of a couple (the r between couples was .72 and after correction for coarse grouping it was .86) to get our overall estimate of the couple's progress, it appears reasonable to conclude that couples had made good CP when they either believed that they had moved closer together (scored 4) or, though they believed that they had not moved closer, they believed that they had retained their good relationship (scored 3). A combined score for the couple of 6 or better, therefore, was considered to be good CP. Those considered to have made poor CP were those whose relationship seemed stable but not very good (2), and those who were further apart than they had been six months earlier, or who had broken up (1). The cutting score for the combined couple's score for poor CP, therefore, was 5 or less. By these classifications, 79 couples showed good CP and 16 showed poor CP.

For the 19 couples of Group II, complete follow-up data was obtained for 17 of them. Only 2 of the 17 couples could be classified as poor CP on the basis of the above criterion and, hence, it would be worthless to investigate which variables were associated with CP.

The CP scale for Group III was further refined to a 5-point scale, the categories being: "We are very much closer than before and moving toward being a permanent couple, or we are a permanent couple" (5); "We continue to have a very close relationship, and we may become a permanent couple although our relationship has not changed radically in the last six months" (4); "We continue to see a lot of each other but we have not really become much closer in the last six months" (3); "We still see each other but the relationship shows a considerable amount of strain. We are further apart than we were six months ago" (2); "We have broken up and/or are not a couple any more" (1).

Categories 4 and 5 were considered to be good CP and categories 3, 2, or 1 indicated poor CP. The correlation between men and women was .96, so the couples' scores could be combined; hence a combined score of 8 or more constituted good CP and less than that was considered to be poor CP. With this dichotomy, 64 couples were classified as good and 34 as poor. The greater number of poor CP couples in Group III compared with Groups I and II was probably due to the fact that couples in Group III had needed only two dates or more to qualify for participation, whereas the requirement for Groups I and II had been "engaged or seriously considering marriage." (Reflecting back, it was unwise to have only accepted subjects who were seriously considering marriage, due to the resulting bias favoring couples making good CP; however, at the time, we were concerned about people who scarcely knew each other volunteering and becoming a "couple" only for the financial compensation. It turned out, however, that the personal nature of the questions, the fact that participation often led to actual discussion of marriage among previously uncommitted couples, and the length of the tests made our fears unjustified.)

THE HYPOTHESES

Some 39 hypotheses have been formulated and tested. These have been grouped into their assumed chronological appearance by stage in the relationship. Physical attractiveness reflects the S stage stimulus. The value consensus hypothesis represents the value stage. The majority of other variables presumably are most operative during the role stage. These are grouped under the rubrics of role perception, personal adequacy, sexism, and sex. Last we consider variables that do not properly fall into any given stage. These include perceptual and expressive style and the attempt to sum a number of variables across different stages to get a more comprehensive measure of equity than that given by the use of single variables.

It should be reiterated that no tests of sequence are being considered in the reported research. Actually two more hypotheses had appeared in an earlier paper (Murstein, 1970), which are not included here. The reason for their exclusion is that after due reflection they seem such weak tests of the sequence part of SVR theory as to merit oblivion in favor of more potent hypotheses. The first of these hypotheses was *"As a stimulus variable, the degree of similarity of physical attractiveness between a couple should not differentiate those individuals making good CP from those making poor CP during the 'role' stage of courtship"* (p. 478). The second was *"Because 'value consensus' is a second-stage variable, it should not differentiate between couples making good and poor CP when progress is measured during the 'role' phase of the relationship"* (p. 478). Both of these hypotheses were substantiated, thus apparently confirming the sequence parts of the theory. However, failure to reject the null hypothesis is admittedly a weak way of supporting the sequence stage aspects of SVR theory. The failure to find significant differences could be due to a multitude of reasons (inadequacy of the test, low reliability, constricted distribution of scores) besides that germane to the hypothesis; hence the omission of these hypotheses from the present report.

The assumption that physical attractiveness is most operative during the stimulus stage, and that, for example, it precedes the appearance of role variables seems quite logical to me. We respond to the way people look before we get to know them. However, any assumption, no matter how logical it may appear, must eventually be verified by research before it can be accepted as a reasonable approximation of a fact. Accordingly, the hypotheses are assumed to test only the exchange portion of the theory.

The methods used to test the hypotheses include mainly the binomial expansion and correlation scores. The binomial expansion seemed an ideal way of testing discrepancies between partners when it is desired to ascertain whether or not discrepancies between partners are due to chance. The method is explained more fully with reference to the data in Hypothesis 1.

In other cases, particularly with Group I, where the data permitted, the coefficient of correlation was used as a measure of relationship. Where this method can be used, it has the advantage of not requiring any comparison group in order to determine significance, as is the case for the use of discrepancy scores. Despite this advantage, we elected to switch to discrepancy scores for most of the analyses with Group III, because these scores seemed to reflect more accurately our desire to find differences in the strengths of variables among our subjects. The coefficient of correlation measures covariation, and even if there are differences in the mean score of a variable between men and women, they might still attain high correlation so long as they covaried. The result of this heterogenecity of approach will be apparent in the report of data when, because of the change in approach, the same hypothesis may be tested by one method for Group I and by another for Group III.

PHYSICAL ATTRACTIVENESS

Earlier I expressed the view that an important variable such as physical attractiveness might be expected to operate within an equity framework despite the possibility of compensating factors. The first hypothesis therefore was

Hypothesis 1. *Premarital couples will show greater than chance similarity for physical attractiveness.*

To test the hypothesis with Group I, it was decided to create a control group of couples whose discrepancies in physical attractiveness could be compared with the discrepancies of the actual couples. The control group was formed by randomly pairing the physical attractiveness scores of the 99 men and women with each other. To ensure stability, this randomization procedure was repeated for a total of five occasions.

The absolute discrepancies between members of each of the actual couples were computed and a cut as close to the median as possible was made. Using this cut, the discrepancies of each random group were examined to determine the number of discrepancies above the cutting point of the real couples. The probability of the event was computed for each randomization and, by a formula found in Edwards (1954), the average probability of the five comparisons was obtained. An example will illustrate the analysis.

For the photo judgments, the mean of the ratings of the eight judges served as the attractiveness score of each subject. (Judges did not know which members belonged in a couple.) The cut closest to the median for the actual subjects showed a discrepancy between the partners of .5 or less units for 60 cases and a discrepancy of greater than .5 for the other 39 cases. The probability of getting a discrepancy score greater than .5 for the actual group is, therefore, .39 (39/99). What was the frequency of cases where the discrepancy was greater than .5 for the first random group? Inspection of the first random group in Table 9.1 shows that 55 of the 99 couples showed a discrepancy greater than .5. What then is the probability by chance of getting a frequency of 55 or more cases with discrepancies greater than .5 when $N = 99$ and the probability of a discrepancy greater than .5 is .39? The answer to this question is found in a table of binomials (Romig, 1953). (Because the tables are given only in intervals of five, the tables of $N=100$ were used with interpolation to obtain the probabilities.) For the present example, this occurrence by chance is most unlikely ($p = .0006$). The subsequent four random replications vary somewhat, as shown in Table 9.1, but the overall probability was

Table 9.1

COMPARISON OF DISCREPANCY SCORES
FOR PHOTO ATTRACTIVENESS
BETWEEN ACTUAL AND RANDOMLY PAIRED COUPLES

	Frequency of Discrepancy > .5	Frequency of Discrepancy ≤ .5	p
Actual couples	39	60	
Random couples			
Trial 1	55	44	.0006
Trial 2	47	52	.0524
Trial 3	45	54	.1111
Trial 4	50	49	.0132
Trial 5	60	39	.0000

Note: χ^2 for overall probability = 52.21 ($p < .01$).

quite significant (p = <.01); hence we conclude that the photo attractiveness of real couples was significantly less discrepant than that of artificially paired couples. The same procedure was used to test the discrepancy between each subject's perception of his partner, and also between the self-concepts for physical attractiveness of the couple. The former comparison was clearly nonsignificant, whereas the latter was highly significant in accordance with the hypothesis (p = <.01). The self-concepts of actual couples, in other words were less discrepant than the self-concepts of randomly paired men and women from the sample. (In an earlier report (Murstein, 1972c), the discrepancy between self-concepts for physical attractiveness was reported as of marginal significance (p <.06). The procedure used then was to take the third largest (median) discrepancy of the five replications of randomized groups as the basis of comparison. Such a procedure is less stable and in essence throws away a good deal of information. Therefore, the procedure described in this chapter was used wherever practical considerations of time and labor did not obviate it.)

Essentially the same study was replicated with 98 new couples from Group III, except that photo attractiveness, which had clearly been significant in the first study, was omitted, and only 3 random replications instead of 5 were employed, since 3 seemed to supply adequate stability and a saving in computing time for the large number of computations envisioned. In the second study, the discrepancy of the partner's physical attractiveness again was not significantly smaller for actual couples than for contrived ones. The self-concepts of the partners for physical attractiveness, however, was significantly smaller for real couples (p = <.01) in accordance with the hypothesis.

After the intended analysis had been completed, it was realized that the best measure of equality of physical attractiveness might be an intraperceptual one in which the subject compared his perception of the partner with his perception of himself. In accordance with the hypothesis, a significant positive correlation should be found between each subject's self-concept for attractiveness and his perception of his partner. The results bore out this expectation, the r for men's perceptions being .50, and for women's perceptions .45, both highly significant (p <.01). The correlation between couples for objective attractiveness (photo) was .38 (p <.01), and for self-perceived attractiveness .31 (p<.01).

The results indicate that physical attractiveness, both as subjectively experienced and objectively measured, operates in accordance with exchange-market rules. Individuals with equal market value for physical attractiveness are more likely to associate in a premarital relationship than individuals with disparate values.

The fact that the comparison for the couple's respective perceptions of the partner failed to follow this rule is probably due to the fact, as the data reveal, that most subjects tend to overvalue the physical attractiveness of the partner and give him a higher rating than they give themselves; thus the mean self-attractiveness ratings for men and women were both 3.4. The men's average rating for women was 4.1 and that of women for men, 3.9. This higher estimation of the partner seems to result in a ceiling effect for attractiveness, which destroys the possibility of differences being found between random and real couples. It is also noteworthy that many individuals' self-concepts for attractiveness are grounded on social reality to a slight extent, the correlation between self-concept for attractiveness and photo attractiveness being .33 ($p < .01$) for men and .24 ($p < .01$) for women.

From the above we may conclude that although the typical subject perceived his partner as slightly above himself in physical attractiveness, he, nevertheless, perceived both himself and his partner as quite comparable on this characteristic. It is readily acknowledged that physical attractiveness is but one of the many factors influencing marital choice. SVR theory holds that value homogeneity and role-compatibility, which represent the last two stages of this three-stage theory, are also quite important in determining marital choice. But, even if one considers only the first (stimulus) stage, physical attractiveness is but one of a multitude of variables that have been enumerated earlier. However, the fact that equality of physical attractiveness tends to influence marital choice even when these other variables are not controlled testifies to its ubiquitousness during the entire course of marital courtship. In sum, we may conclude that Hypothesis 1 is supported.

PHYSICAL ATTRACTIVENESS AND PERCEPTUAL CONGRUENCE ON THE PERSONAL PREFERENCE SCHEDULE

We have seen that members of a couple showed above-chance similarity in physical attractiveness. However, what is more interesting is to know something about the personological correlates of physical attractiveness. Is there greater satisfaction when equity is present than when it is absent? Also, what are the personological correlates of inequity in physical attractiveness? What are the consequences of physical attractiveness for CP? We shall consider some data bearing on these questions, but first it is necessary to formulate some hypotheses.

Rationale for Hypotheses

To understand the impact of physical attractiveness on perceptual congruence in the present situation, it is important to take cognizance of the status of men and women in society and the value of physical attractiveness for each sex. We have noted that men have always occupied a higher status in society than women and have not hesitated to utilize the power implicit in status to accord themselves privileges that were not so readily available to women. One manifestation of such power has been that men can demand that their girlfriends be equal or greater to them in physical attractiveness. Women, occupying a lower stratum in society, are more likely to settle for men of equal or *lower* physical attractiveness. From an exchange point of view, the men can compensate for ugliness by offering the woman economic security, whereas fewer ugly women can offer this to a man in return. However, although men may *seek* to obtain attractive partners with more confidence than women can, *reality* serves to thwart the masculine ambition somewhat. The sex ratio is close to one to one in young adulthood, and in the present generation it is expected that the vast majority of the population will marry. Also, there is no evidence that women are objectively more physically attractive than men although, as a function of their power, men may emphasize women's beauty more than women can emphasize men's attractiveness. Data on the population of subjects in the present study (see Chapter 8) also reveal no differences between men and women on physical attractiveness as judged from photos and self-concepts of attractiveness; hence it is doubtful that the average man marries a woman much more *objectively* attractive than himself.

Photos constitute objective evidence, and self-concepts, although subject to some distortion, are to a degree corrected by the observations of how numerous others react to one's physical presence. There is, however, another measure of physical attractiveness that is important to marital choice but is more capable of being·swayed by psychological needs—the perception of the partner's physical attractiveness. An individual usually does not discuss his partner's physical attractiveness with others, and status is often linked to the physical attractiveness of one's heterosexual partner. The perception of the partner's attractiveness, therefore, is apt to be a more subjective evaluation than either a photo or self-concept, and to be distorted toward the positive end of the continuum.

When the individual compares his perception of his partner's attractiveness with his self-concept for attractiveness, he develops a subjective exchange ratio. If he sees his partner as above him, he should be pleased. If the partner is perceived as below him, there should be dissatisfaction; however, as the man is more powerful than the woman, he may feel that he is entitled to an attractive partner. This need may alter his perception so that he perceives his girlfriend as above himself even if she is not objectively as pretty as he imagines.

Regarding the woman's perceptions, two things may be said. First, due to her inferior status, her satisfactions should be optimal when equality of perception of the partner and self occur. In other words, although it is typical in marital choice to want an attractive partner even if one is not so attractive oneself, the lower power of the woman should make her lower her sights so as to be satisfied with mere perceived equality or less. Second, because of her inferior status, her satisfactions in a relationship should not be as dependent on the physical appearance of her partner as would those of the man. Powerful men in our society can display their status by the attractiveness of their spouse or cohort, though the men themselves be physically unappealing. Common observation leads to the conclusion that the converse is rarely seen. Most unattractive women do not attract handsome men.

The foregoing leads to the following hypotheses:

Hypothesis 2. *When physical attractiveness is measured by (a) photos, or by (b) self-concept, satisfaction with the relationship will be greater the smaller the discrepancy between members of a couple.*

Hypothesis 3. *Where disparities between members of a couple exist with regard to measures of attractiveness, the situation in which the man is less attractive than the woman should be more satisfying to the couple than the situation in which the man is more attractive than the woman.*

Hypothesis 4. *When perceptions of the partners are compared, a discrepancy in which the woman is perceived as more attractive than she perceives the man should lead to greater satisfaction than vice-versa.*

Hypothesis 5. *When the perception of the partner is compared with the self-concept, satisfaction should be greater in those couples in which the man perceives himself as inferior to his girlfriend in physical attractiveness as compared to the converse situation in which the man perceives himself as superior to his girlfriend.*

The assumption is made that satisfaction with the relationship may be indirectly measured by the perceptual congruence (positive intercorrelation) of the concepts of the self, partner, ideal-self, and ideal-spouse on an appropriate personality measure. Because these four concepts are deemed crucial for interpersonal relationships, congruency among them should signify identity of goals, needs, and values.

That perceptual congruence using these or similar variables is empirically related to marital adjustment has been demonstrated by Luckey (1960a, 1960b) and Murstein and Beck (1972). Moreover, as will be demonstrated later, perceptual congruence has been found to be associated with courtship progress, which may be taken as a correlate of satisfaction (Murstein, 1972b); consequently, there appears to be support for the use of these variables as indirect measures of satisfaction with the relationship.

Our measure of perceptual congruence came from the Revised Personal Preference Schedule. It will be recalled that Group I received this test under four different sets (self, ideal-self, perception of boyfriend—girlfriend, ideal-spouse). Since both members of the couple each took the test under four sets, there were eight sets in all, and a total of 28 possible correlations between the different sets. These measures of perceptual congruence (shown in Table 9.2) were investigated regarding their relationship to the three measures of physical attractiveness used in Group I: photo attractiveness, self-concept for attractiveness, and perception of partner's attractiveness.

Findings

To test the hypotheses, it was necessary to construct high and low discrepancy groups for the various measures of physical attractiveness. The main consideration in formulating a group was that it be sizeable enough to represent substantial segments of the subject pool (at least ⅛ of N). Beyond that, the size of the distribution varied considerably as a result of the varying number and crudeness of categories actually used by the subjects and judges in their ratings. All cutting points were, of course, made prior to computation of the perceptual congruence correlations.

Table 9.2

ALL POSSIBLE CORRELATIONS RESULTING FROM INCORRELATION OF
CONCEPTS OF SELF, IDEAL-SELF, PARTNER, AND IDEAL-SPOUSE BY
MEN AND WOMEN

Male Intraperceptions	*Interperceptions*
$self_M$, $ideal$-$self_M$	$self_M$, $self_W$
$self_M$, $ideal$-$spouse_M$	$self_M$, $ideal$-$self_W$
$self_M$, $partner_M$	$self_M$, $partner_W$
$ideal$-$self_M$, $ideal$-$spouse_M$	$self_M$, $ideal$-$spouse_W$
$ideal$-$self_M$, $partner_M$	$ideal$-$self_M$, $self_W$
$ideal$-$spouse_M$, $partner_M$	$ideal$-$self_M$, $ideal$-$self_W$
	$ideal$-$self_M$, $partner_W$
	$ideal$-$self_M$, $ideal$-$spouse_W$
	$partner_M$, $self_W$
Female Intraperceptions	$partner_M$, $ideal$-$self_W$
$self_W$, $ideal$-$self_W$	$partner_M$, $partner_W$
$self_W$, $ideal$-$spouse_W$	$partner_M$, $ideal$-$spouse_W$
$self_W$, $partner_W$	$ideal$-$spouse_M$, $self_W$
$ideal$-$self_W$, $ideal$-$spouse_W$	$ideal$-$spouse_M$, $ideal$-$self_W$
$ideal$-$self_W$, $partner_W$	$ideal$-$spouse_M$, $partner_W$
$ideal$-$spouse_W$, $partner_W$	$ideal$-$spouse_M$, $ideal$-$spouse_W$

Note: M indicates source of perception is the man;
W indicates source is the woman.

Photo Attractiveness

Hypothesis 2a, that photo attractiveness discrepancy was inversely
related to perceptual congruence, was tested by classifying all absolute discrepancies between the couples of between .75 and 1.75 units
as high (N=38) and those from 0.00 to 0.25 as low (N=40). Then t tests
were run between these groups for each of the 28 correlations referred
to above.

By way of illustration, the first perceptual congruence correlation
(the man's self and ideal-self) was transformed to a Fisher's z score for
each couple in order to work with a normalized distribution. The mean

of the 38 z scores for the high absolute discrepancy group was compared with the mean of the 40 scores for the low group, and a t value computed. In like manner, t values were computed for the other 27 perceptual congruence correlations. Not a single significant t value resulted, as indicated in Table 9.3 resulting in a rejection of Hypothesis 2a.

Additional analyses were undertaken in accordance with Hypothesis 3 to determine whether discrepancy scores between the man and woman (M − W) with regard to sign, that is, whether the man was higher in attractiveness (+) or the woman was higher (−), would show any differences in perceptual congruence. Although 2 of the 28 t values were significant, one was in accord with the hypothesis (woman more attractive than man), the other opposed to it.

To check for the possibility of a nonlinear relationship, a third group, which consisted of couples of zero discrepancy, was compared against both the low and high groups. As shown in Table 9.3 under the Photo Attractiveness column, the results were strictly in accordance with chance.

To test whether all-attractive couples showed more perceptual congruence than couples in which the man was attractive but the woman unattractive, standards of attractiveness were set up. All subjects with mean photo attractiveness ratings of 3.50 and higher (from the 8 judges) were called attractive, and those with mean scores of 2.50 or lower were called unattractive. (It will be recalled that a score of 5 was deemed "extremely good looking," 4 "above average," 3 "average," 2 "below average," and 1 "considerably below average." Considering that regression to the mean would be involved in the group judgments of our eight judges, it seems reasonable to select 3.50 and 2.50 as respective cutting scores for attractiveness and unattractiveness.) As Table 9.3 shows, only 1 significant t value was found between the groups. The same was true when handsome men with unattractive girlfriends were compared with unattractive men with attractive girlfriends. In sum, Table 9.3 shows no photo data supporting Hypothesis 3, that couples in which the male is less attractive than the female are more perceptually congruent than vice-versa.

Last, an additional analysis was undertaken to investigate whether handsome as opposed to unattractive men, or beautiful versus unattractive women showed differences in perceptual congruence. For women, results were in accordance with chance, whereas for men, 3 significant t values were found, all indicating greater perceptual congruence among couples in which the man was unattractive.

Strictly speaking, it is impossible to say with certainty what the expected signifcant t values would be by chance, since the multiple

Table 9.3

SIGNIFICANT t VALUES FOR DIFFERENCES IN PERCEPTUAL
CONGRUENCE CORRELATIONS BETWEEN VARIOUS GROUPINGS OF
DIFFERENT PHYSICAL ATTRACTIVENESS MEASURES

	Number of Significant t Values of Total of 28 Computed		
Type of Score	Photo Attractiveness	Self-Attractiveness	Perception of Partner's Attractiveness
|M - W| absolute discrepancy	0 High N = 38 Low N = 40	6— High N = 39 Low N = 59	0 High N = 38 Low N = 60
	2 (1+ 1—) M > W N = 31 M < W N = 28	7— M > W N = 22 M < W N = 17	1+ M > W N = 38 M< W N = 22
(M - W) considering sign	1— M > W N = 31 M = W N = 28	8— M > W N = 22 M = W N = 59	2+ M > W N = 38 M = W N = 38
	1+ M = W N = 18 M < W N = 19	0 M = W N = 59 M < W N = 17	0 M = W N = 38 M< W N = 22
M attractive W attractive vs. M attractive W unattractive	1— attractive-attractive N = 10 attractive-unattractive N = 5	6+ attractive-attractive N = 24 attractive-unattractive N = 19	2— attractive-attractive N = 36 attractive-unattractive N = 27
M attractive W unattractive vs. M unattractive W attractive	1— attractive-unattractive N = 5 unattractive-attractive N = 5	5— attractive-unattractive N = 19 unattractive-attractive N = 14	0 attractive-unattractive N = 27 unattractive-attractive N = 11
Men	3— attractive N = 21 unattractive N = 18	0 attractive N = 43 unattractive N = 55	2+ attractive N = 24 unattractive N = 14
Women	1— attractive N = 24 unattractive N = 19	1+ attractive N = 39 unattractive N = 60	0 attractive N = 71 unattractive N = 28

Note: M = men, W = women. "High" and "Low" refer to the size of the discrepancy. A plus signifies that the first listed group achieved higher mean correlations (perceptual congruence). A minus sign signifies that the second listed group achieved higher mean correlations.

tests of significance are not independent of each other because the same subjects appear in each test. As a rough estimate, however, assuming independent tests, the number of expected significant ($p<.05$) values for 28 tests would be 1.4. The 3 significant t values are, thus, no more than mildly suggestive (at best) of the possibility that greater perceptual congruence was associated with the unattractiveness of the man.

Self - Concept of Attractiveness

Six significant t values were found for the absolute discrepancy comparison, with low discrepancy in self-concepts of physical attractiveness being associated with higher perceptual congruence than the high-discrepancy group. Analysis with respect to sign, as shown in Table 9.3, indicated that in both the case where the woman exceeded the man in self-perception of attractiveness and where there was zero discrepancy, perceptual congruence was greater than the case where the man's self-concept exceeded that of his girlfriend. No difference was found when the equal and woman superior-to-man group were pitted against each other.

The comparison of the all-attractive group with the man-attractive, woman-unattractive group as well as the comparison between the man-attractive, woman-unattractive group with the woman-attractive, man-unattractive group also revealed smaller perceptual congruence for the group in which the man is attractive but his girlfriend is not; thus Hypotheses 2b and 4 are confirmed by the data from self-concepts.

Perception of Partner's Attractiveness

The results of the comparison of perception of partner (Table 9.3) show that neither absolute discrepancy of perception, or discrepancy with sign, or comparison of the subgroups, or analysis of the sexes separately shows other than chance differences for perceptual congruence; accordingly, Hypotheses 3 and 4 are rejected for this variable.

Although not pertinent to any of the hypotheses, it seemed of interest to compare the man-attractive, woman-attractive group against the man-unattractive, woman-attractive group for our various personality measures. The results were that for photo attractiveness there were 2 significant t's out of 28 computed favoring the man-unattractive, woman-attractive group, and no significant t's for self-concept of attractiveness or perception of the partner. The conclusion of no differences between the groups seems justified.

Perception of Partner's Attractiveness minus Self-Attractiveness

The perception of partner in comparison with the self, as shown in Table 9.4, is highly associated with perceptual congruence for the men's perceptions of attractiveness but only marginally so for the women's perceptions. Couples in which the men perceive their partners as considerably more attractive than themselves manifest much more perceptual congruence than couples in which the men perceive themselves as equal or superior to their partners in looks. The zero discrepancy scores had to be pooled with the minus scores (woman perceived by man as inferior to himself) because of the paucity of minus scores. Tables 8.1 and 8.2 (in Chapter 8) which list the ratings of all measures, show that few individuals perceived their partners as inferior to their self-perceptions.

For women, there were three significant t values, as shown in Table 9.4. The direction of these t values was that women who perceived their boyfriends as equal or inferior to themselves in attractiveness (as with men, only a few cases existed in which women perceived their partner as below them in looks) showed greater perceptual congruence than women perceiving their partner as superior to them.

The subgroup comparisons for men shown in Table 9.4 indicate clearly that when a man who perceives himself as unattractive is paired with a woman whom he perceives as attractive, perceptual congruence is greater than when, from the man's point of view, *both* members of the couple are attractive. For women, however, their perception of attractiveness both in their partner and in themselves yields greater perceptual congruence than does the case in which the woman thinks of the partner as handsome and herself as unattractive.

In sum, Hypothesis 5 that men's perception of their girlfriends as superior to them in attractiveness will be associated with perceptual congruence is strongly supported. There is also a suggestion (not formally hypothesized) that women's perception of equality or slight superiority on their part is also associated with perceptual congruence.

The results indicate that the discrepancy between couples with respect to their self-concepts of attractiveness is inversely related to

Table 9.4

*SIGNIFICANT t VALUES FOR PERCEPTUAL CONGRUENCE VARIABLES
FOR (Perception of Partner - Self) ATTRACTIVENESS SCORES*

Type of Score	Groups Compared	Number of Significant t Values of Total of 28 Computed
$(\text{Woman}_M - \text{Self}_M)$	High N = 58 Low N = 40	10+
$(\text{Man}_W - \text{Self}_W)$	High N = 46 Low N = 53	3–
M perceives W attractive M perceives self attractive vs. M perceives W attractive M perceives self unattractive	N = 28 N = 42	8–
M perceives W attractive M perceives self unattractive vs. M perceives W unattractive M perceives self attractive	N = 28 N = 1	computation not possible due to small N
W perceives M attractive W perceives self attractive vs. W perceives M attractive W perceives self unattractive	N = 24 N = 33	4+
W perceives M attractive W perceives self unattractive vs. W perceives M unattractive W perceives self attractive	N = 33 N = 1	computation not possible due to small N

Note: M = men, W = women. M, W as subscripts refer to sex doing the perceiving. A plus sign signifies that the high or first listed group achieved higher mean correlations (perceptual congruence). A minus sign signifies that the low or second listed group achieved higher mean correlations.

perceptual congruence; however, the tendency for the woman's self-perception of her physical attractiveness to be above the man's perception of himself is also beneficial to perceptual congruence. The most disastrous combination relating to the degree of perceptual congruence is that in which the woman's self-percept is lower than the man's self-percept. The perception of the partner-self discrepancy in physical attractiveness is also similarly related to perceptual congruence in that the man's perceiving his partner as above him in physical attractiveness is associated with perceptual congruence, whereas the woman's perception of equality or of herself as a bit superior to him in physical attractiveness is also associated with perceptual congruence.

These findings are consistent with SVR theory, which holds that individuals with equal marital assets are more likely to pair than those of disparate assets. Since men, as a sex, currently have greater power than women, they will be balanced more equally with women and derive satisfaction from the relationship if they perceive their girlfriends as possessing greater physical attractiveness, thus compensating for their inferior status.

Because men can exercise their preferences with regard to physical attractiveness more than women can, it is also to be expected that perceptual congruence would be more related to their perception of physical attractiveness than to women's perception of attractiveness. The fact that 10 significant *t* values of the 28 computed were obtained with respect to the men's perception of partner's attractiveness minus self-attractiveness, whereas only three significant *t* values were found for women's perception of partner's attractiveness minus self-attractiveness supports this conclusion. Also revealing is the fact that of the 10 aforementioned significant values, 5 resulted from the 6 male intraperceptions (comparison of two perceptions stemming from the same person) tested, only 1 from the 6 female intraperceptions tested, and 4 from the 16 interperceptions (comparison of two perceptions each stemming from a different person) tested. In other words, the man's perceptions of his attractiveness and that of his partner resulted in perceptual congruencies within himself and between himself and his partner, but did not affect the congruencies within her perceptions. Of the three significant *t* values resulting from her perceptions of self and partner, all three were interperceptions. In short, her perceptions of physical attractiveness were not significantly related to perceptual congruencies within herself.

The results with the self-concept also generally follow this pattern. The most effective measure within self-concept was the pitting of the zero discrepancy group against that in which the man perceived himself as more attractive than the woman perceived herself. Eight significant *t* values resulted, with higher perceptual congruence found for the zero discrepancy group. Of these values, three were male intraperceptions, five were interperceptions, and *none* were female intraperceptions. The findings for the self and perceived partner minus self-attractiveness variables thus indicate not only relevance to perceptual congruence in general, but their greater influence on the man's perceptual congruence than that of the woman.

It might be argued that woman are less interested in physical attractiveness than men, and it should not be surprising, therefore, that their intraperceptual congruences are not related to physical attractiveness to the extent that men's congruences are related; however, other work with premarital couples indicates that men's perceptions in general are more significantly associated with good courtship progress of the couple than are those of women (Murstein 1972b). This finding makes it conceivable that women are not necessarily less intrinsically interested in physical attractiveness than are men, but may manifest less interest only because they lack the power to exercise their preferences in this area to the extent that men can.

What of the failure of the perception of partner and photo variables to significantly affect perceptual congruence? The perception of partner does not, of itself, seem a promising variable because of the tendency of most subjects to overestimate the attractiveness of the partner (see Tables 8.1, 8.2) and thus restrict the range and usefulness of this variable. Also, unlike the perception of partner-minus-self variable, perception of the partner alone affords no insight into the exchange balance from the subject's point of view; that is, whether or not he believes he is getting a good bargain.

The failure of the photo attractiveness variable to relate to perceptual congruence requires more extended discussion. Objective measures of physical attractiveness (photo) and subjective measures (perception of the partner) showed significant correlations among our couples, who knew each other on the average almost two years (man's photo, woman's perception of him, $r = .32$ $p < .01$; woman's photo, man's perception of her, $r = .26$ $p < .01$). It seems eminently reasonable that this correlation must have been much higher when the individuals were first drawn to each other and their evaluation of the other's physical attractiveness would have been uncolored by the quality of their relationship.

The passage of time, however, should weaken the importance of objective attractiveness, for two reasons. One is that as the partner becomes better known, the effect of objective attractiveness on satisfaction with the partner is largely supplanted by the rewards and costs experienced in interaction with him. Also, in accordance with exchange, persons of disparate physical attractiveness are more likely to have split and not entered into the role stage of courtship in which the present subjects were; consequently, it is not surprising that photo attractiveness is not predictive of perceptual congruence at this stage.

Though photo attractiveness did not relate to perceptual congruence at this late stage of courtship, we noted earlier in Hypothesis 1 that couples were more similar than chance in photographs of physical attractiveness. This suggests that the stage of effective operation of objective physical attractiveness must have occurred earlier and was relatively inoperative after nearly two years of relationship.

At the late stage of courtship in which the subjects were tested, physical attractiveness may function more as a dependent variable than as an independent one regarding interpersonal attraction. Those persons liked may come to be perceived increasingly as physically attractive, those disliked as physically unattractive. The self-perception of attractiveness, on the other hand, may be demeaned in comparison to the attractiveness of the truly beloved. The Freudian explanation for this phenomenon rests on a transfer of libido from the self to the esteemed object, resulting in a feeling of inadequacy of the self until the beloved returns the libido by loving the individual in return (Freud, 1949a). Stendhal (1947), as noted earlier, also observed the exaggeration-of-partners syndrome, which he called *crystallization.*

My own explanation would be that the need to feel that one has made a wise and intrinsically irresistible choice leads to exaggeration of the qualities of the other. Particularly is this the case for those qualities that outside observers *can readily observe* (such as physical attractiveness) and thereby esteem us as "having something" to land such a good "catch." The measure that is subjective enough to reflect this change is the perception of the partner's attractiveness in comparison with self-attractiveness.

The data as a whole thus suggest that objective and subjective indices of physical attractiveness may operate in different strengths at different stages in courtship. It is also conceivable that different exchange rules operate for these indices. Individuals may be drawn to each other initially by a parity basis of marital assets as objectively determined. As the relationship ripens, however, each may subjectively think that he is getting more than he deserves; thus subjectively, there may be two "winners" in such an arrangement, and members of such couples may develop stronger relationships than couples in which one member thinks of himself as equal to his partner.

Two main points emerge from this study. The first is the suggestion that asymmetry of exchange on a given asset (attractiveness) may be conducive to satisfaction for both partners if the asymmetry is reversed on other important assets (status). The term "suggestion" is used because, strictly speaking, the present study only demonstrates the asymmetry, not the compensation. Although, because of their inferior status, it seems logical to assume that women reward men through services in marriage more than vice-versa, this proposition has not been specifically tested in the present study. It might be of interest in future research to select gross examples of asymmetry such as, for example, an attractive man and an ugly woman. It might be predicted that, in enduring relationships, the woman might either possess unusual status, might be unusually competent in interpersonal matters (a household therapist), or might be unusually adequate in providing physical services (a good bedpartner, cook, housekeeper, mother).

The second point is that exchange probably becomes increasingly subjective as courtship progresses because the various services exchanged in later courtship are not readily observable to the outsider. Stimulus characteristics are most important in the early phase of the relationship precisely because the service potential for exchange is not known. Members of a couple possessing striking disparity in stimulus attributes would be expected to have met, therefore, in "closed" situations where the nonstimulus assets of the stimulus-poor individual come to the attention of the stimulus-rich individual without any commitment on the part of the latter. In other words, if an attractive individual will sacrifice prestige in courting an unattractive one, he must first have experienced rewards in the nonstimulus area. Here, too, we have a worthy research project for the future.

Our last question regarding physical attractiveness inquires about its relationship to CP.

Hypothesis 6. *The smaller the discrepancy between partners on physical attractiveness, the better the CP.*

Our measure of analysis was the biserial correlation. The combined scores of the couple were classified as designating good CP or poor CP, as explained earlier. The continuous variable was the discrepancy in the partners' attractiveness, which was measured separately for each of our attractiveness variables.

For Group I, lack of discrepancy in self-concept for attractiveness correlated positively, significantly, and modestly ($R = .21, p < .05$). For Group III, however, the correlation was not significant ($R = -.12$). Lack of discrepancy in photo attractiveness likewise was associated with good CP for Group I ($R = .25$, $p < .05$). Photo attractiveness, it will be recalled, was not among the measures obtained with Group III.

Group I subjects also rated partner attractiveness, and a large absolute discrepancy was significantly associated with good CP ($R = -.21$, $p < .05$). Inspection of the data indicated that the discrepancy associated with good CP was mainly caused by the man's perceiving his partner as more attractive than she perceived him.

In Group III the absolute discrepancy |Partner — Self| was correlated with CP with nonsignificant results ($R = -.01$). When the discrepancy was computed with regard to sign and separately by sex, the picture was quite different. The tendency of the man to see his partner as more physically attractive than he saw himself was significantly correlated with CP ($R = .37$, $p <.01$), whereas the woman's tendency to see herself as inferior in attractiveness was negatively but nonsignificantly correlated with CP ($R = -.11$).

Hypothesis 6 seems to have received only modest support in that several measures of discrepancy showed significance for Group I but not for Group III. As is often the case, the introduction of a measure in Group III not originally anticipated (Partner — Self) yielded interesting findings—the highest correlation with CP for men but a nonsignificant one for women. The research suggests that the man's perception is more influential than the woman's and that when both agree in perceiving her as more attractive than him (though only his perception minus self measure was significant), the result is good CP.

The finding that photo similarity of attractiveness correlated modestly but significantly with CP raises a question to which no ready answer is forthcoming. The photo variable did not relate to perceptual congruence but did relate to CP. Does this suggest that physical attractiveness rises in importance once again as the decision for marriage nears? We have speculated that this may be the case in the theoretical curves describing SVR theory, which show a slight rise in the S curve during the R stage of courtship (see Figure 7.2). On the other hand, the smallness of the correlation induces caution as to whether it might be replicated in future research. Last, perceptual congruence and CP are not equivalent measures. It is conceivable that CP might advance even with only modest perceptual congruence if the partners felt sufficiently committed to each other. In sum, much as I hate to rely on that old researcher's cliché, it seems nevertheless true—that only further research can clarify this question.

CONCLUSIONS ON PHYSICAL ATTRACTIVENESS

My score card indicates considerable support for Hypotheses 1, 2b, 3, 4, and 5, with mixed support for Hypothesis 6, and rejection for Hypothesis 2a. The score is inflated somewhat because not all the measures of physical attractiveness in the successful hypotheses were significant, though the majority were.

Although physical attractiveness seems an important component of marital choice, the various measures of physical attractiveness differed extensively in their influence on perceptual congruence and courtship progress. The most effective predictor of both perceptual congruence and courtship progress was the man's perception of his partner as above him in attractiveness.

This finding illustrates a number of very important points. First, a measure of physical attractiveness that permits an advantageous comparison is superior to measures that do not. The man seeing himself as getting the best possible deal—someone who is better looking than himself—should be quite content. Second, insofar as individuals can get the best possible deal, they should be content. Equity in exchange is not something for which everyone strives. Rather, it is often the best that can be *mutually* achieved. If, however, one member has greater status, in this case the man, he can cash in his status to get someone who he thinks is better looking than himself.

It could be argued that in many cases, especially within individual couples, women may have achieved equal status with men. It should not be surprising, therefore, that for many of our measures, equity of physical attractiveness was also a significant predictor of perceptual congruence and good CP. In no case, however, did we find that male superiority in attractiveness was associated with CP or perceptual congruence. Apparently, there are few men who, possessing both status and attractiveness superiority, are content to remain in the relationship or to be pleased with it while they are in it.

Last, the man's perception of his partner as superior to himself in attractiveness was correlated with CP, but his girlfriend's perception of him in relationship to herself had little influence on perceptual congruence and none on CP. This finding, along with our other findings on physical attractiveness, suggests that CP is male-determined. Our female sample does not seem to have shown an equal influence with men in courtship, perhaps testifying to the fact that women's investment in marriage for our sample was still greater than man's and her power still inferior to his.

NOTE

Chapter 9 is based in part on earlier work (Murstein 1972c; 1972e).

CHAPTER **10**

Values, Roles, and Perception

In this chapter I shall deal very briefly with the second or V stage of SVR theory. The brevity is not due to the lack of importance of the stage, but to the paucity of attention that values have received with reference to marriage research, as we have seen in Chapter 5. The treatment of values in this research has been very elementary, both conceptually and empirically. The recent appearance of Rokeach's (1973) work on values, however, may have a salutary effect on the study of values in marriage.

As noted in Chapter 5, agreement on a wide number of interests and values is not necessarily related to couple satisfaction. What is more pertinent is agreement on interests and values that bear specifically on the couple's relationship. Accordingly, to investigate the influence of values on our premarital couples, I chose as a model Farber's Index of Consensus (Farber, 1957), which deals specifically with family and marital values. I modified it somewhat, changing three of the ten items and rewording several others slightly. The items omitted from Farber's index included "personality development," which seemed difficult to justify as a value as well as being rather abstract and vague. Also omitted were "emotional security," which seemed to be covered by several other items, and "everyday interest," which Farber defined as "Interesting day to day activities having to do with house and family which keep life from being boring" (Farber,

1957, p. 120). I omitted this item because it, too, seemed vague and diffuse.

The items substituted were "satisfaction of being a married person," "enjoying the admiration of others," and "physical comforts of marriage." These items were believed to cover aspects of marriage not covered by other items, and were also less abstractly defined than Farber's items. The major rewording of an item involved changing Farber's euphemistically worded "satisfaction in affection shown" to "satisfactory sex life," which was what Farber's description of the item seemed to intend. The resulting Marriage Value Inventory is shown in Appendix B. Following the belief that value consensus is conducive to CP as developed in Chapter 5, our seventh hypothesis was:

Hypothesis 7. *Individuals considering marriage tend to show greater than chance similarity with regard to their hierarchy of values concerning marriage.*

In Group I, the median Spearman rank order correlation between couples for the ten values was .71. Using the same procedure described earlier in measuring the homogamous tendency for physical attractiveness, the number of actual couples with correlations above, equal to, and below this median was ascertained. Then five successive random pairings of men and women were made, and the number above, equal to, and below the actual group's median value was tabulated. The overall probability as shown in Table 10.1 was $p < .01$, indicating that the correlation between randomized partners on the Marriage Value Inventory was significantly smaller than that of the actual group.

Group II, it will be recalled, consisted of 19 couples who received depth tests and were intensively interviewed. One hundred items describing each individual were sorted into 9 columns from "most like" to "least like" them (the items are listed in Appendix C).

Identifying data had been removed except for knowledge of the sex of the subject, so that it was not known which men and women constituted couples. Items where my associate Rosemary Burns and I disagreed as to column were resolved by discussion. (A fuller description of the depth measures used to arrive at the Q Sort is given in Chapter 12.)

Of the 100 items, 8 were judged by me to represent values. These were "conventionality," "conservatism," "importance of physical attractiveness in others," "moralistic," "concerned with philosophical problems," "committed to intellectual activities," "judges others in conventional terms," and "tends to be rebellious and nonconforming." These variables were individually tested for homogamous selectivity

Table 10.1

COMPARISON OF ACTUAL COUPLES' MARRIAGE VALUE INVENTORY
MEDIAN CORRELATION WITH FIVE REPLICATIONS OF RANDOMLY
PAIRED COUPLES

	Frequency of Couples $\geq$ Median r of .71	Frequency of Couples $<$ Median	p
Actual couples	51	48	
Random couples			
Trial 1	36	63	.0014
Trial 2	41	58	.0231
Trial 3	34	65	.0003
Trial 4	40	59	.0141
Trial 5	43	56	.0556

Note: χ^2 for overall probability = 51.20 ($p < .01$).

by the binomial expansion method described earlier. For example, the column placement by the members of a couple for "conventionality" was recorded and the absolute discrepancy obtained. The median discrepancy was compared against that of randomly paired men and women, and the probability of random discrepancies exceeding that of actual discrepancies was determined. Each of the first six of these variables proved significantly less discrepant (absolute discrepancies) at the .05 level or better for actual couples than for randomly paired ones.

The Marriage Value Inventory was given again to Group III. The median correlation of actual couples was .67, and the binomial expansion method with randomly matched couples showed no significant difference and even a trend contrary to the hypothesis. All in all, therefore, the data offer only moderate support for the hypothesis. The failure to find support with Group III is difficult to assign to any obvious difference between Groups I and III, who seemed to be very homogeneous with respect to their backgrounds (see Appendixes B and D). A clue is provided by reference to Table 10.1. Although the correlation between actual couples is clearly superior to the majority of randomly generated correlations, there are a considerable number of random pairings that are superior to the actual couples' correlations. This suggests that with respect to the values tapped by the Marriage Value Inventory, the actual couples' degree of similarity is only marginally superior to that of the subculture comprising the college population that took the test.

This interpretation is buttressed by a similar failure of Levinger, Senn, and Jorgensen (1970) to replicate the significant findings of Kerckhoff and Davis (1962), all of whom also used college students, a similar value inventory, and a similar measure of courtship to the one employed here.

The similarity of the studies, however, evokes caution. It is possible that the importance of value consensus is not being appropriately measured by the use of a ten-item ranking procedure. Further research on the importance of value homogamy ought to be undertaken with more extensive and refined measures of values.

ROLES AND PERCEPTIONS

There are many tasks that face the couple in the "role" stage before they move into marriage. Rapoport (1963) has listed nine of these, but the limitations of the type of data collected by the present author as well as a somewhat different conceptual framework dictate limiting the analysis to three broad areas: perceived role compatibility, personal adequacy, and sexual compatibility.

Concerning role compatibility, it may be noted that as the couple's relationship ripens, the members increasingly confide in each other and thus become aware of a broader range of each other's behavior than heretofore. They may also become more cognizant of what they desire in a future spouse and more consciously compare these expectations with their perception of the partner. They likewise become increasingly aware of the impact that their own behavior has on the partner and whether he considers these behaviors to be appropriate. Mutual role compatibility should be mutually rewarding and may result in a desire to assure the continuity of satisfaction by putting the relationship on a more-or-less permanent basis through marriage.

A second task is to take the measure of one's own personal adequacy and that of the partner since, for example, such things as moodiness, inability to make decisions, dislike of the self, and neuroticism may be high costs to bear in marriage. A third task involves the necessity of attaining sexual compatibility, whether by achieving a good sexual relationship in practice or by agreement as to the degree of sexuality that will be expressed during the "role" stage prior to marriage. Throughout the three areas, it will be seen that the roles of men and women are not only often dissimilar, but often of unequal importance with respect to CP.

ROLE COMPATIBILITY

Is the Partner Perceived to Be Similar or Opposite to the Self?

We have noted earlier that research on marital choice has offered lukewarm support to the homogamy principle and even less support to the principle of complementary needs. SVR theory, as described so far, has been in accord with the homogamy principle with respect to the "stimulus" and "value" stages. Similarity of roles, however, is not necessarily advantageous during the "role" stage of courtship. The explanation for the lack of usefulness of role-homogamy lies in a distinction between values and roles.

Many values are experienced as part and parcel of the "self," whereas roles are more often situationally and goal determined. Should the situation or goals change, therefore, the roles may also change. For example, the wife may play the role of the loving homemaker so long as she enjoys the rewards of appreciation and affection from her spouse. If she learns that her husband is about to divorce her, however, she may exchange this role for that of "the woman scorned." Since roles are sometimes behavioral means to an end, it is possible that, in some instances, role-similarity may impede the goals of one or both partners. Suppose that both husband and wife desire to essay the role of homemaker and neither wishes to enter the business world. The result is no family income. It is clear, therefore, that what is important is the compatibility of roles with goals, not whether roles are homogamous or complementary.

An individual's ideal-self may be termed a goal more than a role since it is an end he strives towards rather than a part he actually plays. In similar vein, the goal he sets for his partner is embodied in his concept of ideal-spouse. The extent to which an individual is currently able to meet his personal goals is measured by the discrepancy between his self and ideal-self concepts, and the perceived fulfillment of his expectation for his partner is determined by the dicrepancy between his perception of partner and his concept of ideal-spouse.

To understand why role compatibility for some individuals is associated with perceived similarity of self to the partner, whereas for others it involves perceived dissimilarity, we must consider four perceptual concepts: self, ideal-self, perceived partner, and ideal-spouse. Consider first the relationship of the concept of ideal-spouse to ideal-self. It is to be expected that these variables should be highly correlated if a test deals with personality needs and values rather than behavioral roles, because idealized expectations in marriage are generally similar for most of the individuals within the same culture.

The perception of the partner should also be relatively highly correlated with the perceptions of both ideal-spouse and ideal-self in a society such as ours, which emphasizes free choice. The "dating" structure, after all, permits "shopping around" until some tangible approximation of the ideal is discovered. The slightly lower expected correlations of the perceived partner with ideal-self and with ideal-spouse, compared to the ideal-spouse, ideal-self correlation, should merely reflect the fact that the partner, no matter how strongly admired, never quite reaches the ideal. In any event, we should expect that the perceptions of partner, ideal-self, and ideal-spouse should be highly correlated with one another. Whether or not the partner is really as similar to the ideal-self and ideal-spouse as the subject believes he is, is a question that we shall deal with later.

Focusing on the question of perceived similarity to the partner, it is proposed that, if the individual is highly satisfied with himself as determined by a high correlation between the self and ideal-self, and, if it is true, as has been earlier proposed, that the concepts of ideal-self, ideal-spouse, and perceived partner are highly intercorrelated, then it follows that the individual will attempt to marry someone whom he perceives as highly similar to himself on values and needs—provided, of course, that the satisfaction of his partner's need is not seen as precluding the satisfaction of his own similar need.

If, however, the subject is highly dissatisfied with himself (low self/ideal-self correlation), he will still want to marry someone close to his ideal-self and ideal-spouse since, as noted earlier, these variables are largely determined by stereotyped normative values acquired in the process of socialization. The difference between high and low self-acceptance persons with respect to these aforementioned variables, therefore, would not be expected to be very large, since in a socioeconomically homogeneous population like the present one the participants probably share similar ideals; accordingly, if the self is unlike the ideal-self, this will also result in the self being unlike both the ideal-spouse and perceived partner. To the extent that the low self-acceptance person succeeds in meeting a reasonable facsimile of his ideal-spouse, therefore, he will tend to perceive that person as less similar to himself than would be the case for the high self-acceptance person. The perception of the partner as relatively similar or dissimilar to the self is, thus, largely a derivative of the position of the self with respect to the trinity of desiderata, the ideal-self, ideal-spouse, and perceived partner. Figure 10.1 illustrates this state of affairs graphically, with the size of the correlation between concepts

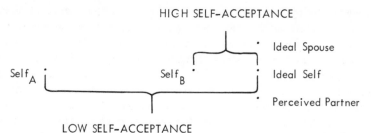

Fig. 10.1. *Where self and ideal-self concepts are far apart (low self-acceptance), "A" sees himself as relatively dissimilar to partner. Where self and ideal-self are close (high self-acceptance), "B" perceives considerable similarity between himself and his partner*

represented by the inverse of the physical distance between them. Our formal hypothesis for this event is as follows:

Hypothesis 8. *Couples with high self-acceptance view their partner as significantly more similar to themselves than couples with low self-acceptance.*

In Group I, the 33 men with the highest self, ideal-self correlations on the Revised Personal Preference Schedule were considered to be high self-acceptance men, while the 33 men with the lowest self, ideal-self correlations were labeled low self-acceptance men. The high self-acceptance men showed a correlation of .73 between the self and the perceived girlfriend, whereas low self-acceptance men showed a correlation of .35, the difference being highly significant ($p < .01$). For high and low self-acceptance women, the correlations were .55 and .30, respectively, the correlations again differing significantly ($p < .01$). Thus, the results of both male and female samples strongly support Hypothesis 8. These data indicate that satisfaction with the self leads to a tendency to choose partners perceived as generally similar to the self, and this tendency is diminished for those persons less satisfied with themselves.

The fact that even the low self-acceptance subjects showed a positive correlation for self and partner is most probably due to the fact that our low self-acceptance subjects were only relatively low in self-acceptance. The fairly high correlations of low self-acceptance subjects between self and ideal-self (.65 for women; .69 for men) may mean that persons volunteering for an extensive study on marital choice generally tend to be quite satisfied with themselves. The second factor contributing to a positive self, partner correlation is that certain items are viewed similarly by most persons of a similar economic status and educational level. Since economic status and educational level are selective for marriage, a certain degree of positive correlation should be found in all items that are not culture-free.

It is not difficult to illustrate that the concepts of homogamy or complementarity, considered without regard to role compatibility, are not very meaningful. Suppose that a man and woman each view themselves as ambitious. If he desires an ideal-spouse who would be low in ambition, but he perceives his partner to be very ambitious, the result will be homogamy of self-characteristics but low perceived role-compatibility. She, on the other hand, may desire an ambitious spouse, and, if she perceives her male partner this way, we have an example of homogamy of self-characteristics leading to high role-compatibility.

The importance of this finding is to support the predominance of role compatibility as a feature of the role stage of SVR theory over the effect of either homogamy or complementarity as predictors of marital choice. Individuals do not seek homogamous or complementary partners. They seek those individuals who meet their ideals, and whether the partner is perceived as similar or complementary depends largely on the individual's self-satisfaction.

Perceptual Congruency, Perceptual Accuracy, and Courtship Progress

The more A likes B, the more he discloses his private world to B. In a "dating" situation, such a disclosure is rewarding to B because it marks him as worthy of receiving intimate information and, accordingly, raises his self-esteem. Moreover, the receipt of intimate information from A encourages B to reciprocate by offering information at equal levels of intimacy. This theoretical sequence of events has received solid empirical verification in the work of Worthy, Gary, and Kahn (1969) among many others.

Once engaged in mutual disclosure, the tendency is for couples to proceed to continuously more intimate cycles of rewarding disclosure. The act of disclosure is not only rewarding to the listener but may serve as a cathartic agent for the discloser. The latter may gain a feeling of relief from expressing himself to a sympathetic listener, as well as acceptance and attention from the other. Individuals who attain ever deeper levels of mutual disclosure, therefore, should make good CP, whereas those who do not reach these levels are more apt to founder in their courtship.

In addition, the level of disclosure reached should have a profound effect on the perception of the partner and on the individual's own perceptual world. Because they have attained deeper levels of disclosure, couples destined to make good CP should become more accurate in predicting each other's self and ideal-self concepts. Also, because intimate disclosure to a friend usually meets acceptance, it increases liking by the discloser; hence, couples reaching an intimate level of disclosure should manifest considerable perceptual congruence between their concept of ideal-spouse and their perception of their partner (partner satisfaction), and this in turn should lead to good CP.

If reciprocity is really operative and couples are equal in depth of feeling and knowledge of each other, then the level of accuracy in predicting the other's responses should be equal. Moreover, the tendency to confirm the other's self image (to see the other as he sees himself) should also be equal, and this equity should lead to good CP. Additionally, if the depth of involvement is equal for both members of the couple, then equal feelings of degree of satisfaction with the relationship ought to exist.

Not everyone in a continuing relationship need feel ecstatic over it. Presumably, individuals with many liabilities and few assets may settle for the best that their market value for others permits. It is likely, therefore, that they may be able to attract only a partner with a similar ratio of deficits to assets. So long as *both* achieve at least a basic minimum degree of satisfaction, both might show good CP if their interest in marriage per se is quite high.

Before turning to our hypotheses, a few comments on the distinction between intra- and interperceptual compatibility seems desirable.

Intra- and Interperceptual Compatibility

From an objective viewpoint, it might be rather difficult for individuals to judge adequately whether their partners would make good spouses. Relatively few persons, strictly speaking, play the role of husband and wife before they are married. Even those persons who live together cannot be said to be completely or even adequately duplicating the marital role, for at least two reasons: (a) each is relatively free to sunder the agreement with little societal disapproval, and (b) the couple does not usually play the role of husband and wife with respect to interactions with the outside world.

The average couple in courtship have seen each other not only for a relatively limited amount of time, but also within only a limited number of roles. In addition, as noted earlier, courtship elicits from individuals the most socially desirable conduct, which, unfortunately, may not be typical of their usual repertoire of behaviors. If couples do not really know each other, but, in accordance with the dictates of society, feel they must be "in love," it follows that (a) the congruence of their perception of their ideal-spouse and partner must be quite high, and (b) if the actual self-concept of one partner and the ideal-spouse desired by the other individual are compared, the congruence would be expected to be relatively low. (It should be noted that part of the difference between the first correlation described above (self$_M$; ideal-spouse$_M$) and the second one (self$_W$, ideal-spouse$_M$) lies in the fact that the first correlation is an intraperceptual one in which both perceptions stem from the same person (man), whereas the second correlation is interperceptual in that it compares the percepts of two different persons; hence, the first correlation should be more reliable since repeated measurements stemming from the same person tend to have less error variance than is the case where percepts stem from two different sources. However, in actual research, the magnitude of the difference between the size of the two correlations in favor of the intraperceptual one makes it highly unlikely that differences in reliability alone could account for this fact.)

From a reward-exchange viewpoint, the origin of liking may be presumed to lie in the similar perceptual outlook of the couple, with the reciprocal rewards this entails. However, although perceived similarity of outlook may initially lead to liking, once individuals are commited to each other, it is the liking that may very well influence the perception (Newcomb, 1961); thus, as we like the other more and more, we perceive him as behaving more and more in accordance with our needs and wishes. If the data for how the partner actually behaves is sparse or absent, we *imagine* that he would behave as we would like him to, nonetheless, because this assumption is necessary to justify our increased commitment to him; thus imagined role-compatibility should greatly exceed actual role-compatibility.

Our preceding discussion leads to a number of hypotheses that I shall list singly, followed by the results pertaining to the particular hypothesis.

Hypothesis 9. *Members of couples will show greater-than-chance equity in ability to predict their partner's (a) self and (b) ideal-self concepts.*

For the hypothesis to be supported, the ability of the man to predict his girlfriend's self-concept had to be closer to her ability to predict his self-concept than was true of the respective predictive abilities of randomly paired men and women. In other words, the hypothesis does not test whether the couple's accuracy is better than chance but whether their equity in predictive ability is better than chance. The same applies to ability to predict the ideal-self.

Only Group III involved the prediction of partner's responses, which were made with respect to the Marriage Expectation Test.

Using the binomial expansion test, both parts of this hypothesis were significantly supported (p <.01). Thus, for example, the absolute difference in the absolute discrepancies |man sees self$_W$ − self$_M$|−|woman sees self$_M$ − self$_W$| was smaller for actual couples than for randomly paired couples. (The subscripts M (man) or W (woman) refer to whether the man or woman is doing the perceiving; man sees self$_W$ indicates the women's prediction of how the man sees himself.)

Hypothesis 10. *The greater the equity between partners for (a) accuracy in predicting the partner's self, and for (b) accuracy in predicting the partner's ideal-self, the greater the CP.*

For Group III, the biserial correlation between equity of accuracy in predicting partner's self and CP was .16, which was not quite significant (p>.05<.10). The biserial correlation between equity of accuracy in predicting the partner's ideal-self and CP was significant (R=.24, p<.5), resulting in partial support for Hypothesis 10.

A more general test of each sex's ability for these predictions occurs in Hypothesis 11.

Hypothesis 11. *Individuals who made more accurate predictions of their partner's (a) self and (b) ideal-self were more likely to later manifest good CP than were poor CP couples.*

As shown in Table 10.2, women in Group III making good CP ten-

Table 10.2

MEAN DISCREPANCY, STANDARD DEVIATIONS, AND t VALUES BETWEEN GOOD AND POOR COURTSHIP PROGRESS (CP) MEN AND WOMEN FOR INACCURACY OF PREDICTION OF SELF AND IDEAL-SELF CONCEPTS

Variable	Good CP (N = 64)		Poor CP (N = 34)		
	Mean	S.D.	Mean	S.D.	t
|Ideal-self$_M$ - M sees his ideal-self|	56.78	13.17	64.32	15.44	2.41*
|Ideal-self$_W$ - W sees her ideal-self$_M$|	58.29	15.52	67.21	15.74	2.66*
|Self$_M$ - M sees his self$_W$|	60.47	11.19	67.06	10.90	2.77*
|Self$_W$ - W sees her self$_M$|	61.09	12.72	61.71	11.85	.23

Note: The higher the discrepancy the more inaccurate the prediction.

*p < .01.

ded to have estimated more accurately at an earlier period how their boyfriends saw themselves ($p < .01$) and their ideal-selves ($p < .01$) than did poor CP women. Similarly, men making good CP were more accurate than low CP men in estimating their girlfriend's ideal-self concepts ($p < .01$), though only a trend was noted for estimating the girlfriends' self-concepts.

Hypothesis 12. *Members of couples will show greater than chance equity between them regarding satisfaction with their partner.*

Satisfaction with the partner was measured by the following absolute discrepancy for men: $|girlfriend_M - ideal\text{-}spouse_M|$. For women the measure was $|boyfriend_W - ideal\text{-}spouse_W|$. Using the binomial method, Group I, who had taken the Personal Preference Schedule, showed extremely significant results in accordance with the hypothesis, but Group III, who had taken the Marital Expectation Test, showed clearly nonsignificant results.

The contradictory evidence may possibly be attributed to the different tests used. The Revised Personal Preference Schedule measures personality needs, and in the present form, at least, it would appear to be sufficiently free of social desirability to have allowed differences to appear in the perceived concepts. The Marriage Expectation Test measures preferences in physique, values, and preferred role behaviors relating to marriage. Possibly, these behaviors are sufficiently stereotyped and loaded with social desirability that when one man's perception of partner was randomly matched with another man's ideal-spouse, the discrepancy was no greater than when both perceptions came from the same person.

It is impossible to rule our completely the possibility that some difference between the subject populations of Group I and III accounts for the conflicting findings; however, this seems unlikely because both groups came from the same collegiate background, recruited only two to three years apart, and their background data indicate that they were highly similar. Another possibility might be that the members of all couples were highly satisfied with each other, so that little variance existed within each group. This possibility may be dismissed when it is noted that Group I possessed a much greater proportion of subjects who made good CP than did Group III, yet Group I showed significant results but not Group III; thus it seems safest to conclude that the contradictory findings are probably due to the "social desirability" effect of the Marital Expectation test.

Hypothesis 13. *The greater the equity between members of a couple for "partner satisfaction" the greater the CP.*

To test this hypothesis, a biserial correlation was computed between the discrepancy of members of the couples for $|\text{partner}_A - \text{ideal-spouse}_A|$ and the dichotomized criterion, good or poor CP. (The subscripts A or B refer to who is doing the perceiving. Two percepts bearing the subscript A indicates that the perceptions stem from the same person—intraperception. Where one subscript is A and the other B, each perception stems from a different member of the couple—interperception.) The result was a significant correlation in Group I ($R = .55$, $p < .01$) and a nonsignificant trend in Group III ($R = .15$, $p > .05$). The explanation for these contradictory findings regarding support of Hypothesis 13 is similar to that advanced earlier for this variable and the tests employed; namely, partner satisfaction is highly vulnerable to social desirability, and this point, in addition to the high social desirability of the Marriage Expectation Test, probably combined to result in nonsignificant findings for Group III.

The general test of the relationship of partner satisfaction to CP is as follows:

Hypothesis 14. *Couples who made good CP showed greater compatibility six months earlier between their conception of ideal-spouse and their perception of the partner than couples making poor CP.*

In Group I, the combined perceptions of both members of good CP couples ($|\text{boyfriend}_W - \text{ideal-spouse}_W| + |\text{girlfriend}_M - \text{ideal-spouse}_M|$) six months earlier in the Revised Personal Preference Schedule showed significantly less discrepancy ($p < .01$) between perception of the partner and the ideal-spouse desired than did the combined scores of poor CP couples; however, the discrepancy scores of either sex alone within the good CP group were not significantly less discrepant than their same-sex counterpart in the poor CP group, though trends existed in both cases. Exactly the same findings occurred in Group III with the Marital Expectations Test. Hypothesis 14, therefore, receives some confirmation, though the effect is not very pronounced.

Hypothesis 15. *Members of a couple will show greater-than-chance equity in their tendency to confirm the partner's self-concept.*

Confirmation of the partner's self-concept in this study was indicated by the tendency to see the partner the way he saw himself. It was measured operationally by $|\text{self}_W - \text{girlfriend}_M|$ and $|\text{self}_M - \text{boyfriend}_W|$. On the Marital Expectation Test (Group III), the results proved to be significantly in accord with the hypothesis ($p < .01$). The question arises as to why confirmation of the partner's self should be significant for Group III, whereas "partner satisfaction" (Hypothesis 12) was not. The answer may lie in the fact that, of the two variables, "partner satisfaction" is more subject to social desirability. Its components are the perception of the partner and that of ideal-spouse, both apt to be highly congruent in a courtship situation. The confirmation of the partner's self on the other hand is less subject to idealization because the percepts stem from two different persons.

Hypothesis 16. *The greater the equity between partners for "confirmation of partner's self," the greater the CP.*

This variable appeared only with Group III. The correlation between it $|partner_A - self_B|$ and CP was nonsignificant ($R = .15$, $p > .05$), despite a trend toward significance. Hypothesis 16 is therefore rejected.

Hypothesis 17. *A perceived compatibility (intraperceptual) variable such as "partner satisfaction" is significantly greater than an actual compatibility (interperceptual) variable, such as confirmation of the partner's self.*

For Group I, a correlation was obtained for each of the 15 need scores in the Revised Personal Preference Schedule between ideal-spouse desired by a subject and his perception of his boyfriend (girlfriend). The mean of these 15 intraperceptual correlations (perceived compatibility) was .63 for women and .60 for men. The mean interperceptual correlations when the ideal-spouse desired by one partner was correlated with the self of the other (actual compatibility) was .20 for $self_M$, ideal spouse$_W$, and .17 for self$_W$, ideal-spouse$_M$. The differences between these intra- and interperceptions are clearly significant in both cases ($p < .01$) and in accordance with the hypothesis.

In Group III, using the Marital Expectation Test, absolute discrepancies between percepts were used instead of correlations between them. The results, nevertheless, remained the same with perceived compatibility for both sexes exceeding actual compatibility ($p < .01$).

Discussions of Findings

Of the 9 hypotheses tested in the perceptual role section, I conclude that four are clearly supported (9, 11, 15, 17), four are partially or weakly supported (by partially supported I mean that a substantial proportion of the tests did not achieve significance, though others clearly did; by weak support I refer to Hypothesis 14, where each sex by itself failed to reach significance, but their combined score did). Only one hypothesis (16) was clearly rejected, though even here a trend in the direction of the hypothesis is apparent. The score-keeping is intended as a summary of the findings rather than as a quantitative measure of the proportion of successes to failures in the theory. This is so because not all of our hypotheses are independent of each other. For example, the fact that the equity hypotheses are substantiated strongly predisposes the general form of the hypothesis toward significance because of the common components in both hypotheses.

Overall, nevertheless, a fairly substantial case for equity with respect to person perception measures has been made. The nature of the variables involved suggests that dynamic reciprocity is involved rather than simple attraction on the basis of similarity. By this I mean that two people are unlikely to be drawn to each other at the beginning of a relationship on the basis of partner satisfaction, accuracy of prediction, or confirming of the self-image. These variables would more likely seem to be affected by interaction and knowledge of each other. Confirmation of a self-image for example, would seem to necessitate some acquaintance with the self-image of the other in order to be able to confirm it. The existence of equity may result from the fact that an individual whose self-image is confirmed tends to reciprocate and confirm that of his partner to the degree that his self-image is confirmed. Those who are hesitant to confirm their partner's self-image probably incur a reciprocal hesitation by the partner with respect to their own self-image.

Accuracy of prediction and person perception scores unfortunately have become almost anathema for many psychologists as a result of criticisms by a number of authors (Cronbach, 1955, 1958; Gage and Cronbach, 1955, Murstein and Pryer, 1959). These authors indicated that accuracy of prediction of another's response is a complex phenomenon with many etiologies other than a simple gift of accurate prediction. For example, some people are accurate because of an ability to differentiate between people, others are sensitive to group normative responses, and still others may become relatively accurate by wisely refraining from extreme judgments when information about the subject is limited. These authors also demonstrated that inadvertantly correlating part and whole scores led to statistical artifacts which marred much of the early research on person perception.

As a result, many researchers have automatically denigrated any research involving person perception scores. Yet the presence of diverse sources of accuracy does not preclude the finding that accuracy of prediction can result from and be a function of the degree and kind of interaction between individuals. Moreover, the fact that equity has been found to exist between couples gives one the choice of concluding that through some mysterious process individuals with identical response sets for item predictions are attracted to each other, or the more reasonable interpretation that accuracy among individuals who know each other over a long period of time is likely to be a product of the kind of relationship they have.

The data in the present system provide some weak support for the conclusion that equity leads to good CP and slightly more robust evidence that partner satisfaction and accuracy of prediction of the partner's responses for self and ideal-self are conducive to good CP. There are several reasons why equity would not be expected to have a high correlation with CP. Many individuals are equitable in their relative lack of satisfaction, accuracy, and confirming tendencies. Such persons would hardly feel the push to advance the courtship, as would be the case for those with strong satisfaction in these areas. Also, it is conceivable that after two years of relationship (the average for our couples), persons perception variables may weaken slightly, whereas variables related to the social network of commitment to parents, relatives, and the partner may become stronger.

A third possible reason for the weak effect of equity on CP is that each sex may not be equal in power to influence CP. I shall discuss hypotheses relating to this power differential shortly. However, we noted earlier that the difference in power between men and women accounted for the difference in satisfaction over the physical attractiveness of the partner, with the man's perceiving the partner as superior in attractiveness leading to greater satisfaction than vice-versa. In similar fashion, confirmation of his image ought to have greater weight than confirmation of her image if he has more power in determining CP.

The difference in the effectiveness of the Personal Preference Schedule and Marital Expectation Test in relating equity to CP deserves further investigation. Whether this is due to their differential susceptibility to social desirability or to the different content of the tests can only be determined by future research.

The greater congruence of the "partner satisfaction" score to the "confirming image" score testifies to the possibility that much premarital compatibility takes place in the eye of the perceiver rather than in the compatibility of the respective perceptions of the partners. Investigation of the possible decreasing divergence in size between intra- and interperceptual scores after marriage and its implication for marital satisfaction would seem worthy of further study.

SUMMARY

A test of the value comparison stage of SVR theory brought partial confirmation of the theory. The question of whether opposites or similars attract was, from a perceptual viewpoint, seen to be artifactual. Perceptual similarity or complementarity was shown to be mainly dependent on self-satisfaction. Equity between couples for the person perception scores as "accuracy of prediction of self and ideal self," "partner satisfaction," and "confirmation of self" was generally greater for actual members of couples than for randomly paired members. The partial exception was speculated to be due to the nature of the test employed.

The association between equity and CP was much weaker, and reasons for the low correlations were described. The superiority of an intraperceptual correlation such as "partner satisfaction" to an interperceptual score such as "confirmation of partner's self-concept" was probably due to methodological factors in part and in part to the tendency of perceived congruence within a single person to generally exceed actual congruence of perception between two persons.

NOTE

Chapter 10 was based in part on these earlier published papers: Murstein 1967a, 1971a, 1972b.

CHAPTER 11

Role Stage Continued:
Self Adequacy; Who's Boss?

The way an individual feels about himself and the degree to which he is neurotic would seem to have an important influence on his attractiveness to others. Feelings of inadequacy and neurotic quirks are not the sort of things an individual wishes to bring to the attention of a prospective heterosexual partner. At first the individual's intention is to win acceptance from the other by putting his best foot forward and to reveal himself slowly until he learns more about his partner and what kind of acceptance he will get if he reveals his private self. For this reason relatively more abstract discussions of values and roles precedes this more intimate level. Somewhere within the role stage, however, the members of a couple learn, directly or indirectly, through extensive observation just how the other views himself, and how well he functions.

It becomes quickly apparent that there are high costs in relating to a neurotic. They often make many unreasonable demands on a relationship, and their perception of the world appears somewhat awry. They often clamor for attention, are quick to take offense for seemingly nonthreatening incidents, and generally demand constant attention and reassurance. Interpersonally speaking they are "heavy."

To a lesser extent the same may be true of low self-acceptance persons. Within the context of our studies, low self-acceptance refers to a large discrepancy or lack of correlation between the self-concept and ideal self-concept. The discrepancy between self and ideal-self on the Revised Personal Preference Schedule correlated .57 ($p < .01$) with the Neurotic Triad score on the Minnesota Multiphasic Personality Inventory (Test-retest reliability of both measures over time varied between .80 and .90.) Although this is a substantial correlation by social science standards, it still suggests that a major portion of the variance of the discrepancy between self and ideal-self is unaccounted for by the Neurotic Triad score. A number of individuals thus may be dissatisfied with their inability to fulfill their ideals and yet not be neurotic. Possibly they have set their ideals too high, or they may think too little of themselves. Whatever the reason, their dissatisfaction with themselves, to the extent that it is expressed to others, is generally a cost to them. It overtly or covertly places a burden on the friend of the low self-accepting person to do something to improve the way he feels about himself.

In a brilliant study, Kipnis (1961) was able to demonstrate that a prime motivation of friendship seems to be to raise one's self-evaluation. Studying changing patterns of person perception over six weeks, she found that the majority of individuals who perceived their best friend more favorably than themselves on a list of personality traits increased in self-esteem over the six-week period. Those who saw their best friend as inferior to themselves tended to decrease their self-esteem. As Kipnis herself notes, "the route to more positive self-evaluations seems to be identification with a positively valued object, even though this means that the self is considered inferior to another individual" (p. 461). Thus, we can better understand another cost of associating with neurotics and persons with low self-esteem; such individuals can do little to raise our own self-esteem. Individuals with high self-concepts generally would not be satisfied with a relationship that promised high costs and little reward in terms of their own self-concept evaluation. If they engage in a relationship with such a person before they are aware of his self-image, they may want to dissolve the relationship once the disparity in adequacy between them and their partner becomes manifest. Thus, high self-acceptance persons should be drawn to high self-acceptance persons, and individuals free of neurosis would likewise seek partners free of neurosis.

But why then should equity work to draw neurotics or individuals dissatisfied with their self-image toward each other? I would argue that the attraction here is a derivative of the inability to attract anyone with fewer costs.

One sometimes gains the impression from the literature on marital choice that everyone sets out to find a partner who can fill his personal needs, and that, somehow or other, each individual more or less manages to find a partner admirably or maliciously suited for himself; hence some psychiatrists (Kubie, 1956; Mittelman, 1944) assume that even neurotics seek each other out. From the conception expressed here that "personal adequacy" is attractive because of its high reward value and low cost, a rather different conclusion is reached. Individuals possessing the greatest number of assets and the fewest liabilities should be able to choose partners appropriately suited to them with a greater probability of success than those who are quite low in marital assets and high in liabilities; consequently, despite the rationalizing process that would tend to force an individual to view his prospective spouse as close to his heart's desire, it is predicted that low self-accepting and/or neurotic persons, for example, should experience less satisfaction with their "steady" or fiancé(e) than high self-accepting and/or nonneurotic persons. Whereas high self-accepting persons "choose" each other because each represents the potential for profitable experience for the other, low self-accepting persons are more apt to "settle" for each other for want of a better alternative.

The preceding discussion gives rise to five hypotheses:

Hypothesis 18. *Individuals tend to choose or settle for partners whose level of self-acceptance is similar to their own.*

Hypothesis 19. *Individuals tend to choose or settle for partners whose level of neuroticism is similar to their own.*

Hypothesis 20. *Individuals are more likely to make good CP when they are going with a partner of comparable self-acceptance than when they are courting a person with a dissimilar degree of self-acceptance.*

Hypothesis 21. *Individuals are more likely to make good CP when they are going with a partner of comparable neuroticism than when they are courting a person with a dissimilar degree of neuroticism.*

Hypothesis 22. *High self-accepting individuals are more likely to perceive their partners as approaching their concept of ideal-spouse than are low self-accepting individuals.*

Hypothesis 18 was tested in Group I by comparing the self-acceptance levels (self, ideal-self *r*) of the girlfriends of high self-acceptance men against the self-acceptance level of girlfriends of low self-acceptance men. High and low self-acceptance were defined as the upper and lower third of the distribution of self, ideal-self correlations on the Revised Personal Preference Schedule disregarding the separate need scores and obtaining one self, ideal-self correlation per person. This correlation was converted to Fisher's Z and treated as an ordinary score. The self, ideal-self correlation of the girlfriends of high self-accepting men was .86, that of low self-accepting men .65, the difference being significant ($p < .01$). Further, the self-acceptance of the boyfriends of high self-acceptance women was significantly higher ($r = .85$) than that of boyfriends of low self-acceptance women ($r = .69$), the difference being significant at the .01 level.

As part of another study, Hypothesis 18 was also tested by the binomial expansion method and confirmed in that members of randomly paired couples (5 replications) showed a significantly greater degree of discrepancy between their self and ideal-self concepts than did actual couples ($p < .01$).

The study was repeated with Group III, who received the Marital Expectation Test. In this case, however, significance was not achieved with members of random couples not showing a significantly greater discrepancy between themselves than did members of actual couples. Hypothesis 18, therefore, receives support in only one of the two independent tests of significance.

Hypothesis 19. *Individuals tend to choose partners whose level of neuroticism is similar to their own.*

In Group I, all subjects had taken the Minnesota Multiphasic Personality Inventory. The 198 profile sheets of the men and women were given to a clinician having some familiarity with the MMPI.[1] Knowing only the profile scores and sex of the subjects, he was asked to sort the sheets into three piles: those with no problems of emotional adjustment, those with slight problems, and those with evidence of considerable disturbance. From his sorting of protocols, the expectancy that both members of a couple would fall into the same category by chance was computed and found to be 51 percent. The actual percentage of times both members of a couple were placed in the same category was 59, and the difference proved to be significant ($p < .03$). An attempt to use a more formal approach was made by correlating the couples for their Neurotic Triad scores. The obtained correlation of .10, although in the predicted direction, failed to achieve significance. Last, the binomial expansion method applied to the Neurotic Triad scores of Group I showed no greater disparity between the scores of randomly selected couples than real ones.

Studies by other researchers, such as Pond, Ryle, and Hamilton (1963), Slater (1946), Willoughby (1936), and Richardson (1939) found significant correlations for neuroticism between marital partners, but these reports, unlike the present study, were done with married couples and did not demonstrate, therefore, that the neuroticism was present before the onset of marriage. In sum, the evidence shows only very slight support for Hypothesis 19. It is believed, however, that the

---

[1] Philip Goldberg was kind enough to serve as the judge of the MMPI protocols.

selective nature of our sample may have restricted the range of neuroticism scores. Our subjects were volunteers from a college group with fairly high self-acceptance. We saw in Chapter 8 that their scores hovered closely around the normal mean. It seems reasonable to assume, therefore, that a more representative population would yield stronger evidence of a positive correlation of neuroticism between couples.

Hypothesis 20. *Individuals are more likely to make good CP when they are going with a partner of comparable self-acceptance than when they are courting a person with a dissimilar degree of self-acceptance.*

For each Group I subject, the sum of the absolute discrepancies between his self and ideal-self concept on the Revised Personal Preference Schedule was converted to a standard score for the distribution of his sex, and the discrepancy between the members of each couple was recorded. This distribution of discrepancies was correlated against the dichotomized criterion Good CP vs. Poor CP. The resulting biserial correlation of .12 although in the predicted direction was not significant.

The occasion arose to test this hypothesis again with Group III as part of another project (Murstein and Roth, 1973). This time, for each subject, the sum of the absolute discrepancies between his self and ideal-self concepts came from the first 76 items of the Marriage Expectation Test (only 76 items were used instead of the 130 item Male and 135 item Female test because the data were initially used as part of another study). The resulting r of .18 just failed to reach significance, and Hypothesis 20 is therefore rejected.

Hypothesis 21. *Individuals are more likely to make good CP when they are going with a partner of comparable neuroticism than when they are courting a person with a dissimilar degree of neuroticism.*

In Group I, the mean correlation between partners on the Neurotic Triad making good CP six months after the administration of the test was .33, whereas for those making poor CP it was −.53. The difference between these coefficients is quite highly significant ($p < .01$) and substantiates the hypothesis; however, a subsequent test of the same data (for purposes other than the present one) showed only a nonsignificant biserial R of .15 between CP and smallness of discrepancy between members of the couple for the Neurotic Triad. The hypothesis was tested somewhat differently in each of the cases and the significant levels would not be expected to be identical. Nevertheless, Hypothesis 21 cannot be said to have gained reasonably clear support.

Hypothesis 22. *High self-acceptance individuals are more likely to perceive their partners as approaching their concept of ideal-spouse than are low self-acceptance individuals.*

In Group I, the correlation for high self-acceptance men between perception of the ideal-spouse and girlfriend on the Marital Expectation Test was .88 whereas for the low self-acceptance men it was .70, a highly significant difference ($p <.01$). For high self-acceptance and low self-acceptance woman, the respective correlations were .86 and .69. These correlations were also significantly different ($p <.01$), thus strongly confirming the hypothesis.

It might be argued that we are dealing here with response sets that have little implication for behavior. In this vein it could be argued that individuals deciding to gloss over their personal failures and to see only "good" (high self-accepters) would naturally extend the same courtesy vis-à-vis their beloved's faults and see the beloved as approaching their heart's desires regarding a spouse (partner satisfaction). However, Hypothesis 14 indicated a small but significant tendency for those perceiving congruency betweeen their partners and their ideal-spouses to make better CP than those less satisfied; hence there is some evidence that this person perception measure has a behavioral correlate.

Other evidence supporting the concept of self-esteem (which appears closely allied to that of self-acceptance) as an important asset influencing interpersonal attraction comes from Walster (1965) and from Kiesler and Baral (1970). The former found that female subjects undergoing an experimentally induced experience that enhanced their self-esteem were more likely to reject the advances of a male research assistant than were subjects who were made to experience a reduction in their self-esteem.

The enhancing of self-esteem presumably added to the self-perceived assets of the women; hence they were probably more likely to perceive themselves as superior to the male assistant who approached them than women whose self-perceived assets had diminished due to a drop in their self-esteem.

Conversely, Kiesler and Baral found that male subjects experiencing a treatment designed to enchance self-esteem were more likely to approach an attractive female confederate for a "date" than were men who received an experimental treatment that lowered their self-esteem. On the other hand, the diminished self-esteem men were more likely than the enhanced self-esteem men to approach a less attractive female confederate. The above studies are consistent with the thesis that low self-esteem persons aim lower in their interpersonal choices than do high self-esteem individuals. The support for the "personal adequacy" hypothesis also indicates that it is a key factor in marital choice.

Hypothesis 23. *Individuals relatively high on the Neurotic Triad scale are less likely to perceive their partners as approaching their concept of ideal-spouse than are persons with low Neurotic Triad scores.*

Individuals in the upper third of the distribution of Neurotic Triad scores for their sex were considered "neurotic," whereas individuals in the lower third were called "normal."

For Group I, taking the Revised Personal Preference Schedule, the correlation of girlfriend and ideal-spouse as perceived by the "neurotic" male was .77. The same correlation for normal men was .84, the difference being significant at the .05 level. For women, the respective correlations were .79 and .83, the difference not being significant. Hypothesis 23, therefore, is confirmed only for men.

One reason for these somewhat equivocal results might be that although neuroticism is considered a liability and neurotics are paired with neurotics at a greater-than-chance expectancy, not all neurotics pair with neurotics. A neurotic who had a compensating quality might be paired with a nonneurotic; hence there would be no reason for the neurotic to be dissatisfied with his partner. As a more stringent test of the hypothesis, therefore, neurotics paired with neurotics might be compared with nonneurotics paired with nonneurotics. With this classification, 13 all-neurotic couples (defined as each member of the couple having a score falling in the lower third of the Neurotic Triad distribution for their sex) were compared with 37 nonneurotic couples (neither partner classified as neurotic). The partner satisfaction (ideal-spouse $_M$, girlfriend $_M$) correlation for neurotic men was .80, that for nonneurotic men .84, the difference not being significant. The partner satisfaction (ideal-spouse $_W$, boyfriend $_W$) correlation was .79 for neurotic women and .80 for nonneurotic women, the difference again not being significant.

One factor contributing to the failure to differentiate neurotics and nonneurotics is that both groups tend to idealize their partner and to find them very close to their ideal-spouse as evidenced by the magnitude of the "partner satisfaction" correlations, which hovered around .80. Given that most of these couples were moving on to marriage, such idealization is not unusual. It does impose a "ceiling effect," however, so that it is rather difficult to differentiate between individuals where the low score signifies partner satisfaction only slightly less than ecstasy.

Another reason Hypothesis 23 may have received only meager support is that our subjects were essentially normal, and the combined effect of two relative small groups and a constricted distribution of people with little real neurosis might cause the lack of association between neuroticism and partner satisfaction. Accordingly, it was decided to utilize the entire population of subjects and to correlate the Neurotic Triad score with the men's and the women's perceived partner, ideal-spouse correlation, treating the latter correlation as a score after converting it for each couple to Fisher's Z. The correlation for men was −.26 and for women −.27, both modest in size but statistically significant (p <.01). Neuroticism, in short, was somewhat inversely related to "partner satisfaction" when the total population was used.

It is possible to argue that neurotics are not really more dissatisfied with each other than nonneurotics; they just complain more, in keeping with their neurosis. According to this hypothesis, a person who gets a high Neurotic Triad score will thereby evince a tendency not only to complain about himself but about his partner as well; thus he should manifest a lower partner satisfaction correlation than the nonneurotic (a noncomplainer) shows with respect to his partner.

The veridicality of the "complaining hypothesis" might be tested by comparing "partner satisfaction" for the case in which a neurotic was courting a normal person with a normal courting a normal person. To make this test, all cases in which a neurotic man (upper third of male Neurotic Triad score) was courting a normal woman (lower third of female Neurotic Triad score) and in which a neurotic woman was courting a normal man were compiled. There were 11 of the former and 10 of the latter; making 21 cases in all.

The "partner satisfaction" mean for this pooled group of neurotics, combining men and women, was compared with the "partner satisfaction" mean of the normals. If the "complaining hypothesis" were true, the neurotics ought to be less satisfied with their normal partners than the normals with their normal partners. According to SVR theory, however, the neurotics should not be dissatisfied with their normal partners for either of two reasons: (1) the neurotic was benefitting from having a close personal relationship with a normal; (2) the neurotic would feel equal to the normal partner because the neurotic would possess compensatory assests of beauty, intelligence, etc. The neurotic courting a normal, in short had little to complain about. A t test between the two groups was clearly nonsignificant (t =.27); hence the neurotics did not complain more about their partner than the normals, and the "complaining hypothesis" received no support.

Neuroticism and Perceptual Congruence

A more general form of Hypothesis 23 would be:

Hypothesis 24. *Neurotics courting neurotics show less perceptual congruence on the Revised Personal Preference Schedule "sets" than do nonneurotics courting nonneurotics.*

This prediction was predicated on the belief that neurotics tend to misperceive both themselves and their partners as a result of their neuroses. Each subject had taken the Edwards test under four sets: self, ideal-self, perceived partner, ideal-spouse. Since each sex had taken the four sets, there were eight sets in all, which when combined into all possible combinations of two sets at a time yielded 28 correlations.

The hypothesis was substantiated in that 8 of the 28 correlations were significantly lower for neurotic pairs than for nonneurotic pairs as shown in Table 11.1.

It might be thought, however, that perhaps the differences in perceptual congruence between neurotics and nonneurotics are due to the difference in perception of needs for the self, ideal-self, spouse, and

Table 11.1

SIGNIFICANT t VALUES BETWEEN NEUROTIC AND NONNEUROTIC COUPLES USING THE REVISED PERSONAL PREFERENCE SCHEDULE ITEMS

Variables Compared	Neurotic Mean r	Nonneurotic Mean r	t
$Self_M$, ideal-self$_M$	.71	.82	2.29*
$Self_M$, boyfriend$_W$	−.13	.03	1.71*
Ideal-self$_M$, self$_W$	−.15	.05	2.33*
Ideal-self$_M$, ideal-spouse$_W$	−.07	.09	1.72*
Ideal-spouse$_M$, ideal-spouse$_W$	−.27	.02	3.18**
Ideal-spouse$_M$, boyfriend$_W$	−.23	.03	3.22**
Girlfriend$_M$, ideal-spouse$_W$	−.19	.01	2.64**
Girlfriend$_M$, boyfriend$_W$	−.19	−.02	2.03*

Note: The subscripts M or W indicate whether the man or woman is doing the perceiving.

*$p <$ .05 for one-tailed test.
**$p <$ .01 for one-tailed test.

ideal-spouse. To test this possibility, *t* tests were computed for each of the 15 Edwards Personal Preference Schedule need scores over each of the 4 perceptual sets, yielding a total of 60 *t* tests for each sex. Neurotic and nonneurotic men differed significantly (p <.05) on only 3 of the 60 *t* tests, and neurotic and nonneurotic women differed on 1 of 60 tests, findings that are consistent with chance expectations. It can be concluded, therefore, that neurotics and nonneurotics did not differ in their expectations for themselves and others for the various needs. It was a general overall difference in perceptual congruence that differentiated the groups.

Regarding this difference, Table 11.1 indicates that apart from the self, ideal-self correlation for the men, all of the other significant differences between the neurotic and nonneurotic groups resulted from negative correlations for the neurotic group and zero-order correlations for the nonneurotic group. In truth, therefore, it is not so much the perceptual congruence of the nonneurotic group which separates them from the neurotics as it is the latter's conflicting perceptions compared to the former's noncorrelated perceptions.

In reviewing the data for neurotics, the conclusion I reach is that the support for neurotics choosing each other is only marginal at best. The repeated statistical tests tend to enhance the probability of finding a significance value eventually. The only justification for badgering the data lies in the fact that there were probably few if any severe neurotics in our population. Not only were all three component scores that make up the Neurotic Triad score well within normal limits, the standard deviation of the distribution was between one-fifth and one-sixth of the mean, about what would be expected in a normal distribution. In short, using the usual cutoff of abnormality on the MMPI — two standard deviations above the mean — it is doubtful that our population contained as much as ten percent of individuals who would be classified as clearly neurotic by the Minnesota test. Yet to work with reasonable numbers in our comparisons, we classified 33 percent of our subjects as "neurotic." The small degree of difference between our "normals" and "neurotics" has undoubtedly adversely affected our attempts to find differences between them on other variables. It would be advisable in future research either to include subjects functioning less well or to use such a large number of subjects that very extreme scores could be chosen and classified as "neurotics" and yet sufficient frequencies would be included so as to permit meaningful analysis.

Discussion

The data on equity in personal adequacy show evidence of statistical support, but, all in all, it is weak support. Among the two variables of personal adequacy, self-acceptance and neuroticism, support is stronger for the former. Among the two tests of adequacy, the existence of equity among couples is easier to demonstrate than equity leading to good CP.

Self-acceptance is probably superior to neuroticism in demonstrating equity because it is less selected out by both a college environment and the process of courtship. Some individuals dissatisfied with themselves are probably very ambitious, and this drive may make them excel in school as well as be attractive to members of the opposite sex lacking in such drive. It is possible to be dissatisfied with oneself and yet have the resources to better this state of affairs.

Neurotics, on the other hand, are dissatisfied with themselves and generally function less well thereby. Their neuroses may prohibit them from drawing on their full capacities, and they expend so much energy on their neuroses that they have little left for personal growth. This inability to capitalize on their resources makes it less likely that severe neurotics can maintain the discipline and concentration necessary to successfully navigate high school and survive the early college period. There are also apt to be more costs for others in relating to them compared to low self-accepters, so that they are less likely to engage in steady relationships.

In sum, it is suggested that our college population was more selected for lack of neurosis than for lack of self-acceptance. Trying to find differences between the extremes of a group in which the most extremely neurotic members have already been screened out is obviously going to be less successful than working with a variable such as self-acceptance in which less selection has occurred.

CP also had probably undergone considerable selection for our subjects. The couples had gone together on the average slightly less than two years. By that point, a considerable number may have decided, without necessarily communicating this to their partner, that they wanted to or felt obliged to marry their partner. Two years is a long time to take up of a post-adolescent's life, and length of courtship undoubtedly breeds commitment in some people regardless of their degree of fulfillment in the relationship. Thus, length of courtship should serve to weaken the influence of personal adequacy variables on CP. Wherever possible, therefore, future research ought to seek to involve not only more representative populations but to study them on a more longitudinal basis than the six months of role stage studied here. In saying this, I am, alas, fully aware that practical considerations of time and money may necessitate departure from the ideal.

The Revised Personal Preference Schedule demonstrated an ability to differentiate real couples from artificial ones on the basis of equity, which the Marital Expectation Test did not. A possible cause for this on the basis of greater sexual desirability of the Marital Expectation Test has been discussed earlier.

A last possibility is that self-acceptance and neuroticism are of only limited influence in consideration of equity and courtship progress. Conceivably some peoples' personal adequacy problems may be largely internal and may not necessarily intrude into their interpersonal relationships to a great extent. The male student with father-authority problems may be much more comfortable in heterosexual encounters. The female student who is convinced that she is stupid in class may avoid, perhaps temporarily, such feelings of inadequacy when her beauty attracts many admirers. In sum, equity in personal adequacy in the present study seems to play a role in courtship, but not a very pronounced one.

WHO'S BOSS?, OR THE GREATER IMPORTANCE OF THE MAN IN COURTSHIP

From the dawn of recorded time, men have manifested greater control over their partner's behavior than have women. In the United States, even as late as the nineteenth century, men denied women full legal status, political franchise, and equal economic opportunity (Murstein, 1947a). Currently, most of these inequities have been greatly reduced, but it is true nevertheless that economic and social power is still disproportionately distributed by sex, with the average woman still less powerful than the average man.

The cost of abstaining from marriage is still perceived by the average woman as greater for her than for the man—for good reason. The status of the unmarried woman is lower than that of the unmarried man; her economic skills are apt to be inferior and, hence, less rewarded in the market. To compound the difficulty, the age difference between marriageable men and women, the women's shorter age range of marriageability, and their longer life-span put them in greater supply and in less demand than men.

Starting in middle age and beyond, the number of unmarried women constantly increases in comparison to the number of unmarried men. This difference in need for marriage is a direct reflection of the difference in power between the sexes.

It is true that many professional women are far from eager to rush into matrimony, but these women constitute a small fraction of the total population of American women. It is further true that, once they are married, many women become aware that traditional marriage roles generally favor men over women. This is hardly surprising since the more powerful generally create more attractive roles for themselves than they assign to those wielding lesser power.

I would also acknowledge that a minority of women exercise more power than men in the relationship. The fact that this is atypical may be gleaned by the way such power is exercised. A domineering man usually makes no bones about his dominance; indeed he may glory in it. A dominant woman is more often a "gray eminence" behind the throne, rarely expressing her dominance publicly, and often ruling more out of a vacuum of leadership provided by the man than from personal desire for the role (Blood and Wolfe, 1960). Our immediate concern, however, is not reactions to marriage roles after marriage, but the motivation for marriage for each sex. Within this context, the woman's greater dependency on marriage for status can scarcely be questioned.

The effect of this greater power and status of men is that, in courting situations, the man is usually . . . the one who usually takes the most active role. He often is the one who actively initiates the relationship by asking for a date. He also is more often the one who is the first to commit himself to the relationship and who, in the everyday aspects of the courtship, decides about such activities as dinner arrangements, movies, and dances. The woman occupies the more passive role as the recipient of the man's wooing. She is not as likely to manifest signs of disturbance during the courtship simply because she has less role-prescribed need to initiate the contact and to make decisions . . . If she accepts the man as a legitimate suitor, he is expected to shoulder most of the interpersonal responsibilities from that point on. (Murstein, 1967b, p. 450)

The result is that although the greatest likelihood of good CP occurs when both members of a couple possess the same degree of neuroticism, the impact of neuroticism for the relationship when only one member is neurotic should be greater when the neurotic partner is the man.

Hypothesis 25. *Courtship progress is impaired more by neuroticism in the man than by neuroticism in the woman.*

The Group I data substantiated this hypothesis in that, by means of a chi-square analysis, good CP was found to be significantly associated with the mental health (low Neurotic Triad score) of the man ($p < .01$) but not with that of the woman.

Turning our attention to the question of correlates of power in marital choice, it can be reasoned that if the man's power in marital choice is greater than that of his partner, confirmation by the woman of his self and ideal-self concepts should have greater consequences for CP than confirmation of the woman's self and ideal-self concepts. The man's tendency to reinforce the woman's self and ideal-self image should make her like him a great deal but should not affect CP as much as in the former case, because it is the man who usually proposes. Moreover, since the initial step is up to him, and because she has more at stake in marriage than he does, the woman will focus on his needs and self-image more than he will on hers; as a result, women who make good CP should be able to predict their boyfriends' self and ideal-self images with greater accuracy than women who do not make good CP. Conversely, the lesser importance of the woman's self and ideal-self images should be reflected in the fact that good and poor CP men should not differ as much in their ability to predict their partners' self and ideal-self concepts.

The greater importance of the man should also make his intraperceptual world more important to CP than the intraperceptual world of the woman. For example, our men were asked to fill out the Marriage Expectation Test under eight different "sets" (1) self, (2) ideal-self, (3) partner, (4) ideal-spouse, and prediction of how his partner perceives his, (5) self, (6) ideal-self, (7) perception of her, (8) ideal-spouse. These sets may be paired with each other to yield 28 possible combinations of two sets. If the man's perceptual congruencies are more important for good CP than are the woman's, then good CP men ought to be distinguished by the smallness of discrepancies between pairs of perceptual sets as compared to poor CP men. If women are of lesser influence in determining CP, no difference would be expected in perceptual congruence between good and poor CP women.

The alleged greater importance of confirming and predicting the man's self and ideal-self and the greater importance of intraperceptual congruence for him lead to the following three hypotheses:

Hypothesis 26. *Confirmation of the man's self and ideal-self concepts through the perceptions of his girlfriend (a) will be followed six months later by good CP, whereas confirmation of the woman's self and ideal-self concepts by the perceptions of her boyfriend (b) will not be as strongly associated with good CP.*

It will be recalled that confirmation of self and ideal-self were measured operationally by the tendency to perceive the partner's self and ideal-self in accordance with the way the partner perceived these concepts. "Confirmation" was interpreted broadly. If, for example, the woman's perception of her boyfriend or her concept of ideal-spouse were similar to his self and ideal-self concepts in all possible pairings, then confirmation was achieved. The four pairings thus tested in Hypothesis 26 were: $|$self$_M$ − ideal-spouse$_W|$, $|$self$_M$ − boyfriend$_W|$, $|$ideal-self$_M$ − ideal-spouse$_W|$, $|$ideal-self − boyfriend$_W|$.

The mean discrepancy scores for each of the variables was computed for the 64 good CP women and the 34 poor CP women of Group III on the Marital Expectation Test and t tests computed. Three of the four variables showed significantly smaller discrepancies for good CP women than for poor CP women at the .05 level or better for a one-tailed test (the $|$self $_M$ − ideal-spouse$_W|$ score was significant in accord with the hypothesis at the .01 level). The $|$ideal-self $_M$ − boyfriend$_W|$ discrepancy was not significant ($t = .92$).

The converse measures with respect to the man's perceptions of the woman and of his ideal-spouse tending to be congruent with her self and ideal-self concepts were likewise tested. Only one of the four t tests was significant. The $|$ideal-self$_W$ − ideal-spouse$_M|$ discrepancy was significantly smaller for good CP women than for poor CP women ($p < .05$).

Hypothesis 27. *The association between predictive accuracy and CP will be greater for women than for men.*

The prediction was confirmed for the self-concept in that the biserial correlation between accuracy of prediction by women and CP was .65 while that for men was .06, the difference being significant at the .01 point. However, contrary to expectation, both men and women showed high correlations between accuracy of prediction of the ideal-self of the partner and CP. The correlation values for men and women respectively were .61 and .63, and the difference was not significant.

Hypothesis 28. *Intraperceptual congruencies (the tendency for any two perceptual sets of a person to be similar) of good CP men (a) should be significantly higher than for poor CP men. Since the perceptions of women have less of a determining significance, (b) the intraperceptual congruencies of good CP women should not differ significantly from those of poor CP women.*

In Group III, on the Marital Expectation Test, good CP men were significantly more congruent (less discrepant) than poor CP men on the following 8 of a total of 28 possible intraperceptual comparisons (all are men's perceptions): $|$ideal-self − ideal-spouse$|$, $|$ideal-self − prediction of how girlfriend perceives ideal-spouse$|$, $|$ideal-self − prediction of girlfriend's ideal-self$|$, $|$ideal-self − prediction of girlfriend's self$|$, $|$ideal-self − woman's prediction of boyfriend$|$, $|$perception of girlfriend – prediction of how girlfriend sees boyfriend|, |self – prediction of how girlfriend sees ideal-self|, |self – prediction of how girlfriend sees self|. Only 1 intraperceptual comparison out of 28 differentiated good and poor CP women: |boyfriend – prediction of boyfriend's perception of ideal-self|.

DISCUSSION

Hypotheses 25, 26, 27, and 28 are reasonably confirmed. CP was more affected by male neurosis than by female neurosis, by confirmation of the male self and ideal-self concepts more than by confirmation of the woman's self and ideal-self concepts, by the woman's greater predictive accuracy of the man than vice-versa, and by perceptual congruency within the man's intraperceptions as opposed to within the woman's intraperceptions. The evidence is somewhat stronger concerning confirmation and prediction of the man's self than for his ideal-self, probably because the former is less subject to culture stereotyping than the latter.

The data stand on their own, but the attribution of the results to the greater power of the man requires further elaboration. Might it not be argued that instead of the women flattering the male self and ideal-self images, those men whose self and ideal-self concepts conform to the images of the partner held by the woman make better CP than those who do not live up to this image? Such an explanation would put the seat of power in the hands of women.

There are several things wrong with such an argument. For one thing, it flies in the teeth of common everyday observation, not to mention the complaints of women's liberation groups. Second, women who accurately predicted the man's self image made good CP, whereas men's accuracy in this regard was unrelated to CP. It is difficult to argue that women have predictions of how men will answer, and men who somehow divine those predictions make good CP. Last, 8 of 28 of the intraperceptions of good CP men were significantly less discrepant than those of poor CP men, but only 1 of 28 of these comparisons of good CP women were significantly less discrepant than those of poor CP women. The intraperceptions of the men cannot in any way be ascribed to conforming to the women's images, because women's perceptions do not enter into the men's intraperceptions. Thus, the "men conforming to women's images of them" explanation does not seem as reasonable as that which holds that the satisfaction of the man is paramount in determining CP.

Satisfaction may occur via perceptual congruence between various perceptions of himself as well as through perceptions of how his girlfriend sees him and her concept of a spouse. This assures him that there is agreement and prompts him to push the courtship along. Within the realm of interperceptions, her ability to confirm and forecast his images of himself probably enables her to modify her behavior accordingly. Happy at being understood, he again pushes the courtship further.

On the other hand, if he suffers from neurosis, he may be much more indecisive about important decisions such as marriage, and neurosis occuring in the more powerful figure is apt to be more detrimental to CP.

These results occurred in the late 1960s, and as egality permeates the relationship between the sexes, it would not be astonishing to see the greater importance of the male in courtship lessen or disappear. Caution is indicated also because of a lack of knowledge of the generalizability of the present findings. However, a partial replication of these findings has been found with young middle-class married couples (Murstein and Beck, 1972), and fuller details of this study are reported in Chapter 14.

SUMMARY

Hypotheses relating to the role stage of courtship and dealing with personal adequacy and sex differences in power exercised in courtship were tested. Some evidence was unearthed that equity of self-acceptance and neurosis play some role in courtship, but the evidence was weak and spotty. Despite the presence of consistent trends, no significance was found for an association between equity on these variables and CP. Some evidence was found that high self-acceptance leads to greater satisfaction with the partner than low self-acceptance, and rather marginal support was found for the hypothesis that "neurosis" is associated with low partner satisfaction and with perceptual incongruence. Reasons for the failures were examined and discussed.

The hypotheses suggesting that the man was more important than the woman in courtship were generally confirmed. His neurosis was more inimical to CP than hers; confirmation of his self and ideal-self concepts was more conducive to CP than his confirmation of her self and ideal-self concepts; her predictive accuracy of these concepts in him was more related to CP than his accuracy in predicting her self and ideal-self concepts; perceptual congruence among his intraperceptions was related to CP; hers was not. An alternative explanation of the data was examined, which stated that she was more powerful than he and that he tried to live up to her image of him. This explanation was found to be inconsistent with certain aspects of the data, and the conclusion that the man played the more powerful role in courtship was retained.

NOTE

Some of the data discussed in Chapter 11 appeared earlier in Murstein, 1967b, 1971a, 1972b, 1973a.

CHAPTER 12

More on Roles:
Sex and Marital Choice

Although psychological and sociological factors associated with marital choice have been extensively researched, the effect of sex drive on marital choice and on the perception of the premarital partner has been largely ignored. At first, the convenient fiction that sex in the United States among "decent" people was essentially a marital phenomenon obviated the need for consideration of its effect on marital choice, and this stand was doubtlessly reinforced by the difficulties in investigating such a personal topic.

The research of Kinsey and associates (1948, 1953) and Burgess and Wallin (1953), among others, rudely dispelled the myth of general premarital chastity for "good folk," especially women. However, Kinsey did not touch upon the relationship of sex drive to courtship progress. Burgess and Wallin's subjects, in retrospect, thought that sex had strengthened their relationship. Kirkendall (1961) thought that sex had had a minimal effect on his subjects' relationships one way or the other. Neither of these studies, however, attempted to measure sex drive per se, nor did they offer quantitative data regarding the relationship of sex drive to person perception and courtship. I do not believe, however, that any current theory of marital choice in the United States which does not include sex within its list of influential variables can be said to be comprehensive. The present chapter represents a modest beginning in this regard.

Drive is defined here as "a tendency initiated by shifts in physiological (or psychological) balance to be sensitive to stimuli of a certain class and to respond in any of a variety of ways that are related to the attainment of a certain goal" (English and English, 1958, pp. 163-164). Drives function in a similar manner to values in that, for a given drive, the more similar the intensity of that drive for each member of the couple, the more compatible the couple. The reason why similarity of sex drive should be rewarding is that it should lead to a similar desire for frequency of sexual contacts by both partners. There are, however, special considerations attached to the sex-drive variable which merit discussion.

It should be noted first that past questionnaire and interview research has indicated that the sex drive of men, in general, is stronger than that of women if sex drive is defined as the consciously experienced desire for relief from sexual tension through sexual activity (Burgess and Wallin, 1953; Terman, 1938; Kinsey et al., 1953; Shuttleworth, 1959). Kinsey reported that men experience a greater number of orgasms over a weekly period and are more easily aroused by a wide variety of stimuli that fail to arouse women to an equal pitch (Kinsey, et al., 1948; 1953).

More recently, a considerable number of experiments have been undertaken on the comparative response of the sexes to a wide variety of erotic stimuli *(Technical Report of the Commission on Obscenity and Pornography,* Vol. 8, 1971). The data vary from reporting no differences between the sexes in sexual arousal and orgasmic reaction following the presentation of the stimuli to statistically significant but not outstanding differences, with males showing greater sexual reactivity. The type of population used and means of recruitment appear to make a difference in the findings (Kaat and Davies, 1971). The younger the subjects, the less their sexual experience, the lower the sexual class, and the less selective the recruiting procedure, the greater the male reactivity compared to the female one.

The differences in responsivity by the sexes to the various stimuli are noteworthy. The work of Schmidt, Sigusch, and their colleagues (Sigusch, Schmidt, Reinfeld, and Wiedermann-Sutor, 1970; Schmidt and Sigusch, 1972), in particular, indicate that women, more than men, respond much more strongly to moderately erotic stimuli that focus on love or suggest some kind of interpersonal relationship between the sexes as compared to more overtly sexual material that either gives no clues as to the relationship of the partner or shows only the opposite sex. Although men also respond strongly to sexual interaction between the sexes, they respond less strongly than women to heterosexual scenes in which the sexual organs are not displayed.

They do, however, respond more strongly to pictures of women in varying degrees of dress than do women in response to comparable male pictures. These data suggest that interpersonal relationships are more important in triggering erotic arousal for women than for men.

There are other data that are consistent with this thesis. Ehrmann (1960), reported that sex with an "acquaintance" was reported as extremely unsatisfactory by women, but sex with a "friend" or "lover" was quite satisfying. On the other hand, male subjects reported that sex with an "acquaintance" was quite satisfying and sex with a "friend" or "lover" only slightly more so.

If men's sex drive is more dependent on overt stimuli and temporal deprivation and less on interpersonal relationships than that of women, the formation of relationships or their termination should affect the orgasmic rate of women more than men. These assumptions are supported by Kinsey's data. Marriage elevated the orgasmic frequency of his male sample only 63 percent, while elevating that of women 560 percent (Shuttleworth, 1959). Conversely, the death of the spouse effected a greater reduction in the orgasm rate of widows than of widowers.

In sum, the more constant nature of the male sex drive should make the discrepancy between masculine and feminine drive more of a problem for the man with his need for a more constant outlet than for the more flexible woman. Since men on the average experience a greater number of orgasms per week than women, couples in which the man experiences a low sex drive (low with respect to his own sex) should be relatively compatible, since the orgasm rate of the partners should tend toward equity. Couples in which the man experiences a high sex drive should, accordingly, experience the greatest sexual incompatibility. To the already present average sex difference in orgasmic rate is added the fact that these men are at the high end of the continuum with regard to their own sex. Although the woman should in part be able to adjust to this rate, there is probably less strain in adapting to a slightly lesser frequency of intercourse than desired than to a considerably greater frequency of intercourse than desired.

It is clear from the mass of literature relating to sex, however, that the implications of differences in sex drive are rarely restricted just to the sexual area. Instead, they are likely to strongly influence the perception of the other person's personality and commitment to the relationship. The stereotyped response of the low-sex-drive woman to the insistence of the high-sex-drive male partner for frequent intercourse is "You are just using me for my body." The high-sex-drive male may perceive his partner, however, as "cold" or indifferent. It is also possible that his concern in satisfying his more imperious sexual needs, compared to the low-sex-drive man, may result in his paying little attention to the personality needs of the partner. In addition, he might use his greater power in the relationship to make the satisfaction of *his* sexual needs more important than the satisfaction of her needs.

The result should be that couples in which the man possesses a high sex drive should be less likely to perceive their partner as meeting their criterion of ideal-spouse (partner satisfaction) than would be the case for couples which include low-sex-drive men. (It will be recalled that "partner satisfaction" is an intraperception score—both percepts within the same person. Interperception scores involve perceptions from both members of the couple.)

The members of couples in which the man has a high sex drive should also be less likely to fulfill the expectations of their partner regarding a potential spouse. In similar vein, the interperceptions (e.g. the ideal of one individual is compared with the self-concept of the partner) should be less congruent for couples where the man possesses a high sex drive than for couples where the man possesses a lower drive. Last, if the relationship between all couples is measured at a future date, it should follow that male high-drive couples should show less CP than male low-drive couples.

For women, whose sex drive is hypothesized to be more influenced by the state of courtship and interpersonal relationships than is the case for men, no differences in either partner satisfaction or actual compatibility should be found between high and low drive. Because women's sexual behavior would seem to be more dependent on involvement with the partner, however, women making good CP should be more sexually active than women not so involved with a partner. For men, in whom the satisfaction of sexual needs is experienced as more pressing and who are less likely to await commitment, no such relationship is expected. The foregoing leads to the following five hypotheses:

Hypothesis 29. *Perceptual compatibility (both intraperceptual and interperceptual) will be significantly less for men and women in male high-sex-drive couples than in male low-sex drive couples.*

Hypothesis 30. *No differences in intraperceptual or interperceptual compatibility will be found between couples in which the woman has a high sex drive and couples in which the woman has a low sex drive.*

Hypothesis 31. *Couples with above-median discrepancies in sex drive will have above-medium discrepancies in intraperceptual and interperceptual compatibility.*

Hypothesis 32. *The CP of male high-sex-drive couples will be (a) significantly less than that of male low-sex-drive couples, but (b) the CP of high-sex-drive women will be greater than that of low-sex-drive women.*

Hypothesis 33. *The CP of couples whose absolute discrepancy of sex drive is below the median will be significantly greater than that of couples whose sex-drive discrepancy is above the median.*

RESULTS OF STUDY WITH GROUP I

The sample consisted of the 99 couples in Group I. The tests analyzed included the Revised Personal Preference Schedule and the four-item sex questionnaire.

The intraperceptual variable tested (partner satisfaction) involved the sum of absolute discrepancies of the perception of the boyfriend by the woman from her concept of her ideal-spouse |boyfriend $_W$ − ideal-spouse $_W$| over the 135 items. Likewise, the man's perception of his girlfriend was compared to his concept of ideal-spouse, |girlfriend $_M$ − ideal-spouse $_M$|. A third, summary score reflected the sum of these discrepancies |boyfriend $_W$ − ideal-spouse $_W$| + | girlfriend $_M$ − ideal-spouse $_M$|.

The interperceptual scores were divided into tests of homogamy where the same sets were compared between partners, and compatibility tests where the expectations of one partner were compared with the self-concept of the other. The homogamy comparisons were | ideal-spouse $_M$ − ideal-spouse $_W$|, | boyfriend $_W$ − girlfriend $_M$|, | self $_M$ − self $_W$|, and |ideal-self $_M$ − ideal-self $_W$|. The interperceptual compatibility comparisons were |self $_M$ − ideal-spouse $_W$|, and |self $_W$ − ideal-spouse $_M$|. A third score involved combining these latter two scores into a summary score |self $_M$ −ideal-spouse $_W$| + |self $_W$ − ideal-spouse $_M$|.

The ten Revised Personal Preference Schedule variables referred to above were each dichotomized as close to the median of the discrepancy scores as possible and compared against each of the likewise dichotomized four sex questions (orgasm frequency, orgasm recency, strength of self-perceived sex drive, and difficulty in controlling sex drive). The comparison of each Preference Schedule variable listed above against each sex variable resulted in 40 χ^2 tests (10×4). However, these tests were computed considering men only, women only, and the |man − woman| discrepancy; thus a total of 120 χ^2 tests ($10 \times 4 \times 3$) were computed. Eighteen of these tests were found to be significant at $p < .05$ or better and are reproduced in Table 12.1.

Table 12.1

SIGNIFICANT χ^2 VALUES BETWEEN REVISED PERSONAL PREFERENCE SCHEDULE AND SEX QUESTION RESPONSES BY MEN, WOMEN, AND |MEN − WOMEN|

Personal Preference Schedule		Sex Questions			
Type of Perception	Absolute Discrepancies	Recentness of Orgasm [1]	Average Rate of Orgasm	Self-Perception of Sex-Drive	Control of Sex a Problem [2]
Interperceptual homogamy	$\mid$Self$_M$ − self$_W\mid$				$\mid$M − W$\mid$*
	$\mid$Ideal-self$_M$ − ideal-self$_W\mid$				
	$\mid$Girlfriend$_M$ − boyfriend$_W\mid$				$\mid$M − W$\mid$*
	$\mid$Ideal-spouse$_M$ − ideal-spouse$_W\mid$		M*		$\mid$M − W$\mid$*
	$\mid$Girlfriend$_M$ − ideal-spouse$_M\mid$		M*	$\mid$M − W$\mid$**, M**	$\mid$M − W$\mid$**
Intraperceptual compatibility	$\mid$Boyfriend$_W$ − ideal-spouse$_W\mid$				$\mid$M − W$\mid$*
	$\mid$Girlfriend$_M$ − ideal-spouse$_M\mid$				
	$\mid$Boyfriend$_W$ − ideal-spouse$_W\mid$	M*, W*			$\mid$M − W$\mid$*
	$\mid$Self$_M$ − ideal-spouse$_W\mid$				$\mid$M − W$\mid$*, M*
Interperceptual compatibility	$\mid$Self$_W$ − ideal-spouse$_M\mid$		M*		$\mid$M − W$\mid$**, M*
	$\mid$Self$_M$ − ideal-spouse$_W\mid$	W*			
	$\mid$Self$_W$ − ideal-spouse$_M\mid$				$\mid$M − W$\mid$**

Note: M = man, W = woman, |M − W| = absolute discrepancy between man and woman. All significant values reflect the finding that low discrepancy scores on the Personal Preference Schedule are associated with low scores on the sex questions.

[1] Low score = not recent.
[2] Low score = no problem.

*p < .05.
**p < .01.

No direct test of overall significance for the number of significant findings is possible since the subjects were the same for all tests of significance, and two of the Revised Personal Preference Schedule variables contain other variables as component scores. Had all significant tests been indepedent, the number of significant findings at the .05 level or better for 120 tests would have been 6. The overall impression, nevertheless, is one of greater-than-chance significance. This impression is strengthened by virtue of the fact that all of the significant findings were in accord with the hypothesis. For tests pertaining to the male sex drive, Table 12.1 shows that 7 of 40 comparisons were significant; for women the rate was 2 of 40, and for | man− woman|, 9 of 40.

Hypothesis 29, which predicted that male low-drive couples would show greater perceptual compatibility than male high-drive ones is supported in that 7 of 40 tests concerning male sex drive proved significant. As predicted also, in Hypothesis 30, the differences between high- and low-sex-drive women did not exceed chance expectations (2 of 40 tests were significant).

Hypothesis 31, which stated that discrepancy in sex drive would be related to discrepancy in perceptual compatibility, is supported by virtue of the 9 significant |man − woman| values found of the 40 tested. These results show that large discrepancies in sex drive are associated with correspondingly large discrepancies in the Revised Personal Preference Schedule variables.

Courtship progress, when tested by chi-square, contrary to the prediction of Hypothesis 32, showed no significant relationship to sex drive in men on any of the four sex questions except for a trend ($p <$ .10) for men perceiving their sex drive as low to make better CP than high-drive men. Women, contrary to prediction, showed a significant ($p < .01$) association between low self-perceived sex drive and good CP. Therefore, Hypothesis 32, which called for (a) low male-drive couples to make better CP than high male-drive couples, and (b) the converse for women, is not supported. The |man − woman| discrepancy, likewise, was not associated with CP, thus resulting in a rejection of Hypothesis 33.

DISCUSSION

Keeping in mind the nonindependent nature of our data, they, nevertheless, are consistent with the assumption that high male sex drive but not high female sex drive is associated with low perceived compatibility. They also reinforce the assumption that equality of sex drive between the sexes facilitates the perception of compatibility. However, the hypotheses dealing with CP were rejected, possibly because of the restricted range of CP.

Also it would be of value to know how emotionally involved with their partners high-sex-drive men were compared to low-drive men. Moreover, were the high-drive men expressing their sex drive in solitary masturbation or through interpersonal contact? If expresed through masturbation, they might not have much different orgasm rates from low-drive men when interacting with their partners and, therefore, less reason to differ from them in perceptual compatibility. A second study, thus, might provide a chance to determine more precisely the state of the relationship between high-drive men and their girlfriends and the source of their orgasms, as well as replicating the findings with Group I. Last, the narrow range of variability of CP in Group I may have inhibited the likelihood of significant findings with this variable. A less committed group of subjects might obviate this problem.

GROUP III STUDY

The procedure was changed in several ways from the Group I study. Recency of orgasm, which seemed to have little direct relevance to the rather stable need patterns and perceptions which were being investigated, was dropped, and a question asking the source of orgasms (intercourse, petting, masturbation, dreams) was substituted and scored on a four-point scale of expressiveness ranging from four points for intercourse to one point for dreams. Also, as noted earlier, the CP scale was broadened from a four-point to a five-point scale.

Tests

Instead of the Revised Personal Preference Schedule, the Marriage Expectation Test, focusing more on heterosexual interpersonal relationships and on factors influencing marital choice, was used. In order to broaden the range of perceptual measurements, each subject filled out the test under 10 different perceptual sets instead of the four (self, ideal-self, boyfriend (girlfriend), ideal-spouse) utilized in the first study. Four of these six additional sets are of importance to the present analysis: boyfriend's prediction of girlfriend's self (W sees self$_M$), boyfriend's prediction of girlfriend's ideal-self (W sees ideal-self$_M$), boyfriend's prediction of girlfriend's perception of him (W sees boyfriend$_M$) and boyfriend's prediction of girlfriend's ideal-spouse (W sees ideal-spouse$_M$). In like manner, the women also took the test under ten comparable sets. The purpose of these additional "sets" was to determine whether ability to focus on the "other" as measured by the accuracy of forecasting the "other's" responses was related to sexual drive.

The first five hypotheses in the second study were the same as in the first study. The additional ones were as follows:

Hypothesis 34. The ability to predict the partner's responses on the Marital Expectation Test will be more accurate for both the man and woman in male low-sex-drive couples as compared to male high-sex-drive couples.

Hypothesis 35. Good CP will be (a) associated with intercourse or petting as the chief source of orgasm in women, but (b) this will not be true for men. The reasoning behind this hypothesis is that women's frequency of orgasm is more apt to be the resultant of the quality of the interpersonal relationship than is true of men. Men's orgasm rate is more apt to be a function of readily identifiable physical discomfort and to be fairly constant through time; hence, the fact that men become committed or engaged to be married should not as profoundly alter their orgasm rate.

RESULTS

The purpose of this second study was to note whether the discrepancy between any two "sets" (we shall call the lack of discrepancy perceptual congruence) was related to sex drive. The comparisons of sets had to be intrasexual because the items for the men's and women's tests were not all identical; thus all sets having the man as the perceptual target could be compared with each other even if the judgments about the man, for example, might come from women. The eight male sets compared were: self$_M$, M sees self$_W$, ideal-self$_M$, M sees ideal-self$_W$, boyfriend$_W$, W sees boyfriend$_M$, ideal-spouse$_W$, W sees ideal-spouse$_M$. There were n (n − 1/2) or 28 possible comparisons between two of the male sets. For female sets there were also 28 possible comparisons, making a total of 56 in all.

Regarding the sex questions, the intention was to compare the upper and lower third of the distribution of each question for degree of perceptual congruence; however, in some cases the coarseness of distribution of the sex variables did not permit an exact cut. The perceptual congruence score for the Marital Expectation Test was obtained by summing the absolute discrepancy between any two sets over all items. A t test was then computed between the summed absolute discrepancy scores (perceptual congruence) for the high and low tails of each sex question.

Turning our attention first to the men, the results showed that for high- versus low-orgasm-frequency men, 28 of the 56 perceptual comparisons were significant at the .05 point or beyond, all showing greater perceptual congruence for the situations in which the man had a low orgasm rate. The significant t values for source of orgasm totaled 15 of 56, for self-perceived sex drive 14 of 56, and for difficulty of control, 7 of 56, all in the predicted direction.

For women, the number of significant values for these four sex variables was respectively 2, 2, 6, and 2, a figure which would not be different from chance if our tests of significance had been independent of each other. Hypotheses 29 and 30 calling for greater perceptual congruence in male low-drive couples than for male high-drive couples, and no significant differences in perceptual congruence between high and low sex-drive women's groups, are both supported.

In the interest of conserving space, the results from only one of the male sex questions (the perceptions associated with high and low orgasm frequency for men) have been listed. Table 12.2 focuses on male-centered perceptions and Table 12.3 on female-centered ones.

A comparison of the high and low absolute $|M - W|$ discrepancies for each of the sex questions showed few significant results. "Orgasm frequency" manifested 4 significant values of 56 comparisons, "source of orgasm" showed 2 significant values of 56, and "control" showed 3 of 56, which are consistent with chance expectations. The "self-perceived strength of sex-drive" question, however, showed 10 of 56 significant values, all indicating that perceptual congruency was associated with smallness of discrepancy in the self-perception of sex-drive of the partners. These 10 values are shown in Table 12.4.

Hypothesis 31 that low $|M - W|$ discrepancies in sex-drive will be associated with perceptual congruence is, therefore, supported only for the self-perceived sex-drive variable.

In accordance with Hypothesis 32, and as shown in Table 12.5, men having a low orgasm rate showed higher CP ($p < .01$) than those with a high orgasm rate, but the other three sex variables showed no significant relationship to CP.

Table 12.2

SIGNIFICANT DIFFERENCES FOR MALE-CENTERED PERCEPTIONS
BETWEEN HIGH AND LOW ORGASM COUPLES [1]

Marital Expectation Test Variable	Type of Comparison	t
$self_M$, ideal-$self_M$	Intraperceptual by man	2.19*
$self_M$, W sees boyfriend$_M$		1.83*
ideal-$self_M$, W sees ideal spouse$_M$		1.95*
boyfriend$_W$, M sees ideal-$self_W$	Intraperceptual by woman	2.27*
ideal-$self_M$, M sees ideal-$self_W$	Forecast by woman of man's self and ideal-self	2.08*
$self_M$, M sees $self_W$		2.43**
W sees boyfriend$_M$, boyfriend$_W$	Forecast by man of woman's perception of boyfriend	2.15*
ideal-$self_M$, ideal spouse$_W$	Interperceptual	2.16*
ideal-$self_M$, boyfriend$_W$		1.87*
ideal-$self_M$, M sees $self_W$		1.77*
$self_M$, ideal-spouse$_W$		3.11**
$self_M$, M_W		2.24*
$self_M$, M sees ideal-$self_W$		2.19*
W sees boyfriend$_M$, ideal-spouse $_W$		2.21*
W sees boyfriend$_M$, M sees ideal-$self_W$		1.95*

Note: This table represents all possible combinations of the eight following variables
that proved significant: $self_M$, ideal-$self_M$, W sees boyfriend$_M$, W sees ideal
spouse$_M$, M sees $self_W$, M sees ideal-$self_W$, boyfriend$_W$, ideal spouse$_W$. Subscripts
refer to who is doing the perceiving, and M and W stand for man and woman; thus
W sees boyfriend$_M$ signifies man's prediction of how his girlfriend sees him.

[1] The discrepancies for low-rate men were always smaller than those for high-rate men.

*$p < .05$.
**$p < .01$.

Hypothesis 32 was supported for women in that a high fequency of
orgasm and achieving this orgasm through intercourse rather than by
other means were both associated with good CP ($p < .01$). Hypothesis
33 was supported for source of orgasm, in that a low discrepancy

Table 12.3

SIGNIFICANT DIFFERENCES FOR FEMALE-CENTERED PERCEPTIONS
BETWEEN HIGH AND LOW MALE ORGASM COUPLES [1]

Marital Expectation Test Variable	Type of Comparison	t
ideal-spouse$_M$, girlfriend$_M$	Intraperceptual by man	2.42**
ideal-spouse$_M$, W sees ideal-self$_M$		1.74*
ideal-self$_W$, W sees ideal-self$_M$	Forecast by man of woman's self and ideal-self	1.76*
self$_W$, W sees self$_M$		2.28*
M sees girlfriend$_W$, girlfriend$_M$	Forecast by woman of man's perception of girlfriend	2.55**
ideal-spouse$_M$, ideal-self$_W$	Interperceptual	3.81**
ideal-spouse$_M$, self$_W$		2.84**
ideal-spouse$_M$, M sees girlfriend$_W$		2.99**
girlfriend$_M$, ideal-self$_W$		3.54**
girlfriend$_M$, self$_W$		2.96**
girlfriend$_M$, M sees ideal-spouse$_W$		2.27*
W sees ideal-self$_M$, self$_W$		1.70*
W sees self$_M$, ideal-self$_W$		2.08

Note: This table represents all possible combinations of the eight following variables which proved significant: self$_W$, ideal-self$_W$, M sees girlfriend$_W$, M sees ideal-spouse$_W$, W sees self$_M$, W sees ideal-self$_M$, girlfriend$_M$, ideal-spouse$_M$. Subscripts refer to who is doing perceiving, and M and W stand for man and woman; thus, M sees girlfriend$_W$ signifies woman's prediction of how her boyfriend perceives her.

[1] The discrepancy for low-rate men was always higher than those for high-rate men.

*p < .05.
**p < .01.

between the couple regarding the means of achieving orgasm (source) yielded higher CP than a high discrepancy ($p < .01$). None of the other three sex variables, however, showed significant differences for the $|M - W|$ discrepancy.

After this analysis had been undertaken, further reflection suggested that discrepancies in the sex drive of the partners in which

Table 12.4

SIGNIFICANT DIFFERENCES IN PERCEPTUAL CONGRUENCE
BETWEEN HIGH (N = 46) AND LOW (N = 52) |MEN - WOMEN|
DISCREPANCY GROUPS FOR SELF-PERCEIVED SEX-DRIVE
STRENGTH [1]

Marital Expectation Test Variable	Type of Comparison	t
$self_M$, ideal $self_M$		3.03**
$self_M$, W sees ideal-$spouse_M$		2.08*
W sees $boyfriend_M$, W sees ideal-$spouse_M$		1.89*
ideal-$self_M$, W sees $boyfriend_M$	Intraperceptual by men	3.10**
ideal-$spouse_M$, $girlfriend_M$		2.23*
ideal-$spouse_M$, W sees $self_M$		1.70*
W_M, W sees ideal-$self_M$		2.44**
W sees $self_M$, W sees ideal-$self_M$		1.88*
$girlfriend_M$, $self_W$	Interperceptual	1.85*
$girlfriend_M$, M sees ideal-$spouse_W$		1.96*

[1] The Marital Expectation Test discrepancies were always greater for high | men - women | self-perceived sex-drive discrepancies.

*$p < .05$.
**$p < .01$.

the woman experienced the greater drive should not be as deleterious to the relationship as the converse, due to the greater flexibility of women, as discussed earlier; accordingly, the discrepancies were recomputed with regard to sign for what suggested itself as the most important indicator of sex-drive, orgasm rate. A cut was made as close to the median as possible. The dichotomies created were: male orgasm rate two units or more greater than that of the female partner, and male rate one unit greater or less (i.e. rate equal or woman higher). A chi-square for the one tailed test proved to be significant ($\chi^2 = 3.86$, $p < .03$) in that couples in which the male orgasm rate was far in excess of that of the female showed significantly poorer CP than the group varying from low male superiority to female superiority orgasm rate group.

Table 12.5

RELATIONSHIP OF MEN'S AND WOMEN'S SEX-DRIVE AND
THE DISCREPANCY BETWEEN THEM TO COURTSHIP PROGRESS
FOR EACH OF FOUR SEX QUESTIONS

	Sex Variable			
	1 *Frequency* *of Orgasm*	*2* *Source of* *Orgasm*	*3* *Self-Perceived* *Sex-Drive*	*4* *Control of* *Sex-Drive* *a Problem*
Men	L**	n.s.	n.s.	n.s.
Women	H*	H**	n.s.	n.s.
|M - W|	n.s.	L**	n.s.	n.s.

Note: The letter L or H refers to whether a low or high score or discrepancy is associated
with good courtship progress (n.s. = not significant). The size of each group for
each sex variable was for men (1) L = 25, H = 25, (2) L = 15, H = 43, (3) L = 54,
H = 44, (4) L = 40, H = 58; for women (1) L = 28, H = 30, (2) L = 29, H = 27,
(3) L = 69, H = 29, (4) L = 65, H = 33; for \|M - W\| (1) L = 32, H = 32, (2) L = 47,
H = 25, (3) L = 52, H = 46, (4) L = 39, H = 59.

*p < .05.
**p < .01.

Hypothesis 34 stated that if male low-sex-drive couples were more
sensitive and aware of each other's interpersonal needs than male
high-drive couples, they should be better able to predict their
partner's various perceptions (self, ideal-self, partner, spouse, ideal-
spouse). The "orgasm rate" variable, which seemed most representative of sex-drive, was used to test this hypothesis. Of the
eight predictive possibilities (forecast of partner's self, ideal-self,
perceived partner, and ideal-spouse by the man, and also by the
woman), Tables 12.2 and 12.3 show that six were significant, all in
accordance with the hypothesis, thus clearly confirming it.

Hypothesis 35, that sexual intercourse and petting to orgasm
would be associated with good CP in women but not for men, is
corroborated as shown by the fact that a χ^2 test computed between
high (n = 30) and low orgasm-rate women (n = 28), showed
significantly higher CP for the former (p < .01) and no significant
difference between high and low orgasm-rate men. (The fact that only
one woman reported masturbation as her primary source of orgasm
indicates that high-orgasm women achieved their high rate through
interpersonal means—petting or intercourse.)

DISCUSSION OF STUDY WITH GROUP III

The data of the second study clearly confirm the finding of the first study that perceived congruence of personality is associated with low sex drive on the part of the man but is not related to the sex drive of the woman. In addition, accuracy in predicting the partner's perceptual world is also more readily found among male low-drive couples than among male high-drive couples. The data also suggest that number of orgasms experienced with the partner is positively associated with good CP for women, but shows no relationship to CP for men. These data are consistent with the thesis advanced earlier that the man's sex drive is more dependent on biological factors than is the woman's, and that her sex drive and satisfaction are more determined by learning and the quality of the interpersonal relationship than is the case for men.

It is possible to demonstrate women's greater dependency on interpersonal relationships by considering the behavior necessary for her to experience orgasm. Most men require little special attention to experience orgasm once intromission has been achieved. This is often not the case with women. The man often must adjust his behavior and focus it on the woman's achieving orgasm. The patience, skill, manner of approach, and time required in this matter would clearly depend on the quality of the interpersonal relationship of the couple. Women making good CP should, in accordance with this thesis, enjoy sex more and indulge in it more frequently, and, in fact, it was noted that their orgasm rate was higher than that of low CP women. The low-sex-drive men, on the other hand, are unlikely to make love more frequently than they wish. Obviously, a man cannot be forced to perform sexually beyond his capacity. The tendency for good CP women to have higher orgasm rates than their boyfriends may have been due to multi-orgasmic capacity, or, more likely, it may have reflected their boyfriend's greater concern for them which is also reflected in their good CP. It might also be thought that women engaging in sex frequently may experience a need to justify such behavior by ascribing it to the closeness of their interpersonal relationship. However, our definition of good CP almost automatically assures that if the woman experiences good CP the man will do so also. Her claim of good CP, therefore, cannot be a rationalization, since the man would also experience good CP.

We referred earlier to several factors that might account for differences between high- and low-sex-drive men other than insensitivity caused by the imperiousness of the former's sex drive. These included the possibility that high-sex-drive men had never been particularly interested in their partners apart from sex. Perhaps this fact rather than only preoccupation with sexual release caused the incompatibility in their relationships? To test this possibility, answers to a background questionnaire filled out at the time of testing were compared for high- and low-orgasm-rate men, orgasm rate being taken as the best individual measure of sex drive. One item on the questionnaire dealt with the men's classification of their relationship with their girlfriends on a six-point scale from "formal engagement" (6) to "date somewhat" (1).

The mean for high-orgasm-rate men of 3.68 [between "date exclusively" (3) and "pinned" (4)] was not significantly different from the mean of 3.77 of low-rate men. There were no differences in length of relationship, age, student status, certainty about marriage, feeling understood by the partner, understanding the partner, or perceived attractiveness of partner. A trend $p < .10$ existed, however, for high-rate men to have had less definite plans for marriage. All in all, however, it does not appear that the high-rate men's lack of psychological compatibility with their partner was based on superficial involvement with their girlfriends.

Another question of interest was whether the high-rate men expressed their high rate in interaction with their partner or by masturbation. If a chief source of orgasm for high-rate were masturbation, it would be difficult to see how the interpersonal relationships of the high-rate men should have suffered any more than those of the low-drive men, since the sexual expression of the former vis-à-vis their girlfriends would not be much different from that of low sex-drive men. However, a four-point item ranging from intercourse as a source of orgasm to erotic dreams yielded a significant t value of 2.40 ($p < .01$). Inspection indicated that more high-rate men utilized inter-course as an outlet as compared to low-rate men. The only other significant difference found between the groups was for the high-rate men to perceive themselves as significantly more physically attractive than the low-rate men ($p < .05$). This finding might be related to the mutually lower perceived satisfaction of members of couples in which the man had a high sex drive. Since men generally are considered to be more powerful than women in terms of status in society, a man who thinks of himself as especially attractive would perhaps believe himself to be a real "cock-of-the-walk." From an exchange orientation of interpersonal behavior, such men might believe that their physical presence and virility were sufficiently rewarding to their girlfriends that they need not take on the burden (cost) of sensitivity to their partner's psyche.

Despite some intriguing results and speculations, there are a number of cautions that must be considered in any questionnaire survey touching on highly personal data. First, was there communication between the members of the couple? In the study with Group I this fact was carefully controlled by separating the couple and having a supervisor present during the entire testing period. In the study with Group III, the woman, who was on campus, was given a packet to fill out and a packet was mailed to her boyfriend when hers was returned. The mailing address of the vast majority of boyfriends was from several hundred to several thousand miles away, and the fact that the packets of the boyfriends were largely collected within three weeks further suggests an absence of collusion. In addition, the participants were told that the importance of the study depended on noncollaborative answers and that any evidence of collaboration would result in nonpayment of the stipulated fees for participation. Last, but perhaps most important, the findings with Group III were essentially replicative of those with Group I, who took the questionnaire under supervision, which prevented collaboration; thus it is doubtful that collaboration seriously affected the results.

A second possible contamination seems more critical. Is the sex questionnaire valid? Do individuals keep track of their orgasm rate per week? Further, is not sexual behavior tied up with morality and concepts of virility to such an extent that it is naive to expect any truthful responses?

There is much to be said for such objections, and doubtless some people did distort, whether from faulty memory that allowed ego-needs to have full play or from direct intent to misrepresent. However, barring a systematic error, the effect would be to increase the error variance and the tendency to accept the null hypothesis when it should be rejected; hence there may be differences that are being overlooked, but it seems probable that whatever differences are found are valid. Inspection of our data generally confirms differences between men and women reported earlier by Kinsey (1953). The men experienced between two and three orgasms per week and the women somewhat less than one, rather similar to the findings of Kinsey a generation earlier.

Finally, the equating of sex drive with orgasm rate can be objected to. Orgasm rate does not necessarily reflect drive strength as might be the case, for example, in a rat. In humans, orgasm rate is more properly considered as drive minus inhibition. Some individuals with strong sexual capacity may be inhibiting their orgasm rate because of unacceptance of these drives or want of a sexual partner. It is readily acknowledged, therefore, that orgasm rate is imperfectly correlated with sex drive, but it was the best measure of drive that could be used in the mass testing study undertaken. In sum, the present study is acknowledged to be crude in the measures used, but the paucity of data in this area suggests that the present findings have value in stimulating further replicative studies to verify or reject our initial findings.

SUMMARY AND CONCLUSIONS

The hypotheses receiving strongest support were those stating that high sex drive in the men would be associated with poor perceived interpersonal compatibility, but that differences in sex drive in women would not be associated with perceived compatibility. The discrepancy in sexual drive between men and women was slightly associated with discrepancy in perceived compatibility, and male high-sex-drive couples and high-discrepancy couples showed a slight tendency to manifest poor CP. High drive in men was related to inaccuracy on the part of *both* partners in forecasting the partner's interpersonal perceptions on the Marital Expectation Test, and last, good CP was associated with the woman engaging in intercourse, but bore no relationship to participation in intercourse on the part of the man.

It appears, therefore, that high sex drive has different connotations for women and men. For women, it is suggested that high drive is a result of involvement and attachment, whereas for men, high drive would seem to be a cause of couple dissatisfaction. The hedging words "appear" and "seem to be" reflect the fact that it is impossible to determine cause and effect in the present two studies. The data, nevertheless, are generally consistent with the conclusions drawn; however, continued replication and better measures of sex drive are badly needed. As far as is known, these two crude studies are the first seeking to measure the relationship of sex drive and courtship progress. It is incumbent on family researchers, therefore, to fill in the lacunae of knowledge in this area with empirical data.

NOTE

Chapter 12 is based mainly on an earlier article (Murstein, 1974b).

CHAPTER 13

Additional Hypotheses

PERCEPTUAL STYLE

In Chapter 7 I noted that individuals were influenced in their attraction by perceptual and expressive styles, but that these variables seemed to cut across the stages rather than operating primarily within one of them. Perceptual style represented the manner of perceiving the world. The test selected to measure perceptual style was the Baughman Ink Blot Test, a modification of the Rorschach Inkblot Test, with the inquiry for the determinants of perception being mainly perceptual rather than verbal, as described earlier in Chapter 8.

We were interested in whether members of couples were alike in their way of perceiving the inkblots; whether they used form predominantly in determining their perceptions, or preferred shading, color, or the other variables listed in Table 13.1.

The Marriage Apperceptive Thematic Examination, which involved making up stories in response to pictures, was scored for 16 variables described earlier in Chapter 8 and listed in Table 13.2. As with the inkblot test, the thinking was that the perceptual style of looking at the pictures and making up stories would be selective in terms of interpersonal attraction. Our hypothesis for the variables analyzed in both the inkblot and thematic tests is as follows:

Hypothesis 36. *Premarital couples will show a greater than chance similarity on variables reflecting perceptual style.*

Table 13.1

LIST OF 48 RORSCHACH VARIABLES ANALYZED

Location Variables

W (whole blot used)
D (large segment used)
Dd (tiny segment used)
S (white space used for perception rather than inkblot)

Determinants of Perception

FC (form predominant, color secondary)
CF (color predominant, form secondary)
C (pure color, no form)
ΣC (composite score weighted as follows:
    ($\frac{1}{2}$FC + CF + 1$\frac{1}{2}$C)**
M (human movement perceived)
M_H (Holtzman variant scoring of human movement)
FM (animal movement)
m (nonliving object movement)
F− (form determined responses of poor accuracy regarding object described)
F+ (form determined responses of good accuracy regarding object described)
ΣF ([F+] + [F] + [F−])**
Total form accuracy %
Pure form accuracy %
Holtzman shading (use of shading to indicate perception, i.e. texture, grayness)

Content and Process Variables

H (human)
(H) (derogated human; e.g. witch)
Hd (part of a human)
(Hd) (part of derogated human)
A animal*
A% (percentage of animal responses to total responses)
(A) (derogated animal)
Ad (part of an animal)
(Ad) (part of derogated animal)
Sex
Blood
Anatomy
X-ray
Barrier
Penetration
Popular (a response occurring with considerable frequency)
Verbalization
Pathological
Integration
Anxiety
Average response time per card
Average reaction time (between receipt of card and first response)
Symbolization
Hostility

Table 13.1 (continued)

Ratio Scores
H + A : Hd + Ad
M : ΣC
W : M
M : FM*
Σ Shading : ΣC*
FC : C + CF*

*p < .05.
**p < .01.

The subjects were the 19 couples from Group II who had undertaken the depth and interview measures in contrast to the largely paper-and-pencil measures undertaken by Groups I and III. The 64 variables (48 inkblot, 16 thematic) were analyzed by the binomial expansion, with actual discrepancies between members of a couple for a given variable being compared against 5 random replications with "artificial" couples.

Two of the 16 thematic variables and 6 of the 48 inkblot variables were significant at the .05 level or above for a one-tailed test, as shown in Tables 13.1 and 13.2. Because the same subjects were used in all tests, and because some of our scores were not completely independent of others, an exact statement of the probability of such an occurrence is not possible. Had each test of significance been indepedent of the others, a total of about three significant values would have been expected by chance. The impression gained, therefore, is that a

Table 13.2

LIST OF 16 THEMATIC TEST VARIABLES ANALYZED

Hostility	Internal punishment
Emotional tone*	Internal punishment/remoteness
Outcome	Internal punishment/hostility
Attitude toward men	Remoteness/hostility
Attitude toward women	Adequacy of interpersonal
Projection	relationship
Remoteness (of hostile expression)	Anxiety
	Affiliation
	Goodness of response*
	Qualifications in story

*p < .01.

statistically significant but very modest tendency toward homogamy of scores has been found. This is reinforced by the fact that all significant values were in the direction predicted.

Various factors probably conspired to reduce the probability of significant findings. Analyzing a large number of variables with only 19 couples means that only very large differences between actual and random couples will be recognized as statistically significant.

Another difficulty found with inkblot scores is that many of them are so low in frequency that they virtually preclude the probability of significant differences between actual and random couples. Suppose, for example, that only 5 persons (3 men, 2 women) out of the total of 38 persons used a white space response in arriving at a percept. This means that 33 persons received a zero score. When the random discrepancies are compared with actual discrepancies, it is almost impossible to expect a significant difference because the predominant score, no matter who is paired with whom, is zero. Had this factor been fully realized prior to the analysis and variables replete with zero scores omitted, the results would undoubtedly have been somewhat more impressive—at least for the inkblot test, where zero scores are more frequent with respect to the variables used.

To check this speculation, we compared the discrepancies of the random pairs with the actual pairs without regard to whether the differences were of sufficient magnitude to reach statistical significance. If the random couples' discrepancy exceeded the actual couples' discrepancy for an inkblot variable, it was scored as a "hit," whereas the opposite occurrence counted as a "miss." In 3 cases there were ties, but for the remaining 45 variables, there were 36 "hits" and 9 "misses." The data thus support the assumption that the nature of the scores impeded significance for the inkblot variables. This did not seem to be the case for the thematic variables, where only 8 "hits" and 7 "misses" (and 1 tie) were recorded for a comparable analysis.

Turning to the inkblot variables that proved significant, inspection of Table 13.1 indicates that the most basic scores, which involved form level and the use of color, predominated among the significant values.

We shall consider briefly the meaning ascribed to these scores by some leading Rorschach experts. It should be kept in mind that this meaning is derived more from the clinical experience of these authors than from their research, and these interpretations are not always accepted by researchers in this field (Murstein, 1965a). Also, because interpretation of these scores depends on the presence of other scores, interpretation can be a very complex process. It would take us too far afield to consider the research findings and the subtleties in depth. We shall have to content ourselves with a rather oversimplified picture of the meaning attributed to these variables, the main purpose being to convey the flavor rather than the letter of the law regarding these variables.

The use of form as opposed to color in determining a response appears to be basically determined by temperament or life style. Form (F) is generally held "to represent those activities which are under the influence of the relatively most intellectual or rational processes" (Piotrowski, 1950, p. 77). Color (C) on the other hand, is alleged to represent subjectively experienced affect; thus form and color represent the two basic human functions of thinking and feeling.

The significance of the ΣF score indicates that actual couples tended to show less discrepancy in their use of responses determined exclusively by the form of the inkblot than did randomly paired couples. The ΣC score significance indicated a similar overall responsivity to color by members of couples. This would indicate equity in affective reactivity according to traditional Rorschach interpreters, although the overall color score tells us nothing about the accuracy and use of control involved in this reactivity.

The couples also showed some tendency toward equity on the number of perceptions of animals. A large number of such perceptions is said to be indicative of low intellectual output or capacity, whereas a moderate number (20-50% of total responses) is within normal range. Less than 10 to 20 percent is typical of artists and scattered catatonics (Piotrowski, 1957). Animal responses are also sometimes interpreted as indicators of more humanistic response potential, given favorable future development (Klopfer, Ainsworth, Klopfer, and Holt, 1954).

The ratio of human movement to animal movement responses (M : FM) is interpreted as follows: Human movement represents how the individual relates to his social milieu, his capacity for human identifications and potential for inner creation (Allen, 1966). Animal movement represents a kind of animal buoyancy. It is said to represent potential for inner resources at a lower level than human movement responses. Not surprisingly, therefore, animal movement is more frequently seen in children than in adults. Animal movement also does not imply the presence of empathy, which is implied in human movement. A ratio in which human movement equals animal movement is said to be in balance in that the impulse life (animal movement) is not in conflict with the individual's value system (human movement). A pronounced imbalance favoring animal movement suggests that immediate needs for gratification rule. A pronounced imbalance in the other direction suggests that impulses are unhealthily quashed in favor of conscious values, suggesting underlying tension and conflict (Klopfer et al., 1954).

The ratio of sum of shading to the sum of color (Σ Shading : Σ C) must be understood in terms of the functions of shading and of color. Shading responses refer to the use of the achromatic shadings from light grey to black to signify diffusion, vista, texture, depth—as the case may be. Shading may represent potential affectivity, but excessive shading represents anxiety. Since color represents affectivity that is more directly expressed, the shading-to-color ratio is somewhat analogous to the animal-movement-to-human-movement ratio. Where the imbalance is too greatly in favor of shading, the individual is too fearful to realize his potential for affectivity by direct expression.

The FC : CF + C ratio compares the mature, restrained use of color with the looser, more amorphous, structureless use of it.

The FC (form color) response represents the desire for adapting the emotionally reactive life to others, whereas the CF (color predominant, form secondary) and C (pure color, no form) responses indicate self-centered emotional impulsiveness that overpowers any drive for adaptiveness (Piotrowski, 1957). A healthy balance between the two would involve FC predominating since it is weighted at $\frac{1}{2}$ as opposed to 1 for CF and $1\frac{1}{2}$ forC.

The inkblot test thus reveals some tendency toward similarity of perception for variables that are largely culture free and unlikely to have been discussed by the partners prior to testing. The importance of such findings could be best determined in future research by finding what behavioral correlates existed with respect to reliably homogamous inkblot scores.

In sum, the inkblot test shows a bit of support for Hypothesis 36, but it is necessary to be rather equivocal because of the modest number of significant findings in comparison to the large number of tests of significance, and because our tests of significance are not independent. However, because so many scores were infrequent, thus biasing toward a conclusion that no significant differences were present, a replication study might be profitably undertaken using only the most frequently occurring scores.

One of the two significant thematic variables was "emotional tone," which indicated less than chance disparity in the emotional tone (positive, negative, or neutral) of the stories told by the partners. The other significant variable was "goodness of response," which measured the adequacy of the thematic story in terms of the subject's ability to follow directions in making up a story and the logical consistency with which the parts of the story hung together. Here too, real couples showed less discrepancy than randomized ones. Our conclusions for the thematic test seem similar to that expressed for the inkblot test—slight support for the hypothesis, but of a very weak order of magnitude.

EXPRESSIVE STYLE

It was noted earlier in Chapter 7 regarding expressive style, that it was impossible to predict whether a variable would be homogamous, complementary, or involve some other relationship unless one knew how the variable fit into the role functioning of the couple. Our prediction for the "expressive style" variables with Group II, therefore, involved inspection of the 100 items used in the Q Sort personality evaluation of this group (see Appendix C-7), in an attempt to determine which of these variables would be best served by complementarity as opposed to homogamy of ownership by the couples.

One variable posited earlier to be complementary (Winch, 1958) is "dominance" (measured by items 41 and 66 in our Q Sort as shown in Table 13.3). If each individual seeks to dominate the other, strife often results, whereas if one follows the other's lead, greater harmony may ensue. Other research (Murstein, 1961b, 1967a) has not supported this finding with the Edwards Personal Preference Schedule for premarital or newlywed couples. It is conceivable, however, that the nine items measuring dominance on the Personal Preference Schedule may be atypical of the way people express themselves in an interview. Also, Winch has criticized this test as having no demonstrable validity and as not getting at the dynamics of interaction as adequately as does an interview. His own and his associates' research (Winch, 1958) showed some support for the idea that dominance, dependency (our items 10, 30, 45, 58, 65, 90), and nurturance needs (item 34) would be negatively correlated between persons who marry. Accordingly, it was predicted that items measuring these needs in the present study would also be negatively associated for couples.

In addition, the present author believed that exhibitionism (items 36, 100) would be negatively related for partners, since a person wanting to be the center of attention would not like to compete with his partner for that honor. Last, the items "masculinity" and "femininity" (item 11, 12) were each also predicted to be negatively

Table 13.3

SIGNIFICANT ITEMS OF THE 100 ITEM Q SORT

conventional*
conservative**
physical attraction of others plays
    important part in relationship***
talkative***
does things spontaneously
    rather than by planning*
control of sex no problem*
introspective about self*
moralistic***
basically anxious*[1]
social poise and presence***
arouses liking in others**
envies others**
uncomfortable with uncertainty
    and complexities
handles anxiety and conflict by
    repression and dissociation**
unrealistic goals*

keeps resentments to self*
regards self as physically
    attractive*
opinionated*
basically hostile toward other
    sex**
not sarcastic**
dependent***[2]
dull**
thin-skinned, sensitive to
    criticism*
egotistical***
coarse*
concerned with philosophical
    problems of life*
ambitious***
high degree of intellectual
    capacity*
strongly committed to
    intellectual endeavours*

[1] Contrary to homogamous prediction.
[2] Complementary prediction.

*$p < .05$.
**$p < .01$.
***$p < .001$.

associated for members of couples. Although sexual energy may be homogamously selective, as worded in our items it should manifest itself in a complementary manner. A "masculine" man, for example, should be drawn to a woman low on "masculinity," that is, a woman who is very feminine. Conversely, a "masculine" woman should be drawn to a "feminine" man.

In sum, Hypothesis 37 predicted that, *in an assessment situation, individuals would be more similar to their partners on a wide variety of "expressive style" behaviors relating to personality except for those items relating to dominance, dependence, nurturance, exhibitionism, masculinity, and femininity, for which a negative relationship was predicted.*

To test the hypothesis, the author and his research assistant independently performed a Q sort based on the typed protocols of the data gathered for Group II (interview, inkblot test, thematic test, sex questionnaire, brief background questionnaire) on each of the 38 subjects. Because the identification was removed from the test data, and because the couples had been interviewed separately a half-year earlier, neither the author nor his assistant could remember who the partner of their particular interviewee was.

Since only one interviewer had been present in interviewing a subject, 16 items that were believed to be dependent on personal observations and therefore not transmittable onto the typed protocol of test behavior, (e.g. "robust") were not judged by the second interviewer. This interviewer placed these items exactly where the first had placed them.

The 100 items are, in the main, highly inferential rather than descriptive; consequently, the interjudge reliabilities were not very high, even with the spurious boost given by the 16 fixed items. A sample of 10 randomly chosen couples yielded reliability Pearson correlation values of from .31 to .74, with a mean of .55. Doubtless these values would have been higher had both interviewers been present when each subject was interviewed, but this had not been feasible. The final Q sort was achieved by the two interviewers comparing their sorts and arriving at a final sort by resolving differences through discussion.

Findings

To determine whether the absolute discrepancy between couples for each item was significantly smaller than chance (homogamous result), a control group was created by randomly pairing the Q sort placements for the men with those of the women. The discrepancies for each of the 100 items of actual couples, it will be recalled, were hypothesized to be smaller than the comparative items for randomized couples, with the exception of those items relating to dominance, dependency, nurturance, exhibition, masculinity, and femininity, for which a complementary relationship was hypothesized.

The data were analyzed by reference to the binomial expansion method described earlier. The median absolute discrepancy between actual couples was found for a given variable, and the frequencies greater than, equal to, and less than the median were listed. This tripartite division was needed because of the crudeness of the scores. The trichotomy was then condensed into a dichotomy according to how closely a 50-55 split could be achieved. For example, the twenty-seventh item "tends to arouse liking and acceptance in other people" showed 9 actual couples with a discrepancy above the median discrepancy of 1, 8 equal to the median, and 2 with a discrepancy below the median; consequently, the data were condensed into the dichotomy above the median (9) versus equal to or below the median (10). Next, the discrepancy between the randomized couples for the same item was compared against the median of the actual group, and the number of randomized couples above versus equal to or below the real couples' median was recorded. The randomization of couples was performed a total of five times and the overall probability again determined.

Examination of Table 13.3 shows that of the 87 items for which discrepancies were predicted to be smaller for actual couples, 28 items were significant at the .05 level or better, 27 being in the predicted direction. Of the 13 items predicted to be complementary, that is, more discrepant for actual couples than for randomized ones, only 1, "dependent," proved to be significant. It appears, therefore, that the homogamous tendency among couples for the type of data in the present study is strongly supported, whereas the complementary tendency for personality items seems no better than chance.

Discussion

The data strongly support the supposition that interpersonal styles are homogamously selective for marriage. Apparently, individual styles of interaction reveal considerable information concerning values and role compatibility, and individuals feel most comfortable when their own style of interaction is duplicated by their partner.

Such an explanation, however, does not seem sufficient. Are not some of the behaviors that were found to be significant highly correlated with social desirability? Is an individual who "envies others," is "physically unattractive," "opinionated," "unrealistic," "coarse," "egotistical," and "possessed limited intellectuality" necessarily drawn to a similar other? As noted earlier, it is not mandatory to assume that individuals possessing socially undesirable characteristics admire these qualities in each other in order that they should come together. According to exchange theory, they are most apt to marry someone who is able to offer them no more and no less than they bring to the marriage; hence similarity of expressive styles of behavior may also reflect the equal status of members of a couple as well as their similar values. In sum, interpersonal assessment through interviews and "depth" tests may well contribute data predictive of marital choice that are not found in questionnaires or personality inventories, although the rather unselective choice of variables in the present study may have dampened this effect.

SUMMING THE VARIABLES IN ORDER TO MEASURE
OVERALL EQUITY

Theoretically, the ideal way to test the validity of exchange theory would be to ascertain all of the variables influencing an individual with respect to marital choice, determine their importance, and weight them accordingly, and also compare the various alternatives (marriage, bachelorhood, cohabitation without marriage, etc.) as well as the field of possible candidates. The researcher would then reduce the data for each candidate to his net profitability for his intended partner. Those with equal net profitability should be most attracted to each other. This was beyond the scope of the present study, and instead, a very rough exploratory study of the summative effects of some five variables was attempted.

Those variables that had been emphasized as key factors in marital choice (Murstein, 1970), were arbitrarily selected for testing exchange theory with respect to Group I. The five variables were sex drive (average orgasm rate), self-acceptance (the sum of the absolute discrepancies between self and ideal-self concepts on the Revised Personal Preference Schedule), neuroticism (Neurotic Triad from the Minnesota test), self-concept for physical attractiveness, and perceived satisfaction with the partner (in the Revised Personal Preference Schedule). No attempt was made to select the variables most pertinent to a given subject, or to weight either their importance or the various alternatives available to him. A crude test indeed! And yet, if these five variables are generally as important as estimated, they might offer some rough test of exchange theory. This test is formulated as follows:

Hypothesis 38. *If a series of variables important for marital choice are converted to standard scores and summed, members of couples will show less than chance discrepancy between these summed scores.*

To test Hypothesis 38, each subject's raw score was transformed to a standardized Z score based on the distribution of his sex for that variable. The five Z scores were then summed for the male partner and for the female partner, and the absolute discrepancy between each partner recorded. The binomial expansion method was used, and the number of randomized couples exceeding the median of the real group is shown for each of five randomized replications in Table 13.4. Inspection of this table reveals that the overall probability of this event occurring by chance is less than .01. In addition, a correlation

Table 13.4

NUMBER OF RANDOMIZED COUPLES ABOVE MEDIAN DISCREPANCY
OF ACTUAL COUPLES (Group I) FOR FIVE SUMMED VARIABLES,
PROBABILITY OF EACH EVENT, AND OVERALL PROBABILITY

	Above Median	Below Median	p of Being Above Median
Actual Couples (Group I)	49	49	.50
Random Couples			
Trial 1	65	33	.00
Trial 2	56	42	.10
Trial 3	59	39	.03
Trial 4	64	34	.00
Trial 5	54	44	.18

Note: $\chi^2 = 41.71$, overall $p < .01$.

was computed between the summed Z scores for men and women and proved to be significant ($r = .37$, $p < .01$). Hypothesis 38 is thus "seemingly" confirmed for Group I. We shall explain this qualification a bit later on.

For Group III, eight important variables were selected, including all of the variables included in Group I except for the Neurotic Triad. This variable was not administered to Group III because it was believed, after the experience of analyzing their data, that the nonneurotic character of the college subjects did not warrant the use of this measure. The four additional variables, selected arbitrarily by the author on the basis of judged importance, were the absolute discrepancy of |Perception of partner's physical attractiveness – self attractiveness| ; confirmation of self-concept of partner (|partner$_A$ – self$_B$|); accuracy of prediction of partner's self (|prediction of partner's self $_A$ – self$_B$ |); accuracy of prediction of partner's ideal-self (|prediction of partner's ideal-self $_A$ – ideal-self $_B$|). (The subscripts A and B are used to indicate that the perceptions stem from different members of the couple.)

As before, the scores were standardized, summed, and the discrepancy obtained between partners. The probability of the discrepancy between actual partners occurring by chance is given in Table 13.5 for each of five random replications. Inspection of this table again apparently indicates strong confirmation of Hypothesis 38, as does the correlation between men's and women's summed Z scores ($r = .61$, $p < .01$).

Table 13.5

NUMBER OF RANDOMIZED COUPLES ABOVE MEDIAN DISCREPANCY
OF ACTUAL COUPLES (Group III) FOR EIGHT SUMMED VARIABLES,
PROBABILITY OF EACH EVENT, AND OVERALL PROBABILITY

	Above Median	Below Median	p of Being Above Median
Actual Couples			
(Group III)	49	49	.50
Random Couples			
Trial 1	70	28	.00
Trial 2	67	31	.00
Trial 3	68	30	.00
Trial 4	62	36	.01
Trial 5	65	33	.00

Note: χ^2 = 81.65, overall p < .01.

Notwithstanding this seemingly solid support, there are reservations to concluding that the summative hypothesis is clearly supported. Although both studies showed significant χ^2s for the probability of the summed scores, as well as significant correlations between the summed scores of the men and women, this does not necessarily demonstrate that the summative effect is responsible for the significance. If, for example, several of the individual variables are significant in their own right (as they were), the overall score might be significant even if one or two of the five variables was not significant and detracted from rather than contributed to the significance level of the summed scores.

One way of ascertaining the effect of summation is to compare the significance level attained by summation with that attained by any of the individual scores. If summation is effective, the significance value of the summed score ought to, at the very least, exceed that of any of the scores considered individually. This was not the case in Group I, where 5 variables were summed but was the case in Group III where eight variables were employed. The summed χ^2 was 81.65, whereas the largest χ^2 for any single variable was 70.49. The difference is small and does not reflect the difference in degrees of freedom (1 for the single variable, 12 for our composite of eight variables). In short, we have no evidence that summing eight haphazardly chosen variables increased over-all equity. Theoretically, of course, the number of variables influencing marital choice must be legion, and one could not hope to encompass all of them in a study.

However, it might be feasible in future research to attempt to ascertain the 10 or 15 most important variables influencing marital choice by more objective means than those employed here and determine whether the summed score yielded greater equity between partners than any variable individually considered.

The effect of summation on CP was also put in hypothesis form.

Hypothesis 39. *If a series of variables important for marital choice are converted to standard scores and summed, equality in summed scores between the members of the couple will be associated with good CP.*

The biserial correlation between the sum of five variables and CP for Group I was not significant despite a trend ($R = .17$), and a similar finding resulted for the sum of eight variables and CP for Group III ($R = .18$). Hypothesis 39 is therefore rejected. The individual biserial R's, which we have discussed earlier, ranged from $-.12$ to $.55$ for Group I and from $-.12$ to $.24$ for Group III. Thus, summation clearly added nothing to the effect produced by the variables considered individually.

The data on summation are thus ambiguous. That equity exists for many variables has been a consistent finding throughout the research, but that it acts summatively has been more difficult to determine. In retrospect, it is apparent to me that equity would not be expected nor necessary for all variables to an equal degree. In the area of sex, for example, what the individuals strive for is sexual satisfaction. Although satisfaction and equity of orgasm may occur for a majority of subjects where each experiences orgasm, equity would hardly be satisfying where each experienced no orgasm. Contrariwise, nonequity might be highly satisfactory to both if they felt no sexual tension after the man experienced 3 orgasms and the woman 10.

Another difficulty with equity of summed scores is that unless you consider all scores and weight them in importance, certain distortions may occur. If it is true, as we have assumed, that men have greater power than women in society, they may be able to obtain rewards from interaction with women that greatly exceed their costs. A man might require his partner to be better looking than himself (as he sees it), and his girlfriend might have to accept him if she wants to be married more than he does. Thus, the extent of power possessed by an individual should be taken into consideration in determining equity. It may well be that as an individual becomes increasingly powerful, it becomes increasingly unlikely that he can find a partner equal in power to himself; consequently, he may engage in a vast amount of exploitive inequitable behavior with respect to his partner, which would certainly foul up any summative attempts at equity.

Adolph Hitler was certainly more powerful than his mistress Eva Braun, whom he married shortly before their deaths. It is also true that she did just about everything the Führer wanted. It could be argued that the arrangement was equitable because Hitler conferred his status on her, which compensated for his exploitive behavior. Aside from the fact that the assumption of status ascription smacks a bit of tautology (that is, if we assume equity must exist, then by working backwards we can always assume that the exploiting partner is equalizing exchange by conferring status), the point is that if the status were not included in the assessment, the relationship would be quite inequitable in terms of services performed. In the present study, of course, we had neither Hitlers nor Eva Brauns. Status was not taken into account in our summation because there was no direct way of measuring it, but it may well have influenced the results.

The failure of summed equity to correlate significantly with CP is in keeping with the generally lower significance levels found for CP than for variables relating only to couple formation. The reasons for this have been discussed earlier.

SUMMARY

"Perceptual style" was predicted to be homogamous for our courting couples and was measured by 48 inkblot and 16 thematic variables. Six of the former and 2 of the latter proved significant. Because of the nonindependent nature of the scores, it was not possible to determine the exact significance of such an occurence, but the fact that all significant values were in the predicted direction supported the conclusion of very modest support for the prediction. A number of reasons for believing that the nature of the scores underestimated the significance levels were discussed.

"Expressive style" of behavior was assessed by a Q Sort based on all of the data from Group II. Homogamy of expressive style was predicted, except for certain items believed to be complementary. However, results confirmed the homogamy hypothesis, but not the complementary one. Twenty-seven of the 87 items predicted to be homogamous were significant, but only 1 of the 13 items predicted to be complementary was found to be so.

An attempt was also made to determine whether summing scores provided a better model of equity than considering the scores individually. Although the summed scores were quite significant, it could not be demonstrated that the effect stemmed from the summation as opposed to concluding that a large number of individually significant items "carried" the data when summation was attempted.

The hypothesis that equity of the summed scores would be conducive to good CP was not supported. With the aid of hindsight, reasons why equity would not automatically influence attraction or CP were expressed.

NOTE

Data reported in Chapter 13 were initially reported in Murstein (1972a) and Murstein (1972d).

CHAPTER 14

A Partial Replication of SVR Theory and Extensions of Exchange and SVR Theory to Other Dyads

In this chapter we shall first consider a study by Hutton (1974), which attempted to test several hypotheses of SVR theory. We shall then consider evidence that is consistent with the exchange aspect of SVR theory obtained from sources other than our premarital couples. We shall also test some of our 39 hypotheses with other than premarital dyads.[1]

THE HUTTON REPLICATION

Hutton (1974) studied engaged or dating couples in which one member was a student in an undergraduate psychology class at Georgia State University. The subjects completed a measure of self-esteem (based on the Leary Interpersonal Checklist), the Allport-Vernon-Lindzey Scale of Values, and two questionnaires measuring self-differentiation, a concept tapping personality functioning and flexibility. Subjects stated the length of time they had been dating and were subdivided into long-term courtships (18 months and over) and short-term courtships (less than 18 months).

Several of her eight hypotheses were very similar to the ones I employed, and I shall indicate the corresponding SVR hypothesis number in parentheses following the description of Hutton's hypothesis. Her first hypothesis was that self-esteem scores of the couples would be significantly related (SVR 18), which was confirmed $(r = .24, p < .05)$.

She next hypothesized that her long-term courtship couples would show greater equivalence of self-esteem than her short-term couples. This hypothesis was not specifically tested by my research but is wholly consistent with the SVR dictum that self-esteem, being primarily a role stage variable, ought to be stronger in the tertiary or role stage of courtship than in earlier stages. The correlation for long-term couples was .45 $(p < .01)$, whereas that for short-term couples was .08, which was not significant, thus confirming the hypothesis.

Hutton also hypothesized that self-esteem similarity between members of couples would lead to good CP measured by question-naires three months later (SVR 20). However, no significant correlation resulted. Her fourth hypothesis was that members of couples would show similarity on their values (SVR 7), which was clearly supported on 4 of 6 values, as noted in Chapter 5.

Hutton's fifth hypothesis called for greater similarity on values for short-term couples than for long-term ones. This followed the SVR thesis that values are more important earlier in courtship than later. No support was found for this hypothesis. Neither was support found for her sixth hypothesis that value congruence would be associated with good CP for short-term couples, but not for long-term ones. No significant correlation was found for either group.

The seventh hypothesis predicted that self-differentiation scores would be equivalent for members of couples. This score was not used in my research, but Hutton's description of it clearly marks it as a role variable. Since most of her subjects knew each other more than 18 months, it could be concluded that the average subject was clearly in the role stage of courtship and hence similarity of self-differentiation ought to be significantly established. Her two self-differentiation scores showed correlations of .39 and .43, both highly significant $(p < .01)$.

Her last hypothesis predicted that equity of self-differentiation would lead to good CP. A strong trend was found for long-term couples $(r = .30, p < .07)$, and a weaker trend for short-term couples $(r = .22, p < .15)$.

Overall her data show fairly good support for SVR theory. They are highly similar to my own findings, with the strongest support being found for equity between couples for which I, too, reported good support, and marginal or nonsupport for correlations with CP, where my data also were weakest. The failure of short-term couples to manifest greater value congruence than long-term couples, and the failure of value congruence for short-term relationships to correlate higher with CP than for long-term relationships to do so are not necessarily blows against SVR theory, as Hutton herself points out. She suggests that value similarity may exert its maximum effect so early in courtship that most "short-term" relationships, which ranged from several months to a year and a half, may actually be too "long-term" at the time of testing to manifest any association with CP. We shall consider the full implications of findings on SVR theory in the last chapter (Chapter 16).

PHYSICAL ATTRACTIVENESS AS AN EXCHANGE VARIABLE

Illsley, cited in Lipset and Bendix (1950), reported that lower-status women who married higher-status men tended to be both taller and healthier than their nonmobile counterparts. Holmes and Hatch (1938) likewise reported a correlation between beauty and probability of marriage in an era when, for a woman, marriage was clearly superior in status to singleness. An investigation by Elder (1969) found that the tendency of a man's social rank to exceed his wife's premarital rank was related to her physical attractiveness. Where a woman had more education than her husband, however, she was more likely to be physically unattractive than physically attractive.

The applicability of Hypothesis 1 (equity of physical attractiveness between partners) was tested by Murstein and Christy (1973) on a middle-aged New England sample of members of a local Connecticut historical society (N=22). The support for the hypothesis was stronger than it had been for our premarital couples. The correlations between members of couples on photos taken by the researchers, self-concepts for attractiveness and perception of the partner's attractiveness were $r = .60$ ($p < .01$), $r = .41$ ($p < .05$), and $r = .43$ ($p < .05$), respectively. These data support the importance of equity of physical attractiveness in marital choice and possibly in maintaining a marriage. It may be that the higher correlations found for middle-aged couples in the Murstein and Christy study as compared to the premarital couples reported on in this book may reflect a selection over time with respect to physical attractiveness; that is, those of disparate physical attractiveness may be more likely to divorce as time progresses. Perhaps up to the point of homogenization of physical attractiveness by old age, the correlation between members of a couple should increase with an increase in the number of years married. The smallness of the sample, however, suggests caution in generalizing.

Data from experiments in matching, at first glance, have not seemed to support Hypothesis 1. Research by Walster, Aronson, Abrahams, and Rottman (1966) on college freshmen who were allegedly matched by a computer but who were actually randomly paired except for height, indicated that physical attractiveness was the major determinant of attraction. The desire to date a physically attractive person was not dependent on one's own attractiveness. Found not of any consequence in the brief two-and-one-half-hour period between the onset of the dance and rating time were measures of social skills, masculinity-femininity, introversion, self-acceptance, intelligence, and high school grade rank. The strong correlation between attraction and physical attractiveness was also supported in computer studies by Brislin and Lewis (1968) and Tesser and Brodie (1971).

The difficulty with these studies lies in the artificial nature of the pairing arrangement. Every individual was in effect guaranteed his date and stood no chance of rejection—at least for the evening. We have noted earlier that *ideally* most people desire to date the best. It is the cost of rejection and/or the tension involved in relating to an individual with greater assets that lowers the aspiration level.

Subsequent experiments that have not guaranteed acceptability have resulted in findings more favorable to the principle of equity. Berscheid, Dion, Walster, and Walster (1971) required subjects to *choose* a dating partner. The attractiveness of the partner varied, as did the probability of being accepted by the potential date. As before, physically attractive dates were most preferred. However, men and women judged to be relatively unattractive by judges tended to choose less attractive dates than did those judged highly attractive. The stated probability of acceptance or rejection did not relate to the attractiveness of the chosen date, however.

A study by Huston (1973a), however, did show this effect. The men were asked to choose a date from an array containing three levels of attractiveness. Half of the men were guaranteed acceptability and half were left in a state of ambiguity regarding their acceptability. Huston found that male subjects assured of acceptance selected a more physically attractive woman than men whose acceptance was ambiguous. Subjects estimated that the more attractive women were less likely to accept them than less attractive women. Also, the subjects' self-evaluated physical attractiveness influenced their estimates of being accepted by the potential date. However, self-estimates of attractiveness did not relate to the degree of attractiveness of their choice of dates.

A study by Stroebe, Insko, Thompson, and Layton (1971) did show, however, that relative to subjects who considered themselves attractive, those evaluating themselves as unattractive were more apt to consider dating unattractive others and less likely to consider dating attractive others.

Although not one of these experiments offers total support for equity of physical attractiveness, taken as a group they do support it somewhat. The physically attractive are preferred first, but the self-evaluation and probability of success serve as moderating influences. It should be noted, nevertheless, that none of these studies approximates very closely the conditions existing with actual ongoing relationships. The game-like atmosphere of these studies must surely have mitigated the fear of rejection and encouraged each person to "go for broke." A high-need achiever may hate to lose under any circumstances, but it is less painful to lose a million dollars in a game of Monopoly than in the stock market. The conclusion that equity of physical attractiveness operates in real-life conditions, where other assets and liabilities are approximately balanced, seems justified. Where the balance of assets is tilted against an individual, physical attractiveness appears to be the *method par excellence* for redressing the balance.

RACE AND MARITAL CHOICE

It might be argued by some persons that whites and blacks are just people under the skin, and, if they interact, they may fall in love and marry for the same reasons that two whites or two blacks marry. However democratic this statement may sound, it has not been accepted by a number of researchers. Well over thirty years ago, an exchange theory was proposed by Robert Merton (1941) who, borrowing heavily from an earlier study by Kingsley Davis (1941), explained the reason for endogamous rules (the tendency to prefer marriage within a particular group, caste, or class) to be so firmly entrenched in all societies.

Endogamy ensures, to a certain extent, that the marriage contractants will have a rough similarity of cultural background inasmuch as they have been socialized in groups with similar cultures. A universe of discourse common to the contractants lessens the likelihood of intra-familial conflict deriving from different sets of values of the spouses. Moreover, by precluding diverse group loyalties of the mates, the conjugal unit is integrated with the larger social structure. Both class and caste endogamy prevent that familial instability which occurs when children identify themselves with the upper-status parent and condemn the lower-status parent in terms of the cultural values which they have assimilated. This potential split of loyalties becomes especially disruptive within a racial-caste system where the child's animosity may be directed against himself as well as the lower-caste parent who bears the invidious racial marks. (Merton, 1941, pp. 368-69)

From this point, Merton goes on to explain that deviations from the norm involving upper- and lower-caste groups elicit a kind of exchange in which the lower-caste person gives something extra to the relationship to compensate for the higher status of the "upper" person. Merton deals with color (white) as one example of status, and socioeconomic class as another. He then makes three hypotheses:

1. The marriage of a white lower-class female to a black lower-class male will occur no more frequently than that of a black lower-class female to a white lower-class male. The dimensions of status are equally distributed in such an arrangement.

2. A white lower-class female should marry a black upper-class male more frequently than any other combination. Presumably, the "whiteness" of the lower-class female should balance off the upper-classness of her consort. (It might be thought that a lower-class white male and an upper-class black female should be equally balanced in rewarding power; however, Morton does not deal with this possibility.) Many other combinations would not provide for a balancing of caste and class. Marriage where both the white and black were either of the lower or the upper class would be imbalanced to the detriment of the white, and white upper-class/black lower-class marriage would be even more imbalanced.

3. The least frequent type of marriage should be one in which race and class hypogamy exists; i.e., one in which a white upper-class female marries a black lower-class male.

The evidence bearing on these hypotheses is rather skimpy, but the data of Wirth and Goldhammer (1944) on black-white marriage in Boston between 1914 and 1938 do not support any of the hypotheses. Regarding Merton's first hypothesis, marriages of lower-class white females to black lower-class males, contrary to prediction, occurred three times as frequently as that of lower-class black females and white males.

The second hypothesis calling for a white lower-class female/black upper-class male marriage to be the most frequent was not supported either. Marriage was far more prevalent when the black groom and white bride were in identical or nearly identical occupational levels. The tendency for homogamy in socioeconomic status to be most prevalent in interracial marriages is also reported in a study of Los Angeles county in the fifties and sixties (Burma, Cretser, and Seacrest, 1970).

Merton's third hypothesis has not yet been tested, but the failure of his first two hypotheses puts his theory in question. Their failure, however, does not necessarily imply that the romantic notion of two persons in love being blind to color is correct. We know, for example, that race is the most endogamously selective variable for marriage. Even an adherent of the romantic school, therefore, would have to acknowledge that before a black person and a white person can be struck by Cupid's arrow, they must come within range of his bow. The probability of a black and a white marrying, therefore, can be seen as involving two distinct probabilities: first, the probability that they will ever meet in a relationship in which marriage is at least conceivable (certain contacts are relatively unconducive to marriage possibilities—such as janitor/secretary, stock clerk/buyer, waitress/ employer; hence the necessity of stipulating reasonable status equivalence, which makes the possibility of marriage conceivable); second, the probability that they will marry, given that they meet in a potentially marriageable situation.

A study by David Heer (1966) bears on the probability of the first part. Studying the state of California, he found a strong correlation ($r = .85$) between the actual and expected intermarriage rate for whites based on the proportion of blacks in each of 26 aereal units. The greater the proportion of blacks: the greater the intermarriage rate. Using a measure of residential segregation, he found that this index correlated ($r = - .57$) with the ratio of actual to expected intermarriage. In other words, the greater the segregation, the less the intermarriage rate. Last the ratio of white-collar whites to white-collar blacks correlated ($r = - .83$) with the ratio of actual to expected intermarriage. Thus, the greater the proportion of white-collar blacks, the greater the intermarriage rate. In sum, these data show that the intermarriage rate depends conclusively on the number of blacks in the area, their degree of residential segregation, and the kind of jobs they hold. Heer's data do not, of course, tell us *which* blacks will marry *which* whites, although they do suggest that occupational equality may be a factor.

We are now at the second step of probability, in which we need a theory to explain the probability of a black/white marriage once the possibility of a meeting exists. We shall try to do this within the framework of SVR theory. First, we may note that in the "stimulus" stage the black is not apt to be considered by the white as a marriage partner, because within most white subcultures blacks are perceived as being of inferior status to whites. In like manner, most blacks are uninterested in marrying whites, who, thus, also fail to pass the stimulus stage. The stimulus barrier is further strengthened by the finding that white individuals with some degree of prejudice against blacks tend to believe that the blacks will have different attitudes and values than they (Rokeach, Smith, and Evans, 1960).

Regarding the actual compatibility of values between blacks and whites, research indicates that some differences exist even after controlling for income and education (Rokeach, 1973). Thus, value incompatibility would probably be somewhat more frequent for mixed-race couples than for those of the same race.

Role functioning offers perhaps the least hindrance to black/white couples considering marriage who have negotiated the first two stages successfully. Roles to some extent are open to choice, depending on the structure of personality as well as the demands of the en- vironment. Yet roles are also influenced by the mores of society and the effects of child-rearing. Because the discrimination in jobs has fallen most heavily on the black male, his role in the family has often been more tenuous than that of the white male. On the other hand, the extended family (grandparents, cousins, nephews, aunts, uncles, nieces) has traditionally been much closer in black families; thus the differences in cultural prescription for roles between black and white would ensure an additional problem for the longevity of black/white couple relationships.

ANOTHER LOOK AT EXCHANGE

In the face of the difficulties outlined above, it is scarcely surprising to note that the black/white marriage percentage for the country as a whole reported in the 1960 census was 0.15 percent. Although the precise figures for 1970 have not yet been published, preliminary estimates indicate a large relative percentage increase, but an overall figure of still less than one percent. But what of this fraction of one percent—the exceptions? Are these individuals insensitive to color so that they interact simply as two people? I wish to suggest that few persons, if any, are insensitive to color, and that *whites marrying blacks profit consciously or unconsciously from the higher status of* whites by marrying partners with higher marital assets than they themselves possess.

Although Merton's use of the exchange model did not result in support for his hypotheses, the difficulty may have rested in his choice of socioeconomic class as the variable on which to base his exchange theory. Marrying a person of another class is a rare occurrence, because it would raise the specter of intrafamilial dissension through a clash in the different values associated with class, a view expressed earlier by Davis and by Merton himself.

Merton would have been on firmer ground had he predicted that although class is homogamously selective for black/white marriage, it is not as selective as in all-white or all-black marriage; he might have noted then that when there are differences in status, they will be in the direction of black superiority and white inferiority with respect to the average of each race.

There is little reliable data to test this view with respect to class, but it is supported by the data on education taken from the 1960 census as shown in Table 14.1.

Table 14.1

PERCENT DISTRIBUTION BY YEARS OF SCHOOL COMPLETED
BY HUSBAND AND WIFE, BY RACE OF HUSBAND AND WIFE:
UNITED STATES, 1960

	White husband		Negro husband	
Years of School Completed	*White wife*	*Negro wife*	*White wife*	*Negro wife*
All married couples [1]	100.0	100.0	100.0	100.0
Husband:				
No high school (0-8)	16.9	34.4	30.2	40.0
High school (9-12)	54.2	48.1	49.7	49.9
College (13 or more)	28.9	17.5	20.1	10.1
Wife:				
No high school	11.3	24.8	25.4	27.0
High school	68.4	60.6	59.1	62.3
College	20.3	14.6	15.4	10.7

[1] Married couples with husband and wife in first marriage, married between 1950 and 1960, and excluding couples with either spouse other than white or Negro.

Source: US Bureau of the Census, *US Census of Population: 1960, Subject Reports, Marital Status,* Final Report PC(2)—4E, table 12.

Inspection of this table indicates that the black husband of a white wife possesses an education superior to that of a black husband of a black wife but not to that of a white husband of a white wife. Likewise, the black wife of a white husband typically has an education superior to that of a black wife of a black husband but not to that of a white wife of a white husband. In short, compared to all-black marriages, black-white marriages are completely in accord with the exchange theory predictions. Compared to the white educational levels, however, black-white marriages do not support the predictions, because the educational level of the black is always lower than that of his same-sex counterpart in an all-white marriage.

In comparing educational levels, however, it should be kept in mind that blacks average less education than whites; if we assume that races are approximately equal in intelligence, then the absolute level of education for a black might tend to underestimate his intelligence; hence a white marrying a black with a slightly inferior education might actually be marrying an individual slightly superior in intellectual status. Perhaps a fairer test of educational status, therefore, might be to compare each person with the norm for his race rather than the absolute level of education attained. In any event, if one takes cognizance of the difference in educational level attained between the races, the data in Table 14.1 generally support exchange theory.

There is another variable influencing the exchange balance in marriage that should be considered—the sex factor. If men at present possess more power in marital choice than women, it follows that men ought to be better able to traverse the color barrier than women; accordingly, more black men should marry white women than black women marry white men. Data on recent marriages in the 1970 census supported this assumption in that there were 41,223 of the first kind of marriage and 23,566 of the second.

It is also noteworthy that the proportion of black man/white woman marriages of the total black/white marriages (figures were available only on the 1960 census) was highest in the North and West (62 percent) compared to the South where it was only 42 percent (Carter and Glick, 1970). If we make the reasonable assumption that the black man enjoys more status in the West and North than the South, then the figures are consistent with exchange theory.

There is another variable that probably is not as homogamously selective as socioeconomic class or education, and would, therefore, be more readily available for "trading" to achieve equal exchange in interracial marriage. This variable is physical attractiveness, which, perhaps because it was not a sociological or psychological variable, has been ignored until recently by most researchers in these disciplines. According to the exchange component of SVR theory, an individual possessing higher race status might select a partner from a lower race status who was more attractive than a partner he might obtain within his own race. Regrettably, this hypothesis has not yet been put to empirical test.

There is some evidence, however, which indicates that judgments of physical attractiveness are influenced by status. A study was undertaken in which 3 photographs of black men, of black women, of white men, and of white women were judged for physical attractiveness by black and white judges (Parrott and Coleman, 1971). Each picture represented a gradation of culturally acknowledged racial characteristics. The extreme black picture, for example, depicted the photo of an individual with thicker lips, wider nose, and more prominent cheekbones than the other pictures. The most extreme photograph of a white represented thinner lips, narrower nose, and smoother cheekbones than the other types. Both white men and black men prefered the extreme white type, whereas black and white women showed no such distinction; however, black women showed less liking for all physical types.

If we assume that preferences for physical types are culturally learned rather than innate, then these differences suggest the effect of higher white status on standards of sexual attractiveness. The lower ratings by black women to all of the pictures may reflect the dual handicap of being black and a woman in a society discriminating against blacks and women. These twin handicaps on the one hand may generally dampen the probability of black women/white men marriages and reduce the black woman's sexual interest in white men who are seen as too distant in status to be interested in them. On the other hand, there may be resentment against black men because, as *men*, they have the option, and are increasingly exercising it, of courting white women.

The power of color in mate selection is also seen in another recent study which investigates the effect of lightness of color on educational level, occupation, and socioeconomic mobility within black marriages (Udry, Bauman, and Chase, 1971). For long-standing marriages, lightness of skin color was positively associated for both sexes with higher educational level, occupation, and mobility. For more recent marriages, however, darkness of skin color for the man was positively associated with these variables, whereas women still continued to show a positive association between lightness of skin and these variables. Not surprisingly therefore, whereas light skin colored men and women were highly likely to be paired in earlier marriages, the more recent marriages showed more dark-skinned men paired with light-skinned women. These data, collected in the latter part of 1965 in Washington, D.C., suggest that for that sample and time period, at least, black was more beautiful for men than for women.

That color of skin enters not only into evaluations of the other's physical attractiveness but also of one's own attractiveness is demonstrated in a study by Rosenberg and Simmons (1971). Black interviewers rating black children were more apt to rate the light rather than the dark children as good-looking. Moreover, 70 percent of the black children rated as light by the interviewers considered themselves "very" or "pretty" good-looking, as opposed to only 47 percent of such ratings for children described by the interviewers as darker.

These studies suggest that, unromantic as it may sound, two people do not simply fall in love, disregarding "stimulus" characteristics such as color. The members of an interracial couple may be personally quite unprejudiced, but, either consciously or unconsiously, they follow the weighting assigned to color by society. The color that is "up" in the particular strata in which they operate probably trades that status asset in return for better looks, intelligence, personality adequacy, economic standing, or education on the part of the member of the "down" color.

APPLICATION TO ONGOING MARRIAGES AND FRIENDSHIP

Several of the hypotheses on marital choice have been carried over into two studies that my associates and I have done on marriage (Beck, 1970, Murstein and Beck, 1972) and friendship (Murstein and Lamb, 1973). The married sample consisted of 60 volunteer couples, none of whom had less than a high school degree and all of whom had been married at least one year. The mean age of the wives was 25.01, that of the husbands 26.54, the standard deviations being 2.42 and 3.15 years respectively. The average length of time married was 3.07 years (S.D. 1.79), the range being from 1 to 9.82 years. In 36 of the couples at least one spouse was a student. Other occupations of participants included teachers, nurses, and social workers. Overall, the sample was middle to upper-middle class and relatively homogeneous.

The friendship population consisted of 26 women residing in a cooperative college house at a northeast women's college. The typical age was the late teens, and the mean length of residence was 10 months, with a range extending from 4 months to 3 years and 4 months. The house had voted unanimously to participate in the study of personality and friendship. The nature of a cooperative house with the sharing of many decisions and duties of housekeeping and cooking—duties not borne by the regular college student at a residential college—quickly leads to each member getting to know other members quite well.

In addition to our own data, information from selected other studies will be cited where pertinent. Where the hypotheses from the work on marital choice have not been carried over intact, they have been changed by substituting marital adjustment for courtship progress in the original hypotheses. Otherwise, for the purpose of comparison, the numeration of the original hypotheses is retained.

MARRIED COUPLES

Hypothesis 8, that self-acceptance is positively associated with the tendency to perceive the partner as similar to the self, has been tested in a relatively large number of studies. Kogan and Jackson (1964) gave 24 middle-aged women the Interpersonal Check List, which they took under the following sets: self, ideal-self, perceived husband. Dividing the women into two groups on the basis of their perception of similarity of their husband to themselves, the high group (r ranged from .54 to .98) showed a mean self, ideal-self r of .82, whereas the low perceived similarity group (r ranged from .36 to −.40) showed a mean self, ideal-self r of .46, the difference being significant at the .05 level.

Goodman (1964) worked with both members of married couples to whom he administered the Edwards Personal Preference Schedule and a direct measure of self-acceptance, the Bill Index of Adjustment and Values. He found that high self-acceptance individuals manifested a good deal of actual similarity with respect to the spouse, whereas low self-acceptance individuals showed negative (complementary) correlations. The results of this study are similar to those found in our work on premarital couples, except that actual similarity was used as a measure by Goodman instead of perceived similarity.

A study by Murstein and Levy (1973), also with middle-aged couples, dichotomized 15 married men into high and low self-acceptance subjects based on an adjective checklist. The seven high men showed a mean perceived similarity to spouse r of .47, the value of r being .19 for the low men, and the difference quite significant ($p <$

.01). Comparable values for high and low women were .74 and .31 respectively, and the difference was again significant ($p < .01$).

The research of Karp, Jackson, and Lester (1970) involved unmarried couples and an adjectival phrase checklist. In general, the actual self resembled the perceived partner's self; however, in the case where the self and ideal-self were very discrepant, the partner was perceived as close to the ideal-self rather than the self.

Last, Beck (1970) found an r of .21 ($p < .05$) between self-acceptance and perceived similarity to the spouse for 60 husbands using an adjective trait list. For women, the same correlation reached a high .76 ($p < .01$). Hypothesis 8, thus, has been overwhelmingly supported in studies with married people.

Hypothesis 11, which stated that ability to predict the partner's self and ideal-self concepts is associated with marriage adjustment, has been supported for women's predictions but not for those of men in a study by Murstein and Beck (1972). The correlations for women's predictions of their husband's self and ideal-self were .37 ($p < .01$) and .22 ($p < .05$). The correlations for men's predictions were .05 and .10 respectively, both nonsignificant. These data are consistent with the position that the ability to accurately gauge the partner is more important for the less powerful member than for the more powerful one.

Hypothesis 14, which stated that partner satisfaction (correlation of partner$_A$, ideal-spouse$_A$) would be correlated with marital adjustment, was confirmed ($p < .01$) by Murstein and Beck (1972). The correlation for men's perceptions was .44, for women .57, the difference between the sexes not being significant. The same hypothesis had been confirmed earlier by Luckey (1960a) and Kotler (1965).

Hypothesis 17, that intraperceptions would educe significantly greater correlations than interperceptions, was tested by Beck (1970). The most objective way to compare intraperceptual and inter-perceptual correlations is to do so for similar concepts. When, therefore, the four perceived similarity correlations (the tendency of men and of women to perceive themselves as similar to their spouses and their ideal-selves as similar to their ideal-spouses) were averaged, they yielded a mean r of .28. Actual similarity between the couples' selves, ideal-selves, perception of partner, and ideal-spouse yielded a mean r of .26, the difference between perceived and actual similarity not being significant. However, the two perceived partner satisfaction correlations (perception of the spouse by one individual compared to the same person's ideal-spouse concept) averaged .48, whereas the eight actual role-compatibility correlations (self-concept of one individual compared with the way he is perceived by his spouse) showed a mean value of .30. By an exact probability test, this difference approached significance ($p < .07$). Thus, there seems to be a trend toward some support for Hypothesis 17, although strictly speaking it is not supported.

Hypothesis 21, that marital adjustment is greater when two partners possess the same degree of mental health, has been indirectly tested by Boxer (1970). He found marital adjustment to be low in couples where one member of the couple had been hospitalized because of a psychiatric disorder. (Boxer did not measure marital adjustment per se. However, his description of these couples plus the fact that they showed poor confirmation of the partner's self | self $_A$ – spouse $_B$| suggest that they were dissatisfied in their marriages.) Compared to two control groups, the members of the psychiatric group had significantly greater discrepancies on a wide variety of measures of mental health. The data are not terribly strong, nonetheless, because the measurements occurred after hospitalization, and there was no way of determining the scores prior to commitment. Moreover, the couples were selected for discrepancy in that the group was defined as having *one* member who was hospitalized; accordingly, the fact that such couples diverged on mental health scores compared to non-psychiatrically selected couples was not astounding. The best test of this hypothesis would obviously be a longitudinal study of intact couples.

Hypothesis 22, that high self-accepting persons are more likely to see their spouse as approaching their ideal spouse concept than are low self-accepting persons, was significantly demonstrated via a *t* test for both husbands ($p < .01$) and wives ($p < .01$) in a study of young married couples (Beck, 1970).

The greater importance of the man than of the woman in courtship led to a number of hypotheses regarding his possibly greater role in determining marital adjustment. Hypothesis 25, for example, stated that the effect of neuroticism in the man on marital adjustment would be greater than would neuroticism in the woman. There is very little evidence on this question. Terman (1938) found little difference between the correlation of neuroticism and marital adjustment either for men or for women. Both correlations were low and of minimal significance. His measure of neuroticism (Bernreuter's Introversion Score), however, is not considered an adequate measure of neuroticism by current standards. It is probably best to await further evidence before any definitive conclusions can be drawn with respect to this question.

Hypothesis 26, that confirmation of the man's self-image should have greater impact on marital adjustment than confirmation of the woman's self-image, received a direct test in the Murstein and Beck (1972) article. The tendency of women to confirm the self-image of their husbands was significantly associated with marital adjustment ($r = .32$, $p < .01$), but, as predicted, no significant correlation was found between marital adjustment and the confirmation of the wives' self-images by their husbands ($r = .02$).

Hypothesis 27, that the predictive accuracy of the spouse's self and ideal-self concepts would be significantly more positively correlated with marital adjustment for female predictors than for male predictors was also largely verified by this study. Women's accuracy ($r = .37$) was significantly greater ($p < .01$) than men's accuracy ($r = .05$) in predicting the self-concept of the spouse, but did not quite reach significance for the prediction of his (her) ideal-self concept (women's $r = .22$, men's $r = .10$). However, the women's r of .22 did attain significance, whereas the men's r did not.

Hypothesis 28 stated that if the man's role in marriage is more crucial to the success of the marriage than that of the woman, his intraperceptions should be more closely associated with the couple's marriage adjustment than his wife's intraperceptions. In the Murstein and Beck study (1972), four intraperceptions were obtained for each subject: | self − ideal-self |; | self − spouse |; | ideal-self − ideal-spouse |; | spouse − ideal-spouse |. The average correlation for the men's perceptions was .32 and for the wives' .47. Although the difference is not significant, a trend exists contrary to that predicted by the hypothesis and contrary to the findings in the earlier work on premarital couples.

Taken as a totality, the data are consistent with the thesis that the husband is the central perceptual object in early marriage. Unlike the data on premarital couples, however, the present data do not support the conclusion that the husband is of major importance *both as perceiver and as object*. Said otherwise, the confirmation of his perceptions of himself as well as the ability to accurately predict these perceptions by the woman are associated with marital adjustment. However, unlike the case in courtship, his intraperceptions are no more important for marriage adjustment than are hers, and may even be somewhat less important.

The interpretation of this difference in findings probably rests on the difference between courtship and marriage. Unless the man's various perceptions of himself and his girlfriend are congruent, he is not apt to propose to her no matter how congruent her intra-perceptions may be. Once married, however, her perceptions become more important. If they are not congruent she may feel unhappy, and this unhappiness is transmitted to him with the result that both become unhappy. The possible lesser importance of his intra-perceptions after marriage may reside in the fact that men, more often than women, have alternatives to marriage as a source of contentment – for instance, a career.

The suggestion that the woman may be of key importance as the perceiver and the man as the perceived is quite consistent with the view, in American marriage, that the woman is called upon to adjust to the man much more than vice-versa (Burgess & Locke, 1945). If that is true, then it would be expected that her perceptions would correlate more highly with marital adjustment than his do (they do in this study, though not quite significantly). Also, correlations in which he is the perceptual target would correlate more highly with marital adjustment than when she is the perceptual target (this is largely the case). Whether this state of affairs represents an injustice to women or is an essential role differentiation necessary for optimal family functioning is a moot point, but one not capable of being answered by the present data.

There are alternate interpretations that could account for the data. Could it be that women are in general more astute about interpersonal matters than are men? Perhaps so, but the data of Murstein and Beck (1972) do not reveal this. There were eight correlations in the study that measured the ability to predict the partner's responses (the self, ideal-self, spouse, ideal-spouse, concepts held by the husbands and by the wives). Four of these correlations were significant at the .05 point or better; two by men, two by women. Thus, no sex difference in accuracy was observed.

When the correlations were inspected more closely, however, a pattern clearly emerged. The significant perceptions by wives were those in which they predicted their husbands' self and ideal-self concepts. The significant perceptions by husbands were those in which they predicted how their wives perceived their spouses and ideal-spouses. All four significant correlations, therefore, related to the man as the perceptual object and confirm the centrality of the way the husband is perceived being a major factor in marital adjustment.

There is, nevertheless, yet another plausible explanation of the data. It could be argued that the role of husbands in society is more clear-cut than that of women. The American husband stereotype has always called on the man to occupy the role of provider who aggressively surmounts any kind of difficulty while yet manifesting only tenderness and sensitivity toward his wife. The role of the wife, however, is still in transition and involves several choices, so that no single stereotype has won wide acceptance. There is the stereotype of the traditional submissive wife who doesn't work but stays home and seeks to fulfill the role of good mother and homemaker. There is the stereotype of the career-housewife who works, tends the house, and raises the children, and may feel anxious about not doing any of her jobs quite right. Then, there is the egalitarian stereotype who believes that everything—career, work in household, raising of children—should be shared fifty-fifty.

If individuals project their stereotype in their forecast of the responses of the other sex and also for themselves, then from our preceding discussion women following the norms should find it easier to predict the self-concept of the husband than vice-versa. Further, to the extent that the individual conforms to the expected role for him, the couple should be happy. Since the role expected of men is still more clearly defined than that expected of women, we would expect that satisfaction of the role norm by men should be more associated with marriage adjustment than stereotyped role conformity by women.

There is a study by Corsini (1956), which bears on this question. Working with University of Chicago couples, he used a 50-item adjective Q sort to measure personality. A mean correlation, resulting from correlating every man's self sort with every other man's self sort, served as an index of conformity to the male stereotype. A similar procedure was used to obtain a female index of conformity. The conformity index was then correlated with a measure of marital adjustment. The correlation between the marital adjustment of both husband and wife with the male conformity index was very significant; that between the female conformity index and marital adjustment nonsignificant. In other words, the husband's playing a stereotyped masculine role made for a happy marriage. The wife's playing such a role was independent of marriage adjustment.

With reference to the Murstein and Beck data, therefore, it may be that the accuracy in predicting the man's role is an artifact. Perhaps most of the wives predicted a socially desirable masculine role for their husbands, but only happy husbands saw themselves in this light, thus accounting for the association between accuracy and marital adjustment. The separation of these confounded explanations is a task for future research.

In sum, the research on early marriage, although skimpy, tends to support many of the hypotheses first formulated for marital choice and courtship progress. Many, but not all of the factors associated with choice seem to be important in maintaining adjustment in the early years of marriage.

FRIENDSHIP

Most of the studies of friendship have utilized same-sex friends, and our conclusions are most applicable, therefore, to this kind of relationship. In the premarital data referred to earlier, the hypothesis that, in accordance with the exchange process, members of couples would show greater than chance similarity of physical attractiveness was significantly confirmed (Hypothesis 1). Few would question, however, that marriage has more of the physical in it than friendship. Also, physical appearance would appear at first glance to have greater social stimulus value in a marriage than it has in same-sex friendship.

It may be, however, that physical attractiveness plays a role of some importance, but in a rather convoluted way. Research indicated that physical attractiveness is appreciated by same-sex peers as well as opposite-sex (Berscheid and Walster, 1974). The beautiful are assumed to have many admirable qualities, though other research indicates that the beauty stereotype has some unattractive traits assigned to it as well (Dermer, 1973).

For women, in particular, a beautiful female friend may be at the same time both a boon and a bane. If a woman is somewhat unattractive, she may find it hard to meet interesting men. All sorts of men, however, hover around a beautiful woman. The unattractive friend may think that she may cull the rejects of her beautious friend, or she may think that other traits of hers might lead her eventually to win over the boyfriend once a "closed field" situation exists.

On the other hand, a beautiful friend is deadly competition. If the mediocre-looking girl has a boyfriend, she may live in fear that once he meets her beautiful friend she will lose him. As a result, the null hypothesis of no association between the attractiveness of friends was relied on since I had no adequate information as to which direction the correlation would fall.

The hypothesis was tested in a study of a girl's college cooperative (Murstein and Lamb, 1973) in which everyone (N = 26) ranked every other person for physical attractiveness, the mean ranking attributed to a subject serving as the criterion. Reciprocal best friends within the group (those who chose each other among their top three friends), were correlated for physical attractiveness. The resulting r of $-.49$ ($p<.05$) was rather unexpected. It suggests that, since physical intimacy is probably not crucial to the relationship per se, physical attractiveness may serve as a negotiable asset on the part of an attractive woman to be traded for assets that the nonattractive friend possesses. Perhaps equal physical attractiveness on the part of girlfriends would put them in competition for men. It may be, therefore, that the more attractive partner serves as a supplier of men and as a model for the less attractive one on how to deal with men, which is compensated by the less attractive girl's services to the more attractive one in other areas. The data serve only to whet the appetite for more extensive research on this question.

That friends tend to share common values much more than nonfriends (Hypothesis 7) has been extensively documented by Richardson (1939, 1940), Newcomb (1961), and numerous others. The occasional failure of this variable to hold (Marsden, 1966) may be a function of the nature of the control group used to compare against the friends. Marsden's data showed a significant association of values among friends, but this was no greater than the value obtained by randomly matching college girls from the same college population. If the measuring instrument deals in very general values, and if the population from which the sample is drawn is itself a homogeneous group, then it may well occur, as was the case with Marsden, that friends are no more homogeneously selected than strangers.

The tendency for self-acceptance and perceived similarity to the fiancé(e) or spouse to correlate (Hypothesis 8), as we have seen, was well documented for engaged and married persons. The relationship also holds when best friends are substituted for the fiancé(e) and spouse (McKenna, Hofstaetter, and O'Connor, 1956; Murstein and Levy, 1973; Murstein and Lamb, 1973). Hypothesis 18 called for a greater-than-chance association for self-acceptance among reciprocal best friends. In the study on the girl's cooperative (Murstein and Lamb, 1973), this was significantly demonstrated ($p < .01$). Last, several researchers (Vreeland and Corey, 1935; Bonney, 1946) have reported a significant correlation among friends for neuroticism (Hypothesis 19). In sum, the data on friendship closely follow the findings for premarital couples, with the noted exception of the inegality of physical attractiveness.

CONCLUSIONS

In reviewing the data, it appears that SVR theory is consistent with much of what we know about marital choice, and that it has applicability to variables such as skin color which were not tested in my own research. Further, many of the hypotheses, slightly modified, apply to married relationships and to friendships. The sole clearcut exception, the lack of homogamy of physical attractiveness among college women friends, is hardly surprising. Same-sex friends who are not homosexual would presumably find physical attractiveness of less personal concern than would opposite-sex lovers. However, with reference to competition for men, reasons were advanced why women of disparate physical attractiveness might be drawn to each other.

It seems reasonable from the support tendered our hypotheses from data in marriage and friendship to conclude that much of SVR theory may apply to dyadic relationships in general rather than solely to marital choice. The testing of more hypotheses in future research should determine the extent of generalizability.

NOTES

Portions of Chapter 14 were based on other works by the author (Murstein, 1971b; 1973b).

1. All hypothesis numbers henceforth in this chapter refer to their SVR counterparts.

CHAPTER 15

Multiple Predictors
and Other Correlates
of Courtship Progress

At the end of the data collection of Group I, we wished to see how well CP could be predicted by combining a number of variables in linear fashion to obtain a multiple correlation. We were also interested in ascertaining the degree to which each of our variables could predict the CP criterion. The results of this analysis will be described both for Group I and Group III. Group II, it will be recalled, is omitted from consideration because of the small number of subjects and because almost everyone in this group had achieved good CP.

GROUP I

The criterion to be predicted was the combined CP score of the couple, which could range from 2 to 8. The number of predictor variables was 109, and they were selected in most cases on the arbitrary basis that they ought to have something to do with CP. A few variables were selected on the basis of having already proved to be significantly associated with CP. The items chosen included Revised Personal Preference Schedule scores, the sex questionnaire, background data, Marriage Value Inventory, measures of physical attractiveness,

275

Minnesota scores, and various Marital Expectation Test Satisfaction scores.

These Marital Expectation Satisfaction scores were obtained as follows: each subject had filled out the Marriage Expectation Test according to how important each item was with regard to his expectation for marriage regarding his spouse. The rating that could be assigned to each item ranged from (5), very important to (1), of no importance. In addition, the subject filled out the same test according to how he perceived his partner, and this test was factor analyzed (orthogonal solution). Only the first nine factors extracted for each sex were utilized, on the basis of convenience, although many more factors had eigenvalues somewhat greater than one. The satisfaction score for a given item in a given factor was computed by multiplying the importance weight (rating) the subject had assigned the item by the rating of the item given in judging the perceived partner. This product was then multiplied by the square of the factor loading for the item. A "factor score" was obtained by summing all items on a factor where the loading was at least .30. The satisfaction factor score was thus described by the following equation:

Marital Expectation Test Satisfaction Factor $_i = \Sigma_i^n$ (Importance weight j × perceived partner j × factor loading j) where $j \ldots n$ equals the items on the given i-th factor.

A total of 18 factor scores (1 for each of 9 factors for each sex) were standardized and included in the pool of 109 variables correlated with CP.

(No extensive description of the factor analysis and dimensions of marital expectation is given here, because it is not specifically tied to a testing of SVR theory. The first nine factors extracted for men for perception of the partner were labeled, in order of extraction: (1) Madonna (altruistic, perfect woman), (2) Traditional Submissive Wife, (3) Family Approved Spouse, (4) Physical-Sex Orientation, (5) Social Skills, (6) Even-Tempered, Understanding, (7) Non-Dominant, (8) Loving and Accepting, (9) Authoritarian, Conventional Sex Views.

For women's perceptions, the 9 factors were (1) All-American Boy (altruistic, perfect man), (2) Traditional, Dominant Husband, (3) Intellectual, Controller, Non-Religious, (4) Narcissistic, Materialistic, (5) Family Approved, Conventional Sex Views, (6) Egalitarian, Tolerant, (7) Social, Gregarious, (8) Don Juan, (9) Love and Involvement.

The factor analysis was done with 130 items for men and 135 for women, selected via earlier factor analyses from an original pool of 262 items for each sex. Because the number of subjects (99 of each sex) was smaller than the number of variables factor analyzed, the reliability of the factors would be expected to be low. However, the factors are used here as a rough selection device for 18 variables rather than as a description of stable marital expectation dimensions; consequently, the use of "factor scores" derived from these factors would seem permissible. A subsequent replication with a larger American and French population (Murstein, 1975) tended to largely support the dimensions extracted in this earlier study.)

Because of the advanced stage of courtship of subjects in Group I at the onset of testing, it was not expected that the correlation of any of our 109 variables with the criterion would be very high, and we were justified in that expectation. The highest correlation with CP was the women's factor score 9 for perceived partner ($r = .32$), which we have labeled "Perceived Love and Involvement by the Man." The variable adding most to the magnitude of the multiple correlation coefficient was the lack of absolute discrepancy in physical (photo) attractiveness, which boosted the multiple correlation to .39. Lack of photo attractiveness by the woman was the third contributing variable, increasing the r to .44. The woman's lack of expectation of an egalitarian, tolerant husband as derived from the Marital Expectation Test was the next variable added, raising the correlation to .50, followed by the man's perception of his girlfriend as physically attractive, which raised the correlation to .56.

With our large battery of variables it is no feat ultimately to approach unity in predicting the criterion; however, only the first ten variables are shown in Table 15.1 along with the successive increments in r as they are added. Even after only five variables, the multiple r is a respectable .56 ($p < .01$). A "shrinkage" formula given by Guilford (1956) indicates that on retest the estimated correlation would be .53. This supposes, however, that five variables represented the entirety of variables. In actuality, these five represent the best selection from 109 variables; hence we have surely capitalized on chance factors in selecting these five, and cannot, therefore, put much credence in the "shrinkage" result. The only way to determine the predictive efficiency of our beta coefficients therefore would have been to do a cross-validation study with a new group (Group III). Our main purpose in the Group III project, however, was to investigate a number of new perceptual variables; thus the multiple correlation computed for Group III data was only a partial replication of Group I.

Before turning to this project, however, some observations regarding the significant correlations with the criterion for Group I seem in order. Table 15.2 lists these for a two-tailed distribution. A

Table 15.1

MULTIPLE CORRELATION OF COURTSHIP PROGRESS OF COUPLES
AND BEST PREDICTING VARIABLES FROM GROUP I

Variable No.	Variable	Multiple r
1	Woman's perception of love and involvement by man (MET Factor 9)	.32
2	Low absolute discrepancy in physical attractiveness (photo)	.39
3	Lack of woman's photo attractiveness	.44
4	Woman's lack of expectation for egalitarian-tolerant spouse (MET Factor 6)	.50
5	Man's perception of partner as physically attractive	.56
6	High absolute discrepancy in perception of physical attractiveness of partner	.59
7	Length of time going together	.62
8	Smallness of F (validity scale) on MMPI	.65
9	Low absolute discrepancy self-perceptions for physical attractiveness	.67
10	Smallness of $\left| \text{self}_M - \text{ideal-self}_M \right|$	.69

Note: Marital Expectation Test is abbreviated to MET, Minnesota Multiphasic
Personality Inventory to MMPI.

Variables in this and succeeding tables have sometimes been phrased to
indicate direction of the relationship.

note of caution is in order in interpreting these significant values, due
to the large number of correlations computed (109). Had each test of
significance been independent (which they were not), the number of
values significant by chance alone would have been about five.

The table is consistent with the observations made earlier that the
man is the main perceptual target in marriage, but Table 15.2 also
suggests that the woman's perception of him as a "wonderful" person
is also a correlate of good CP. Contrariwise, there is little evidence
that the man's perceptions of his partner's personality are related to
CP. The only Marriage Expectation Test factor operative for men was
their perception of their girlfriends as "even-tempered and understanding"; but this factor sounds very much as if the understanding by
the girlfriend is being done about him and, thus, does not indicate that

Table 15.2

VARIABLES FROM THE 109 INVESTIGATED FOR GROUP I
CORRELATING SIGNIFICANTLY WITH THE COUPLES' CP (One-Tailed Test)

Variable	r
Woman's perception of "love and involvement by man" (MET Factor 9)	.32
Woman's perception of man as "Don Juan" (MET Factor 8)	.29
Small discrepancy in physical attractiveness (photo)	.25
Woman's satisfaction with man as "intellectual and controlled' (MET Factor 3)	.25
Woman's perception of partner as "all-American boy" (MET Factor 1)	.24
Man's perception of woman as "even-tempered and understanding" (MET Factor 6)	.24
Woman never contemplated breaking up	.24
Woman has never wished they had not gone together	.23
Woman's L (Lie) scale score in MMPI	.23
Woman reports relationship has never broken up	.22
Small $\mid$ boyfriend$_W$ − ideal-spouse$_W$ $\mid$ discrepancy	.22
Woman unattractive in photo	.22
Small discrepancy in self-perception of physical attractiveness	.21
Male perception of sex-drive as low	.21
Man never contemplated breaking up	.21
Man's schizophrenia score low on MMPI	.21
Large discrepancy in subjects' perception of partner's physical attractiveness	.20
Age at which I would like to be married $\leq$ 21	.20

$r = .20.$ $p < .05.$
$r = .27.$ $p < .01.$

he is very much focused on her personality needs. The same kind of finding has been reported for young married couples (Murstein and Beck, 1972). In that study, the tendency for the husband to be the perceptual target of the couple's person perceptions was significantly associated with marital adjustment, but the tendency of the husband to confirm his wife's self and ideal-self concepts, for example, was not related to marital adjustment.

Table 15.2 also indicates that the importance of physical attractiveness appears to carry through the stimulus and value stages of courtship into the role stage. Self evaluation of attractiveness seems to follow an equal exchange principle in that the smaller the discrepancy, the better the CP, but the variable "perception of the partner's attractiveness" follows the opposite principle—namely the larger the discrepancy, the better the CP. We have seen the explanation for this finding in Chapter 7. It was noted there that, all other assets and liabilities of a couple being equal, exchange theory permitted the man to marry a woman whom he perceived as more physically attractive than himself in exchange for his greater status in marriage. Inspection of Tables 8.1 and 8.2 in Chapter 8 supports this position in that the men perceived the women as somewhat more attractive than the women perceived them ($\chi^2 = 6.34, p < .01$).

Interestingly enough, women's low photo attractiveness was slightly but significantly correlated with CP ($r = .22$). Although the women's acknowledged self-concept of attractiveness did not correlate significantly with CP ($r = .02$), it is possible that the objective (photo) lack of attractiveness of the women coupled with the men's apparent tendency to subjectively overestimate their attractiveness may have combined to accelerate CP.

Personality adjustment seems related to CP in different ways for the sexes. Inspection of the complete correlation matrix of the 109 variables with CP suggested that for men, low MMPI scores were slightly associated with good CP, whereas for women, high scores were so associated. To check out this possibility, a chi-square for our 18 MMPI scores was computed for the sign of the correlation (+ or −) between the dichotomies men, women, and good or poor CP. Of the 18 variables, men showed positive correlations 15 times and negative correlations for only 3 of the variables. Women on the 18 variables showed positive correlations 6 times, and negative correlations 12 times, resulting in a significant χ^2 value of 7.31 ($p < .01$). Since high scores in this case were toward the deviant end, whereas low scores hovered about the mean (normalcy of the normative population on whom the test was standardized), the results suggest that normal scores for the men but slightly deviant scores for the women were associated with good CP. The correlations with CP were quite small, as might be predicted from the finding in Chapter 8 that the scores of both sexes were almost always within what is generally considered the "normal" zone (less than one standard deviation above the mean). For the eighteen MMPI scores, the correlation with CP for men ranged from +.21 to −.06. For women the range was from +.19 to −.23.

Overall, the 109 correlations of Group I point to a male-centered relationship in which the man is "built up" by his girlfriend. The MMPI data offer mild support to the idea that the women, who are psychologically slightly deviant in their scores, are apt to be drawn toward matrimony and toward cool, competent men.

GROUP III

The criterion of the multiple correlation study for Group III was a five-point scale of CP instead of a four-point one as in Group I; the range of summed couples' CP scores was therefore from 2 (relationship had broken up) to 10 (very much closer than before). The summed CP score was correlated with 151 variables selected as possibly contributing to CP. Of these variables, the vast majority (120) were obtained from the Marriage Expectation Test. Only the first 76 items of this test are identical for both sexes, and only these items were used, in order to obtain all possible comparisons of two perceptual sets and to correlate these with CP. It will be recalled that the eight sets taken by each sex included self, ideal-self, partner, ideal-spouse and the prediction of how the partner would perceive the self, ideal-self, partner, ideal-spouse. The totality of sets is 16 for both members of a couple taken together. The total number of combinations of two perceptual sets taken two at a time, therefore, is n(n-1)/2 or 120 combinations. Each combination became a score by taking the sum of the absolute discrepancies between any two perceptual sets across the 76 items.

Other variables included the Marriage Value Inventory correlation between members of a couple, church membership, church attendance, and the belief that the subject understood his partner and that his partner understood him. Physical attractiveness measures included the discrepancy of self-concepts of attractiveness (both absolute and signed), and the signed discrepancy of the partner's attractiveness minus the self-percept for attractiveness. Last, the sex questions relating to weekly rate of orgasm, self-perceived sex-drive, source of orgasm, and difficulty in controlling sex-drive were obtained for men, women, and the absolute and signed discrepancy between the partners.

The multiple R is shown in Table 15.3. This table shows that the belief by the man that his partner understood him was the variable most closely associated with CP. The woman's tendency to experience most of her orgasms through intercourse also added somewhat to the correlation, as did the man's perceiving his sex drive as strong.[1] This finding is opposite to that reported for Group I, where the man's tendency to perceive his sex drive as low was significantly correlated with CP. It is difficult to understand why the two samples should differ in this respect. Unfortunately, the possibilities seem endless. The relationships in both cases were quite modest, and considering the numerous computations, it would not be unusual if one of these significances were a chance event.

In general, for both Groups I and III, a positive relationship was found between perceptual congruence and CP over most of the "set" comparisons, and a negative relationship between strength of self-evaluated sex drive and perceptual congruence. Only for the comparisons between CP and the self-evaluation of sex drive for men and for women did the results vary in that the relationship was negative for Group I but positive for Group III. It may be that Groups I and III tended to evaluate their similar sexual behaviors somewhat differently psychologically. Conceivably, although only three years separated the groups, Group I may have been more socialized to think that marriage-oriented people were not at the mercy of bestial passions, whereas the changing social climate made it more acceptable to accept the connection between passion and marriage three years later.

Returning to the variables contributing to the multiple correlation, it may be noted from inspection of Table 15.3 that a slight increment is added by several of the Marriage Expectation Test discrepancy scores. Only the ten most important variables contributing to the size of the multiple correlation have been listed.

[1]The above finding is not in agreement with the finding reported in Chapter 12 that CP was not related to self-perception of sex drive for men. The discrepancy is explained by the somewhat different analyses performed. In Chapter 12, CP was dichotomized as was self-perception of sex drive and a χ^2 computed. For the multiple correlation, neither the CP nor self-perceived sex-drive scores were collapsed into dichotomies, but were treated as continuous data.

The χ^2 procedure "throws away" information, which the correlative procedure, using interval data, does not. Apparently, in this case, the difference in procedure resulted in a change from a nonsignificant to a significant finding.

Certain significant findings for Group III reported in Chapter 12 are not always found to be significant in Table 15.4. For example, low frequency of orgasm for men was reported to be significantly associated with good CP ($p < .01$) in Table 12.5, but it is not significantly correlated with CP in Table 15.4. The apparent contradiction has to do with the population analyzed. In Chapter 12 we were attempting to demonstrate the existence of a relationship and chose the upper and lower third of the distribution of orgasm frequency for men. In Table 15.4, the attempt is to predict CP for all subjects; hence all of the male subjects were utilized, which in this case reduced the association between CP and orgasm frequency below the significance level.

Table 15.3

MULTIPLE CORRELATION OF COURTSHIP PROGRESS OF COUPLES AND BEST PREDICTING VARIABLES FOR GROUP III

Variable No.	Variable	Multiple r
1	My partner understands me (man)	.54
2	My partner understands me (woman)	.62
3	Source of orgasms primarily by intercourse (woman)	.67
4	Sex drive of self perceived as strong (man)	.71
5	$\mid$ Ideal-self$_W$ – girlfriend sees me$_M$ $\mid$	.75
6	$\mid$ Boyfriend sees ideal-spouse$_W$ – boyfriend sees self$_W$ $\mid$	.77
7	$\mid$ Ideal-spouse$_M$ – girlfriend sees me$_M$ $\mid$	.78
8	$\mid$ Ideal-spouse$_M$ – boyfriend sees ideal-self$_W$ $\mid$	.79
9	$\mid$ Boyfriend sees ideal-spouse$_W$ – boyfriend sees me$_W$ $\mid$	.80
10	$\mid$ Boyfriend$_W$ – boyfriend sees ideal-self$_W$ $\mid$	.81

Note: All correlations are highly significant ($p < .01$). Discrepancy scores are to be interpreted such that the smaller the discrepancy the better the CP.

In view of our experience with Group I data, we were able to make predictions about the direction of correlation in Group III 'and, therefore, used a one-tailed test of significance. Table 15.4 shows all of the variables that correlated very significantly ($p < .01$) with the criterion, CP. Thirty-six of the 151 variables reached the criterion. The highest correlations included being understood and understanding the partner, and various sex measures reflecting a high self-perceived sex drive on the part of the man and woman and a low discrepancy in orgasm frequency between them. A considerable number of Marriage Expectation Test discrepancy scores were significant, all indicating that perceptual congruence of the various sets was associated with good CP. As with Group I, the intraperceptions of the man were more apt to be correlated with CP (six significant at $p < .01$) than was the case for women (one significant at $p < .01$).

Because Group III was not as far advanced in courtship as Group I, the correlations with CP were noticeably higher. The person perception measures, although not very highly correlated with CP, were nevertheless consistently associated with it. Of the 120 such measures, 26 were significant beyond the .01 point despite our truncated version of the Marital Expectation Test, attesting to the possible value of person perception measures in predicting CP.

Table 15.4

VARIABLES FROM THE 151 INVESTIGATED FOR GROUP III
CORRELATING SIGNIFICANTLY WITH THE COUPLES' CP (Two-Tailed Test)

Variable	r
My partner understands me (man)	.54
I understand my partner (man)	.50
Source of orgasm is intercourse (woman)	.45
My partner understands me (woman)	.41
I understand my partner (woman)	.40
Lack of discrepancy (absolute) in source of orgasm $\mid$ M - W $\mid$	.40
Lack of discrepancy (signed) in source of orgasm (M - W)	.39
Strong self-perceived sex-drive (woman)	.36
$\mid \text{Self}_M - \text{boyfriend sees his ideal-spouse}_W \mid$	.31
Strong self-perceived sex-drive (man)	.30
$\mid \text{Ideal-spouse}_W - \text{girlfriend sees me}_M \mid$	.30
$\mid \text{Ideal-self}_W - \text{girlfriend sees me}_M \mid$	.30
$\mid \text{Ideal-self}_W - \text{girlfriend sees ideal-self}_M \mid$	.30
$\mid \text{Self}_M - \text{boyfriend sees ideal-self}_W \mid$	.30
$\mid \text{Self}_M - \text{ideal-self}_W \mid$	.30
$\mid \text{Ideal-spouse}_W - \text{girlfriend sees self}_M \mid$	.29
$\mid \text{Ideal-spouse}_M - \text{ideal-self}_W \mid$	.29
$\mid \text{Self}_M - \text{boyfriend sees self}_W \mid$	.29
$\mid \text{Ideal-self}_W - \text{girlfriend sees self}_M \mid$	.28
$\mid \text{Ideal-self}_M - \text{girlfriend}_M \mid$	.27
$\mid \text{Girlfriend sees me}_M - \text{boyfriend sees ideal-spouse}_W \mid$	.27
$\mid \text{Self}_M - \text{boyfriend}_W \mid$	.27
$\mid \text{Ideal-spouse}_W - \text{girlfriend sees ideal-self}_M \mid$	.26
$\mid \text{Ideal-self}_M - \text{girlfriend sees ideal-spouse}_M \mid$	.26
$\mid \text{Ideal-self}_M - \text{girlfriend sees ideal-self}_M \mid$	.26
$\mid \text{Ideal-self}_M - \text{girlfriend sees self}_M \mid$	.26
$\mid \text{Ideal-self}_W - \text{girlfriend sees ideal-spouse}_M \mid$	.26
$\mid \text{Ideal-self}_M - \text{girlfriend sees me}_M \mid$	.25
Frequency of orgasm high (woman)	.25
$\mid \text{Girlfriend sees me}_M - \text{boyfriend sees me}_W \mid$	.25
$\mid \text{Self}_M - \text{girlfriend sees me}_M \mid$	.25
$\mid \text{Self}_M - \text{ideal-spouse}_W \mid$	.25

Table 15.4 *(continued)*

Variable	r
| Self$_W$ − boyfriend sees me$_W$ |	.25
| Girlfriend$_M$ − ideal-spouse$_W$ |	.24
| Ideal-self$_M$ − ideal-self$_W$ |	.24
| Girlfriend$_M$ − ideal-self$_W$ |	.24

Note: All discrepancy scores are in the direction such that the smaller the discrepancy the better the CP.

$p < .01.$

In view of the finding that understanding and being understood by the partner were so important to CP, I was curious as to just how much foundation there was in the accuracy of forecasting of the partner on the Marriage Expectation Test. Accordingly, the five-point rating scales for being understood and for understanding the partner (5 = extremely well, 4 = fairly well, above average, . . . , 1 = doesn't understand me very well) were correlated with the partner's attempts to forecast the partner's responses to the self, ideal-self, ideal-spouse, and partner percepts.

It should be mentioned that the skewed distribution and small variability of being understood (men $\bar{x}$ = 4.18, S. D. = .77; women $\bar{x}$ = 4.40, S. D. = .69) and understanding the partner (men $\bar{x}$ = 4.27, S. D. = .70; women $\bar{x}$ = 4.42, S. D. = .67) ratings predisposed toward less than high correlation. It could also be said that being understood is not completely reducible to forecasting someone's responses to 76 items on the Marriage Expectation Test. On the other hand, the percepts involved and the content area of the items should have some relevance for the subjects. In any event, as shown in Table 15.5, the results show some significant but low correlations between men's feelings of being understood and accuracy of forecast by their partners, but nothing approaching significance for women being understood.

There is some faint statistical support for both the men and women's feeling of understanding their partner, but the size of the correlation does not support the confidence exhibited in the ratings. Despite this failure to document the feeling with a great deal of evidence, the belief that one is understood and understands is apparently sufficient to enable the courtship to forge ahead.

Table 15.5

CORRELATIONS OF RATINGS OF BEING UNDERSTOOD AND UNDER-
STANDING PARTNER WITH FORECASTS ON MARRIAGE EXPECTATION
TEST

Marriage Expectation Test Variable	Rating of Being Understood	Rating of Understanding
Forecast by Women	(By Man)	(By Woman)
$\mid$Self$_M$ − boyfriend sees self$_W\mid$	−.38**	−.14
$\mid$Ideal-self$_M$ − boyfriend sees ideal-self$_W\mid$	−.11	−.03
$\mid$Ideal-spouse$_M$ − boyfriend sees ideal-spouse$_W\mid$	−.04	−.08
$\mid$Girlfriend$_M$ − boyfriend sees me$_W\mid$	−.27**	−.21*
Forecast by Men	(By Woman)	(By Man)
$\mid$Self$_W$ − girlfriend sees self$_M\mid$	−.08	−.18*
$\mid$Ideal-self$_W$ − girlfriend sees ideal-self$_M\mid$	−.04	−.04
$\mid$Ideal-spouse$_W$ − girlfriend sees ideal-spouse$_M\mid$	−.08	−.06
$\mid$Boyfriend$_W$ − girlfriend sees me$_M\mid$	−.09	−.22*

Note: A negative correlation supports the validity of the forecast in that low discrepancy
between prediction and partner's response is correlated with a high rating of understanding and being understood.

* $p < .05$.
** $p < .01$.

CP AND BACKGROUND QUESTIONS

Group I

The 12 background questions were dichotomized as close to the
median as possible and compared with CP for men and for women.
Table 15.6 shows the hypotheses made and the significant values for
the various x^2 tests. Inspection of this table indicates that good CP

Table 15.6

CHI-SQUARE VALUES FOR BACKGROUND QUESTIONS
FOR MEN, WOMEN, AND COURTSHIP PROGRESS (Group I)

Variable No.	Hypothesized that good CP is associated with:	*p* Men	*p* Women
1	Positive attitudes toward having children	n.s.	n.s.
2	Boyfriend's (girlfriend's) positive attitudes toward having children	n.s.	n.s.
3	Parents still married (as opposed to broken homes)	n.s.	n.s.
4	High social status of parents	n.s.	n.s.
5	Belonging to many community organizations	n.s.	n.s.
6	Confidence that marriage will be happy	.05	n.s.
7	Never having broken off the relationship	.01	.01
8	Never contemplated breaking off the relationship	.05	.05
9	Never wished they had not gone together	n.s.	n.s.
10	Report of parents' marriage as happy	n.s.	n.s.
11	Being a church member	n.s.	n.s.
12	Degree of certainty about marriage to partner	.05	.01

Note: n.s. = not significant.

both for men and for women was related to never having broken off the relationship or having contemplated breaking it, and degree of certainty about marrying the partner. In addition, confidence that the marriage would be happy was associated with good CP for men but not for women. This finding probably reflects the man's greater role in the determination of CP.

Group III

The 14 background questions for Group III were compared in a similar fashion to Group I. The summary of significant findings and significance levels is given in Table 15.7. The actual frequencies for Groups I and III may be found in Appendix B-5 and D-2, respectively.

Inspection of this table indicates that the majority of background questions did not relate significantly to CP when analyzed separately by sex. The nonsignificant relationships for both sexes included age, church membership, frequency of church attendance, whether the subject was now a student, the future schooling planned, the length of

Table 15.7

TESTS OF SIGNIFICANCE FOR BACKGROUND QUESTIONS
FOR MEN, WOMEN, AND COURTSHIP PROGRESS (GROUP III)

	p	
Hypothesis that good CP is associated with:	*Men*	*Women*
Age	n.s.	n.s.
Being a church member	n.s.	n.s.
Frequency of church attendance	n.s.	n.s.
Not being a student	n.s.	n.s.
Advanced class in college [1]	.05	n.s.
Extent of college degree sought	n.s.	n.s.
Length of time going together	n.s.	n.s.
Present relationship classification	.01	.01
Certainty of marriage to partner	.01	.01
Perceived attractiveness of partner	n.s.	n.s.
Perceived attractiveness of self	n.s.	n.s.
Definite plans for marriage	.05	.05
Months to marriage (for those planning marriage)	n.s.	n.s.
Self-evaluation of closeness as couple	.01	.01
Answering yes to "My partner understands me"	.05	n.s.
Answering yes to "I understand my partner"	n.s.	n.s.

Note: n.s. = not significant.

[1] $\bar{x}_{\text{Good CP}} = 3.0$, $\bar{x}_{\text{Poor CP}} = 2.2$ years.

time the couple had known each other, the degree of physical attractiveness, the number of months to the wedding (for those who had answered intentions to wed), and the belief that the subject understood his partner.

The variables significantly associated with CP for both sexes included the classification of the relationship. Good CP men had a mean classification of 3.94 where 3 represented a rating for "date exclusively" and 4 a rating for "pinned or its equivalent." Poor CP men achieved a mean rating of 2.56 where 2 represented "date partner a lot." A *t* test showed a highly significant difference $p < .01$. The mean ratings for women were 3.73 and 2.59 respectively, the differences also being highly significant ($p < .01$).

To the question, "How sure are you that you will marry (the partner)?" good CP men achieved a mean rating of 4.61 and poor CP men a score of 3.59, where (3) represented "somewhat uncertain," (4) signified "pretty sure" and (5) indicated "barring unforeseen circumstances." The good and poor CP women scored 4.69 and 3.56

respectively, and in both cases the differences were highly significant ($p < .01$).

Regarding definite plans for marriage, a 2×2 χ^2 analysis (definite plans, indefinite plans, good or poor CP) for men and women separately were both significant ($p < .05$). The results indicated that although both men and women with definite plans for marriage were in the minority, they were proportionately still more likely to occur among those destined to make good CP than among potentially poor CP individuals.

The men's and women's evaluations of their closeness as a couple also related significantly to CP. The mean for good CP men was 4.45, that for poor CP men, 3.85; the mean for good CP women, 4.55, poor CP women 4.00, where (5) signified "Very much in love, very close to perfect compatibility," (4) indicated "closer than average couple" and (3) represented "about as close as the average couple." Both sex comparisons were significant beyond the .01 level.

For some items only the men could be differentiated by CP. Good CP men, for example, were further along in school. Noting that (4) stood for Senior class, (3) for Junior, and (2) for Sophomore, good CP men showed a mean of 3.02 to poor CP men's 2.24 ($p < .01$).

In sum, these findings indicate that the subsequently good CP subjects were already more strongly involved with each other and more strongly committed to each other at the time of testing than were subsequently poor CP couples.

Concerning the items of being understood by the partner and understanding him, only the man being understood by the partner differentiated good and poor CP couples, though trends were apparent in the expected direction. The weakness of these variables in the present analysis may seem surprising in view of their correlation with CP in the multiple correlation analysis. However, the t test used in the present analysis is a test of location. The coefficient of correlations is a measure of covariation; hence these tests of significance do not measure the same thing. Also, for purposes of the t test, the dichotomy good or poor CP was used, whereas for the multiple correlation finer degrees of courtship progress could be used.

SOCIOECONOMIC CLASS, VALUE HOMOGAMY, AND CP

For Group I, the McGuire Index of Socioeconomic Status was computed for each person and the correlation between good CP couples and poor CP couples computed. The Pearson r for the 64 good

CP couples was .13, that between poor CP couples .28, the difference not being significant. Apparently, the homogeneity of the population precluded high correlations from ensuing between members of a couple.

The correlation of the couple's Marriage Value Inventory congruency and CP was a nonsignificant .09 in Group I, and a barely significant .19 ($p < .05$) in Group III, indicating that this variable did not play a large role in CP at an advanced stage of the relationship.

SUMMARY AND CONCLUSIONS

We have examined a multitude of correlates of CP and found that the man's understanding and being understood by his partner were most strongly correlated with the criterion, with the woman's feeling understood and understanding her partner being slightly less important. Variables relating to sexual compatibility also were significantly related, as were a number of perceptual congruence measures.

The qualities of being understood by and understanding the partner were found to be very weakly grounded in reality insofar as ability to forecast the partner's responses on the Marriage Expectation Test was concerned. This, however, is not the most desirable test of understanding since it does not permit the weighting of what is important to the individual and what is trivial. The finding that the man's understanding and being understood is more important than the woman's position with regard to these variables supports the thesis that has been developed of the man's role in marital choice being stronger than that of the woman.

It is noteworthy also that measures of physical attractiveness such as perception of the partner's attractiveness (determined by additional analysis for Group III), perception of partner's attractiveness minus the self-evaluation of attractiveness, and self-evaluation of attractiveness did not correlate significantly with CP in Group III, although several of the attractiveness measures correlated minimally but significantly in Group I (see Table 15.2).

The relative unimportance of physical attractiveness and value compatibility at this final role stage of courtship is compatible with SVR theory but does not provide a stringent test of the theory, because it would be necessary to demonstrate that both measures had been very important at earlier stages.

Regarding physical attractiveness, there is a good deal of indirect evidence, which we have already reviewed, supporting (along with common sense) the conclusion that physical attractiveness precedes other variables in initiating attraction. The indirect evidence for value compatibility as a second variable, as we noted earlier in Chapter 5, is much more clouded.

The variables most closely associated with CP (understanding, sex, and person perception) would seem to be readily classified as role stage variables. However, once again this conclusion rests on logic rather than empirical support. For example, it seems unlikely that understanding, sexual compatibility, and perceptual congruence could precede the considerable development of a relationship, but "unreasonable" things have occurred in social science research, and the measurement of these variables in the early stages of courtship would be necessary for solid confirmation of this thesis.

CHAPTER 16

Failures, Successes, Omissions, and Conclusions

I have often wondered in perusing the professional journals, how many failures went unreported. Journals cater almost exclusively to successes, so that although we may learn that Professor Wigglebottom has demonstrated a significant relationship ($p < .05$) between variable A and B, we do not always learn how many unsuccessful analyses or studies were done *before* the successful one that merited publication. Such an event, of course, capitalizes on chance. If one does enough studies, one is bound to eventually come out with a significant result. The probability of a chance occurrence could be better ascertained if a successful replication were undertaken; but this rarely occurs, in part because journals manifest little interest in publishing replications, in part because the researchers themselves, fearing the hazards of a replication study, are content to let well enough alone.

It is therefore with a sense of historicity that I modestly present the report of a study that failed. My desire to do so does not stem from masochistic needs, but because the problem is very important, and because others may profit from my fruitless pursuit and address themselves to perhaps more promising avenues of approach.

In attempting to predict marital choice, the "desire to marry" should serve as an "enhancer" or "supressor" variable. That is, to the extent that this variable is experienced as a drive-state, the importance of the other factors, such as assets in the marriage market and role compatibility, should be lessened. On the other hand, to the extent that marriage is seen as a distant or arbitrary goal, near-perfect compatibility between the partners would be necessary to arouse motivation to marry.

Marriage is not entered into simply because of the compatibility of two people. Marriage as a status has a value in its own right, which may be considered as the summation of its positive and negative aspects as seen by the potential candidates.

This being the case, I assembled a series of questions that on face value seemed to be associated with the desire to marry. I called the test Scale E (for expediency, or desire to marry) and included it in the battery of inventories administered to Group I. (The questions and scoring key appear in Appendix B-4.) Some questions were subtle indeed ("I am an orphan or have lost one of my parents."), whereas others came right to the point ("Would you like to be married right now?"). With but very few exceptions, it made no difference: Considered as a scale, summing correct answers to the questions, or doing an item-by-item analysis, the results relating desire to marry to CP were almost uniformly nonsignificant.

Specifically, neither the men's Expediency score, the women's Expediency score, or an average of the two related to the couple's CP. A χ^2 of each of the 22 items for women dichotomized at the median and compared with the dichotomy good or poor CP yielded no significant findings. A similar analysis for the men's Expediency score showed one barely significant finding at the .05 level for the question "Would you like to be married now?" Last, comparison of the Expediency score with a variety of Revised Edwards Personal Preference Schedule, Minnesota Multiphasic Personality Inventory, sex, and background items revealed no significant findings above chance.

A comparison of the items for sex differences showed several significant findings. More men than women thought that a well-adjusted person could be married to anyone ($\chi^2 = 5.39, p < .01$), more men than women were interested in getting away from living at home ($\chi^2 = 7.26, p < .01$), more women than men had broken off with someone they had hoped to marry ($\chi^2 = 4.35, p < .05$), and more "other" men had earlier wanted to marry the woman in the couple than had "other" women wanted to marry the man in the couple ($t = 2.40, p < .01$). However, none of these items related to CP.

Although the subject has by no means been mined by these questions, it is difficult to avoid the conclusion that the desire to marry is not a very simple concept. It may depend not only on personality factors and the kind of partner one is involved with, but with *timing, societal inculcation, critical incidents,* and *social network* or "conveyor belt" influences as well, issues that have been discussed earlier in Chapter 4. These factors are not part of the dyadic interaction, which is what SVR theory is largely concerned with. Yet they are important in marital choice, and they show us that marital choice is generally precipitated by more than a simple act of volition by the two involved partners.

The aforementioned factors, however, do not themselves determine the selection of the partner. Rather, they serve as accelerators or depressors with regard to the field of eligibles with whom the nubile individual interacts. Marital choice, in sum, is the result of the interaction of a marriageable couple within a societal context. No dyadic marital theory, therefore, can of itself attempt to forecast with great accuracy whether a marriage will take place and when it will occur, unless knowledge of these nondyadic factors is available as well as information pertaining to dyadic interaction.

This lack of inclusiveness of SVR theory does not vitiate its potential contribution to understanding marital choice. Couple compatibility is surely a big component of any marital choice equation, and to the extent that we increase our knowledge of why individuals attract each other, we inevitably increase our ability to predict marital choice, albeit with something less than perfection. Additionally, SVR theory would seem to have applicability beyond marital choice. Our brief coverage of early marriage and friendship suggested that SVR theory theory is almost wholly applicable to interpersonal relationships in general, although the importance of the various stages will vary according to the nature of the relationship.

SUMMARY OF SVR FINDINGS

We have considered 39 hypotheses, of which a considerable majority received some support, if not always very strong support. My own (subjective) evaluation of the outcome lists 15 hypotheses as receiving fairly strong or moderate support, 18 receiving weak or mixed support, and 6 as being very equivocal or not reaching significance, often despite trends in the right direction.

Far more important than a "batting average," however, is the significance of the findings and their relevance to the theory. The two pillars of the theory are that equity of exchange is conducive to dyadic formation and CP, and that the progression of the relationship follows the SVR sequence. Most of the data collected have focused on the exchange principle, and, taken as a whole, considerable support for this principle has been found.

Some of the Equity Principle variables found to be of similar strength among members of couples were: physical attractiveness (self-evaluation and photo), confirmation of the other's self-image, accuracy in predicting the self and ideal-self image. Many other variables supported the equity of exchange principle in a somewhat weaker fashion; either statistical significance was reached but the proportion of "hits" to "misses" did not seem to indicate the presence of a strong effect, or the variable supported the equity principle with one group, but not with another. Included within this category were perceptual and expressive styles on the unstructured tests, partner satisfaction, self-acceptance, and neuroticism. Sex-drive discrepancy between the couple was inversely related to perceptual congruence on the Revised Edwards test. Homogamy of values among couples was found in Groups I and II, but not for Group III.

The relationship between equity and CP was also apparent for some variables on some occasions and not others. Equity of partner satisfaction, accuracy in predicting the partner's self and ideal-self, equity in self-evaluation of physical attractiveness were each found to be significant for one of the groups studied, but not for another group.

If we make the assumption that men possess greater social status than women, then additional findings can readily be incorporated as support for the exchange framework. The woman as the less powerful member of the couple must be more alert to the man's interpersonal needs and percepts than he need be to hers in order to advance the courtship. Thus, accuracy in predicting both the man's self-concept and ideal-self concept leads couples to good CP, but only prediction of the woman's ideal-self leads to good CP. Confirmation of the man's self and ideal-self was much more strongly associated with good CP than confirmation of the woman's self and ideal-self concepts. Intrapersonal congruence for the man was fairly strongly associated with good CP, but it was not significantly associated with CP for the woman. Also, neuroticism in the man had a significant, deleterious effect on courtship, but neuroticism in the woman was not significantly related to CP. Likewise, the man's sex drive was more closely tied to perceptual congruence than was the woman's sex drive.

Another clear indication of imbalance of the sexes with regard to status was the finding that perceptual congruence on the Revised Edwards test was most strongly associated with the man's perception of his girlfriend as more physically attractive than himself. Indeed, when this group was compared with a group in which the man perceived his girlfriend as about equal to himself in attractiveness, perceptual congruence was found to be stronger for the former group than for the latter.

Turning to the consequence of possession of highly valued assets, it was argued that self-acceptance was of value not only to the individual possessing it, but to his partner, who thereby avoided the costs of relating to and meeting the great needs of a low self-acceptance person. Accordingly, it was predicted and subsequently verified that the high status of high self-acceptance subjects would enable them to pick partners who more closely met their ideal-spouse expectations than would be the case for low self-acceptance persons.

The argument that this finding was merely a response set, in that individuals placing themselves in a socially desirable light (high self-acceptance) were apt to also distort in claiming above-average correspondence between their ideal-spouse percept and that of their partner, was not accepted because satisfaction with the partner was found to have valued behavioral correlates—those more satisfied with their partner showed better CP six months later than those less satisfied with their partner.

These data show not only the importance of equity, but also that equity involves less cost for the man than for the woman because his greater status serves as compensation for her extra costs. Good CP is more apt to ensue if *his* self-concepts are accurately diagnosed, and *his* views or self are confirmed, than contrariwise.

On the debit side of the ledger, his deficiencies also influence the relationship more than hers. His neurosis affects CP more than hers does, and the strength of his sex drive is negatively related to perceptual congruency within the couple, whereas hers is not related at all.

Physical attractiveness plays an important role in courtship. Homogamy of attractiveness is characteristic of couples, but from the subjective point of view the man's perception of his girlfriend as more attractive than himself is associated with the couple's high perceptual congruity on personality items compared to his perception of himself as superior to her in physical attractiveness, which results in lower perceptual congruity. Presumably, in the former case he should be quite satisfied with his success, but in the latter case he is losing out by marrying someone inferior in attractiveness. Ideally, most people would probably prefer someone more attractive than themselves. But when the man's wishes in this regard are satisfied, perceptual congruence is much greater than when the woman's wishes are satisfied, thus testifying to his greater power in the relationship.

That equity of confirmation of the partner's self-concept and accuracy in predicting the partner's concepts are greater for actual couples than for randomized ones suggests that disclosure and perhaps sensitivity work on a reciprocal basis. Each member of the couple probably discloses an increasingly personal aspect of himself to his partner. This action connotes trust and affection and probably serves as a model for the other to reciprocate. The mutuality of disclosure probably leads to mutuality of acceptance (confirmation) and of predictability.

Despite the fact of considerable support for the equity thesis, the evidence was not overwhelming, and some explanation ought to be attempted for the exceptions. The first consideration is the roughness of the measures used. For example, men and women have died for their values, but, regrettably, no really adequate test of value compatibility existed at the time of the research. The literature is replete with evidence of value homogamy (see Richardson 1939, and Chapter 5 in this book), but the best scale that I could come up with relating to marriage (Marriage Value Inventory) was a ten-item ranking one, probably heavily influenced by social desirability.

When this consideration is added to the fact that we were working with an extremely homogeneous group of upper-middle-class college students, it is not remarkable that despite the fact that value homogamy always existed among couples, it was not always significantly greater than that existing among the college population at large.

Another measure that might be questioned is the use of orgasm frequency as a measure of sex drive. But research is the art of the pragmatic. We were not in a position to use chemical array tests nor to test measures of sexual inhibition. Orgasm frequency seemed a useful index of sexual behavior that would also provide an indirect, rough measure of sex drive. No doubt, however, the crudeness of our measures took their toll and magnified the possibility of accepting the null hypothesis of no difference in groups when we ought to have rejected it (Type II error).

The use of photos to depict physical attractiveness also has inherent limitations in that photos do not possess depth or reflect contours well. Neither can they show the subject in animation, which often tells us of his grace, musculature, energy level, and power— all factors influencing judgments of attractiveness.

The modest degree of success in our hypotheses involving self-acceptance and the rather marginal findings involving neuroticism no doubt were influenced by the fact that our population of highly self-accepting and essentially nonneurotic subjects was rather too selected to expect outstanding differentiation. Last, the constricted range of scores with regard to CP resulting from using a heavily committed group also negatively influenced our hypotheses. Overall, the results, not surprisingly, were mixed where our measures were most suspect.

Unsupported Hypotheses, or "The Lights That Failed"

Six of our hypotheses showed little or no support. It may be useful to review these briefly in order to attempt to understand the causes of these failures. The hypotheses were: (4) When perceptions of the partner's physical attractiveness are compared for members of a couple, the perception of the woman as more attractive than the perception of the man will lead to greater couple satisfaction (peceptual congruence) than vice-versa. (16) The greater the equity in each couple member's tendency to "confirm" the self-image of his partner, the greater the CP. (20) The greater the correspondence (equity) between degree of self-acceptance for each member of a couple, the greater the CP. (33) Below median discrepancy in sex drive is associated with good CP. (38) If a series of variables judged important for marital choice are converted to standardized scores and summed, members of couples will show less than chance discrepancy between these summed scores. (39) Equity between members of couples for the summed scores will be associated with good CP.

The failure of Hypothesis 4, in my opinion, rests on two bases. First, the perception of the partner's attractiveness is subject to intense social desirability effects. Accordingly, there is a constricted range of scores (making for difficulty in differentiating the groups) because *there are almost no ugly partners* (see Table 8.2). Second, exchange must be seen from the eyes of the participants. Whether it is exceedingly gratifying to have an attractive partner or merely *de rigeur* depends on how attractive the subject perceives himself to be. Consideration of only the "perception of partner" variable does not take this into account, and, consequently, offers no insight into the subjective perception of exchange. When the self-concept was taken into account together with perception of the partner, the results were quite significant (Hypothesis 5).

The failures of Hypotheses 16 and 20 point to a problem with equity theory that needs more attention. Equity seems to work better in predicting who goes with whom than in predicting which couples will make good CP six months later. Equity seems to be more important in attracting couples initially than in maintaining the relationship over a considerable period of time. One reason may be that internal reward systems do not play an important part in influencing courtship behavior until a relationship jells to some extent. An individual is not obligated to continue a relationship with someone he has seen a few times and for whom he no longer cares, and he is unlikely to think ill of himself for dropping the partner or think well of himself for continuing the relationship because he is "committed." Individuals who have courted for a year or two, however, may find these considerations of some importance, even if they find the relationship somewhat "inequitable."

Turning to equity itself leads to the observation that equity of a *lack* of tendency to confirm the partner's self-concept should not advance CP. It is only when equity is found for a mutual tendency to *reinforce* the partner that it leads to good CP; hence, not surprisingly, our general equity score is not always predictive of good CP.

In addition, if the status of the principals is imbalanced, inequity in behavior may be a means of compensating for this imbalance. Thus, person perception measures have been most related to CP when the woman confirmed the man's images of self than vice-versa. In short, it is equity over all relevant variables including status, services, attractiveness, etc. that would be most predictive of couple pairing, with given variables sometimes being inequitable because of existing power and status differentials between the sexes.

Our Hypothesis 38, which attempted to test the equity of summed variables, did not lead to clear results. Although, statistically speaking, equity between actual couples was greater than for randomized couples, we were unable to ascertain that a summative effect was operating rather than several individual variables "pulling" several useless variables to significance. Even had we been able to use a larger pool of variables after determining which were important to CP, there would still be another reason why equity of itself would be a less-than-perfect predictor of CP, as was seen, for example, in Hypothesis 39.

Assuming perfect equity, there must still be a minimum of satisfaction in the relationship—the comparison level threshold must be met, otherwise the person may simply decide that the costs of matrimony outweigh the possible gains. The factors determining this threshold of the desire to marry are important but, as noted earlier, have not yet been adequately measured.

Last, the weakness in predicting CP is also due to forces outside the dyad, such as parental and peer pressures, and job changes. It is possible, therefore, that very high accuracy in predicting CP will never be found barring theoretical advances, improved instrumentation, and changes in styles of courtship.

The Sequence Principle

Although there has been no explicit testing of the SVR sequence, the review of the literature does provide some indirect evaluation of it. The various computer matching and contrived choice of dating partner paradigms have stoutly indicated that physical attractiveness, the prime stimulus attribute, is the first factor influencing attraction in newly formed dyads.

Does the V stage follow the S stage and precede the R stage? Kerckhoff and Davis's research (1962) supported the conclusion that V preceded R, or, in their terms, value consensus preceded psychological compatibility. Thus, we had strong indirect support for the SVR sequence until Levinger, Senn, and Jorgensen (1970) were unable to replicate Kerckhoff and Davis's findings.

In my own research, value homogamy received support sometimes and not at other times. The real question is not whether the individual's value homogeneity is greater than chance, but whether pair selectivity for values is greater than class selectivity. In short, is the selectivity accomplished by virtue of the fact that the couple attend the same university and join the Newman club, or is there any individual system of values that operates in pairing beyond these broader cultural factors?

As the matter stands, therefore, I believe that the S and R portions of the SVR sequence have considerable support. Whether V is important enough to retain its place in the theory remains to be determined. My suspicion is, following Hutton (1974), that, if it is important, this importance occurs early in the courtship. All of the studies on marital choice have occurred too late in the sequence of courtship to provide a fair test of the importance of value comparison. It is only by testing couples earlier in the development of their relationship, using a more profound measure of values than those used hitherto, that we can determine whether V precedes R or operates concomitantly with it.

FINAL WORDS

We have arrived at the finish line, and I should like to discuss briefly some of the implications deriving from the research described. It is also customary—so customary that it is almost ritualistic—to add a few notes of caution about generalizability at the end of the research. These "sins" are inevitably viewed by the author as more catechismic than cataclysmic—if they were cataclysmic, the author would never have published the research.

I shall follow this convention to a certain extent; however, I should like to add another necessary feature for a theoretical treatise—the need to make as explicit as possible the biases that have shaped the course of the theory.

First, the cautions about generalizability. The subjects were almost exclusively a college sample derived from middle-class or upper-middle-class backgrounds and stemming mainly, but far from exclusively, from the middle Atlantic and Northeastern states. The "warning flag" extends beyond the fact that these are college students—after all, almost half the people of college age in the United States are college students. Our subjects were college students *interested in volunteering* for a study on marriage. Further, they were individuals who, for the most part, were willing to commit themselves to a possible marriage while still undergraduates (mainly the women were undergraduates). It is safe to assume, therefore, that these individuals had an above average facility in heterosexual relationships and an above average interest in marriage.

Would our results be found with other premarital groups? The evidence is too sparse to permit a strong statement. Hutton's (1974) work, which tested only a few of our numerous hypotheses, showed results rather similar to those we found. Also, our findings with very young married couples, described earlier, were quite similar to those found with our premarital couples, suggesting that our premarital data may have some generalizability.

There is also the question of time lag. Our research was done in the late sixties, and attitudes toward marriage are always changing. Would less support for SVR theory be found today? My guess is that the converse would be true. SVR theory is essentially a theory of dyadic compatibility. Although marital choice in the United States depends substantially on dyadic compatibility, it is not an exclusive dependence. I have indicated earlier the importance of nondyadic factors such as desire to marry, external pressure, critical incidents, and timing in determining marital choice.

Today, pressures toward marriage appear to be lessening. A considerable number of young people are cohabiting and drifting into marriage rather than leaping into it. Interpersonal compatibility and self-actualization as goal-models are gaining, and the status of marriage is waning somewhat. In this climate, a theory such as SVR, which places a premium on interpersonal compatibility, should become even more relevant than it was in the past, when marriage was a highly desirable status in itself and less emphasis was placed on interpersonal relationships.

A bias much more difficult to eradicate stems from an author's formal training. Research topics and the approaches to them do not, like Minerva, spring full-blown from Zeus's head. Our graduate school training often outfits us with a set of blinders that causes us to evaluate problems through the schema considered correct for our particular profession. Psychologists often focus on the individual and his differences from other individuals, his variability and role playing, and the richness of his intrapsychic world—perhaps at the expense of neglecting the social context of his socialization. Sociologists are more apt to study man from a social-institutional standpoint and to focus on the person as a member of a group and on interactions between members rather than on the process within a person.

I have tried to take account of the biases implicit in my training as a psychologist and to be sensitive to the forces outside of the individual and of the dyad that influence marital choice. I have avoided discussion of homogamous selection by such sociologically oriented factors as race, religion, age, socioeconomic status, and propinquity for several reasons. For one thing, these factors have been written about for many decades and their association with marital choice is generally known. Secondly, it is interesting to note that few researchers have bothered to deal with the exceptions. How does it happen that a black marries a white despite homogamous selection by race? Instead of treating these exceptions as "errata," I have tried to develop a theory that would account for them on the basis of social exchange. Last, I have avoided preoccupation with these traditional variables because I do not believe that they influence the specific choice of a partner but largely serve to define the field of eligibles from which the choice is made.

Nevertheless, I do not wish to pretend to an inherent sensitivity to the sociological viewpoint or to claim that I have done full justice to the concerns of the sociologist regarding marital choice. The study of marriage is best achieved from an interdisciplinary point of view, but few of us can claim to be adequately trained in psychology, sociology, and anthropology, to name the three most relevant disciplines that come to mind. If SVR theory over-emphasizes perceptual processes, therefore, and does not give sufficient attention to societal influences, if the characters seem to have too vitalistic a role in choosing a spouse, whereas the pressures and influences of society are not emphasized enough, the origins of sins may be more readily understood.

A perusal of our many findings leads to the conclusion that marital choice is a more cognitive process than the "mystique of love" had led us to believe. Partner choice is associated with consideration of the partner and the self with respect to looks, and sensitivity to important perceptual concepts like self and ideal-self, and the degree to which the partner corresponds to the ideal-spouse image.

Our subjects did not behave like Tristan and Isolde, who were caught in the fiery passion of a burning love. There seemed to be a controlled cadence to the recitations of what led the individuals to love each other, and these events seemed no more spontaneous than the practiced faints of the Victorian heroine, who always seemed to pick out a comfortable spot in which to delicately swoon.

The cognitive nature of our results also gainsays the statement of Lawrence Kubie (1956) that marital choice is an unconscious process. Good CP, as we have seen, is associated with role compatibility consciously attributed over a number of variables.

Our data also caution against acceptance of simple, undemanding theories of marital choice. Complementary needs theory, we have noted, has garnered no empirical support in the present research and little elsewhere. Our data do suggest, however, that complementarity of personality may be most operative where one or both of the partners are strongly insufficient in some area, and an attempt is made to find a partner whose personality makeup is as different as possible from the unacceptable or unfulfilled aspects of oneself.

Similarity of personality in our research, as in so much earlier research, was faintly supported. Members of couples, for the most part, showed correlations ranging between .00 and .20 on the Minnesota Multiphasic Personality Inventory and the Revised Edwards Schedule. Such low relationships indicate that personality similarity, of itself, is an insignificant contributor to marital choice.

I have sought to develop a theory capable of treating the marriage process from the first contact of nubile individuals to the point of their marriage. The price for such a grand scope is a loss of parsimonious elegance in the theory. SVR theory is at once eclectic and complex. Temporally, it is a successive filter theory: viewed at any given point of time from a transactional point of view, it is an exchange theory; viewed teleologically from the individual's standpoint, it is a hedonistic reinforcement process.

I have tried to make the processes involved in the theory sufficiently clear to derive a large number of hypotheses that were capable of being supported or rejected by empirical research. A good theory must carry within itself the potential seeds of its eventual acceptance or destruction. A theory that endures some length of time because it is sufficiently ambiguous so as to be impervious to empirical research is, in the long run, of little heuristic value.

SUMMARY AND CONCLUSIONS

A review of our findings indicates no support for a monolithic theory of marital choice such as complementary needs or similarity of personality needs. The equity principle of SVR theory received considerable support, but equity, of itself, was shown to be too simplistic to serve as a good predictor of courtship. For example, equity in behavior is not necessary for courtship to advance. One member of the couple may perform more valued services for the partner than vice-versa, but the partner's contribution may depend on his status. The necessity of measuring status and services in the same units poses great difficulties for empirical research on equity.

Other problems include the fact that equity of mutual non-reinforcement of each other by members of a dyad would not normally lead to marriage; hence the individual's threshold for sufficient rewards to push him toward matrimony (desire to marry) must be ascertained. My initial attempt in this regard did not prove successful.

A further problem may be that individuals' satisfactions do not only come from rewards from the dyadic partner. They may come from peers, society, and family; thus a situation apparently imbalanced with respect to the partner may actually be equitable within the total "life space" context of the individual. Further, the individual may serve as a self-rewarding instrument so that his ability to fulfill a role model he sets for himself may compensate for inequitable exchange with the partner. It was suggested that this factor becomes more important as the relationship develops, being weakest initially in dyadic pairing, increasing in strength when commitment has been achieved, and becoming even stronger after marriage.

If to all of these complexities we add the uncontrollable fluctuations of environmental changes, critical incidents, and timing, it becomes doubtful that we can ever achieve a very high predictive index of marital choice early in courtship. Dyadic pairing, apart from necessarily including marriage, should be easier to predict. In sum, equity is quite important, but it is not all-pervasive in dyadic formation.

Concerning the second important axis of SVR theory, sequence, little direct empirical information was available due to the difficulties of conducting a required longitudinal study. Indirect evidence supported the initial importance of the S factor and the importance of R variables in advanced courtship. Remaining to be resolved is the importance of V in the sequence.

Like most research efforts, our findings have answered several questions and produced new questions to prod further research: Can a useful scale measuring "desire to marry" be constructed? Are stimulus variables really more muted in a "closed" field? What is the relationship of sex drive and marital choice, given the more permissive atmosphere of the seventies? How soon, if ever, will women be able to discount male status in choosing a spouse? It is my hope that the present volume may aid in stimulating research to answer these and other questions in understanding who will pair with whom and who will marry whom.

REFERENCES

Adams, B. N. *The American Family: A sociological interpretation.* Chicago: Markham, 1971.

Allen, G. Falling in love. *Fortnightly Review,* 1886, *46,* 432-462.

Allen, R. M. *Student's Rorschach manual.* New York: International Universities Press, 1966.

Altman, I. & Taylor, D. A. *Social penetration.* New York: Holt, Rinehart & Winston, 1973.

Andrews, R. O., & Christensen, H. T. Relationship of absence of a parent to courtship status: repeat study. *American Sociological Review,* 1951, *16,* 541-544.

Aronson, E. Some antecedents of interpersonal attraction. In W. J. Arnold and D. Levine (Eds.), *Nebraska symposium on motivation 1969.* Lincoln, Nebraska: University of Nebraska Press, 1970. Pp. 143-173.

Astell, Mary. *Reflections upon marriage.* London: R. Wilkin, 1706.

Atkinson, J. W. (Ed.). *Motives in fantasy, action, and society.* Princeton, N. J.: Van Nostrand, 1958.

Banta, T. J., & Hetherington, M. Relations between needs of friends and fiancés. *Journal of Abnormal and Social Psychology,* 1963, *66,* 501-404.

Bardwick, J. *The psychology of women: a study of bio-cultural conflicts.* New York: Harper & Row, 1971.

Barron, F. An ego-strength scale which predicts response to psychotherapy. In G. S. Welsh and W. G. Dahlstrom (Eds.), *Basic readings on the MMPI in psychology and medicine.* Minneapolis: University of Minnesota Press, 1956. Pp. 226-234.

The batchelor's directory. London: Richard Cumberland, 1696.

Baughman, E. E. A new method of Rorschach inquiry. *Journal of Projective Techniques,* 1958, *22,* 381-389.

Beck, G. D. *Person perception and marital adjustment.* Master's Thesis, Connecticut College, 1970.

Becker, G. The complementary-needs hypothesis, authoritarianism, dominance, and other Edwards Personal Preference Schedule scores. *Journal of Personality,* 1964, *32,* 45-56.

Beckman, L. Assortive mating in man. *The Eugenics Review,* 1962, *54,* 63-67.

Beier, E. G., Rossi, A. M., & Garfield, R. L. Similarity plus dissimilarity of personality. Basis for friendship? *Psychological Reports,* 1961, *8,* 3-8.

Bell, A. G. Upon the formation of a deaf variety of the human race. *Mem. National Academy of Science,* 1883, *2,* 179-262.

Bellamy, C. J. *An experiment in marriage.* Albany, N. Y.: Albany Book Co., 1889.

Benson, P. The common interests myth in marriage. *Social Problems,* 1955, *3,* 27-34.

Bermann, E. A. Compatibility and stability in the dyad. Paper presented before the American Psychological Association, New York, September, 1966.

Berscheid, E., Dion, K. K., Walster, E., & Walster, G. W. Physical attractiveness and dating choice: A test of the matching hypothesis. *Journal of Experimental Social Psychology,* 1971, *7,* 173-189.

Berscheid, E., & Walster, E. H. *Interpersonal attraction.* Reading, Mass.: Addison-Wesley, 1969.

Berscheid, E., & Walster, E. Beauty and the best. *Psychology Today,* 1972 (March), *5,* 42+.

Berscheid, E., & Walster, E. Physical attractiveness. In L. Berkowitz (Ed.), *Advances in experimental social psychology.* Vol. 7. New York: Academic Press, 1974. Pp. 157-215.

Blau, P. M. *Exchange and power in social life.* New York: John Wiley, 1964.

Blazer, J. A. Complementary needs and marital happiness. *Marriage and Family Living,* 1963, *25,* 89-95.

Blood, R. O., Jr., & Wolfe, D. M. *Husbands and wives.* Glencoe, Ill.: Free Press, 1960.

Boalt, G. *Family and marriage.* New York: McKay, 1965.

Bolton, C. D. Mate selection as the development of a relationship. *Marriage and Family Living,* 1961, *23,* 234-240.

Bonaparte, M. *Female sexuality.* New York: International Universities Press, 1953.

Bonney, M. E. A sociometric study of the relationship of some factors to mutual friendships on the elementary, secondary, and college levels. *Sociometry,* 1946, *9,* 21-47.

Boswell, J. *Life of Samuel Johnson.* Chicago: Encyclopedia Britannica, 1952.

Bowerman, C. E., & Day, B. R. A test of the theory of complementary needs as applied to couples during courtship. *American Sociological Review,* 1956. *21,* 602-605.

Bowman, C. C. Uncomplimentary remarks on complementary needs. *American Sociological Review,* 1955, *20,* 466.

Boxer, L. Mate selection and emotional disorder. *The Family Coordinator,* 1970, *19,* 173-179.

Brislin, R. W., & Lewis, S. A. Dating and physical attractiveness. Replication. *Psychological Reports,* 1968, *22,* 976.

Bruner, J. S., & Postman, L. Symbolic value as an organizing factor in perception. *Journal of Social Psychology,* 1948, *27,* 203-208.

Buckingham, J. S. *The eastern and western states of America.* 2 Vols., London: Fisher, Son & Co., 1867.

Burgess, E. W., & Locke, H. J. *The family.* New York: American Book Co., 1945.

Burgess, E. W., & Wallin, P. *Engagement and marriage.* Philadelphia: Lippincott, 1953.

Burma, J. H., Cretser, G. A., & Seacrest, T. A comparison of the occupational status of intramarrying and intermarrying couples: a research note. *Sociology and Social Research,* 1970, *54,* 508-519.

Byrne, D. *The attraction paradigm.* New York: Academic Press, 1971.

Campbell, Sir George. Sir George Campbell on scientific marriage-making. *The Spectator,* 1886, *59,* 1206-1207.

Capellanus, A. *The art of courtly love* (Translated by J. J. Parry). New York: Frederick Ungar, 1959.

Carter, H., & Glick, P. C. *Marriage and divorce: a social and economic study.* Cambridge: Harvard University Press, 1970.

Cattell, R. B., & Nesselroade, J. R. Likeness and completeness theories examined by sixteen personality factor measures on stably and unstably married couples. *Journal of Personality and Social Psychology,* 1970, *7,* 351-361.

Centers, R., & Granville, A. C. Reciprocal need gratification in intersexual attraction: A test of the hypotheses of Schutz and Winch. *Journal of Personality,* 1971, *39,* 26-43.

Chamber's Journal, The choice matrimonial, 1898, *1,* 498-500.

Coan, T. M. To marry or not to marry. *The Galaxy,* 1869, *7,* 493-500.

Commins, W. D. Marriage age of oldest sons. *Journal of Social Psychology,* 1932, *3,* 487-490.

Coombs, R. H. A value theory of mate-selection. *Family Life Coordinator,* 1961, *10,* 51-54.

Coombs, R. H. Reinforcement of values in the parental home as a factor in mate-selection. *Marriage and Family Living,* 1962, *24,* 155-157.

Coombs, R. H. Value consensus and partner satisfaction among dating couples. *Journal of Marriage and the Family*, 1966, *28*, 165-173.

Corah, N., Feldman, M. J., Cohen, I. S., Gruen, W., Meadow, A., & Ringwall, E. A. Social desirability as a variable in the Edwards Personal Preference Schedule. *Journal of Consulting Psychology*, 1958, *22*, 70-72.

Corsini, R. J. Understanding and similarity in marriage. *Journal of Abnormal and Social Psychology*, 1956, *52*, 327-332.

Cozby, I. Self-disclosure in human relationships. *Psychological Bulletin*, 1973, *79*, 73-91.

Cronbach, L. J. Processes affecting scores on "understanding of others" and "assumed similarity." *Psychological Bulletin*, 1955, *52*, 177-193.

Cronbach, L. J. Proposals leading to analytic treatment of social perception scores. In R. Tagiuri and L. Petrullo (Eds.), *Person perception and interpersonal behavior*, Stanford, Calif.: Stanford University Press, 1958. Pp. 353-379.

Dalhstrom, W. G., & Welsh, G. S. (Eds.). *An MMPI handbook*. Minneapolis: University of Minnesota Press, 1960.

Davis, K. Intermarriage in caste societies. *American Anthropologist*, 1941. N. S. *43*, 376-395.

Day, D. *The evaluation of love*. New York: Dial Press, 1954.

Defoe, D. *The use and abuse of the marriage bed*. London: T. Warner, 1727.

Dentler, R. A., & Hutchinson, J. G. Socioeconomic versus family membership status as sources of family attitude consensus. *Child Development*, 1961, *32*, 249-254.

Dermer, M. *When beauty fails*. Unpublished doctoral dissertation, University of Minnesota, Minneapolis, 1973.

Eckland, B. K. Theories of mate-selection. *Eugenics Quarterly*, 1968, *15*, 71-84.

Edwards, A. L. *Statistical methods for the behavioral sciences*. New York: Holt, Rinehart, & Winston, 1954.

Edwards, A. L. *Edwards Personal Preference Schedule*. New York: The Psychological Corporation, 1959.

Edwards, A. L. *The measurement of personality traits by scales and inventories*. New York: Holt, Rinehart, & Winston, 1970.

Edwards, J. N. Familial behavior as social exchange. *Journal of Marriage and the Family*, 1969, *31*, 518-526.

Edwards, W. A theory of decision-making. *Psychological Bulletin*, 1954, *51*, 380-417.

Edwards, W. The prediction of decisions among bets. *Journal of Experimental Psychology*, 1955, *50*, 201-214.

Ehrmann, W. *Premarital dating behavior*. New York: Bantam, 1960.

Eidelberg, L. Neurotic choice of mate. In V. W. Eisenstein (Ed.), *Neurotic interaction in marriage*. New York: Basic Books, 1956. Pp. 57-64.

Elder, Jr., G. H. Appearance and education in marriage mobility. *American Sociological Review*, 1969, *34*, 519-533.

English, H. B., & English, A. C. *A comprehensive dictionary of psychological and psychoanalytical terms*. New York: David McKay, 1958.

Epstein, S. The measurement of drive and conflict in humans: theory and experiment. In M. R. Jones (Ed.), *Nebraska symposium on motivation*. Lincoln, Nebraska: University of Nebraska Press, 1962. Pp. 127-205.

Epton, N. *Love and the French*. Cleveland: World, 1959.

Eron, L. D. A normative study of the Thematic Apperception Test. *Psychological Monographs*, 1950, *64*, No. 9.

Evans, R. *Conversations with Carl Jung*. Princeton: Van Nostrand, 1964.

Farber, B. An index of marital integration. *Sociometry*, 1957, *20*, 117-134.

Farber, B. *Family: organization and interaction*. San Francisco: Chandler Publishing Co., 1964.

Festinger, L. A theory of social comparison processes. *Human Relations*, 1954, *7*, 117-140.

Fiedler, F. E. The psychological distance dimension in interpersonal relations. *Journal of Personality*, 1953, *22*, 142-150.

Fisher, S., & Cleveland, S. E. *Body image and personality*. Princeton, N. J.: Van Nostrand, 1958.

Fowler, L. N. *Marriage, its history and ceremonies*. New York: S. R. Wells, 1855.

Fowler, O. S. *Matrimony*. Boston: O. S. Fowler, 1859.

Freud, S. *New introductory lectures on psycho-analysis*. New York: Norton, 1933.

Freud, S. *Three contributions to the theory of sex*. New York: The Modern Library, 1938.

Freud, S. On narcissism. In *Collected papers*, Volume 4. London: Hogarth Press, 1949, P. 44-50. (a)

Freud, S. *An outline of psychoanalysis*. New York: Norton, 1949. (b)

Freud, S. Group psychology and the analysis of the ego. In *The major works of Sigmund Freud*. Chicago: Encyclopedia Britannica, 1952. Pp. 664-696. (a)

Freud, S. *Civilization and its discontents*. In *The major works of Sigmund Freud*. Chicago: Encyclopedia Britannica, 1952. Pp. 767-802. (b)

Gage, N. L., & Cronbach, L. J. Conceptual and methodological problems in interpersonal perception. *Psychological Review*, 1955, *62*, 411-422.

Goethe, J. W. *Elective affinities*. Chicago: Henry Regnery, 1963.

Goldstein, J. W., & Rosenfeld, H. M. Insecurity and preference for persons similar to oneself. *Journal of Personality*, 1969, *37*, 253-268.

Goods, W. J. The theoretical importance of love. *American Sociological Review*, 1959, *24*, 38-47.

Goodman, M. Expressed self-acceptance and interspousal needs: a basis for mate selection. *Journal of Counseling Psychology,* 1964, *11,* 129-135.

Gordon, M., & Bernstein, M. C. Mate choice and domestic life in the 19th-century marriage manual. Unpublished manuscript, University of Connecticut, 1969.

Greenfield, S. M. Love and marriage in modern America: A functional analysis. *Sociological Quarterly,* 1965, *6,* 361-377.

Greller, J. C. Dating by computer? *Cosmopolitan,* 1967 (June), 73-74.

Gross, L. Effects of verbal and nonverbal reinforcement in the Rorschach. *Journal of Consulting Psychology,* 1959, *23,* 66-68.

Guilford, J. P. *Fundamental statistics in psychology and education* (3rd edition). New York: McGraw-Hill, 1956.

Hamilton, G. V., & MacGowan, K. *What is wrong with marriage.* New York: Albert & Charles Boni, 1929.

Harmon, H. H. *Modern factor analysis.* Chicago: University of Chicago Press, 1967.

Harris, J. A. Assortative mating in man. *The Popular Science Monthly,* 1912, *80,* 476-492.

Hathaway, S. R., & McKinley, J. C. *Minnesota Multiphasic Personality Inventory.* New York: The Psychological Corporation, 1967.

Hawkins, J. L. A theory of companionate interaction. Unpublished manuscript, Indiana University, 1968.

Heer, D. M. Negro-white marriage in the United States. *Journal of Marriage and the Family,* 1966, *28,* 262-273.

Hegel, O. W. F. *The philosophy of right.* Chicago: Encyclopedia Britannica, 1952.

Heiss, J. S. Variations in courtship progress among high school students. *Marriage and Family Living,* 1960, *22,* 165-170.

Heiss, J. S., & Gordon, M. Need patterns and the mutual satisfaction of dating and engaged couples. *Journal of Marriage and the Family,* 1964, *26,* 337-339.

Hobart, C. W. Emancipation from parents and courtship in adolescents. *Pacific Sociological Review,* Spring, 1958, *1,* 25-29. (a)

Hobart, C. W. Disillusionment in marriage and romanticism. *Marriage and Family Living,* 1958, *20,* 156-162. (b)

Hobart, C. W. Some effects of romanticism during courtship on marriage role opinions. *Sociology and social research,* 1958, *42,* 336-343. (c)

Hobart, C. W. The incidence of romanticism during courtship. *Social Forces,* 1958, *36,* 362-367. (d)

Hobart, C. W. Attitude changes during courtship and marriage. *Marriage and Family Living,* 1960, *22,* 352-359.

Hobart, C. W., & Lindholm, L. The theory of complementary needs: a re-examination. *Pacific Sociological Review,* 1963, *6,* 73-79.

Holmes, S. J., & Hatch, C. E. Personal appearance as related to scholastic records and marriage selection in college women. *Human Biology,* 1938, *10,* 65-76.

Holtzman, W. H. *Guide to administration and scoring Holtzman Inkblot Techniques.* New York: Psychological Corporation, 1961.

Holz, R. F. Homogamy and heterogamy in the marital dyad: The effects of role on need dispositions. Paper presented at the American Sociological Association Convention, San Francisco, 1969.

Holz, R. F. Similarity and complementarity in marital interaction: The effects of role on need patterns. *CRC Report,* Boston U., 1970, No. 46.

Homans, G. C. *Social behavior: its elementary forms.* New York: Harcourt, Brace & World, 1961.

Horst, P., & Wright, C. E. The comparative reliability of two techniques of personality appraisal. *Journal of Clinical Psychology,* 1959, *15,* 388-391.

Huston, T. L. Ambiguity of acceptance, social desirability, and dating choice. *Journal of Experimental Social Psychology,* 1973, *9,* 32-42. (a)

Huston, T. L. A decision-making model of the initiation of heterosexual pair relationships. Paper presented at the National Council in Family Relations, Toronto, October, 1973. (b)

Huston, T. L. A perspective on interpersonal attraction. In T. L. Huston (Ed.), *Foundations of interpersonal attraction.* New York: Academic Press, 1974.

Hutton, S. P. *Self-esteem, values and self-differentiation in premarital dyads.* Unpublished doctoral dissertation, Georgia State University, 1974.

Izard, C. Personality similarity and friendship. *Journal of Abnormal and Social Psychology,* 1960, *61,* 47-51. (a)

Izard, C. Personality similarity, positive effect, and interpersonal attraction. *Journal of Abnormal and Social Psychology,* 1960, *61,* 484-485. (b)

Izard, C. Personality similarity and friendship: A follow-up study. *Journal of Abnormal and Social Psychology,* 1963, *66,* 598-600.

Jacoby, S. Forty nine million singles can't all be right. *The New York Times Magazine,* February 17, 1974, 12-13, 41, 43, 46, 48-49.

Kaat, G. A., & Davis, K. E. Effect of volunteer biases on sexual behavior and attitudes. *Journal of Sex Research,* 1971, *7,* 26-34.

Kant, I. *The science of right.* Chicago: Encyclopedia Britannica, 1952.

Karp, E. S., Jackson, J. H., & Lester, D. Ideal-self fulfillment in mate selection: A corollary to the complementary need theory of mate selection. *Journal of Marriage and the Family,* 1970, *32,* 269-272.

Katz, I., Glucksberg, S., & Krauss, R. Need satisfaction and Edwards PPS scores in married couples. *Journal of Consulting Psychology,* 1960, *24,* 205-208.

Kelly, E. L. Marital compatibility as related to personality traits of husbands and wives as rated by self and spouse. *The Journal of Social Psychology,* 1941, *13,* 193-198.

314   *References*

Kenkel, W. F. *The family in perspective* (2nd ed.). New York: Appleton-Century-Crofts, 1966.

Kent, D. P. Subjective factors in mate selection: an exploratory study. *Sociology and Social Research*, 1951, *35*, 391-398.

Kerckhoff, A. C. Patterns of homogamy and the field of eligibles. *Social Forces*, 1964, *42*, 289-297.

Kerckhoff, A. C. Status-related value patterns among married couples. *Journal of Marriage and the Family*, 1972, *34*, 105-110.

Kerckhoff, A. C. The social context of interpersonal attraction. In T. L. Huston (Ed.), *Foundations of interpersonal attraction*. New York: Academic Press, 1974. Pp. 61-78.

Kerckhoff, A. C., & Bean, F. D. Role-related factors in person perception among engaged couples. *Sociometry*, June, 1967, *30*, 176-186.

Kerckhoff, A. C., & Davis, K. E. Value consensus and need complementarity in mate selection. *American Sociological Review*, 1962, *27*, 295-303.

Kernodle, W. Some implications of the homogamy-complementary needs theories of mate selection for sociological research. *Social Forces*, 1959, *38*, 145-152.

Kiesler, S. B., & Baral, R. L. The search for a romantic partner: the effects of self-esteem and physical attractiveness on romantic behavior. In K. Gergen and D. Marlowe (Eds.), *Personality and social behavior*. Reading, Mass.: Addison-Wesley, 1970. Pp. 155-165.

Kinsey, A. C., Pomeroy, W. B., & Martin, C. E. *Sexual behavior in the human male*, Philadelphia: Saunders, 1948.

Kinsey, A. C., Pomeroy, W. B., Martin, C. E., & Gebhard, P. H. *Sexual behavior in the human female*. Philadelphia: Saunders, 1953.

Kipnis, D. Changes in self-concepts in relation to perceptions of others. *Journal of Personality*, 1961, *29*, 449-465.

Kirkendall, L. A. *Premarital intercourse and interpersonal relationhips*. New York: Julian Press, 1961.

Kirkpatrick, C. A statistical investigation of the psychoanalytic theory of mate selection. *Journal of Abnormal and Social Psychology*, 1937, *32*, 427-430.

Kirkpatrick, C. Familial development, selective needs, and predictive theory. *Journal of Marriage and the Family*, 1967, *29*, 229-236.

Kirkpatrick, C., & Caplow, T. Courtship in a group of Minnesota students. *American Journal of Sociology*, 1945, *51*, 114-125.

Klopfer, B., Ainsworth, M., Klopfer, W. G., & Holt, R. R. *Developments in the Rorschach Technique: Technique and theory*. New York: World, 1954.

Knapp, M. *Nonverbal communication in human interaction*. New York: Holt, Rinehart, & Winston, 1972.

Knupfer, G., Clark, W., & Room, R. The mental health of the unmarried. *American Journal of Psychiatry*, 1966, *122*, 841-851.

Kogan, K. L., & Jackson, J. K. Perceptions of self and spouse: some contaminating factors. *Journal of Marriage and the Family*, 1964, *26*, 60-64.

Komarovsky, M. Functional analysis of sex roles. *American Sociological Review*, 1950, *15*, 508-516.

Kotler, S. L. Middle-class marital role perceptions and marital adjustment. *Sociology and Social Research*, 1965, *49*, 281-294.

Ktsanes, T. Mate selection on the basis of personality type: A study utilizing an empirical typology of personality. *American Sociological Review*, 1955, *20*, 547-551.

Kubie, L. S. Psychoanalysis and marriage: practical and theoretical issues. In V. E. Eisenstein (Ed.), *Neurotic interaction in marriage*. New York: Basic Books, 1956. Pp. 10-43.

Leslie, G. R., & Richardson, A. H. Family versus campus influences in relation to mate selection. *Social Problems*, 1956, *4*, 117-121.

Levinger, G. Note on need complementarity in marriage. *Psychological Bulletin*, 1964, *61*, 153-157.

Levinger, G., Senn, D. J., & Jorgensen, B. W. Progress toward permanence in courtship: A test of the Kerckhoff-Davis hypothesis. *Sociometry*, 1970, *33*, 427-443.

Lewin, K., Dembo, T., Festinger, L., & Sears, P. Level of aspiration. In J. M. Hunt (Ed.), *Personality and the behavior disorders*, Volume 1. New York: Ronald Press, 1944. Pp. 333-378.

Lewis, R. A. A developmental framework for the analysis of premarital dyadic formation. *Family Process*, 1972, *11*, 17-48.

Lewis, R. A. A longitudinal test of a developmental framework for premarital dyadic formation. *Journal of Marriage and the Family*, 1973, *35*, 16-25.

Lipetz, M. E., Cohen, I. H., Dworin, J., & Rogers, L. S. Need complementarity, marital stability, and marital satisfaction. In K. J. Gergen & D. Marlowe (Eds.), *Personality and social behavior*. Reading, Massachusetts: Addison-Wesley, 1970. Pp. 201-212.

Lipset, S. M., & Bendix, R. *Social mobility in industrial society*. Berkely: University of California Press, 1959.

Locke, H. J., Sabagh, G., & Thomes, M. M. Interfaith marriage. *Social Problems*, 1957, *4*, 333-340.

Locke, J. Concerning civil government. In *Locke, Berkeley, Hume*. Chicago: Encyclopedia Britannica, 1952. Pp. 25-81.

Lu, Y. C. Marital roles and marital adjustment. *Sociology and Social Research*, 1952, *36*, 364-368.

Luckey, E. B. Implications for marriage counseling of self perceptions and spouse perceptions. *Journal of Counseling Psychology*, 1960, *7*, 3-9. (a)

Luckey, E. B. Marital satisfaction and congruent self-spouse concepts. *Social Forces*, 1960, *39*, 153-157. (b)

Luther, M. *Letters of spiritual counsel*. Philadelphia: Westminster Press, 1955.

Mangus, A. H. Relationships between young women's conceptions of intimate male associates and of their ideal husbands. *Journal of Social Psychology*, 1936, *7*, 403-420.

Marsden, E. Values as determinants of friendship choice. *Connecticut College Psychology Journal*, 1966, *3*, 3-13.

McCall, A. B. The tower room. *Women's Home companion*, 1911, *28* (Sept.), 24.

McGuire, C., & White, G. D. The measurement of social status. Report No. 3, Laboratory of Human Behavior, Department of Educational Psychology, The University of Texas, 1955.

McKenna, H. V., Hofstaetter, P. R., & O'Connor, J. P. The concepts of the ideal-self and of the friend. *Journal of Personality*, 1956, *24*, 262-271.

Merton, R. K. Intermarriage and the social structure. *Psychiatry*, 1941, *4*, 361-374.

Military clinical psychology. TM8-242-AFM160-45. Washington: United States Government Printing Office, 1951.

Miller, N., Campbell, D. T., Twedt, H., & O'Connell, E. J. Similarity, contrast, and complementarity in friendship choice. *Journal of Personality and Social Psychology*, 1966, *3*, 3-12.

Milton, J. *Paradise lost.* Chicago: Encyclopedia Britannica, 1952.

Mittelman, B. Complementary neurotic reactions in intimate relations. *Psychoanalytic Quarterly*, 1944, *13*, 479-491.

de Montesquieu C. *The spirit of laws.* Chicago: Encylopedia Britannica, 1952.

Moreau de Saint-Méry, M.L.E. The bitter thoughts of president Moreau. In O. Handlin (Ed.), *This was America.* Cambridge: Harvard University Press, 1949. Pp. 88-103.

Morgan, E. S. *The puritan family.* Boston: Public Library, 1944.

Morris, C. *Varieties of human value.* Chicago: University of Chicago Press, 1956.

Murray, H. A. *Explorations in personality.* New York: Oxford University Press, 1938.

Murray, H. A. *Thematic Apperception Test manual.* Cambridge, Mass.: Harvard University Press, 1943.

Murstein, B. I. The projection of hostility on the Rorschach and as a result of ego-threat. *Journal of Projective Technique*, 1956, *20*, 418-428.

Murstein, B. I. Factor analyses of the Rorschach. *Journal of Consulting Psychology*, 1960, *24*, 262-275.

Murstein, B. I. Assumptions, adaptation-level, and projective techniques. *Perceptual and Motor Skills*, 1961, *12*, 107-125. (a)

Murstein, B. I. The complementary need hypothesis in newlyweds and middle-aged married couples. *Journal of Abnormal and Social Psychology*, 1961, *63*, 194-197. (b)

Murstein, B. I. *Theory and research in projective techniques: Emphasizing the TAT.* New York: John Wiley, 1963.

Murstein, B. I. (Ed.). *Handbook of projective techniques.* New York: Basic Books, 1965. (a)

Murstein, B. I. New thoughts about ambiguity and the TAT. *Journal of Projective Techniques & Personality Assessment,* 1965, *29,* 219-225. (b)

Murstein, B. I. Possession of hostility and accuracy of perception of it in others: a cross-sex replication. *Journal of Projective Techniques & Personality Assessment,* 1966, *30,* 46-50.

Murstein, B. I. Empirical tests of role, complementary needs, and homogamy theories of marital choice. *Journal of Marriage and the Family,* 1967, *29,* 689-696. (a)

Murstein, B. I. The relationship of mental health to marital choice and courtship progress. *Journal of Marriage and the Family,* 1967, *29,* 447-451. (b)

Murstein, B. I. Effect of stimulus, background, personality, and scoring system on the manifestation of hostility on the TAT. *Journal of Consulting and Clinical Psychology,* 1968, *32,* 355-365.

Murstein, B. I. Stimulus-value-role: a theory of marital choice. *Journal of Marriage and the Family,* 1970, *32,* 465-481.

Murstein, B. I. Self ideal-self discrepancy and the choice of marital partner. *Journal of Consulting and Clinical Psychology,* 1971, *37,* 47-52. (a)

Murstein, B. I. (Ed.). *Theories of attraction and love.* New York: Springer, 1971. (b)

Murstein, B. I. What makes people sexually appealing? *Sexual Behavior,* 1971, *1,* (No. 3), 75. (c)

Murstein, B. I. Interview behavior, projective techniques, and questionnaires in the clinical assessment of marital choice. *Journal of Personality Assessment.* 1972, *36,* 462-467. (a)

Murstein, B. I. Person perception and courtship progress among pre-marital couples. *Journal of Marriage and the Family,* 1972, *34,* 621-627. (b)

Murstein, B. I. Physical attractiveness and marital choice. *Journal of Personality and Social Psychology,* 1972, *22,* 8-12. (c)

Murstein, B. I. A thematic test and the Rorschach in predicting marital choice. *Journal of Personality Assessment,* 1972, *36,* 213-217. (d)

Murstein, B. I. Physical attractiveness and person perception. Unpublished manuscript, New London: Connecticut College, 1972. (e)

Murstein, B. I. Perceived congruence among premarital couples as a function of neuroticism. *Journal of Abnormal Psychology,* 1973, *81,* 22-26. (a)

Murstein, B. I. A theory of marital choice applied to interracial marriage. In L. E. Abt. and I. Stuart (Eds.), *Interracial marriage: Expectations and realities.* New York: Grossman, 1973. Pp. 17-35. (b)

Murstein, B. I. *Love, sex and marriage through the ages.* New York: Springer, 1974. (a)

Murstein, B. I. Sex-drive, person perception, and marital choice. *Archives of Sexual Behavior,* 1974, *3,* 331-348. (b)

Murstein, B. I. Dimensions of marital expectation in an American and French college population: a cross-cultural comparison. Unpublished paper, Connecticut College, 1975.

Murstein, B. I., & Beck, G. D. Person perception, marriage adjustment, and social desirability. *Journal of Consulting and Clinical Psychology,* 1972, *39,* 396-403.

Murstein, B. I., & Christy, P. Physical attractiveness and marital adjustment. Unpublished manuscript, Connecticut College, 1973.

Murstein, B. I., & Lamb, J. The determinants of friendship in a girl's cooperative. Unpublished paper, Connecticut College, 1973.

Murstein, B. I., & Levy, M. Self-acceptance and perceived similarity of spouse and best friend. Unpublished manuscript, Connecticut College, 1973.

Murstein, B. I., & Pryer, R. S. The concept of projection: a review. *Psychological Bulletin,* 1959, *56,* 353-374.

Murstein, B. I., & Roth, R. D. Stimulus-value-role theory, exchange-theory, and marital choice. Unpublished manuscript, Connecticut College, 1973.

National Bureau of Standards. *Tables of the binomial probability distribution.* Washington, D.C.: U.S. Government Printing Office, 1950.

Newcomb, T. M. *The acquaintance process.* New York: Holt, Rinehart & Winston, 1961.

Orlinsky, D. The psychology of romantic love: a conceptual model. Paper delivered at American Psychological Association Convention, Washington, D.C., 1971.

Paine, T. *The writings of Tom Paine,* Volume 1. New York: G. P. Putnam's Sons, 1894.

Palmer, J., & Byrne, D. Attraction toward dominant and submissive strangers: Similarity versus complementarity. *Journal of Experimental Research in Personality,* 1970, *4,* 108-115.

Parrott, G. L., & Coleman, G. Sexual appeal in black and white. *Proceedings, 79th Annual Convention, APA,* 1971, 321-322.

Patten, S. N. The laws of social attraction. *Popular Science Monthly,* 1908, *73,* 354-360.

Pearson, K. Assortative mating in man. *Biometrika,* 1903, *2,* 481-498.

Piotrowski, Z. A. A Rorschach compendium. In J. A. Brussel, K. S. Hitch, & Z. A. Piotrowski (Eds.), *A Rorschach training manual.* Utica, N.Y., State Hospitals Press, 1950. Pp. 33-86.

Piotrowski, Z. A. *Perceptanalysis.* New York: Macmillan, 1957.

Pollis, C. A. Dating involvement and patterns of idealization: a test of

Waller's hypothesis. *Journal of Marriage and the Family,* 1969, *31,* 765-771.

Pond, D. A., Ryle, A., & Hamilton, M. Marriage and neurosis in a working-class population. *British Journal of Psychiatry,* 1963, *109,* 592-598.

Preston, A. The ideals of the bride to be. *Ladies Home Journal,* 1905, *22* (March), 26.

Prince, A. J., & Baggaley, A. C. Personality variables and the ideal mate. *Family Life Coordinator,* 1963, *3,* 93-96.

Rapoport, R. Normal crises, family structure and mental health. *Family Process,* 1963, *2,* 68-80.

Rapoport, R. The transition from engagement to marriage. *Acta Sociologica,* 1964, *8,* 36-55.

Rapoport, R. The study of marriage as a critical transition for personality and family development. Unpublished manuscript, Harvard Medical School, Cambridge, Boston, 1965.

Rapoport, R., & Rapoport, R. N. New light on the honeymoon. *Human Relations,* 1964, *17,* 33-56.

Rapoport, R., & Rapoport, R. Work and family in contemporary society. *American Sociological Review,* 1965, *30,* 381-394.

Rapoport, R., & Rapoport, R. Family transitions in contemporary society. *Journal of Psychosomatic Research,* 1968, *12,* 29-38.

Reader, N., & English, H. B. Personality factors in adolescent friendships. *Journal of Consulting Psychology,* 1947, *11,* 212-220.

Reilly, M. A., Commins, W. D., & Stefic, E. C. The complementarity of personality needs in friendship choice. *Journal of Abnormal and Social Psychology,* 1960, *61,* 292-294.

Reiss, I. L. Toward a sociology of the heterosexual love relationship. *Marriage and Family Living,* 1960, *22,* 139-145.

Reiss, I. L. *The family system in America.* New York: Holt, Rinehart, & Winston, 1971.

Reiter, H. H. Similarities and differences in scores on certain personality scales among engaged couples. *Psychological Reports,* 1970, *26,* 465-466.

Rich, R. O. Value balance and engagement to marry. Paper presented at National Council in Family Relations, Toronto, Canada, Oct., 1973.

Richardson, H. M. Studies of mental resemblances between husbands and wives and between friends. *Psychological Bulletin,* 1939, *36,* 104-120.

Richardson, H. M. Community of values as a factor in friendship of college and adult women. *Journal of Social Psychology,* 1940, *11,* 303-312.

Rokeach, M. *The nature of human values.* New York: The Free Press, 1973.

Rokeach, M., Smith, P. W., & Evans, R. I. Two kinds of prejudice or one? In M. Rokeach (Ed.), *The open and closed mind.* New York: Basic Books, 1960. Pp. 132-168.

Romig, H. G. *50-100 binomial tables.* New York: Wiley, 1953.

Roos, D. E. Complementary needs in mate selection: A study based on R-type factor analysis. Unpublished doctoral dissertation, Northwestern University, 1956.

Rosenberg, M. & Simmons, R. G. *Black and white self-esteem: The urban school child.* Arnold and Caroline Rose Monograph Series. Washington, D.C. American Sociological Association, 1971.

Rosow, I. Issues in the concept of need complementarity. *Sociometry*, 1957, *20*, 216-233.

Rotter, J. B. *Social learning and clinical psychology.* New York: Prentice-Hall, 1954.

Rubin, Z. The measurement of romantic love. *Journal of Personality and Social Psychology*, 1970, *16*, 265-273.

Rubin, Z., & Levinger, G. Theory and data badly mated: A critique of Murstein's SVR and Lewis's PDF models of mate selection. *Journal of Marriage and the Family*, 1974, *36*, 226-231.

Rychlak, J. F. The similarity, compatibility, or incompatibility of needs in interpersonal selection. *Journal of Personality and Social Psychology*, 1965, *2*, 334-340.

Ryder, R. G., Kafka, J. S., & Olson, D. H. Separating and joining influences in courtship and early marriage. *American Journal of Orthopsychiatry*, 1971, *4*, 450-464.

Saper, B. Motivational components in the interpersonal transactions of married couples. *Psychiatric Quarterly*, 1965, *39*, 303-314.

Schellenberg, J. A. Homogamy in personal values and the "field of eligibles." *Social Forces*, December, 1960, *39*, 157-162.

Schellenberg, J. S., & Bee, L. S. A re-examination of the theory of complementary needs in mate selection. *Marriage and Family Living*, 1960, *22*, 227-232.

Schmidt, G., & Sigusch, V. Sex differences in reactions to pictorial and narrative stimili of sexual content. Paper read at the 4 Meeting, Czecho-Slovakian Sex Research Association, Praha, June 8-9, 1972.

Schutz, W. C. *FIRO: A three dimensional theory of interpersonal behavior.* New York: Rinehart, 1958.

Shuttleworth, F. K. A biosocial and developmental theory of male and female sexuality. *Marriage and Family Living*, 1959, *21*, 163-171.

Sigall, H., & Aronson, E. Liking for an evaluator as a function of her physical attractiveness and nature of the evaluations. *Journal of Experimental Social Psychology*, 1969, *5*, 93-100.

Sigusch, V., Schmidt, G., Reinfeld, A., & Wiedemann-Sutor, I. Psychosexual stimulation: sex differences. *Journal of Sex Research*, 1970, *6*, 10-24.

Simkins, L. Examiner reinforcement and situational variables in a projective testing situation. *Journal of Consulting Psychology*, 1960, *24*, 541-547.

Simpson, G. *People in families.* New York: Crowell, 1960.

Slater, E. An investigation into assortative mating. *Eugenics Review*, 1946, *38*, 27-28.

Snyder, E. C. Attitudes: a study of homogamy and marital selectivity. *Journal of Marriage and the Family*, 1964, *26*, 332-334.

Spencer, H. *An autobiography*. Vol. 1. London: Watts & Co., 1926.

Spinoza, B. *Ethics*. Chicago: Encyclopedia Britannica, 1952.

Stendhal (H. Beyle). *On love*. New York: Liveright, 1947.

Strauss, A. The ideal and the chosen mate. *American Journal of Sociology*, 1946, *52*, 204-208. (a)

Strauss, A. The influence of parent-images upon marital choice. *American Sociological Review*, 1946, *11*, 554-559. (b)

Stroebe, W., Insko, A., Thompson, V. D., & Layton, B. D. Effects of physical attractiveness, attitude similarity, and sex on various aspects of interpersonal attraction. *Journal of Personality and Social Psychology*, 1971, *18*, 79-91.

Strong, E., Wallace, W., & Wilson, W. Three-filter date selection by computer. *The Family Coordinator*, 1969, *18*, 166-171.

Strong, E., & Wilson, W. Three-filter date selection by computer—phase II. *The Family Coordinator*, 1969, *18*, 256-259.

Stuart, I. R. Complementary versus homogeneous needs in mate selection: a television program situation. *The Journal of Social Psychology*, 1962, *56*, 291-300.

Swedenborg, E. *Conjugial love*. New York: Swedenborg Foundation, 1954.

Swift, J. *Gulliver's travels*. Chicago: Encylopedia Britannica, 1952.

Swift, J. Letter to a very young lady on her marriage. In I. Schneider (Ed.), *The world of love*, 2 vols., New York: George Braziller, 1964. Pp. 447-454.

Szondi, L. Contributions to fate analysis: an attempt at a theory of choice in love. *Acta Psychologica*, 1937, *3*, 1-80.

Technical Report of the Commission on Obscenity and Pornography, Vol. 8. *Erotica and Social Behavior*. U.S. Government Printing Office, Washington, D.C., 1971.

Terman, L. M. *Psychological factors in marital happiness*. New York: McGraw-Hill, 1938.

Tesser, A., & Brodie, M. A note on the evaluation of a "computer date." *Psychonomic Science*, 1971, *23*, 300.

Tharp, R. G. Psychological patterning in marriage. *Psychological Bulletin*, 1963, *60*, 97-117.

Tharp, R. G. Reply to Levinger's note. *Psychological Bulletin*, 1964, *61*, 158-160.

Thibaut, J. W., & Kelley, H. H. *The social psychology of groups*. New York: John Wiley, 1959.

Thompson, W. R., & Nishimura, R. Some determinants of friendship. *Journal of Personality*, 1952, *20*, 305-314.

Trost, J. Some data on mate-selection: complementarity. *Journal of Marriage and the Family*, 1967, *29*, 730-738.

Turner, E. S. *A history of courting*. London: Michael Joseph, 1954.

Udry, J. R. Complementarity in mate selection: A perceptual approach. *Marriage and Family Living*, 1963, *25*, 281-290.

Udry, J. R. Structural correlates of feminine beauty preferences in Britain and the United States: A comparison. *Sociology and Social Research*, 1965, *49*, 330-342. (a)

Udry, J. R. The influence of the ideal mate image on mate selection and mate perception. *Journal of Marriage and the Family*, 1965, *27*, 477-482. (b)

Udry, J. R. Personality match and interpersonal perception as predictors of marriage. *Journal of Marriage and the Family*, 1967, *29*, 722-725.

Udry, J. R., Bauman, K. E., & Chase, C. A. Skin color, status, and mate selection. *American Journal of Sociology*, 1971, *76*, 722-733.

Vital statistics of the United States, 1969. Vol. 3. *Marriage and divorce*. Rockville, Md.: U.S. Department of Health, Education and Welfare, 1972.

Vreeland, F. M., & Corey, S. M. A study of college friendships. *Journal of Abnormal and Social Psychology*, 1935, *30*, 229-236.

Waller, W. *The family: a dynamic interpretation*. New York: Cordon, 1938.

Walster, E. The effect of self-esteem on romantic liking. *Journal of Experimental Social Psychology*, 1965, *1*, 184-197.

Walster, E., Aronson, V., Abrahams, D., & Rottman, L. Importance of physical attractiveness in dating behavior. *Journal of Personality and Social Psychology*, 1966, *5*, 508-516.

Walster, E., & Walster, G. W. Effect of expecting to be liked on choice of associates. *Journal of Abnormal and Social Psychology*, 1963, *67*, 402-404.

Walster, E., Walster, G. W., Piliavin, J., & Schmidt, L. "Playing hard to get": Understanding an elusive phenomenon. *Journal of Personality and Social Psychology*, 1973, *26*, 113-121.

Ward, L. F. *Pure sociology*. New York: Macmillan, 1916.

Warner, W. L., Junker, B. H., & Adams, W. A. *Color and human nature*. Washington, D.C.: American Council on Education, 1941.

Weininger, O. *Sex and character*. New York: Putnam's, 1906.

Wells, S. R. *Wedlock: or the right relation of the sexes*. New York: Samuel R. Wells, 1869.

Welsh, G. R. Factor dimensions A and R. In G. S. Welsh & W. G. Dahlstrom (Eds.), *Basic readings on the MMPI in psychology and medicine*. Minneapolis: University of Minnesota Press, 1956. Pp. 264-281.

Welsh, G. S., & Dahlstrom, W. G. (Eds.), *Basic readings on the MMPI in psychology and medicine*. Minneapolis: University of Minnesota Press, 1956.

Westermarck, E. *The future of marriage in western civilization.* New York: Macmillan, 1936.

Wickes, T. A. Examiner influence in a test situation. *Journal of Consulting Psychology,* 1956, *20,* 23-26.

Williams Jr., R. M. *American society: A sociological interpretation.* New York: Knopf, 1954.

Willoughby, R. R. Neuroticism in marriage. IV homogamy: V summary and conclusions. *Journal of Social Psychology,* 1963, *7,* 19-31.

Winch, R. F. The relation between courtship behavior and attitudes toward parents among college men. *American Sociological Review,* 1943, *8,* 167-174.

Winch, R. F. Interrelations between certain social background and parent-son factors in a study of courtship among college men. *American Sociological Review,* 1946, *11,* 333-341.

Winch, R. F. Primary factors in a study of courtship. *American Sociological Review,* 1947, *12,* 658-666.

Winch, R. F. The relation between loss of a parent and progress in courtship. *Journal of Social Psychology,* 1949, *29,* 51-56. (a)

Winch, R. F. Courtship in college women. *The American Journal of Sociology,* 1949, *55,* 269-278. (b)

Winch, R. F. Some data bearing on the Oedipus hypothesis. *Journal of Abnormal and Social Psychology,* 1950, *45,* 481-489.

Winch, R. F. Further data and observation on the Oedipus hypothesis: the consequence of an inadequate hypothesis. *American Sociological Review,* 1951, *16,* 784-795.

Winch, R. F. The theory of complementary needs in mate-selection: An analytic and descriptive study. *American Sociological Review,* 1954, *19,* 241-249.

Winch, R. F. The theory of complementary needs in mate-selection: a test of one kind of complementariness. *American Sociological Review,* 1955, *20,* 52-56. (a)

Winch, R. F. The theory of complementary needs in mate-selection: final results on the test of the general hypothesis. *American Sociological Review,* 1955, *20,* 552-555. (b)

Winch, R. F. *Mate-selection.* New York: Harper, 1958.

Winch, R. F. Another look at the theory of complementary needs in mate-selection. *Journal of Marriage and the Family,* 1967, *29,* 756-762.

Winch, R. F. Complementary needs and related notions about voluntary mate-selection. In R. F. Winch and G. Spanier (Eds.), *Selected studies in marriage and the family.* New York: Holt, Rinehart & Winston, 1974. Pp. 399-410.

Winch, R. F., Ktsanes, T., & Ktsanes, V. The theory of complementary needs in mate-selection: an analytic and descriptive study. *American Sociological Review*, 1954, *19*, 241-249.

Winch, R. F., Ktsanes, T., & Ktsanes, V. Empirical elaboration of the theory of complementary needs in mate-selection. *The Journal of Abnormal and Social Psychology*, 1955, *51*, 508-513.

Winch, R. F., & More, D. M. Quantitative analysis of qualitative data in the assessment of motivation: reliability, congruence, and validity. *The American Journal of Sociology*, 1956, *61*, 445-452. (a)

Winch, R. F., & More, D. M. Does TAT add information to interviews? statistical analysis of the increment. *Journal of Clinical Psychology*, 1956, *7*, 316-321. (b)

Winer, B. J. *Statistical principles in experimental design.* New York: McGraw-Hill, 1962.

Wirth, L., & Goldhammer, H. The hybrid and the problems of miscegination, In O. Klineberg (Ed.), *Characteristics of the American Negro.* New York: Harper, 1944. Pp. 249-369.

Wolfe, H. A theory of mate selection based on interaction. Unpublished paper, Dept. of Sociology, Pennsylvania State University, 1973.

Worthy, M., Gary, A. L., & Kahn, G. M. Self disclosure as an exchange process. *Journal of Personality and Social Psychology*, 1969, *13*, 59-63.

Zelditch Jr., M. Role differentiation in the nuclear family: A comparative study. In T. Parsons & R. F. Bales (Eds.), *Family, socialization and interaction process.* Glencoe, Ill.: The Free Press, 1955. Pp. 259-351.

Appendices

Appendix A

List of Tests and Questionnaires Used in Research

Group I Measures (Appendix B)

Entire testing sequence included:
  Minnesota Multiphasic Personality Inventory
  Marriage Value Inventory*
  McGuire Socioeconomic Index*
  Revised Edwards Personal Preference Schedule taken under four sets:
    self, ideal-self, perception of partner, ideal spouse*
  Expediency Scale*
  Background Questions*
  (Sex Questionnaire)**
  Follow-up Questions and Information (6 months later)*

Group II Measures (Appendix C)

Entire testing sequence included:
  Interview*
  Baughman Rorschach Modification
  Marriage Apperceptive Thematic Examination*
  Background Questions*
  Sex Questions
  Follow-up Questions (six months later)*
  Evaluation Q Sort by Interviewers*

Group III Measures (Appendix D)

Entire testing sequence included:
10 "sets" of Marital Expectation Test as follows:

Men	*Women*
1. Self	Self*
2. Ideal-self*	Ideal-self
3. Girlfriend	Boyfriend
4. Ideal spouse	Ideal spouse
5. How girlfriend sees self	How boyfriend sees self
6. How girlfriend sees ideal-self	How boyfriend sees ideal-self
7. How girlfriend sees me	How boyfriend sees me
8. How girlfriend sees ideal-spouse	How boyfriend sees ideal-spouse
9. Importance of self items	Importance of self items
10. Importance of ideal-self items	Importance of ideal-self items

Marriage Value Inventory***
McGuire Index***
Background Questions*
Sex Questions*
McGuire Index Frequencies*
Courtship Progress Question Follow-up (six months later)*

* Given in full in the Appendix. In the case of tests given under several perceptual sets, only one "set" is listed since the others are identical except for slight grammatical alterations. Only three of the 13 pictures used from the Marriage Apperceptive Thematic Examination are included.

**The Sex Questions for Group I were listed in Chapter 8, pages 140-141.

***Text appears under Group I (Appendix B).

Appendix B

Group I Measures

Group I

1. MARRIAGE VALUE INVENTORY

Below are listed standards by which marital success has been measured. Look through the list and mark *1* after the item you consider the most important value of marriage to you personally (in the column headed *Rank*). Look through the list again and mark *2* after the item you consider next in importance. Keep doing this until you have a number after each item.

There is no order of items which is correct; the order you choose is correct for you. Remember, there can be only one item marked *1*, one item marked *2*, one item marked *3*, . . . one item marked *10*.

Rank

Healthy and happy children _____

Satisfactory sex life _____

Companionship with spouse. Someone to be with, talk to, to relate to emotionally _____

Satisfaction of being a married person with all the social and psychological benefits this status allows in the community as opposed to being single _____

Economic security. Being sure that the family will be able to keep up or improve its standard of living _____

A home where one feels one belongs apart from outside relationships with other persons; the feeling of having identity; a place to relax where other people do not interfere _____

Moral and religious unity. Trying to live a family life according to religious and moral principles and teachings _____

Enjoying the admiration of others because of the attractiveness of my spouse (physical, intellectual, personality) and our family _____

Physical comforts of marriage (non-sexual) such as eating better meals, motivation to prepare meals, having good clothes, living in comfortable surroundings, enjoying labor-saving conveniences, etc. _____

A place in the community. The ability of a family to give its members a respected place in the community and to make them desirable citizens _____

2. MCGUIRE SOCIOECONOMIC INDEX

Code No._____

Please be as specific as possible about the following information as this information will bear no names when analyzed.

Profession of father_____ Yearly Income _____

Profession of mother (if any)_____ Yearly Income _____

Total family income_____

MAJOR SOURCE OF FAMILY INCOME (check appropriate choice)

_____ 1. Inherited saving and investments: "old money" reputed to provide basic income.

_____ 2. Earned wealth; "new money" has provided "transferable" investment income.

_____ 3. Profits, fees, royalties, includes executives who receive a "share of profit."

_____ 4. Salary, commissions, regular income aid on monthly or yearly basis.

_____ 5. Wages on hourly basis; piece work; weekly checks as distinguished from monthly or bi-weekly.

_____ 6. Incomes from "odd jobs" or private relief; "sharecropping" or seasonal work.

_____ 7. Public relief or charity.

_____ 8. Other.

330

EDUCATIONAL ATTAINMENT OF FATHER OR PARENT LIVED WITH IF ONLY ONE

_____ 1. Completed appropriate graduate work for a recognized profession at highest level.

_____ 2. Graduate from a four-year college, university, or professional school with a recognized bachelor's degree, including four-year teacher colleges.

_____ 3. Attended college or university for two or more years; junior college graduate; teacher education from a normal school; R.N. from a nursing school.

_____ 4. Graduate from high school or completed equivalent secondary education; includes various kinds of "post-high" business education or trade school study.

_____ 5. Attended high school, completed grade nine, but did not graduate from high school.

_____ 6. Completed grade eight but did not attend beyond grade nine.

_____ 7. Left elementary or junior high school before completing grade eight.

Scored as follows: The number of points obtained is equal to the number in the item checked. "Source of income" is multiplied by 4 and then added to 3 times the point checked for "Educational Attainment."

3. REVISED EDWARDS PERSONAL PREFERENCE SCHEDULE*

Please answer each item by writing the abbreviation for the item in the space provided on the answer sheet. For example, if an item says: *I like to swim*, you have a choice of one of five answers. These are:

Very important to me	(V)
Somewhat important to me	(S)
Average importance to me	(A)
Little importance	(L)
Almost no importance	(N)

If swimming were somewhat important you should write the capital letter *S* in the space provided for the item on the answer sheet.

There are a few items to be answered differently. These items have the choice of:

Very frequently	(V)
Somewhat frequently	(S)
Occasionally	(O)
Rarely	(R)
Almost never	(N)

Answer these items with one of the letters above. For example, the item *I go to the movies* (Very frequently, Somewhat frequently, Occasionally, Rarely, Almost never), might be answered *R* in the space provided.

Your choice in each instance should be in terms of what you like and how you feel at the present time, and not in terms of what you think you should like, or, how you think you should feel. This is not a test. There are no right or wrong answers. Your choices should be a description of your own personal likes and feelings. Please make sure you have answered every item.

4. EXPEDIENCY SCALE (SCALE E)

Code No._____

Please answer the following questions to the best of your ability by putting a number or check mark on the appropriate line.
(Circled responses or responses below the median for some of the questions were counted as unit points for expediency [desire to marry]).

	Men		Women	
	Yes	No	Yes	No
1. What is the best age for someone of your sex to marry?	Below median age 23 = 1[a]		Below median age 22 = 1[a]	
2. Would you like to be married right now?	(59)	40	(71)	28
3. Do you think a well-adjusted person could be married to anyone?	(31)	68	(17)	82
4. (a) Is a woman over 25 who is still single at a real disadvantage socially speaking?			(36)	63
(b) Is a man over 30 who is still single at a real disadvantage socially speaking?	(32)	67		
5. Do you experience a great deal of pressure from your parents to marry?	(2)	97	(5)	94
6. Would you want to marry within the next 5 years even if it could not be to your present boyfriend (girlfriend)?	(60)	39	(66)	33

	Men		Women	
	Yes	No	Yes	No
7. At what age would you like to marry?	Below median age 23 = 1^b		Below median age 22 = 1^b	
8. Should one be "in love" in order to marry?	97	(2)	92	(7)
9. Do you find a single life a lonely unsatisfactory existence despite some advantages?	(55)	44	(50)	49
10. Would you like to get away from living at home?	(74)	25	(56)	43
11. Having children is the most meaningful thing about marriage.	(32)	67	(31)	68
12. I have broken off with someone I hoped to marry.	20	(79)	33	(66)
13. I have been turned down by someone I hoped to marry.	(12)	87	(12)	87
14. Most of my close friends are married.	(16)	83	(12)	87
15. I am an orphan or have lost one or both of my parents.	(6)	93	(7)	92
16. How many people have wanted to marry you?	Below median = 2^c		Below median = 3^c	
17. How many persons have you wanted to marry?	Below median = 1^d		Below median = 1^d	
18. Do you have a close family relationship?	75	(24)	73	(26)
19. Do you have difficulty getting to meet eligible marriage partners?	(7)	92	(7)	92
20. Have you found that all of the "good" men (women) with respect to marriage are already married or otherwise unavailable?	2	(97)	2	(97)

	Men		Women	
	Yes	*No*	*Yes*	*No*

21. Does the thought of not being able to live completely according to your own preferences make you hesitate to marry? 18 (81) 10 (89)

22. Do you have any future educational plans after you get your degree? 69 (30) 46 (53)

[a] Men's mean = 23.63, S.D. = 2.20; Women's mean = 21.93, S.D. = 1.40.
[b] Men's mean = 23.50, S.D. = 3.00; Women's mean = 21.94, S.D. = 1.63.
[c] Men's mean = 1.99, S.D. = 1.49; Women's mean = 2.59, S.D. = 1.96.
[d] Men's mean = 1.44, S.D. = 0.96; Women's mean = 1.23, S.D. = 0.86.

Note: Numbers represent responses of Group I to the questions (N = 99).

5. BACKGROUND DATA

Code No._____

How long have you been going together with your boyfriend (fiancé)
or girlfriend (fiancée) on a regular basis?   Mean = 21.62 months
                                                     S.D. = 14.77 months

	Men	*Women*
1. What is your attitude toward having children?		
desire children very much	80	86
mildly desire them	14	10
mild objection to them	3	2
object very much to having them	2	1
2. What is your fiancé(e)'s attitude toward having children?		
desires children very much	89	88
mildly desires them	7	9
mild objection to them	2	0
objects very much to having them	1	2
3. Marital status of your parents:		
married (both living)	83	86
separated	1	1
divorced	5	5
both dead	0	0
mother dead, father alive	2	2
mother alive, father dead	8	4
4. What do you consider to be the social status of your parents in their community?		
one of the leading families	7	2
upper class	6	6
upper-middle class	42	53
middle class	35	26
lower class	9	11
no status as they are dead	0	1

	Men	Women

5. How many organizations do you belong to or attend regularly, such as church club, athletic club, social club, luncheon club (like Rotary, Kiwanis, Lions), fraternal order, college fraternity, college sorority, civic organization, music society, patriotic organization, YWCA, YMCA, YMHA, CYO?

	Men	Women
None	28	19
One	22	17
Two	28	28
Three or more	21	35

6. How confident are you that your marriage will be a happy one?

	Men	Women
very confident	68	72
confident	28	22
a little uncertain	2	5
very uncertain	1	0

7. Has your steady relationship with your fiancé(e) ever been broken off temporarily?

	Men	Women
never	69	69
once	19	23
twice	7	4
three or more times	4	3

8. Have you ever contemplated breaking your relationship?

	Men	Women
never	44	49
once	26	27
occasionally	28	23
frequently	1	0

9. Do you ever wish you had not gone together?

	Men	Women
never	77	83
once	7	5
occasionally	13	10
frequently	2	1

10. Your appraisal of the happiness of your parents' marriage:

	Men	Women
very happy	48	48
happy	24	25
average	13	13
unhappy	11	7
very unhappy	3	3

11. Are you a church member?

	Men	Women
yes	68	83
no	31	16

12. How sure are you that you will marry the individual taking the questionnaire with you?

	Men	Women
absolutely sure	1	0
barring unforeseen circumstances I will	36	46
pretty sure	52	40
somewhat uncertain	5	6
other (write in space)	4	7

6. FOLLOW-UP QUESTIONNAIRE

	Men	*Women*

1. Is the relationship between you two different from what it was last fall or winter when you filled out the first questionnaire?

	Men	Women
We are farther from being a permanent union	10	14
It is about the same, but not necessarily very good	5	2
It is about the same but very good	34	27
We are married, or we are nearer to being a permanent couple	48	54

2. How confident are you that your marriage will be a happy one?

	Men	Women
very confident	51	53
confident	34	27
a little uncertain	5	7
very uncertain	3	8

3. Has your steady relationship with your fiancé(e) ever been broken off temporarily?

	Men	Women
never	61	63
once	20	20
twice	8	6
three or more times	4	6

4. Have you ever contemplated breaking your relationship?

	Men	Women
never	37	38
once	25	30
occasionally	28	22
frequently	3	5

5. Do you ever wish you had not gone together?

	Men	Women
never	71	72

	Men·	Women
once	6	8
occasionally	14	15
frequently	2	0

6. What is the size of your home town?

less than 5,000	8	12
5,000 to 10,000	14	17
10,000 to 25,000	11	19
25,000 to 100,000	34	31
100,000 to 250,000	15	11
250,000 to 1 million or more	9	3

7. Where did you two first meet?

Blind date	6	6
Through mutual friend or relative	18	21
Dance or social event	25	24
In school or work	27	27
Chance occurrence	16	16

8. Your religion:

Catholic	24	23
Protestant	37	52
Jewish	17	14
None	15	16
Other (explain)		

9. How close do you feel to your father? (If parent is deceased, check relationship up to death and state age of termination of relationship).

Very close	18	20
Closer than average	21	21
As close as average	37	30
Below the average	9	13
Not close at all	8	11

10. How close do you feel to your mother? (If parent is deceased, check relationship up to death and state age of termination of relationship).

	Men	*Women*
Very close	22	25
Closer than average	25	22
As close as average	36	31
Below the average	7	11
Not close at all	3	6

11. If you could, would you prefer to marry later than the date you plan to marry that you have given us? If your answer is yes, please explain.

yes	20	22
no	69	68

12. Would your fiancé(e) (steady) prefer to marry later than the date you have given us? If answer is yes, please explain.

yes	17	17
no	72	76

Group II Measures

1. INTERVIEW QUESTIONS

Family Relationships

Here we are interested in the subject's relationship to his/her parents and siblings. We would like to know S's perception of each parent, the degree of contact and involvement with parents and siblings, the salient issues between S and his/her family and their way of dealing with one another. Particularly important is the response of the family to S's impending marriage and the manner in which S copes with family relationships in the present.

1. Could you tell me something about your family—what they are like and how you get along together? (Probe about position regarding siblings.)

   (Follow with specific question not touched upon above.)

(Mother)

2. How would you describe your mother as a person? (temperament, style of activity, etc.).

3. How close were you to her in growing up?

4. Has your relationship changed much?

5. Was she strict or lenient?

6. Does she have much "say" over what you do now?

7. Do you talk over your decisions with her?

8. Confide in her?

9. Spend much time with her?

10. How would you say she sees you now: as her child or as a grown-up person?

11. What do you do when you have a difference of opinion?

12. How has she reacted to your getting engaged and your decision to marry?

13. What does she think of your fiancé(e)?

14. What happened the first time they met?

15. How do they get along?

16. How does he/she like her?

17. Has she helped much in your wedding plans?

18. Has she made things difficult in some ways?

19. How comfortable do you feel with your mother when you are with your fiancé(e)?

20. How much do you think you will miss her when you get married?

21. How much do you think you would miss her if you should leave town?

22. How often do you plan to see her when you are married?

(Father)

23. How would you describe your father as a person? (temperament, style of activity, etc.).

24. How close to him were you in growing up?

25. Has the relationship changed much?

26. Was he strict or lenient?

27. Does he have much "say" over what you do now?

28. Do you talk over your decisions with him?

29. Confide your feelings in him?

30. Do you spend much time with him?

31. How would you say he sees you now—as his child or as a grown-up person?

32. What do you do when you have a difference of opinion?

33. How had he reacted to your getting engaged and your decision to marry?

34. What does he think of your fiancé(e)?

35. What happened the first time they met?

36. How do they get along?

37. How does he/she like him?

38. Has he helped much in your wedding plans?

39. Has he made things difficult in some ways?

40. How comfortable do you feel with your father when you are with your fiancé(e)?

41. How much do you think you will miss him when you get married?

42. How much do you think you would miss him if you should leave town?

43. How often do you plan to see him when you are married?

(Parents as a Couple)

44. What are your parents like as a couple?

45. How close are they?

46. How do they get along in general?

47. Does one parent have more "say" than the other in some areas?

48. What is their pattern? (Is one more talkative, affectionate, etc.?)

49. Did your parents express much affection in front of the children?

50. Were there some things that mother was dissatisfied with about father?

51. He about her?

52. Which parent are you more like?

53. Were you closer to one than the other?

54. Are there some things you plan to do differently from them in your marriage?

55. In raising your children?

56. How satisfied are you with your present relationship to your parents?

57. How did you happen to meet_____?

58. How long ago?

59. Were you consciously seeking a spouse at the time?

60. Were you aware of any "tests" you were using to eliminate unworthy candidates?

61. What was your first impression?

62. When did you notice a change in your feelings about _____?

63. In _____'s feelings?

64. When did you decide you might want to marry _____?

65. Was there any particular event associated with this decision?

66. To what extent has this relationship been similar and different from earlier relationships?

67. Were there any fights or disagreements which played a significant role in the development of the relationship?

68. Were there any separations or breaks that were important?

69. Are you in love with _____?

70. What do you mean by love?

71. Does _____ love you?

72. What does love mean here?

73. In which area do you feel closest to _____? (social, intellectual, affectional, sexual)

74. Which least?

75. Do you like to share all your troubles and feelings with _____?

76. How about he/she with you?

77. What kind of things do you generally talk about together?

78. Can you remember the last time you had a disagreement?

79. Could you describe what happened?

80. How did you resolve it?

81. How satisfied are you with the way it worked out?

82. Was this something that has come up before?

83. Would you like to see the amount of emotional contact between you changed in any way?

84. How?

85. Has talking with and about one another ever been a problem?

86. Any particularly difficult areas to talk about?

87. How do you feel about the future of the relationship?

88. Do you or have you ever regretted getting this deeply involved?

89. Could you break off the relationship now if you wanted to?

90. How would you go about doing it?

91. If you could have your sexual and personality needs satisfied without marrying, would you marry?

92. (If yes,) Why?

93. Have you ever been sorely disappointed in love?

94. How did you react to (each of these)?

95. Do you believe marriage may be broken off if the couples are no longer in love?

96. Under what conditions?

97. Do you think _____ is emotionally mature? Explain.

98. Do you feel you are mature?

99. Do you think _____ likes you more than you like him or vice versa? Explain.

100. Have you met any obstacles to getting married?

101. What are they?

102. How have you dealt with them?

103. How satisfied are you with the way things seem to be working out?

104. Does _____ view the relationship differently from you?

105. What sort of things do you like to do with _____?

106. Do you think you'll be able to continue these interests after marriage?

107. Can two people be "too close" together?

108. Do you feel your relationship "smothering" in any way?

109. Do you ever get bored with _____?

110. Were there certain personality traits of yours you were concerned about and tried to hide when you first started going together? Which?

One important part of the relationship of an engaged couple is physical closeness; we'd like to talk a little about how this is for you.

111. What are your feelings about sexual relations for an engaged couple?

112. Do you and your fiancé(e) talk much about your sexual relationship?

113. What are his/her feelings about it?

114. What has been the pattern in your relationship?

115. How far have you gone? (necking, petting, intercourse)

116. Has one of you been more eager than the other to go further?

117. (If they do not have intercourse) Does one of you usually stop first?

118. Are there any differences between you and your fiancé(e) in your sexual temperaments?

119. Do you enjoy being with him/her sexually? Explain.

120. Is there a difference between your feelings about it at the time and afterwards?

121. What do you like best about _____?

122. What else?
     (Get at least 3)

123. What do you like least?

124. What needs does he/she fulfill?

125. What objectively speaking would you say are your best qualities?
     (At least 3)

126. Your worst?

127. What do think _____ likes best about you?

128. Least?

129. What needs of his/hers do you think you fulfill?

130. Do you think a man has many chances to marry?

131. What limits his chances?

132. What's the best age for a man to marry? Why?

133. Do you think a woman has many chances to marry?

134. What limits her chances?

135. What's the best age for her to marry?

136. How do you feel about _____'s physical attractiveness?

137. What physical qualities of _____ appeal to you most?

138. Is physical attractiveness very important to you?

139. How distressed would you feel if it changed for the worse after marriage?

140. How do you feel you stack up physically?

141. How do you feel when you know someone doesn't like you?

142. When you want to do something very much and _____ doesn't, what happens?

143. When _____ wants to do something very much and you don't?

144. Would you describe yourself as unconventional? In what way?

145. How about _____?

146. Do you feel a wife should take care of the home?

147. What other responsibilities are primarily a woman's?

148. What are a man's responsibilities?

149. (For women) Do you want to work after marriage? At what sort of job and for how long?

150. What is the purpose of marriage for you?

151. For _____?

152. What does _____'s father think about you?

153. _____'s mother?

154. _____'s friends?

155. What do your friends think about _____?

156. How do you feel about helping people?

157. Will you tell me about some times when you have helped people?

158. Do friends bring their troubles to you?

159. How do you go about consoling them?

160. Do you find yourself often consoling _____?

161. Would you say that he/she consoles you more than you console him/her?

162. What kinds of things make you upset and worried?

163. Will you give me an example of a time when you were worried?

164. Just how did you feel at that time?

165. When you have been faced with the problem of making some important decision, how did you go about making it?

166. Did anyone help you decide? Who?

167. When you are faced with decisions now, to whom do you turn? (If stuck, investigate college entrance, fraternity membership, course of study, major, etc.)

168. If someone insults you when other people are around, what do you do?

169. What do you do if you are the only two people present?

170. Do you become angered easily?

171. How do you act when you are angry?

172. What kinds of things make you angry?

173. Will you tell me about the last time you were angry?

174. Do you ever get angry at _____?

175. When you are standing in line waiting for a movie or to be seated in a restaurant and someone pushes you or steps in front of you in line, what do you do?

176. What are your feelings at this time?

177. (If response is "do nothing," then:) Under what circumstances would you do something?

178. Do you ever have the feeling that you would like to "blow off steam?"

179. How do you go about doing it?

180. How do you feel when you have to meet many people who are strangers to you?

181. Is it easy for you to talk to strangers?

182. Are you embarrassed at times like these?

183. All of us have dreamed about the future and the things we would like to have, the sort of life we would like to lead. Will you tell me the sort of life you have imagined for yourself?

184. Now, this is the kind of life you would like to have. Is this the kind you believe you will have or is there a difference between what you would like and the life you think you will actually have?
(Explore for differences between fantasy and actual expectations.)

185. How do you feel about having children of your own?

186. How many would you like to have?

187. How does _____ act when he/she has had four or five drinks?

188. How do you feel when he/she shows the effects of a few drinks?

189. How do you feel when you are a little high?

Self-Anchoring Scaling: Marital Relationship and Marriage

The following are a few structured questions we would like you to consider concerning your ideas about marriage.

(Administration instructions: Ask the following questions in the order presented. Do not make any specific probes other than to restate the question using synonyms if necessary. If S uses very general descriptive terms such as "maturity," "happiness," "getting along well," etc., ask for clarification of these terms; ask S what they mean to him in as concrete terms as he can define them. If S has trouble with the initial statement of the question, it is permissible to say "think of other marriages you know, what do you think are good or bad points about them?")

1. *Ideal marriage one year hence.*

People have different ideas about what constitutes a happy relationship between husband and wife. When you think about your future marriage, what are your wishes and hopes for it? In other words, if you imagine your future marriage in the best possible light, what would it look like one year after marriage if you are to be happy? Take your time answering; such things aren't easy to put into words.

Worst state of affairs one year hence.

Now, taking the other side of the picture, what are your fears and worries about your future marriage? In other words, if you imagine your marriage after one year in the *worst* possible light, what would it look like then? Again, take your time in answering.

Here is a picture of a ladder. Suppose we say that at the top of the ladder *(pointing)* is the very best state of affairs you have just described; at the bottom *(pointing)* is the very worst state of affairs.

1A. Where on the ladder *(moving finger rapidly up and down ladder)* do you feel you and your fiancé(e) as a couple stand *at the present time*? Step number _____.

1B. And where do you think you will be on the ladder by the time you actually get married? Step number _____.

2. *Man and woman most ready for marriage.*

Each person who gets married enters a new kind of life. What would you regard as the most desirable characteristics for a man to have to make him most ready for marriage, that is, for being a husband? In other words, when you think of yourself and other engaged couples, what are the characteristics of those men you think most ready for marriage? Take your time in answering.

Repeat for opposite sex.

Man and woman least ready for marriage.

Now, take the other side of the picture. Think of engaged couples you know and describe the characteristics of the man, woman, couple that make the person (couple) least ready for marriage.

Repeat for opposite sex.

Once again, let's say the top of the ladder *(pointing)* are the characteristics you have described as making a person (couple) most ready for marriage; at the bottom *(pointing)* is the worst set of characteristics.

2A. Where on the ladder *(finger moving rapidly up and down ladder)* do you feel you stand with regard to being personally ready for marriage? Step number _____.

2B. Where on the ladder do you feel your fiancé(e) stands with regard to being personally ready for marriage? Step number _____.

2. SELECTIONS FROM MARRIAGE APPERCEPTIVE THEMATIC EXAMINATION

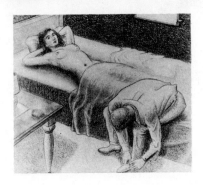

3. BACKGROUND DATA

	Men	*Women*
	(N = 19 couples)	

1. Age of subjects:

	Men	Women
Mean	21.42	20.05
S.D.	1.9	1.5

2. Are you a church member?

	Men	Women
Yes	15	17
No	4	2

3. Are you now a student?

	Men	Women
Yes	15	18
No	4	1

4. Class?

	Men	Women
Freshman	0	3
Sophomore	5	3
Junior	2	6
Senior	4	4
Graduate Student	4	2
Not a student	4	1

5. Degree planned?

	Men	Women
Baccalaureate	5	11
Masters	7	5
Ph.D.	4	0
Other	3	3

6. Length of courtship (months)

	Men	Women
Mean	18.79	18.74
S.D.	11.7	11.8

7. Present classification of relationship:

	Men	Women
Date a lot	0	0

	Men	Women
Date exclusively	4	2
"Pinned" or similar commitment	4	4
Consider selves engaged	4	7
Formal announcement of engagement	7	6

8. How confident are you that your marriage will be a happy one?

	Men	Women
Very confident	15	12
Confident	2	7
A little uncertain	2	0
Very uncertain	0	0

9. Has your relationship with your present partner ever been broken off?

	Men	Women
Never	16	15
Once	3	4
Twice	0	0
Three or more times	0	0

10. Have you ever contemplated breaking your relationship?

	Men	Women
Never	14	14
Once	5	2
Occasionally	0	3
Frequently	0	0

11. Do you ever wish you had not gone together?

	Men	Women
Never	16	15
Once	2	2
Occasionally	1	2
Frequently	0	0

12. How sure are you that you will marry the individual taking the test with you?

	Men	Women
Absolutely sure	7	8
Barring unforeseen circumstances	10	9
Pretty sure	2	2
Somewhat uncertain	0	0
Other	0	0

Men   Women

13. Perception of partner's physical attractiveness:

	Men	Women
Extremely good-looking	5	7
Better than average	12	8
Average	2	4
Somewhat below average	0	0
Considerably below average	0	0

14. Self-perception of attractiveness:

	Men	Women
Extremely good-looking	0	0
Better than average	8	3
Average	10	16
Somewhat below average	1	0
Considerably below average	0	0

15. Do you have definite plans for marriage with each other?

	Men	Women
Yes	17	14
No	2	5

4. SEX QUESTIONNAIRE

1. Average weekly frequency of orgasm:	*Men*	*Women*
1	0	3
2	0	1
3	0	3
4	2	3
5	2	1
6	2	0
7	0	0
8	3	2
9	1	4
10	2	1
15-21	6	1
≥ 22	1	0

2. Self-perceived sex drive:		
Above average	5	1
Average	12	16
Below average	2	2

3. Sex is a problem:		
Little or no problem	10	11
Something of a problem	5	5
A definite problem	1	2
A difficult problem	3	1
A very difficult problem	0	0

5.   FOLLOW-UP QUESTIONNAIRE*

	Men	*Women*
	$(N = 17)^a$	

1. Courtship progress at the end of six months:

	Men	Women
Married or nearer to being a permanent union	10	11
About the same, but very good	7	7
About the same, but not necessarily very good	1	0
Farther apart from being a permanent union	1	1

2. How confident are you that your marriage will be a happy one:

Very confident	9	9
Confident	6	6
A little uncertain	1	2
Very uncertain	1	0

3. Has your relationship with your present partner ever been broken off:

Never	13	14
Once	2	2
Twice	1	1
Three or more times	1	0

4. Have you ever contemplated breaking your relationship?

Never	11	7
Once	3	7
Occasionally	2	3
Frequently	1	0

5. Do you ever wish you had not gone together?

Never	15	13
Once	0	4
Occasionally	2	0
Frequently	0	0

	Men	*Women*

6. What is the size of your home town?

	Men	Women
less than 5000	2	3
5000 to 10,000	2	3
10,000 to 25,000	7	2
25,000 to 100,000	3	4
100,000 to 200,000	2	3
more than 200,000	1	2

7. How did you two meet?

	Men	Women
Blind date	2	2
Friends	7	7
Social event	3	3
School	2	2
Chance	3	3

8. What is your religion?

	Men	Women
Protestant	6	6
Catholic	5	6
Jewish	4	5
Other	2	0

9. Height, Weight

	Men	Women
Mean Height[b]	6' 0"	5' 4"
Mean Weight[c]	170 lb.	117 lb.

10. How close are you to your father?

	Men	Women
Very close	3	4
Closer than average	7	6
As close as average	5	4
Below average	2	3
Not close at all	0	0

11. How close are you to your mother?

	Men	Women
Very close	3	5
Closer than average	4	4
As close as average	6	6
Below average	3	1
Not close at all	1	1

Men   Women

12. Would you prefer to marry later than planned?

	Men	Women
Yes	2	5
No	15	12

13. Would your fiancé(e) prefer to marry later than planned?

	Men	Women
Yes	2	3
No	15	14

[a] The Follow-up Questionnaire for Group II was not received for two couples.
[b] Correlation between couples = .03
[c] Correlation between couples = .14.

6.   Q SORT USED TO ASSESS SUBJECTS

1. anxiety re sexual adequacy

2. high energy level

3. critical, skeptical, not easily impressed

4. conventional

5. need to communicate, be close to people

6. conservative

7. physical attraction of other plays important part in relationship

8. talkative person

9. does things spontaneously rather than planning out

10. seeks reassurance

11. behaves in feminine style and manner

12. behaves in masculine style and manner

13. facially or gesturally expressive

14. enjoys sex a great deal

15. control of sex no problem

16. nervous

17. difficulty expressing real love and attachment

18. rapid personal tempo, behaves and acts quickly

19. introspective and concerned with self as object

20. moralistic

21. perceptive of wide range of interpersonal cues

22. aloof

23. attractive, combination physical and psychological

24. basically anxious

25. social poise and presence, appears socially at ease

26. affected

27. tends to arouse liking and acceptance in people

28. envies others

29. uncomfortable with uncertainty and complexities

30. dependent on father

31. handles anxiety and conflicts by in effect refusing to recognize repressive or dissociative tendencies

32. low frustration level

33. unrealistic aspiration level, unrealistic goals

34. arouses nurturant feelings in others

35. keeps people at a distance, avoids close interpersonal relations

36. needs attention very badly

37. interprets basically clear-cut and simple situations in complicated and particularizing ways

38. emotionally bland, flattened affect

39. likely to keep irritations and resentments to himself

40. very anxious to be approved of

41. genuinely submissive, accepts domination comfortably

42. outspoken

43. sex drive high

44. evaluates the motivation of others in interpreting situations

45. creates and exploits dependency in others

46. basically hostile toward own sex

47. has readiness to feel guilt

48. robust

49. concerned with own body and adequacy of its physiological functioning

50. hides personal thoughts and feelings

51. interesting, arresting person

52. regards self as physically attractive

53. interested in fiancé as person rather than as narcissistic extension

54. tends to be self-punishing

55. judges self and others in conventional terms

56. opinionated

57. tends to be rebellious and nonconforming

58. dependent on mother

59. basically hostile toward other sex

60. inhibited

61. not sarcastic

62. not critical of other's minor flaws

63. unselfish

64. needs to run the show always

65. dependent

66. gives up and withdraws where possible in the face of frustration and adversity

67. dull

68. thin-skinned, sensitive to anything that can be construed as criticism or an interpersonal slight

69. egotistical

70. coarse

71. reluctant to commit self to any definite course of action, tends to delay or avoid action

72. behaves in a giving way toward others

73. evasive

74. appreciative

75. basically distrustful of people in general, questions their motivations

76. uncomplaining

77. sees self as very desirable as person, highly satisfied with self

78. immature

79. concerned with philosophical problems, e.g., religions, values, the meaning of life

80. friendly

81. verbally fluent, can express ideas well

82. cooperative

83. good relationship with father

84. personally charming

85. generally confident person

86. flexible, can adapt self to other's needs

87. calm, relaxed in manner

88. appears straightforward, forthright, candid in dealing with others

89. ambitious

90. is turned to for advice and reassurance

91. has warmth, the capacity for close relationships, compassionate

92. happy

93. appears to have a high degree of intellectual capacity

94. optimistic

95. strongly committed to intellectual activities

96. humorous

97. good relationship with mother

98. insight into own motives and behavior

99. skilled in social techniques of imaginative play, pretending and humor

100. self-dramatizing, histrionic

Appendix D

Group III Measures

1. MARITAL EXPECTATION TEST

Ideal-Self MET* (for men)

Directions: Please consider and score each of the traits, behaviors, and attitudes listed below according to how you would ideally like to be. If you think the item describes your ideal self very well, put a 5 in the space next to the item. If you think the item is generally true but not completely so, put a 4. If you don't know, are not sure or believe the item is as applicable at times as it is inapplicable at other times, put a 3. If you believe the item is generally untrue of your ideal self but not always untrue, put a 2. If you think the item describes a person completely opposite to your ideal self, put a 1. Be sure you have not skipped any items.

Summary:

Describes your ideal self very closely	5
Generally true of your ideal self but not completely or always	4
Don't know, not sure, just as much true as untrue, etc.	3
Generally untrue, but not always or completely untrue	2
Completely opposite of your ideal self	1

*The forms of all other men-centered MET "sets" were identical except for slight rewordings for grammatical reasons.

1. I am admired by my girlfriend _____

2. I don't mind a good argument _____

3. I think that almost any woman is better off in her own home than in a job or profession _____

4. The church knows best in all things _____

5. My girlfriend can confide in me _____

6. I am able to criticize myself _____

7. I am a good dancer _____

8. I let others make decisions _____

9. I don't try to dominate my girlfriend _____

10. I like all the members of my girlfriend's family _____

11. It is all right for both husband and wife to contribute to the financial support of the family regularly _____

12. I have lots of friends including those of the opposite sex _____

13. I enjoy my girlfriend's friends _____

14. I am liked by my girlfriend's friends _____

15. My girlfriend likes my friends _____

16. I join in the fun and humor at parties _____

17. I do not feel I must always have my way _____

18. I am very honest _____

19. My intelligence is greater than that of my girlfriend _____

20. My intelligence is less than that of my girlfriend _____

21. I am not jealous and overpossessive _____

22. I am a good listener _____

23. I listen to reason in argument _____

24. I listen to and help solve my girlfriend's problems _____

25. I am a good lover _____

26. I mix easily socially _____

27. Only in emergencies should the wife contribute to the financial support of the family _____

28. The husband should have the major voice in financial matters _____

29. It is all right if the wife earns as much money as her husband and contributes equally _____

30. I would prefer a wife of the same nationality as me _____

31. I make much of neatness and manners _____

32. I am not nervous _____

33. I do nice things at the right time _____

34. I am optimistic _____

35. My girlfriend's mother likes and accepts me _____

36. My girlfriend's father likes and accepts me _____

37. My father likes and accepts my girlfriend _____

38. My mother likes and accepts my girlfriend _____

39. I am passionate _____

40. I make my girlfriend feel passionate _____

41. I enjoy being with people _____

42. I am physically strong _____

43. I am popular socially _____

44. I am popular with women _____

45. I am a religious person _____

46. I am very respectful to authority _____

47. I like responsibility _____

48. I accept the responsibilities of being a spouse _____

49. I would want my wife to have sexual intercourse anytime I wanted it provided she wasn't unusually tired or ill _____

50. I believe sexual intercourse is permissible if you are engaged _____

51. I believe sexual intercourse is permissible if you like each other _____

52. I want to have sex relations with my future wife before marriage _____

53. I am sexually experienced, i.e., not a virgin _____

54. I am not shy _____

55. I am not lacking in social grace _____

56. I have a family of higher social standing than my girlfriend _____

57. I am straightforward and direct _____

58. I can be strict if necessary _____

59. I react pleasantly to suggestions _____

60. I am not suspicious of my girlfriend _____

61. I don't fly off the handle for every little thing _____

62. The husband should decide whether or not the wife may work outside the home _____

63. My wife will take full responsibility for care and training of our children so that I can devote my time to my work _____

64. I will leave the care of the children to my wife when they are babies _____

65. I will make the majority of the decisions concerning the children such as where they will go and what they may do _____

66. It will be exclusively my wife's duty to do the cooking and keeping the house in order _____

67. An education is important for my wife whether or not she works outside the home _____

68. My major responsibility to our children will be to make a good living, provide a home and make them mind _____

69. My wife should not be taller than me _____

70. My wife and I will share responsibility for work around the house if both of us work outside the home _____

71. If there is a difference of opinion, I will decide where to live _____

72. My wife will be as well informed as me concerning the family's financial status and business affairs _____

73. It will be my responsibility and privilege to choose where we will go and what we will do when we go out _____

74. The husband should help wash and dry dishes _____

75. My wife should love and respect me regardless of the kind of work I do _____

76. I am not fat _____

77. I admire my girlfriend _____

78. I don't take advantage of my girlfriend _____

79. I am affectionate _____

80. I like the same amusements as my girlfriend _____

81. I appreciate what my girlfriend does for me _____

82. I always need to ask advice before acting _____

83. I maintain balance and emotional control in emergencies _____

84. I am calm _____

85. I want children _____

86. I desire many children _____

87. I believe that the most important task of a wife is the physical care of the children _____

88. The wife should take part in community affairs only after she has finished her household responsibilities _____

89. I confide in my girlfriend _____

90. I am generally cooperative _____

91. I expect my wife to play a dependent role _____

92. I can accept disappointment and adjust to change _____

93. I can pull my girlfriend "out of the dumps" _____

94. I believe the "end justifies the means" _____

95. I am in good physical condition _____

96. The husband should take a share in the household tasks (especially if the wife has the constant care of small children) _____

97. I enjoy and see humor in situations and jokes that are funny to my girlfriend _____

98. I have a family with more money than my girlfriend _____

99. I indulge my girlfriend in her little whims _____

100. I have high intelligence _____

101. I am not irritable _____

102. I believe it is hard to spend leisure time together _____

103. I love my girlfriend _____

104. I need my girlfriend's love _____

105. I am not psychologically dependent on my parents _____

106. I don't want my girlfriend to replace my mother and/or father _____

107. I am passive and unaggressive _____

108. I am patient with my girlfriend _____

109. I have the same political beliefs as my girlfriend _____

110. Husband and wife should each respect the other's religious, political or ethical convictions and not strive to change them _____

111. I respect my girlfriend _____

112. I am someone whom my girlfriend can respect _____

113. I am not self-centered _____

114. I can exercise self-control when needed _____

115. My sex drive is compatible with that of my girlfriend _____

116. I believe sexual intercourse is permissible if you love each other _____

117. I am sexually attractive _____

118. I am fond of social gatherings _____

119. I am tolerant of different viewpoints _____

120. I need understanding _____

121. I feel unloved _____

122. I would respect my wife's choice if she preferred to have a career to having children _____

123. It's O.K. with me if my wife wishes to combine a career and motherhood _____

124. My wife should fit her life to mine _____

125. My wife should not be more than 8 inches shorter than me _____

126. I appreciate a good homemaker _____

127. I am willing to do things around the house _____

128. I am willing to help with the housework _____

129. If I help with the housework, my wife will help with outside chores such as keeping the yard, painting or repairing the house _____

130. My wife's opinion will carry as much weight as mine in money matters _____

131. I appreciate my wife's staying at home to care for me and the children instead of using time attending club meetings and entertainment outside the house _____

132. My wife can work if she likes to even if she doesn't have to _____

133. My wife's age should be at least three years less than mine _____

134. I have a good physique _____

135. I am very muscular _____

Self MET* (for women)

Directions: Please consider and score each of the traits, behaviors, and attitudes listed below *according to how you see yourself.* If you think the item describes yourself very well, put a 5 in the space next to the item. If you think the item is generally true but not completely so, put a 4. If you don't know, are not sure or believe the item is as applicable at times as it is inapplicable at other times, put a 3. If you believe the item is generally untrue of yourself but not always untrue, put a 2. If you think the item describes a person completely opposite to yourself, put a 1. Be sure you have not skipped any of the items.

Summary:

Describes yourself very closely	*5*
Generally true of yourself but not completely or always	*4*
Don't know, not sure, just as much true as untrue, etc.	*3*
Generally untrue, but not always or completely untrue	*2*
Completely opposite of yourself	*1*

1. I am admired by my boyfriend   _____

2. I don't mind a good argument   _____

3. Almost any woman is better off in her own home than in a job or profession   _____

4. The church knows best in all things   _____

5. I confide in my boyfriend   _____

6. I am able to criticize myself   _____

7. I am a good dancer   _____

8. I let others make decisions   _____

9. I don't try to dominate my boyfriend   _____

10. My entire family is liked by my boyfriend   _____

*The forms of all other women-centered MET "sets" were identical except for slight rewordings for grammatical reasons.

11. It is all right for both husband and wife to contribute to the financial support of the family regularly   _____

12. I have lots of friends including those of the opposite sex   _____

13. I enjoy my boyfriend's friends   _____

14. I am liked by my boyfriend's friends   _____

15. I have friends my boyfriend likes   _____

16. I join in the fun and humor at parties   _____

17. I do not feel I must always have my way   _____

18. I am very honest   _____

19. I am more intelligent than my boyfriend   _____

20. I am less intelligent than my boyfriend   _____

21. I am not jealous and overpossessive   _____

22. I am a good listener   _____

23. I listen to reason in argument   _____

24. I listen to and help solve my boyfriend's problems   _____

25. I am a good lover   _____

26. I mix easily socially   _____

27. I think that only in emergencies should the wife contribute to the financial support of the family   _____

28. I think the husband should have the major voice in financial matters   _____

29. I think it is all right if the wife earns as much money as her husband and contributes equally   _____

30. I would prefer a husband of the same nationality as me   _____

31. I make much of neatness and manners   _____

32. I am not nervous   _____

33. I do nice things at the right time   _____

34. I am optimistic   _____

35. My boyfriend's mother likes and accepts me   _____

36. My boyfriend's father likes and accepts me   _____

37. My father likes and accepts my boyfriend   _____

38. My mother likes and accepts my boyfriend   _____

39. I am passionate   _____

40. I make my boyfriend feel passionate   _____

41. I enjoy being with people   _____

42. I am physically strong   _____

43. I am popular socially   _____

44. I am popular with men   _____

45. I am a religious person   _____

46. I am very respectful to authority   _____

47. I like responsibility   _____

48. I accept the responsibility of being a spouse   _____

49. I would have sexual intercourse anytime my husband wanted it provided I wasn't unusually tired or ill   _____

50. I believe sexual intercourse is permissible if you are engaged   _____

51. I believe sexual intercourse is permissible if you like each other   _____

52. I want to have sex relations with my future husband before marriage   _____

53. I am sexually experienced, i.e., not a virgin   _____

54. I am not shy   _____

55. I am not lacking in social grace   _____

56. I have a family of higher social standing than my boyfriend   _____

57. I am straightforward and direct   _____

58. I can be strict if necessary   _____

59. I react pleasantly to suggestions   _____

60. I am not suspicious of my boyfriend   _____

61. I don't fly off the handle for every little thing   _____

62. I think that the husband should decide whether or not the wife may work outside the home   _____

63. I will take full responsibility for care and training of our children so that my husband can devote his time to work   _____

64. I will take complete care of the children when they are babies   _____

65. My husband will make most of the decisions concerning the children, such as where they will go and what they will do   _____

66. It will be exclusively my duty to do the cooking and keep the house in order   _____

67. An education is important for me whether or not I work outside the home   _____

68. My husband's major responsibility to our children will be to make a good living, provide a home, and make them mind   _____

69. I prefer a husband no shorter than me in height   _____

70. My husband and I will share responsibility for housework if both of us work outside the home   _____

71. If there is a difference of opinion, my husband will decide where to live   _____

72. I should be as well informed as my husband concerning the family's financial and business matters   _____

73. It is my husband's responsibility and privilege to choose where we will go and what we will do when we go out   _____

74. I would appreciate my husband's helping to wash or dry dishes   _____

75. I will love and respect my husband regardless of the kind of work he does   _____

76. I am not fat   _____

77. I stimulate the ambition of my boyfriend   _____

78. I am very anxious to be approved of _____

79. I am attentive _____

80. I would have handsome children _____

81. I always crave my boyfriend's company _____

82. My complexion is fair, not dark _____

83. I radiate confidence _____

84. I am not critical of my boyfriend _____

85. I am not critical of myself _____

86. I can take criticism well _____

87. I am dependable _____

88. I am a dependent person _____

89. I have more education than my boyfriend _____

90. I am efficient _____

91. My financial prospects are good _____

92. I am forgiving _____

93. My heredity is normal _____

94. I do not need to be the important person in every activity _____

95. I think it is more serious if the wife becomes involved with another man than if the husband becomes involved with another woman (infidelity) _____

96. I have insight into myself _____

97. I join lots of organizations _____

98. I am the "life of the party" _____

99. I relieve my boyfriend's loneliness _____

100. I don't feel lonely much of the time _____

101. I have good manners _____

102. I like the opposite sex generally _____

103. I am orderly _____

104. I strive to keep promises _____

105. I am of the same religion as my boyfriend _____

106. I want to make a plan for saving and spending money _____

107. I would want my husband to have sexual intercourse anytime I wanted it provided he was not unusually tired or ill _____

108. I have conventional sex standards _____

109. I share and discuss my problems with my boyfriend _____

110. I don't smoke excessively _____

111. I am fond of social gatherings _____

112. I am emotionally stable _____

113. I have good table manners _____

114. I hardly ever talk back _____

115. I will yield my point of view to avoid arguments _____

116. I am interested in often trying new things; not a creature of habit _____

117. I prefer a husband older than me (at least three years) _____

118. I don't value children over a husband _____

119. A man should want a woman who has not had sexual intercourse with any other man before marriage _____

120. I want a husband to be the "boss" who says what is to be done and what is not to be done _____

121. My husband and I will have equal voice in decisions affecting the family as a whole _____

122. If my husband is a good worker, respectable and faithful to my family, other personal characteristics are of considerably less importance _____

123. Since doing things like laundry, cleaning, and child care are woman's work, my husband will feel no responsibility for them _____

124. My husband will decide all money matters _____

125. I enjoy sex very much   _____

126. I am a good, neat and orderly homemaker   _____

127. I think that weekends are to be a period of rest for
     my husband, so I will not expect him to assist with
     the housework   _____

128. I have well-developed breasts   _____

129. I have good-looking legs   _____

130. I have a very good figure   _____

2. BACKGROUND DATA

	Men	Women
1. Age of subjects:		
Mean	21.0	19.85
S.D.	2.1	1.3
2. Are you a church member?		
Yes	69	86
No	20	12
No response	9	
3. What is your religion?		
Protestant	35	49
Catholic	32	26
Jewish	19	15
Other	4	4
No response	8	4
4. How often do you attend church?		
At least once a week	7	23
From time to time	33	39
Rarely	32	31
Never	25	2
No response	1	3
5. Are you a student now?		
Yes	88	98
No	10	0
6. Class in school:		
Graduate	12	0
Senior	20	13
Junior	22	30
Sophomore	23	21
Freshman	13	34
Not a student	8	0

	Men	Women
7. What degree do you have concrete plans for attaining?		
Ph.D.	32	1
Master's	29	29
Bachelor	32	67
Other	5	1
8. How long have you been going together?		
1-12 months	31	31
13-24 months	30	30
25-36 months	24	23
37-48 months	6	8
>48 months	7	6
9. Present classification of relationship:		
Date somewhat	12	5
Date a lot	19	29
Date exclusively	17	21
"Pinned" or similar committment	21	22
Informal engagement	20	13
Formal engagement	9	8
10. How sure are you that you will marry the present partner?		
Absolutely sure	21	15
Barring unforeseen circumstances	33	35
Pretty sure	11	18
Somewhat uncertain	18	19
Doubt it	14	10
Absolutely sure won't	1	1
11. Do you have definite plans to marry your partner?		
Yes	31	33
No	67	65
12. If yes to above, when?		
In 0-12 months	8	9
13-18 months	7	10
19-24 months	3	0

	Men	Women
25-36 months	9	8
>37 months	4	6

13. How do you currently evaluate yourself as a couple?

Very much in love	41	52
Closer than average	40	36
As close as average	15	8
Less close than average	2	2
Considerably less close than average	0	0

14. How well does your girlfriend (boyfriend) understand you?

Extremely well	35	50
Fairly well, above average	50	40
About as well as most others	9	7
Less well than most others	4	1
Doesn't understand me very well	0	0

15. How well do you understand your girlfriend (boyfriend)?

Extremely well	39	50
Fairly well, above average	47	43
About as well as most others	11	3
Less well than most others	1	2
Not very well	0	0

3. SEX QUESTIONNAIRE

	Men	Women

1. What is your best estimate of your average rate of sexual orgasm per week?

	Men	Women
0	3	28
1	7	18
2	17	23
3	23	11
4	8	0
5	15	3
6	6	2
7	5	6
8-14	12	4
15-21	1	3
≥ 22	1	0

2. Source of orgasms (if two or more sources checked, the one closest to intercourse is listed):

	Men	Women
Sexual intercourse	43	27
Petting	40	42
Masturbation	11	1
"Dreams"	2	1
No response or no orgasm	2	27

3. As you see yourself in relation to other members of your sex and your age would you rate your sex drive as

	Men	Women
Much stronger than average	6	3
Somewhat stronger than average	37	26
About the same as average	50	62
Not quite as strong as average	5	5
Considerably below average	0	2

4. Please rate the extent to which control of your sex drive is a problem. "Control" here means to exercise effort to get your mind off sex, to get to

	Men	Women

concentrating on something else; efforts to subdue, to cope with sexual desires in some manner.

	Men	Women
Control is little or no problem	40	65
Control is something of a problem	45	24
Control is a definite problem	10	4
Control is a difficult problem	3	5
Control is a very difficult problem	0	0

4. McGUIRE SOCIOECONOMIC INDEX

Score	Men	Women
5-10	2	2
11-15	14	19
16-20	18	21
21-25	26	28
26-30	18	14
31-35	18	9
≥ 36	2	5

Note: High score = high status.

FOLLOW-UP QUESTIONNAIRE

Considering your relationship with your partner with whom you participated in the Interpersonal Relationship study, how does it compare currently with the way it was when you filled out the inventories approximately six months ago.

	Men	*Women*
We are very much closer than before and moving toward being a permanent couple, or we are a permanent couple.	50	52
We continue to have a very close relationship and we may become a permanent couple although our relationship has not changed radically in the last six months.	15	15
We continue to see a lot of each other, but we have not really become much closer in the last six months.	7	7
We still see each other, but the relationship shows a considerable amount of strain. We are further apart than we were six months ago.	10	8
We have broken up and/or are not a couple any more.	16	16

Other (do not use this category except if you feel that for special reasons none of the above items fit your situation). If you check this category, please explain.

INDEX